SURVIVE
&THRIVE

SURVIVE
& THRIVE

ENTREPRENEURSHIP
FRAMEWORKS THAT WORK

Easy to follow how-to guides, to create
your entrepreneurial initiative

PAUL KEWENE-HITE

MĀTANGA HĀPAI

First Edition

PUBLISHED IN 2020 BY MĀTANGA HĀPAI LIMITED

ISBN 978-0-473-53503-2 (Paperback)

ISBN 978-0-473-53504-9 (eBook)

ISBN 978-0-473-53505-6 (Audiobook)

COVER DESIGN Sarah Gifford

BOOK DESIGN Shawn Dahl, dahlimama inc

PROOFREADING AND COPYEDITING Sasha Kewene-Hite and Kristine Haglund

PHOTOGRAPHS

Author archives (pages 5, 224, 252)

C. Amos Hopkins (page 9)

Manahi Taber-Kewene via manahivisuals.com (pages 14, 22, 34, 36, 74, 144, 146, 184, 226, 254, 268, 270, 294, 350, 360, 358, 382, 405, 412)

Riccardo Annandale on Unsplash (page 17)

ThisisEngineering RAEng on Unsplash (pages 76 and 384)

Christina @ wocintechchat.com on Unsplash (page 112)

National Cancer Institute on Unsplash (page 181)

AdobeStock (page 292)

Kalen Emsley on Unsplash (page 313)

Larm Rmah on Unsplash (page 314)

Rachel Hite Eng for TRUEAfrica.org (page 346)

Janko Ferlič on Unsplash (page 408)

PAINTING Rochelle Heywood (page 359)

For Natasha, Elijah, Sasha, Joshua, Ellie, and
those who will one day join our family.
I've wanted to give up a thousand times,
but each time I thought of you.

§

For my big brother Steven who has made
countless sacrifices to guide me on my path,
and without whom I would never have made it
to Harvard (and everything that followed
would have been much less likely).

I am the little kid to the left of my
brother Steven. This was the early
1970s. I am now the much bigger
little brother.

TABLE OF CONTENTS

Interludes [Short Stories]

WHY I WROTE THIS BOOK

Things happen. We have ideas, dreams, experience; sometimes things work out and other times not so much. Some things go to plan while other things change, shift and move, evolve and devolve, pivot, flip on their head, and implode or explode. The question is not will things happen; the question is how will you respond when things happen? I will call all things that happen change.

I have learned that:

> ▶ When you adapt effectively to change you are more likely to survive.
> ▶ The better you adapt to change the more likely you are to thrive.

As you adapt to change, what can be done about your ideas, interests, needs, wants, and the things that change?

As I have traveled the world teaching and building as an entrepreneur people have repeatedly asked me what they can do to be an entrepreneur. What can they do about their ideas? What can they do about the things that are happening in their lives and businesses?

You know how sometimes your mind will replay very complex detail in a flash, something that might have lasted hours or years, but it is relived in a flash of light in an instant when you are asked a question? The following is what I think about whenever I am asked if entrepreneurship can be taught or what a person can do about their idea or business:

As a child and teenager, I had uncountable ideas for things that I wanted to invent. I remember dreaming about flying cars and wondering how I could make one for all of my family members and friends. (I had a version with a thousand "reverse vacuum blowers" pointing down under the vehicle and another that had a compact helicopter propeller under the vehicle.) I remember thinking that jetpacks were very doable; I drew seemingly endless pages of examples of how 1. a jetpack would be controlled by the wearer, 2. the wearer would not get burned by, or catch on fire because of, the jet exhaust, and 3. the fuel would be air. I dreamt about how to build food replicators (inspired by the TV show Star Trek) so that my family could eat better and we could feed other food-insecure families. I puzzled through how to make a whipped cream gun for food fights (inspired by the 1976 kids' movie *Bugsy Malone*). I drew pages of ideas for an unbreakable, unjammable clothing zipper. I looked at different materials to see how to make a tangle free phone cord. I had a long list of other ideas. I wasn't the only one dreaming as a kid. I remember conversations with friends, especially my best friend Mark Probert, about what we thought needed to exist. Kids are creative machines.

When I was around 15 years old, I told my mom and one of my sisters that I wanted to write a book that would help kids like me who were struggling in school, being bullied, and feeling hopeless and anxious the way that I did. I had already written quite a few pages. This conversation around our kitchen table made my mom cry. Regretting that I had told her how I felt to the point of making her cry, I destroyed the pages of that early writing and promised her that I wouldn't write the book.

When I was 19 years old (in early 1984), I left for two years of volunteer missionary service for The Church of Jesus Christ of Latter-day Saints in Thailand. Walking up and down the streets of Bangkok, I saw waterways and vacant land filled with rubbish, and I wanted to do something about it. I dreamt about being involved in a company that cleaned up garbage and rubbish. Thailand would be first, and then the solution would expand to the rest of the developing world. I had no idea how to do it, but I worried about garbage and its impact on the lives of people who lived around it. At the time I felt too small when faced with the reality of such a big challenge. On 27 November 1985 (the day after Thanksgiving Day in America) I returned to the USA feeling like Superman after my experience as a missionary. I felt refreshed and renewed, hopeful, fully empowered, and able to accomplish great things in life. I was going to attend university and return to Thailand to clean the waterways and streets.

In my early 20s, when I was a student at Harvard, to my embarrassment I admit that I let other people talk me out of my dream to clean up the garbage in the developing world. When I would tell people about my dream, they would scrunch up their faces and ask me if I was serious. I stopped talking to people about it. I didn't have a word for it back then, but now I would say

that I lost all psychological safety around the topic. People would laugh, tell me it was weird, and make me feel silly for dreaming about it. So, with regret, I dropped the idea.

My next dream was to launch a company that offered personalized tours around countries. I had the idea that fellow returned missionaries from every corner of the world would be excellent personal guides on tours of "the real" (rather than touristy) corners of planet earth. There would be tours focusing on food, fitness, culture, and more. Travelers could work side by side with locals to build homes for the homeless (for a day or a week or more, as able and interested), they would volunteer to help restore historical ruins (even if only for a few hours or a day), they would care for rescued elephants (and other animals), and they could work in rice fields or train with martial arts masters, etc. I imagined former missionaries taking travelers into the homes of locals where everyone would share a freshly cooked meal after learning how to shop in local markets for fresh ingredients and cook alongside the family. Then the traveler would potentially stay the night in a guest room or in some cases sleep on the open floor with a family in the developing world. They would shower out of rain barrels just as locals do (unless they had access to indoor plumbing). No souvenirs would be sold, travelers and locals would also gain perspective and insight into the real lives of people they would otherwise never have the opportunity to meet. The money made from the tours would be shared

This is the only photo that I can find from my years at Harvard. (My roommate was testing out his new camera.) My wife framed this photo and keeps it on our dresser.

with the locals who were involved in the personalized experiences.

I sat down with business professionals at the Small Business Administration (SBA)[1]. One of those volunteers was a professional investor in Boston who, when I was mid-story, told me to stop talking about the travel idea. He said that he was already an investor in a guided tour company, and he didn't want to know too much detail about my "excellent and exciting idea." I asked him what I should do, and he said, "just do it and you'll figure out what works and what doesn't work." I then told him about the idea to clean up garbage in the developing world and he told me that "garbage isn't sexy" and even worse, that the task was too big with too little profit so to forget about it. I walked out of the SBA 100% unsure of how to "just do it."

I knocked on the doors of professors, and none knew how to help me make my personalized tour idea into a real company. One professor said to me, "I have ideas of my own. If I knew how to create a company out of an idea I wouldn't be here, I'd be out doing it." I didn't know anyone who had created their own company, other than my father who was a barber and had opened multiple barbershops. He was not interested in talking about my ideas.

I spent hours in the libraries at Harvard. The librarians were very patient and helpful, but even in the second-largest library system in the world after the US Library of Congress, we could not find any workbooks that I could use to develop my idea, step-by-step, into a viable company.

While staring at the cathedral ceiling in Widener Library one day, wondering how to cross a seemingly invisible bridge that I could not find over a chasm of understanding that was blocking my path forward, it occurred to me that I needed to develop the very workbook that I could not locate and might not yet exist. (Which means that my idea for the book that you are reading struck me in ~1987 and I am writing this introduction in 2020.)

> "Furious activity is no substitute for understanding."
> —H.H. Williams

I now realize that one of my mistakes back then was confusing my feverish and furious busywork with a path to understanding what needed to be done. A flurry of activity does not necessarily result in improvement. When you know what you are doing, you may work quickly but that is not the same as a frenzy that just kicks up dust that creates an illusion of advancement. Watch a top chef, or a professional fighter, or any other practical master of their craft—they might go fast and move swiftly but it is clear that they know what they are doing, and they aren't just "doing stuff" fast. A maelstrom of "doing stuff" is a poor proxy for progress.

While I was a student, I sold computers (and calculators, cameras, TVs, etc.) at the Harvard Coop in Harvard Square to pay my bills and feed myself. When I graduated from Harvard, I took a job selling computers in Portland, Oregon USA. I then took a job at a startup software company in Portland doing technical support, and within a year I was promoted to international sales. I kept trying to figure out how to convert the idea in my notebook into a real company; I told myself that the technical support and international sales jobs were all learning for my future company. I considered taking a job in the travel industry but I could see, in 1992, that technology was becoming a major factor in everyday life in the world; it seemed to me that staying involved with technology was what I should be doing to learn how to make my own startup one day.

---

1   sba.gov The SBA was founded in 1953 to help small business owners and entrepreneurs across the USA.

I took a job as a Technology Evangelist (yes that was my job title) at Apple in the Silicon Valley. I worked with engineers, product managers, executives, and more. At Apple I learned countless lessons about how both hardware and software is planned, engineered, marketed, and sold successfully. Working at Apple was a dream, I was surrounded every day by smart and creative people. I loved every second of it. It dawned on me, while working at Apple, that entrepreneurs do more than build startups, they work inside companies. It was around this time that I started seeing entrepreneurs everywhere I looked.

While I was at Apple, I realized that I could not find my notebook filled with the details for my personalized travel company. It must have been lost in one of my moves from house to house. I needed to decide whether to work to recreate all of that detail or to let it go. I let it go and focused on my career in technology. I still think my idea for a travel business would be an interesting approach to giving people an intimate insight into the everyday real lives of people in cultures and countries around the world. I also believe there is still a meaningful business opportunity in cleaning up the world's garbage.

After Apple I became President of a software company with offices in the Middle East, the Silicon Valley, and Utah, USA. Our engineers did excellent work to create compelling software. We went through the hard work to take the company public, but we never actually listed the company publicly. I learned volumes about software development, leading teams across offices around the world, financial planning and accounting, cash management, raising investment capital, the process to take a company public, and all of it was a powerful learning experience.

I then invested time helping other entrepreneurs in the Silicon Valley writing their business plans and creating their presentations, planning out their technology development, working with lawyers, financial planners and accountants, working to raise investment capital, and more. In the mix I worked on my own ventures as well. I could not count the hours of work invested, the number of presentations made, the lessons that I learned, or the notes taken. Helping others was a powerful learning experience, and my understanding of how things work grew leaps and bounds. Helping others helped me. This moment in time powerfully informed the shape and details of the frameworks in this book.

I then joined NEC[2] Computers. My talented team and I worked diligently to close new business. I interfaced with operations, sales, marketing, engineering, and other departments. I built relationships that reached well beyond my assigned role. Adding to what I learned at Apple, at NEC I learned tremendous lessons about how large enterprises function, and how to work like an entrepreneur inside a big machine.

I left NEC and joined another startup. I initially filled in temporarily for a friend who had an accident, but it became a permanent full-time opportunity. I learned increasingly valuable lessons from the talented CEO, I learned from the excellent engineers about their work on innovative new hardware and software, I improved my understanding of operations, leading teams, human resources, and more.

I then had a new idea and worked to create a tech startup around it. I then briefly consulted to MIT's Media Lab Europe. I then joined a startup venture capital firm that never fully launched, so I pivoted and joined a consulting group that helped companies and governments around the

---

2   NEC is the Nippon Electric Company. NEC is headquartered in Tokyo, Japan, I worked in the Mountain View, California office.

world. We consulted to startups, small and medium enterprises, family businesses, and governments around the world. We helped repair struggling businesses and build new initiatives, we authored business plans, did financial modelling, wrote white papers for technology, worked to raise investment capital, and more.

I was recruited to become the CEO of a startup in Ireland. We were passionate about our technology, we loved working together, and had great fun in the process. I learned more lessons about teams, investment capital, partnerships, product launches, and more. We genuinely believed in what we were working to achieve. During this time, I also volunteered with Social Entrepreneurs Ireland (SEI) to help social venture entrepreneurs around Ireland succeed. During my volunteer work with SEI, it was more fully impressed on my understanding that social ventures need to think and operate like for-profit ventures. When a social venture is planned and executed with the business rigor of a for-profit they stand the best chance to survive, and the better they are at the business side of doing good, the more likely they are to thrive.

Over those years of working in companies big and small, I kept track of the questions asked by gatekeepers. "Gatekeepers" are the decision makers who can block you or let you enter (making everything better or worse); investors, lawyers, accountants, boards of directors, shareholders, strategic partners, your own team, customers, suppliers, government employees in key departments, etc. I inventoried the questions, monitored the frequency of repeated questions, noticed what worked and didn't work, and I used all of those years of critical thinking to build frameworks that would predictably open doors that were otherwise shut and often locked.

After two years in Ireland, I was offered a job at INSEAD in France working in the INSEAD Centre for Entrepreneurship (ICE). I started teaching a 48-hour Startup Bootcamp, which meant that I now had a forum to apply my startup framework to help many people at once rather than one at a time as I had been doing up to that point. INSEAD asked me to start teaching the Business Planning Workshop to MBA students in addition to my Startup Bootcamp. In 2010, INSEAD offered me a position as an Affiliate Professor of Entrepreneurship and Family Enterprise; a position I held at INSEAD for 10 amazing years. I used my frameworks in the classroom and in private mentoring sessions with my students. INSEAD had me teach weekend short courses called bootcamps on creating a company out of basic ideas and how to partner with scientists to build a company around their intellectual properties. I taught evening seminars on professional sales, and how to pitch and present to investors and strategic others. I also taught full courses on how to be a corporate entrepreneur, how to acquire and turn around a failing business, and more.

Participants have commented to me over the years that they are surprised that my frameworks "make sense." I've been asked why I don't include complex mathematical or logic problems that unlock some unfathomable hidden mystery. I always smile to myself, because I remember when the process to make a company out of just an idea was an unfathomable hidden mystery to me. I tell people that I now realize that creating a company, or a new business unit inside of a company or government, is not that hard once you know how.

I tell people that these are a few of the keys:

▶ Get out of your own way. We can be our own worst enemy and biggest barrier. The biggest thing holding you back is most likely you. (This goes for people in the developed and developing world, people from privileged and challenged backgrounds; this applies to all people.)

▶ Find a teacher who has a curriculum and a pedagogy (method of teaching) that works for you. Being able to do something is not the same as being able to explain how to do it or being able to coach and train someone to do it. In business, the teachers might be professors, lawyers, accountants, advisors who are experts in the field, investors, or other members of your team, etc. The curriculum might be formalized or informal; what matters is that it represents their knowledge of how to coherently explain what needs to be done.

▶ Learn the vocabulary, grammar, and syntax of what you want to accomplish just like you are learning a new language.

▶ Practice, practice, practice (continuing with the learning new language example, this would be practicing with native speakers even if it is only a few words ... and being willing to make mistakes and to learn from those mistakes).

▶ Write everything down, then look up from the book and go outside and start applying your bright idea to the real world.

I believe that what we think are mysteries are very often truths and realities that are hidden in plain sight. The details of my frameworks are commonly available information, yet I could not count the number of times I have personally witnessed an "Aha!" moment when someone has woken up to an insight that converted a tangle of thoughts in their mind into ordered understanding.

> "Common sense is
> not so common."
> —Voltaire

What I have found is that everything that people need is around us everywhere ... it is simply a matter of the details being presented in a digestible and usable format.

Questions are more powerful than answers. Answers are only as good as the question. This workbook is filled with questions. My hope is that you find value in bringing your questions and testing them against the questions in this book. You could say that all of my frameworks are inventories of questions in specific orders with some editorial comments for each, to help you think about each question and what to do about it. You can do the work out of order, but I have found that when you do the work in the order of the steps that each builds to the next, so there is less need to circle back and redo steps.

One of my goals is that these frameworks will help you refine your questions. You will likely have questions that are not addressed in this book, so use the questions as they are framed here to think about your own questions so that you can refine them.

My hope is that you will find enough information and help in this workbook to kickstart your entrepreneurial dream with easy-to-follow how-to guides to create your entrepreneurial initiative.

No book or framework will offer you everything that you need. Anyone who tells you otherwise is selling you something.

None of my frameworks are exhaustive, factoring for all possible questions. You are very likely to have questions that I have not inventoried. These frameworks are simply intended to give you a place to start. In my experience, knowing where to start and being brave enough to start are often the most difficult parts of the journey. Following through and getting it done with no excuses are the next most difficult parts.

My sincere hope is that you will discover comfort and empowerment through your work exploring one or more of these frameworks.

May the guards at the gates along your path let you pass.

HOW TO USE THIS WORKBOOK

I hope that this workbook is helpful and straightforward to use. You might use one of the frameworks, or more than one. It is unlikely that you will use them all (but you never know!). You are welcome, of course, to read and explore all of them.

I have learned a lot by going through the processes necessary to create each framework. If you have the time and interest, exploring all of the frameworks will allow you to see the common steps between them, and the ways all entrepreneurship paths are both different and overlapping to varying degrees, like concentric circles or a Venn diagram.

The word "framework" is used in business and education as well as other industries but used less frequently in everyday life. It may be helpful to establish a definition of the word "framework" so that we can better appreciate why the word is being used in this book.

Framework (noun) 1. a basic conceptional structure (as of ideas),
2. a skeletal, openwork, or structural frame.

Our skeleton is our body's framework; our muscles and connective tissues hold our frame together and help it work. In education the structured plan for how and what you will study and hopefully learn is the framework. It is common for potential clients and students to ask a professor for the framework before they decide to engage in a program or take your class. This workbook presents entrepreneurship frameworks with steps, explanations, and assignments. There is an order to the operations, and the order is very deliberate—just like every bone has a purpose for where it is located in the skeleton. The order of the steps, the explanations, and assignments build the frame of what you will be working to accomplish as an entrepreneur.

You will officially start on the page where it says START HERE. That first framework has four parts: 1. an exercise on what produces Trust, 2. an exercise around the connection between what creates fear and what produces calm, 3. an exercise on what strategy is and how to think about it in practical terms, and 4. an exercise on being prepared so that you are always ready.

Once you have finished START HERE, you should move to whichever framework is most in line with your interests.

For example:

▶ If you want to think through your career first, you might go straight to the framework at the back of the book called BUILDING AND REBUILDING YOUR CAREER.

▶ If you would like to learn about buying a company (anybody can buy a company if they know how), then you might go straight to the framework called ACQUISITIONS.

▶ If you are an employee and you need to work on an initiative inside your organization, then go straight to the framework called CORPORATE, FAMILY BUSINESS, SCHOOL, AND GOVERNMENT ENTREPRENEURSHIP.

▶ You might be a scientist, or you might know nothing about science, but you know a scientist, and you want to build a company around a set of intellectual properties (IP) that is currently in the lab. You would then go straight to the SCIENCE AND TECHNOLOGY framework and get started.

▶ Chances are very high that if you are building around technology of any type you would also complete the OFFERING REQUIREMENTS DOCUMENT (ORD) framework. There will be some duplication of steps and content between the two frameworks; you will then see how the two frameworks overlap and fit together like two puzzles that make one expanded more complete picture. The OFFERING REQUIREMENTS DOCUMENT (ORD) framework is interesting because you might use it as part of your new STARTUP or your CORPORATE, FAMILY BUSINESS, SCHOOL, AND GOVERNMENT ENTREPRENEURSHIP initiative, or the SOFTWARE DEVELOPMENT that you are working on or any of the other frameworks.

▶ You might use the SALES framework with any of the other frameworks, or SALES might be the only framework that you use.

If you are unsure which framework best applies to you, look at the TABLE OF CONTENTS or review the summaries for each framework that begin on page 32 of the START HERE framework. If you still don't know which framework or type of entrepreneurship best suits your interest, then you might read the first few pages of a given framework until you find one that feels like it works for you.

I have had participants in my classes that have gone halfway through one of the frameworks before deciding that the type of entrepreneurship that we were exploring in that framework didn't work for them. That is perfectly okay. Once the participant shifted onto another entrepreneurial path, they were more excited and motivated to dig in and work. Not all paths work for everyone. For example, you might think in the beginning that you want to do a STARTUP, but when doing that work you realize that you just aren't connecting with it as well as you thought that you would. So, you shift gears and start working on ACQUISITIONS to buy an existing company, and you find that really works for you. Again, that is okay.

So, explore and work to find the path that works best for you!

▶ **One more note for those who explore more than one framework:**

Most of the frameworks have at least one overlapping step (finance for example, or presentations). If you see anything that looks like a duplication of a step that you have already done in a previous framework, just do a quick review to see if there are differences (which there sometimes are), review your thinking and work, and then press forward. Keep in mind that no entrepreneurship path is 100% different from the other forms; entrepreneurs of all stripes have work that must be done in common whether they are sitting at a desk in governments or corporations, building in a science lab, crammed into tiny rented offices, working from home, pushing a cart, or waist deep in a marshland.

▶ A Note About Questions

"If I had an hour to solve a problem and my life depended
on the solution, I would spend the first 55 minutes
determining the proper question to ask,
for once I know the proper question, I could solve
the problem in less than five minutes."
—Albert Einstein

Throughout these frameworks, there are assignments, each of which includes an instruction to "Explore and refine your questions." Asking good questions is the key to finding good answers, and ultimately, you will have to both 1. ask your own questions and 2. find good answers. This book will start you on that path.

A few years ago, I was having an open conversation about questions with a class filled with MBA students. The topic of the conversation was the role of questions. We discussed which was more important, a question or an answer and how to ask, refine, and explore questions. One of my students (who was an emergency room (ER) surgeon before pursuing an MBA at INSEAD) said, "When someone is rushed into my ER following some life-threatening event there are many things that I need to know as soon as possible. I need to understand what vital systems in their body have been harmed so that I can prioritize and get to work. I start by quickly inventorying what I can see, and then I do the more pressing work of inventorying what I cannot see." Then my MBA student who is a doctor said something that sounds obvious, but it struck me as profound: "A cut on the skin, for example, is more obvious than a cut on the heart. I might lose the patient if I waste time cleaning a scratch on their arm when something more vital needs my attention immediately." As we explored the process of an ER doctor performing triage (which is the assignment of degrees of urgency to wounds or illnesses to decide the order of treatment) a few things became clear to me:

> ▶ Very often what you cannot see is more vital than what you can see. Thus, the art of science is learning how to see what isn't obvious to the untrained eye.

> ▶ The art of relevant questions followed by appropriate action directly impacts the ability of science to save life.

This reinforced my long-held belief that prioritizing accurately and then taking action according to those priorities produces wins. Relationships, everyday life, and business are this way.

Throughout the frameworks in this book you will see the encouragement and instruction to explore and refine your questions. If you work to answer a question that is off target, then the answer will also be off target. Imagine if you start walking in a direction (or driving or flying) and you are off just a little in the direction you travel. In the beginning being off a little does not matter that much because you are still going in the general direction, but over time that uncorrected misalignment could become an issue. Imagine if you walk (or drive or fly) that line for a day or a week or a month—at the end of the journey you will be off by a very wide margin. This is why we make refinements and adjustments to our direction and path as we walk, drive, and fly (in business we call those adjustments "pivots" whether they are big or small). The same thing happens with questions. Questions need to be refined, adjusted, and updated as you go. A refined and adjusted question stands the best chance of resulting in an on-target answer.

In Hal Gregersen's book *Questions Are the Answer: A Breakthrough Approach to Your Most Vexing Problems at Work and in Life* (2019) he asserts that "by getting better at questioning, you raise your chances of unlocking better answers." He then emphasizes the powerful idea of "catalytic questions [that] dissolve barriers—which in idea generation, usually come in the form of false assumptions—and channel energy down more productive pathways." Therefore, "some questions knock down the walls that have been constraining a problem solver's thinking."

READ "Better Brainstorming," Hal Gregersen, *Harvard Business Review* (HBR) (March–April 2018)

In the article In the article, "Better Brainstorming," Hal Gregersen presents a 3-step process to harness the power of the "Question Burst." He says the Question Burst "helps people adopt a more creative habit of thinking and, when they're looking for breakthroughs, gives them a sense of control. There's actually something they can do other than sit and wait for a bolt from the blue."

Here is a simplified summary, quoting material directly from Gregersen's 3 steps:

1. **Set the stage**:
   "Include two or three people who have no direct experience with the problem and whose cognitive style or worldview is starkly different from yours... Engage others in the cause in a non-threatening way... making yourself vulnerable by sharing the problem—but you're also summoning empathy, which fosters idea generation...

   Select a challenge you care deeply about... Invite people to help you consider the challenge from fresh angles... Give yourself just two minutes to lay out the problem for them... Just hit the highlights [then] clearly spell out two critical rules: First, people can contribute only questions... Second, no preambles or justifications that frame a question will be allowed, because they'll guide listeners to see the problem in a certain way—the very thing you're trying to avoid."

2. **Brainstorm the questions**
   "Now set a timer and spend the next four minutes collectively generating as many questions as possible about the challenge. As in all brainstorming, don't allow pushback on anyone's contributions. The more surprising and provocative the questions are, the better... In this exercise the emphasis is on quantity... Write every question down verbatim on paper, a laptop, or a tablet instead of a white-board so that you can capture everything accurately."

   As you brainstorm, you should ask others to check your work so that you don't commit "unconscious censoring." As you are brainstorming questions you must resist offering answers when questions are being generated. Finally, generate as many questions as possible—Gregerson suggests that you should try for at least 15, but the more the better.

3. **Identify a quest—and commit to it.**
   "On your own, study the questions you jotted down, looking for those that suggest new pathways... Now try expanding those few into their own sets of related or fol-low-on questions. A classic way of doing this is the 'five whys' sequence developed

by Toyota Industries' founder Sakichi Toyoda—or the variation on it suggested by Stanford's Michael Ray in *The Highest Goal*. Ask yourself why the question you chose seemed important or meaningful. Then ask why the reason you just gave is important—or why it's a sticking point. And so on. By better understanding why a question really matters and what obstacles you might face in addressing it, you deepen your resolve and ability to do something about it and further broaden the territory of possible solutions... Finally, commit to pursuing at least one new pathway you've glimpsed."

Gregersen recommends "doing at least three rounds of the Question Burst exercise for a given issue... The more you do it, the deeper you'll go in your thinking."

Three rounds should take less than 20 minutes. Gregerson promises that "The process will also get easier the more you do it, [and that] people must hold themselves accountable for follow-up [and] must take responsibility for exploring the pathways those questions open up and discovering valuable answers."

ALSO READ THESE HBR ARTICLES
▶ "Use Catalytic Questioning to Solve Significant Problems," Hal Gregersen (July 2013)
▶ "Yes, You Can Brainstorm Without Groupthink," Vijay Govindarajan and Jay Terwilliger (July 2012)
▶ "Are You Solving the Right Problems?," Thomas Wedell-Wedellsborg (January–February 2017)

As a final note from me, always remember that when someone asks a question, it indicates what was unclear and needs more attention. Questions shine a light on what is working and what needs more effort to make it work. Embrace and be patient with questions. Questions unlock doors that are currently closed.

> "The secret of getting ahead
> is getting started."
> —Mark Twain

COMMON TO ALL FRAMEWORKS

Trust is important in life and relationships. All forms of thriving business and entrepreneurship require trust. Some people believe that trust is earned while others believe that trust is lost. Preparing to build trust will have a positive effect no matter which perspective you encounter.

Please do the preparatory framework on trust (part 1), visibility, control, and support (part 2), strategy (part 3), and due diligence (part 4) *before* you begin work on the specific framework for the type of entrepreneurship that you are pursuing (i.e., startups, science & technology, software, corporate, family enterprise, school, government, acquisitions, turnarounds, crisis leadership, lifestyle, social, volunteers, sales, reimagining and rebuilding your career, etc.).

Grit is another important word—and way of living—that is common across all frameworks in this book (and life). Grit is important no matter what you do.

> **Grit** (noun) 4: firmness of mind or spirit: unyielding courage in the face of hardship or danger.

Grit is the ability to get up in the morning even when you don't feel like you can. It is the ability to push through resistance to do what must be done. It is the difference between finishing and dropping out. It is a primary characteristic of winners, and it can be learned and developed. Build grit into the normal practice of how you do everything. You can do it.

PREPARATORY
FRAMEWORK

PREPAREDNESS, PROFESSIONALISM, EXECUTION, CRITICAL THINKING, PROBLEM SOLVING, TO PRODUCE TRUST

Trust (noun) 1 a: assured reliance on the character, ability, strength, or truth of someone or something, b: one in which confidence is placed.

Trust is a power. When you are trusted, you will be given access to do things that people who are not trusted will struggle to accomplish. My experience in business is that trust is built by Preparedness, Professionalism, Critical Thinking, and Problem Solving. These are made more compelling when combined with the character traits and behaviors of only needing to be asked once, doing what you say you will do, following through, consistency, creating psychological safety[1], and being honest about what happened or is happening.

READ *Fearless Organizations: Creating Psychological Safety in the Workplace for Learning, Innovation, and Growth,* Amy Edmondson (2019)

Preparedness

> "By failing to prepare, you are preparing to fail."
> —**Reverend H.K. Williams** (often misattributed to Benjamin Franklin)

Mastery is the direct result of practice. Whatever you practice most is what you will be good at (ranging from the procrastination of everything to full engagement of anything). Everything that you have done in your life has been preparation for this moment, which means that you might be prepared for this opportunity or not. It is not possible for anyone to be perfectly prepared for all potentialities in any moment, but it is possible to practice preparedness.

Consider a sports team that practices set plays[2] repeatedly. The specific detail of any practiced play is less important than learning what options are possible during a play, along with strengths and weaknesses of the players; and then what work works well and less well. Be deliberate in what and how you practice. In business, you and your team need to practice like a team of athletes practices their sport. Practice preparedness, professionalism, critical thinking, problem solving, execution, trust, and then consider how those apply to planning, messaging, meetings, presentations, execution, and more.

The reality of your preparedness (or lack of it) is obvious to other people who need you to be prepared.

---

1   Psychological Safety is when individuals bring their authentic best selves to a situation. They show their real opinions and ideas because they feel safe doing so. Google maintains that Psychological Safety is the #1 factor in successful teams: https://rework.withgoogle.com/blog/five-keys-to-a-successful-google-team

2   A "set play" applies to both team and individual sports. A set play is when athletes plan positions and movements that are likely to result in advancement and scoring. For example, where players position themselves on a field or court, and time when they will move, and how they will move, to best advantage themselves and potentially assist others on their team. Set plays factor for the movement of their opponent(s).

Professionalism

It might sound obvious but being professional is essential (and not everyone is professional in their business dealings and practices). "Professional" typically means that you are paid for what you do. By professional what I mean is that you listen before talking and that your method of engagement is based on integrity, truthfulness, and following through with what you say you will do.

Critical Thinking

Critical Thinking is the gathering of fact-based data to inform an opinion that in turn is used in good planning and subsequent execution. Critical Thinking is not guesswork, or opinion based on emotion or hearsay (what someone said someone said). Use primary sources as able.

Problem Solving

Problem Solving is applied critical thinking. Robust preparation and professionalism will meaningfully improve your critical thinking and problem solving. Keep in mind that problem solving is an ongoing process that will need to adapt to new data and changing circumstances.

Execution

Execution is the most commonly missing detail in business planning. This is the detail of who will do what, when, where, and how. When someone asks you about your execution plan, be prepared to give representative detail. Think of it like someone asking how a traditional clock works. Most people would make the mistake of saying "a clock tells time," when the question might be looking for mechanical detail. So, you might ask if the questioner is looking for the answer to the question of what it does (tell time) or the answer to the question of how the mechanism moves the hands of the clock to indicate time.

When asked how it tells time they might say that the big hand points at the minutes and the little hand points at the hour. What you need to be able to do is open the clock face and point at a few representative cogs and springs, and demonstrate that you understand how that cog and that spring operate in the system of moving pieces that, in turn, move the hands that you use to tell time. Again, you may not need to explain in intricate detail, just give representative examples.

Another analogy would be to think of it like skipping stones across a pond. You can point to the area around the pond and the body of water and then touch on a few details that would be struck across the surface where a skipped stone might hit from this side to the other side. Your ability to explain even a few things from here to there will help persuade the listener that you actually understand how to do what you are planning to accomplish.

> **ASSIGNMENT** Write at least one paragraph on this section. Specifically detail how you will prepare, think critically, solve problems, and execute to create trust. Show with supportive telling in all of your work. Showing is more powerful than telling; showing is when you give specific, practical examples of what you are doing rather than saying that you are doing it. Explore and refine your questions.

PART 2

VISIBILITY, CONTROL, AND SUPPORT

For a moment let's consider lessons from a rollercoaster:

People sometimes use the word "rollercoaster" to describe a troubled or difficult time, and with good reason. Being shaken and rattled around, with uncomfortable ups and downs, can make for a crazy ride. When climbing onto a rollercoaster in an amusement park, we board it knowing that it will be over in minutes, and we expect to be unsettled by it. When crazy rides happen at work or in regular life, we don't have the luxury of knowing when (or if) the uncomfortable ride will end.

There is more to the rollercoaster comparison than ups and downs and being shaken around. There are at least three specific lessons from a rollercoaster that can make your life and work unhappy when they are absent and happy when they are present.

Visibility

If you cannot see where you are going, and you are going there at speed, you will become anxious. The rollercoaster shows you where you are going then takes that visibility away, then shows you again, then takes it away, all to make the ride exciting. If you've never ridden on a roller coaster, imagine riding in a speeding car with a blindfold on, then the blindfold is taken off and put back on repeatedly, as the car swerves dangerously in and out and around traffic. It is not a pleasant sensation when you feel there is a real possibility of being hurt or worse. These rides sometimes happen at work (and in life) when the person in charge does not consistently and transparently show what is happening and where you are headed.

Control

While the rollercoaster cars whip around, up and down, outside of your ability to control what is happening, your only choice is to hang on and wait for it to end. This creates anxiety. There are times that the rollercoaster will slow down, making breaking sounds and sensations, etc. to create the impression that someone or something is controlling things. The rollercoaster plays with visibility and control in combinations, giving and taking it away. Back to the example of riding in a car, when you don't have control of the car and it feels like the driver has poor control of the car it can create anxiety and fear of the worst happening (do not be that driver and do not ride with that driver). This happens at work (and in life) when it is unclear whether or not the person who is supposed to be in control of the critical details really is able to drive safely.

Support

On the rollercoaster when you can't see what is holding you up, your worry compounds. Not all beams and bars in a rollercoaster are physically necessary; some are put there to give your mind a calming idea that there is support involved in the structure. In the driving example, wondering where your support is could be you questioning the safety of the physical car or doubting that the driver is listening to your requests for them to slow down or drive more carefully. This happens at work (and life) when you feel that your voice is not being heard, and you doubt that the way things are being run will support you if you need it.

Most people crave visibility, control, and support. Even if we don't have those three things, we need to know that someone has them and that they are competent.

> **HINT** Share. If people feel that they can contribute to the visibility, share the controls, and be part of the support, then the odds that they will be calm go up. Empower others by asking questions; it is a type of control sharing. If people can ask questions and then hear from your responses that you are working to understand them, that you value what they said, and that the sound when they spoke was not just in the air around your ears but that the meaning of their message entered your mind and heart, then that moment will go a long way to calming them down. If you can integrate their questions, comments, and suggestions into your progressively refined questions, their calm can become happiness.

When we sit through a presentation by a CEO (whether we are shareholders and board of directors or the leadership team and employees or people at home watching the news), we need to know where the company is going, whether the CEO understands the controls and who has them, and whether the systems are in place to do what needs to be done when it needs to be done. If we leave a presentation doubting the clarity of the CEO's vision, or control, or support structure, it can create problems for the audience which comes back around as a problem for the speaker. "Did I miss something? The CEO talked for 30 minutes and I still have no idea what is happening."

When you build your slides, or explain what you are doing or plan to do, when you speak with employees, boards/shareholders, bankers, customers, suppliers, the press, the community, and every other stakeholder, (kids, parents, friends), think … do your messages create visibility as well as a clear understanding of the controls and what support is available?

Visibility, control, and support being given and taken away in combinations is fun when it is a rollercoaster for a few minutes, but it is exhausting, frustrating, and potentially terrifying when it is your everyday life and work.

Supply these three things during every interaction, and the people around you will have a better chance of staying calm.

> **ASSIGNMENT** Write at least one paragraph on this section. Show what you are doing to create visibility on where you are planning to go and how you will get there. Show where the controls are and that you know how to use them. Bonus points for showing how you will share controls. Then show where the support is and how it will work. Explore and refine your questions.

PART 3

STRATEGY AND TACTICS
APPLY TO EVERYTHING

Strategy is the what and why. Tactics are the how.

Strategy (noun) 1. a plan of action designed to achieve a long-term or overall aim.

> "Real strategists get their hands dirty digging for ideas, and real strategies are built from the nuggets they uncover."
> —**Henry Mintzberg**, writer and educator ,
> in the January–February 1994 Harvard Business Review article titled
> *The Fall and Rise of Strategic Planning*

> "In today's complex business world, strategic planning is indispensable to achieving superior management."
> —**George Steiner**, professor of management, author on strategy, and co-founder of
> The California Management Review, from his book *Strategic Planning*

In 2015, one of the foremost experts on strategy, Harvard Business School professor Michael Porter, said, "Most companies don't have a strategy. Everybody works hard. Everybody goes to the office everyday. Everybody does many many things. But there is really no strategy in any meaningful sense of that word." Professor Porter taught that "[Strategy] means deliberately choosing a different set of activities to deliver a unique mix of value."

In my personal experience, strategy is variously defined and interpreted, often misunderstood and underappreciated, yet it has great value when it is done well.

Not only do many people disagree about what strategy actually means, but, even worse, few people make any meaningful effort to deliberately formulate and execute a strategy by any definition. Most people (and companies) simply "do stuff." They have meetings about meetings, and talk about talking, and then they just do what they want to do anyway and sometimes it works and sometimes it works less well and sometimes they know why but usually they don't understand why something worked or did not work as planned.

When I carried a business card with the title Director of Strategic Planning at a major technology company, one day I attended a meeting along with other vice presidents and directors. During the meeting one of the VPs in the room looked across that conference room table and said to me "You are our Director of Strategic Planning? So that means that you do nothing but think about things that don't matter and nobody cares about. Get a real job and do something that actually matters." Regardless of what I actually achieved in my strategy role, an important leader in our company thought that the words "strategic planning" meant that I did nothing that mattered. That is a problem.

So what is strategy in practical terms and why does it matter?

▶ Strategy is deliberately selecting, planning, and executing activities that deliver value. Value is when a thing increases in its meaning, transaction potential, and power, as well as its capacity and ability to accomplish its potential.

▶ Strategy is knowing what must be done to accomplish a results-defined end-goal, and most specifically knowing WHY are you going to do WHAT you plan to do.

▶ Tactics are then HOW you are going to do WHAT you plan to do. So a Strategy or Strategic Plan includes reasoning as to HOW you will do WHAT and WHY to create and capture value.

Jack Welch[3] wrote that "Strategy is not a lengthy action plan. It is the evolution of a central idea through continually changing circumstances." My personal experience has led me to this paraphrase that I find myself repeating like a mantra: Strategy is not a lengthy action plan etched in stone, it is the practical capacity to stay flexible around a central idea.

Staying flexible around a central idea means that you should explore and experiment with what works best for you until you find a combination that clicks and works for you and your circumstances. Individuals, couples, friendships, businesses, governments, don't all need the same things but they all need to do the same thing—stay flexible in their thinking, planning, and execution.

The best athletes, professionals, etc, succeed because they plan, practice, and flexibly engage.

Be strategic, be tactical, be flexible, then drive to get things done.

How will you incorporate flexibility into your strategy and supporting tactics? Engage powerful critical thinking, apply that critical thinking to powerfully problem solve, then take deliberate action.

Being an entrepreneur requires calm, agility, and an ability to see through the distortions that happen in life. Some people are exceptionally skilled at dealing with uncertainty and chaos. It is something that can be learned and developed as a skill.

> **ASSIGNMENT** Write a strategy statement for what you will be working to accomplish and why you are doing it (identify the intended outcome or result of the work). Write a tactics statement as to how you will work to accomplish that strategy. A paragraph will do. This Assignment is to frame your thinking and commitment to the work that you are about to undertake.

---

3 John Francis Welch Jr. was an American business executive, chemical engineer, and writer. He was chairman and CEO of General Electric between 1981 and 2001.

PART 4

DUE DILIGENCE APPLIES TO EVERY TYPE OF ENTREPRENEURSHIP

Due diligence (DD) is a common term and process in the world of investment capital; it is when an investor works to determine that your assertions and claims about your company and what you are doing are accurate. We do DD in normal life as well, we just don't call it due diligence or DD. Before we buy a house or a car we walk around the house and drive the car, we ask questions and seek the advice of a home inspector and an auto mechanic to confirm that there are no problems or issues. This is all DD. If the homeowner and car owner have good paperwork, showing regular maintenance and care was given to the home and car, it makes the DD easier and comforts us as the potential buyer. Most people wait to organize the paperwork until someone asks them for details and documentation, I recommend that you start keeping track of all documentation right now. Save your future self the headache of scrambling to find and put together what you can easily start organizing today.

Call it documentation, or filing, or organizing, or a paper trail, or whatever else you are comfortable calling it. Start keeping track of the details of what you are doing.

Keeping track of your work and all associated documentation is critical. It applies to everything, not just the uses that the business world typically associates with due diligence (DD), which is the investigations that you do in advance of an investment to make certain (to the best of your ability) that you are buying what you think you are buying. If you keep track of all of your files and records at the level of professional grade DD then it will help you with your filing of taxes, applications for grants, applications with banks for loans, presentations to shareholders and the board, and countless other uses. Good records will save you time and money and will make everything better. For the purposes of this workbook I am categorizing all good housekeeping of your documentation as DD.

DD is something that you need to do on every new opportunity. DD is the process of determining that everything is in good working order and as it should be. Traditionally DD is performed during an investment or acquisition to make certain that all details are as they were represented to be. DD, in my opinion, is something that you should be preparing for from Day 1 and every time anything happens SO THAT when a moment comes, and someone asks you to account for the details of your work you will be ready.

DD is when you take the car that you want to buy to a mechanic whom you trust to look at every detail of the car and tell you what is wrong with it before you buy. If you are the owner of that car, the DD that is performed by a potential buyer will be much simpler if you can show them every receipt and piece of paper associated with every regular service, oil change, new set of tires, etc. If you cannot show the potential buyer evidence of regular servicing on the car it will create doubt in their mind that you changed the oil and paid careful attention to the health of the car that you are asking them to buy from you.

DD is when you bring in a qualified inspector to look at every little detail of the house and property before you buy. In business DD is a standard process, whether you are selling or buying you will be part of the process of discovery. It is best to be prepared for it.

If the government decides to audit your tax filings, and you do not have good records supporting the details in your tax filings, then you are going to find yourself having a difficult and potentially expensive conversation with the tax authority. Keep good records of everything that might be needed in the future.

Regardless of the type of entrepreneurial initiative you are pursuing and creating, you need to keep track of all details as you go. Every time you make an agreement or sign a document with a lawyer, an accountant, an investor, the government, a bank, a supplier, a customer, or anybody for anything, keep the original and make a copy. Make two folders or binders, one for the originals and one for a copy. Do not keep them in the same place; keep one at your office and one in a fireproof safe deposit box at a bank or some other secure offsite location (just in case, because you never know what might happen).

Then when you are in a conversation with a potential investor, or the bank, or a lawyer, or an accountant, or the government, or the board, or shareholders—whoever needs to see the details of the agreements and contracts which represent the decisions that you've made—you have everything together in one place ready to go.

Take for example the situation where you are raising investment capital and the investor gives you a list of questions they need answered (which is their due diligence into you to make sure that you are doing what you say you are doing and you are who you say you are); the time it could take to gather all of the details so that you can answer all of those questions is not going to be trivial. I have known people and startups that have lost their lead over their competition while gathering all of the information requested by a potential investor. Do not let this happen to you. When you start the process to raise capital, anticipate the questions that will be asked by an interested investor, and be ready to hand them a binder with COPIES (not originals) of everything that you have to get them started. Then you can get back to work staying ahead of (or catching up with) the competition.

My grandmother cleaned the kitchen as she cooked. As soon as she used a dish or a pan or a utensil, she washed it. Then when she was done cooking a meal the kitchen was clean; the only dirty dishes that remained were the dishes being used to eat the meal. Do the same in your venture no matter what type of entrepreneurship you are engaging. Keep good records as you go. Keep track of every detail, every receipt, every contract, as you go. Stay organized. Then the only not yet organized detail is the one that you are actively engaging in a moment; when that detail is completed, organize it too.

Be prepared. Organize as you go starting right now. A potential structure for your DD binder(s) might be:

- ▶ Corporate Records
- ▶ Public Filings and Financial Information
- ▶ Corporate Agreements
- ▶ Human Resources
- ▶ Insurance and Securities
- ▶ Governmental Regulations and Environmental Compliance
- ▶ Legal
- ▶ Intellectual Property (IP)
- ▶ Other

ASSIGNMENT Get two binders, one for original documents and the other for duplicate copies. Start putting copies of everything in those binders. Every Friday make sure that the binders are up to date (the original in the original binder and a clean copy in the duplicate folder). Keep the duplicate binder in a lockable drawer or filing cabinet near your desk; keep the originals in a separate secure location. Be sure that: 1) the secure place is actually safe and dry (a deposit box at your bank is one example), 2) you won't forget where that place is located, and 3) at least one other trusted person (e.g., a co-founder or your lawyer) knows the location and has access.

NEXT STEP

Now that you have completed all four parts of the Preparatory Framework, please advance to the framework that best suits your interests and needs. If you aren't sure which framework is right for you, keep in mind that you might ultimately do more than one, consider the following brief snapshot of each type:

▶ Startup
People who have an idea (or no idea) and want to create a company but don't know how or where to start.

▶ Science & Technology
Scientists who have intellectual property (IP), and they want to build a company around it. Or a non-scientist who wants to partner with a scientist to build a company around the scientist's IP.

▶ Software Development
People who have an idea for an app for a smart device or enterprise software but don't know how or where to start.

▶ Corporate, Family Enterprise, School, and Government
People who want to create a new initiative inside their organization. This is "Corporate Entrepreneurship" which is sometimes called "Intrapreneurship."

▶ Acquisitions
People who want to be entrepreneurs by buying an existing company, and need to understand the basics of how it is done.

▶ Turnarounds
People with a struggling or failing organization who need structure to help them think through how to make repairs and effect change.

▶ Crisis Leadership
People who need to prepare for a crisis or help working through a crisis in their organization.

▶ Building and Rebuilding Your Career
People who want to take stock of what they've been doing to line it up with their dreams and aspirations, to create a new path forward.

▶ Lifestyle
People who want control of their time, working enough to fund the lifestyle that they want, so that they can spend more time living life than at a job.

▶ Social

People who want to create and capture value by doing something to help people and the planet by building a non-profit or charity.

▶ Volunteers

People who are managing or leading volunteers.

▶ Professional Sales

People who need to persuade others and could use some structure.

▶ Offering Requirements Document (ORD)

The ORD is an evolution of a Market Requirements Document (MRD) to help people think through their ideas for software or science and technology. If you are making any type of thing, working through the ORD could be helpful.

One last thought before you head off to your framework(s) ... Do not worry about what you do not know. Nobody knows everything. Everybody needs to continue to learn. Learning is essential to good health. Be a person who learns and create an entrepreneurial initiative that learns. Ask and refine your questions. Explore. Puzzle through the things that you know and the things that you do not know. You won't have enough time, or information, or resources, and that just means that you are normal ... it also means that you are living the life of an entrepreneur.

"Go confidently in the direction of your dreams!
Live the life you've imagined." —Thoreau

FEAR MOTIVATES

There is a meaningful and important difference between being afraid and being scared. Fear is a knot in your gut, or maybe a pounding in your thoughts, but it keeps you focused and deliberate about whatever is causing the fear. Being scared produces irrational behavior and panic that can result in you and others being hurt.

When something comes at you quickly (whether it is a bee or a fist or a car or a job loss or a company failure or an economic upheaval, etc.), if you experience fear, you take action to deal with whatever is happening. If you get scared, you might freeze or flail around, creating chaos and not necessarily saving yourself from what is happening; you might make it worse.

When I started training in martial arts in 2013, I was filled with fear about it. I had a lump in my throat as I walked in to Evolve MMA in Singapore. My heart was pounding. I was sweating before the first class started. My friend Chatri Sityodtong had persuaded me that martial arts are a great way to get fit. I was very overweight and needed to do something. The myriad things that I had already tried were not working. Chatri is a successful martial artist himself, as well as one of the most successful business moguls in the world of martial arts. He is passionate about helping people "unleash their unquenchable warrior spirit" through martial arts. He is succeeding.

I quickly realized that training in Muay Thai[1] (the martial art that I chose) was not scary. Not only was I not scared during the training, but my fears about the training disappeared once I started doing it. My fear of being out of shape and overweight remained, however. Fear of poor health, fear of disease, fear of shortened lifespan, and other fears around being unfit drove me to work harder. I became fit. Eight months into my training (4 to 6 days a week for at least one hour each day), I was promoted to level 2 in Muay Thai, which meant that I could spar, going face to face with someone who was trying to hit me and knock me down. I experienced fear in the first moments of sparring, but I wasn't scared. My fear caused me to focus on what was happening, and to learn how to not get hit and knocked down.

---

1   Muay rhymes with "boy" and it means to box. Thai sounds like "tie" and means pertaining to Thailand.

It took regular, focused practice to stay standing during sparring.

In time, my fears were replaced by confidence. Very importantly, every time I sparred, I knew that I might get hit and knocked down. Over-confidence can be as dangerous as being scared. You can become reckless and might get hurt.

There is an important blend of fear and confidence that keeps us on our toes. A healthy blend of fear and confidence makes you a safe driver on the road, and a safe pedestrian walking down the side of that same road. You know that things can happen, so you stay alert. With practice, you can enjoy your drive and your stroll down the road.

Entrepreneurship is the same. Deliberate, focused practice of correct principles and techniques can produce a blend of healthy, productive fear, and confidence.

Over the years, all over the world, people have asked me about their fears. "Can I do it?" "How do I know if I have what it takes to succeed?" If they are asking good questions, being rational, and are simply unsure or even anxious, I suggest that they embrace their fears as motivation and fuel for what they are doing. It is when people are obviously panicked and authentically scared that we sit down and focus on breathing and process through what is happening and what they can do about it. Sometimes, professional help is what they need. Sometimes, they see that there is a solution and that they don't need to be scared, and they settle into a space with productive fear and even confidence.

For me, a big part of converting fear into confidence is knowing what to do. I was blessed to have access to Evolve MMA in Singapore. It is arguably the best martial arts training on planet earth.

Seek out the best teachers and training so that you can deal with what scares you. Learn to master what scares you until it becomes productive, healthy fear, blended with confidence. Learn how to respond when things happen. Fear can be a fuel if you let it. Embrace your fear and do something about it.

This workbook is designed to help you learn what to do. If you are reading this book with trepidation or fear, that is okay. As I have taken the steps to publish this workbook, I have needed to process through my fears about doing it. I have needed to practice what I preach. As an entrepreneur, confronting and embracing fear is a way of life. Use fear to learn to be confident about what you want to accomplish.

Being either scared or over-confident will not serve you well in life or work (or a fight). Fear can motivate you to pay attention and succeed. Butterflies are good, even when they feel more like bats. Train your butterflies to fly in formation toward your goal, and get on with it.

STARTUP
ENTREPRENEURSHIP

"Genius is one percent inspiration
and ninety-nine percent perspiration.
Accordingly, a 'genius' is often merely
a talented person who has done all of
his or her homework."

—**Thomas Edison**

Whether you are working on a startup by choice or out of necessity, you are to be congratulated for taking your first steps on the grand adventure of startup entrepreneurship.

Just in case you feel like you are too young to start a company, you are not. If you wonder if you are too old, you are not. For the latter, read: *Late Bloomers*, Rich Karlgaard (2019).

No matter what your social, economic or education level or background, or whatever other thing you think might disqualify you from starting a company, it will not stop you unless you let it. You can do this.

The safest harbor is not found working a job at a big company. Big companies sometimes fail and go out of business. Good workers sometimes lose their jobs. Your safest harbor is in you and your ability to dust yourself off, focus on an opportunity with a willingness to work and puzzle through what must be done. That is your greatest security. You don't need to know everything; your greatest asset is an open heart and mind, along with a willingness to focus and work.

Contrary to a common belief, entrepreneurs are not necessarily "risk takers." They are, however, willing to embrace risk to create stability and security for themselves and their families. What is more, most startup entrepreneurs are not anti-corporation, anti-job, or anti-working-for-someone-else. A vast majority of the entrepreneurs I know love to work, crave paychecks and benefits; they want their small startups to become big companies that offer stability for themselves and other workers. A comparatively small percentage of entrepreneurs do not want to create a job or even a company with other employees—they want to create a lifestyle with flexibility and control over their time. Everyone has personal goals and what works for them. If you are seeking a lifestyle then consider working on the Lifestyle Entrepreneurship framework (read the first page of the framework to see if that is more in line with what you need and want). If you are interested in creating a startup company that may create jobs for others and scale into a bigger company, then you are in the right framework.

Startups can be very exciting and can also be the cause of anxiety and worry if you have never done it before, or if you have done it before and it didn't go well, or if you did it before and it went well but you aren't sure why and if you can be so lucky again. I have worked with people from around the world and all of the above feelings are common. You may just not be sure how to get started.

I remember when I was starting my career as an entrepreneur. I asked every entrepreneur and successful businessperson I knew how to build a startup, what books I should read, if there were any step-by-step guides that I could get my hands on. I was told by everyone to just throw myself into it and I would figure out what worked and what did not. I then experienced the compounding anxiety and worry that I would waste time and money that I didn't have as I worked to reinvent the wheel. I yearned for even a little insight from someone experienced who could give me guidance and hints as to what I should do. I felt very isolated and alone even though I had people all around me.

As I experimented with startups over the years, I kept track of what worked, what worked less well, what didn't work at all, and what created problems. I kept track of the questions that were asked, and started mapping the trends of what questions were asked repeatedly by lawyers, accountants, potential investors, shareholders, boards of directors, experienced potential hires, my teams, customers, suppliers, etc. This framework is the result of decades of experimentation and experience with what works.

I have used this framework to help others create fundable startups that went on to succeed. Most of the people whom I have taught had never been involved in building a startup before they worked through my framework with me. I am confident that even if you have never built a startup before,

this framework will help you during your early steps to be a startup entrepreneur. There is more to do than what is in this framework, but this is a kick-off point for you to think through your first planning of how to frame a startup that can succeed. I know that this framework works and can help you. I have personally seen it help startup entrepreneurs of all ages and education levels around the world.

Every now and then I see former students walking around wearing my startup bootcamp shirt. It always makes me smile. On the back, I wrote:

Dropped headfirst, learned to land on my feet.

Starting a company might feel as disorienting as being dropped headfirst. If you remember to breathe, staying flexible around the central idea, you can land on your feet.

The following is a 19-step framework for Startup Entrepreneurship training that I have created over my career. The foundation of the framework is my personal experience and knowledge of what is expected from strategic others and what works in practice. This framework is not exhaustive but is designed to kick-start planning and execution to give you a path forward. People around the world, from all social, economic and education levels and backgrounds have successfully created viable pitch- and launch-ready startups across industries using this framework.

Before you start this framework: If you have not already done so, please go back to the page called START HERE and complete parts 1, 2, 3, and 4 of the preparatory frameworks. Once that is completed, come back to this page and move forward to the following:

PREAMBLE **Write Everything Down**

STEP 1 **A Firm Foundation**

STEP 2 **The Basic Idea**

STEP 3 **The Big Play**

STEP 4 **The Offering**

STEP 5 **Value Proposition, Unique Selling Proposition (USP), or Why-to-Buy**

STEP 6 **Go to Market**

STEP 7 **Team and Execution**

STEP 8 **Business Modeling**

STEP 9 **Financial Modeling**

STEP 10 **Fundable Event Timelines**

STEP 11 **Capital Modeling**

STEP 12 **Liquidity and Exits**

STEP 13 **Founderitis**

STEP 14 **Boards: Advisory and Governance**

STEP 15 **Marketing, Sales, and Business Development**

STEP 16 **Call to Action or The Ask**

STEP 17 **Executive Summaries and Business Plans**

STEP 18 **Pitching and Presentations**

STEP 19 **Save Your Work, Update It Regularly, and Refer to It Often**

The purpose of the framework is to help individuals and teams structure their ideas into an execution ready condition so that they can: A. Persuade investors to invest, and B. allow the individual and teams to actually launch their startup. This framework can be taught in-person, or via technology, or worked on privately by an individual or team. The 20-step framework is as follows:

WRITE EVERYTHING DOWN

It is common that people have a bright idea, which they think and dream about but never write down the details. Then they forget. At the time, the idea seemed so obvious and so clearly brilliant, but an hour later, or the next morning, it is gone. Get into the habit of writing down all of your bright ideas in a book that you protect and keep track of where you keep it (or a folder in an obvious location on your computer that you regularly back up).

Once you have an idea for a product and/or startup company, the first thing that you need to do is write down all of your thoughts about it. Don't worry about the structure of the writing yet; write down everything that you can think of that you want the product or startup to do. If writing does not work for you then record yourself talking. If you can't do that then draw pictures. If you can't do that then ask someone to help you with one of the options. Once you've documented your thoughts, get started with the 20-step framework and refer to your documented thoughts as you go. Do not delete any of your thoughts, drawings, or recordings. Use all of it as a reference as you work. Special note: Stay flexible around the central idea. Things will be evolving and moving around. Keep track of the details. Let's get started.

ASSIGNMENT If you already use the cloud to back up all of your work securely, that is excellent. If you regularly use software that keeps track of versions of your work, so that you never invest hours editing the wrong version of a document, that is superb. If, however, for any reason, you are not yet able to back-up in the cloud or you do not have access to software that keeps track of versions of your documents, you will need to do these things manually. If you are working on a computer, create a folder with a logical name that you will not forget. Put that folder in an obvious location on the computer (not a clever place, but a clear and easy to remember place), that will still be obvious to you tomorrow and the next day. Create a new document and save it in the folder that you just created. Name the file something easy to remember and give it today's date; then every day you edit it, save a version with that day's date so that you can tell the difference between files. Always work on the most recent date and version of the file. If you do not have a computer, buy a spiral binder with lined paper (or an equivalent that is available to you). Put your name and contact information on it and keep it in a safe place. Do all of your work in the document or binder.

A FIRM FOUNDATION

Once you have decided to create a startup company, a good first move is to seek out qualified legal and accounting guidance on questions such as where to incorporate, where to operate, agreements between the founders on ownership, etc. These are critical questions that people take for granted as they enthusiastically rush to create their product. Where you incorporate will impact the taxes that you pay, access to support from the government including grant money, and more. Where you operate will impact the cost of operating your company, your access to skilled employees, and more. Building a solid foundation when you start will save you the trouble of realizing later that you should have incorporated in a different country or state, that you should have incorporated as a different type of legal entity, that you should have opened an office somewhere else, and that now you need to move everything around, which may mean losing money and key employees. Start with interviewing lawyers and accountants who understand the type of business you plan to create. Seek their counsel before you do anything.

ASSIGNMENT Identify a lawyer and accountant whom you can approach and with whom you can work. Identify where you will incorporate and where you plan to operate as a company (where you will have an office and employees). Write at least one paragraph on this section. Explore and refine your questions.

THE BASIC IDEA

If you have an idea to work on, that is good news. If you aren't sure whether your idea is good enough, take a chance on it and start working; you can always pivot—try it from a different angle or approach, taking it in a different direction—or you can view the exploration as practice and start over with a completely different idea if this first idea doesn't fly for some reason. Do not overthink it. Chances are, you have had several excellent ideas over the years, but if you are like most people you talked yourself out of those ideas saying something along the lines of "If it is such a good idea, then someone would have done it by now." The truth is that you might be the "someone" who thought of it who is doing it right now.

In the Silicon Valley the conventional wisdom is that if you are and I are talking about it, then there are other teams of people within driving distance who are already working on it. Don't worry about other people working on an idea that is similar to your idea; competition is validation. You could still be the one to win with the execution of that idea, so embrace it and see what you can do with it.

If you cannot think of a "once in a lifetime" idea, you might look around you. What doesn't exist (as far as you can tell) that would make your life better? Look at your home life, your hobbies, your work, and think, "what does not exist that would be really helpful?" or "I have an idea of how to make that already helpful thing even better."

I know from experience that people have more ideas than they give themselves credit for. I have led hundreds of trainings around the world with groups of colleagues, friends, and strangers, and at the beginning of the brainstorming ideas section of the training people say they have no good ideas. But then we talk about it, and within an hour we have dozens of ideas for products and startup companies.

To start things off, it is very important to realize a couple things about an idea:

▶ The idea will change. It will morph and evolve, and in the end, it might be very similar to the original idea, or radically different. Or you might abandon it completely, in preference for a new idea that evolves out of your work on that original idea. All of those outcomes are okay.

▶ If you or any of your collaborators are too attached to the details of your original idea, it could become a problem when the idea evolves and changes. Thus, it is very important that you become attached to doing something entrepreneurial rather than becoming too attached to specific ideas or details. This is why the original idea is important but not more important than picking your best idea (whatever it is) and getting started, then seeing what happens over time.

▶ A special note about your potential idea:

In all of my startup entrepreneurship teaching to individuals and groups around the world, the most common basic idea is food. Whether it is food delivery, a food cart, drink stand, kiosk, bar, café, restaurant, food packaging or bottling company, etc. There is something about food and beverage (F&B) that people find irresistible. It might be because food is one of the core essentials of life along with air and water. (Of the three I would suggest doing something with water. Clean water, make water more available to those who live without it, etc.)

There is something about F&B ideas that many people cannot resist. But you need to know that F&B are very high failure rate businesses. That reality doesn't mean that you shouldn't pursue your F&B dream; you just need to understand the risk in the reality of it before you jump in. If you do F&B anything, keep in mind that the business details and execution of the venture itself are more important than whatever food or beverage you prepare and serve. You could be the best culinary experience in town and go under. The right location, a long line of customers every day, superb food, etc. will not save you from bad business practices.

> **HINT** You need to become an expert or hire experts in forecasting, procurement, supply chain, inventory control, and portion control, and then you have a chance to succeed.
>
> **BONUS HINT** This is also the secret to a successful business manufacturing any physical thing (aka any "widget").

There are 5 fundamental areas of **need**: 1. Everyone is born, 2. Everyone needs to breathe clean air, 3. Everyone needs to eat healthy food and drink clean water, 4. Everyone needs to eliminate what their body does not use of what they eat and drink, 5. Everyone dies. Consider how far away your idea falls from those fundamental 5 vital areas of need. The further away from the 5 you go, the less your idea is a need and the more it becomes a *want*, or even worse, a curiosity (a useless thing looking for someone who cares). Whatever you choose, do no harm.

If you are genuinely stuck and cannot think of an idea, do not worry; there are resources that you can explore.

Once you have an idea to work on, keep in mind that the idea will evolve, move around, and potentially change completely. Do not anchor too tightly onto the specifics of the idea, rather, stay flexible around the central idea.

"After pitching and working with others your idea should change and evolve. If it didn't then you need to take a step back and question whether or not you were listening carefully enough." —Sami Kizilbash

The idea is important but not the most important ingredient in the creation of a startup. A powerful idea is very helpful, but there are many examples in the world of weak ideas that succeed, and great ideas that do not. Do not let the lack of a great idea (in your opinion) get in the way of you starting a company.

> **HINT** "The right team and execution can make gold out of rubbish. The wrong team and execution will make rubbish out of gold." —Paul Kewene-Hite

This framework is geared around execution, and we will get to the formation of the right team in later steps.

ASSIGNMENT Explore your basic idea. This is not yet an inventory of features and benefits, this is simply stating what it is that you plan to offer (e.g., RFID[1] tagging of polar bears, female plumbers in Shanghai, alternative schools in Bulgaria, a FinTech solution for microloans to farmers in Africa, etc.) Write at least one paragraph on this section. Explore and refine your questions.

---

1   RFID is Radio Frequency Identification. Invented in 1945 it is a mature technology that is used across industries from retail to the military. It uses transmitters and readers to keep track of the details of items, their location, and movements.

THE BIG PLAY

Beyond the creation of your idea as a product (for example), it is important to identify the bigger-picture impact of what you are working to create.

Investors, shareholders, boards of directors/governors, and your eventual team will need to understand A. Is your startup a one-trick pony, meaning will your company ever do more than whatever you have decided to do as a first offering (e.g., product, service, solution?). B. How does the first offering (and the follow-on offerings that you are lining up) fit into a bigger opportunity for the company, shareholders, and stakeholders?

Consider companies like McDonalds, Amazon, and Tesla. What is the bigger play for those companies? Even though the average person thinks of McDonalds as a fast food restaurant, it is also a real estate company that has realized significant wealth from controlling and creatively deploying its real estate holdings. It is important to note that real estate being a part of the value creation and value capture at McDonalds was not part of their beginning; it came later, thanks to Corporate Entrepreneurship[2].

Most people think that Amazon is an online store where you can buy books, clothes, toys, etc. Thanks to Corporate Entrepreneurship, however, Amazon is a company that does much more than e-commerce of books and consumer electronics; Amazon as a company controls a meaningful percentage of the transactions in the cloud, thanks to Amazon Web Services (AWS).

Next, consider Tesla. Most people think of Tesla as a maker of high-end electric cars. But thanks to Corporate Entrepreneurship, Tesla is becoming a power company that produces various products from the shingles on roof tops harvesting solar energy to power stations that you install in your garage to power your house and your car.

So, the question for you at this point is: What is the bigger picture for your company in light of your entrepreneurial engagement right now? You may be working on a specific solution or product or service, but what is the potential bigger impact on the company? Clarifying and defining your intention up front will help you as you go. The intention that you establish now may change and evolve as you go, and that is normal.

> **HINT** An evolutionary step happens when startup entre-
> preneurs eventually become corporate entrepreneurs
> inside the company that they build. It is how companies
> continue to grow and stay viable and relevant over time.

---

2   Corporate Entrepreneurship is simply the work of an entrepreneur inside of an existing organiza-
    tion (e.g., a company, school, government, etc.)

STEP 4

THE OFFERING

Once you decide on the basic idea and your intention for the bigger play, you need to articulate some meaningful detail into what you will offer your customers; this is your product, service, and/or platform. Remember to include the standard features and benefits that are required for your type of offering; do not focus exclusively on special or differentiated features and benefits.

If your startup is gearing around any type of science or technology, it will be helpful to use my framework for an **Offering Requirements Document (ORD)**. My ORD is a specially customized science and technology development framework, based on a traditional Market Requirements Document (MRD).

You should consider which of the following is a factor in your offering:

Invention ▶ Uncommon. This is when you work to achieve what has never been before. This can be done but it is comparatively rare, and it is often the most expensive in both cost and time.

Innovation ▶ Common. This is when you take an existing thing and materially change, modify, adapt, and reposition it into a new and improved thing. The key here is that innovation is done to something that already exists. This is significantly more common than invention and typically less expensive in both cost and time. Importantly, innovation does not necessarily stay positioned where it is at the moment; part of the innovation is that it might be repositioned and/or relocated.

Renovation ▶ Common. Renovation makes material modifications and adaptations to something that already exists, but it differs from innovation in two respects: 1. The renovated thing is typically intended to stay positioned where it already is, and 2. The primary goal is to uplift and refresh the thing so that it can be revived and stay relevant.

Revolution ▶ Uncommon. This is when you engage (maybe even fight against) the way that things are to effect significant change from the status quo, so that things can become what they should be. Revolution commonly requires invention as well as innovation, and the renovation of many things rather than effecting change to only one specific thing.

Nothing ▶ *This fifth option is the most common.* Most companies do more of the same, even when they know that they need to change. Doing something just to be doing something, or because you can, is also not good enough, and might be value destructive rather than value creative. Do not break something that is working and should not be changed. Think about this carefully; WHY are you doing whatever it is that you plan to do?

At the beginning of your explanation of what you hope to do, I suggest that you first identify whether (and why) you intend to invent, innovate, renovate, or revolutionize as part of creating a startup.

Next, in the context of that declared intention, you need to give some detail about the thing itself that you intend to work on and accomplish. Define what it currently is and what it can and should become in as much detail as possible. (It is helpful if you can connect it back to the "why.")

This is where you will inventory features and benefits. What will what you are offering actually do and how will it do it? What features and benefits are standard, and which make it unique and different?

Keep in mind that the "what" will likely evolve over time, and that is normal. You will be experimenting and exploring, trying different approaches, possibly pivoting once or more, until you find the right combination to open the lock on this opportunity.

> **ASSIGNMENT** Write at least one paragraph in your own words about what you plan to do. Then identify whether or not this work will require invention of something new, an innovation or renovation of an existing thing, or a revolution to overthrow something. Then inventory the standard and differentiated features and benefits. Explore and refine your questions.

STEP 5

VALUE PROPOSITION, UNIQUE SELLING PROPOSITION (USP), OR WHY-TO-BUY

Now that you have inventoried the features and benefits of your offering, you need a simple-to-understand statement of why anyone will care about it and who they are to you (e.g., shareholders, Board of Directors, employees, customers, suppliers, etc.) You might need multiple statements of value; do not assume that one statement fits all purposes. Each stakeholder may have a unique perspective on what part of what you are doing is valuable to them.

Establishing the value of the offering to intended beneficiaries (meaning the people who will buy and use what you are selling) is key. Why would someone buy it? Especially, why should they do what you want them to do rather than doing nothing differently? You need to think about value, USP, and why-to-buy from several perspectives: the end user, the buyer, your strategic partners, your own team, investors, and shareholders.

This is another opportunity to think in the context of standards and differentiators. People have standard motivations to buy, such as needing a product or service or solution that actually works as advertised and as suits their needs. But they are also motivated by the values around the offering that are different and set your offering apart from any other offerings. When puzzling through the value of the offering and reasons someone would buy it, think about their specific requirements and pain points.

For example, as to the value proposition for your own company itself, answer the question of how this offering increases the value of the company. Does it enhance your brand, or does it conflict or detract from the brand? If so, how? Does the offering create and capture shareholder value? If so, how? Will it make processes more efficient and/or effective? If so, how?

As another example, regarding the value proposition for your target customer: As a base line, does your offering satisfy their fundamental needs and requirements? Once that is established (hopefully easily and quickly), start thinking about their motivations. Are they motivated at all? (Keep in mind that the most common competition is "nothing," meaning the user does nothing to change what they are currently doing.) If they are motivated to change, what is behind that motivation? Everyone has a drive that is separate and distinct from the thing that they are buying. For example, they might have a leadership or man-agement problem, or a workflow problem, or a budget or cash problem, or they are losing market share, etc. There is something that is causing your customer to be frustrated or stressed or to lose sleep. You need to figure out what that is so that you can address it.

As an example, when I worked at a technology company, we were presenting for a signifi-cant contract worth millions of dollars. We figured out that a primary motivation for our potential customer was around the fact that they had a unified global P&L anchored on a single currency and they needed to purchase in that single currency everywhere in the world. We figured out how to make it possible for the client to buy in their single currency anywhere in the world, and that very heavily biased them toward buying our technology. The features and benefits of the technology mattered less than how it met the client's spe-cific need (as long as the technology met the basic technical specifications.

So, what you need to do right now is to think about two value propositions:

1. For your own company and what is the value that your initiative will deliver to your company?

2. For your primary target customer/user. What is their primary motivation and therefore the top three most compelling values that you are offering them?

GO TO MARKET

STEP 6

You need to plan how to deliver your offering to the target customer and market. Where, when, how, and to whom the offering will be delivered should be detailed to a meaningful degree.

It is often helpful to think backward from the hands of the customer. Imagine how what you are offering will make it into the hands of the person who will use it. Then take one step at a time back to where you are now. Will you be manufacturing a physical product? Will it be software that is downloaded from the cloud or used at-will via a web browser and delivered from a cloud-based server (including the delivery of installers and plug-ins)? Is it a service that will be delivered over the cloud or in person? Think through all of the moving parts as if you were building the clockworks inside of a mechanical watch.

Let me give you a high-level example that begins with the goal and works backwards. In the business world, this is commonly called "Reverse Engineering"—taking a process or product apart to see how it was built so that you can build the same thing without starting from scratch. This timeline is for example only and will differ for every product and market as every delivery involves unique considerations that must be factored into planning.

Let's say that your startup will be designing, engineering, manufacturing, and then delivering a physical electronic device to the market. (I'll use a physical product that needs to be manufactured as an example, because it tends to be more complicated than engineering and delivering software.) Let's further assume that there are seasonality considerations for your target market.

1. **Product in stores (online as well as brick-and-mortar)**
    Let's say that you need to have the product in stores (online and in physical locations) by November (for example), so that you can hit the big selling season for your product in late November through late-December.

2. **Pallets[3] of finished goods shipping to distribution, fulfillment, and stores**
   Which means that you need to have pallets of boxes of your physical product
   in distribution by October so that it can be delivered to stores in October
   and November.

3. **Active manufacturing**
   Which means that you should be actively manufacturing by August or no later
   than September so that you can begin shipping in September to hit distribution
   in October.

4. **Raw materials to manufacturing**
   Which means that you need to have all raw materials, casts, tools, and manufac-
   turing BOMs (Bill of Materials) and specifications, etc. to the manufacturer by
   August, but ideally in July for manufacture in August.

5. **Testing complete**
   Which means that you need to have the product finalized and tested and ready for
   manufacturing no later than July.

6. **Active Beta and Alpha testing along with bug regression and fixes**
   Which means that you should have been in beta testing no later than May, and
   alpha testing (for example) as early as February or March, giving your team time
   for bug regression and fixes. This is also the time that you should be ordering all
   of the raw materials to make sure that they arrive at the manufacturer's facility
   on time.

7. **Technical Specifications and other engineering completed**
   The freeze on modifications to all technical specifications for the product should
   happen by February, with engineering and design completed by that time.

8. **Research and Development (R&D)**
   You need to work with engineering to ensure that you have time to complete
   that work between now and January-February, which also means working with
   Marketing and all other internal parties to ensure that the device that you are
   making is correctly planned and aligned with all relevant expectations.

9. **Marketing and Sales Activities well in advance**
   Then you have considerations for all marketing and sales activities. You need to
   advertise to stores and distribution so that they can order the product and have it
   in stores in time, and that needs to be done far in advance. You also need to plan
   when you will advertise to the customer, so that they are motivated to buy once
   the product is in stores and online.

---

3   A pallet is a type of low profile platform typically made of wood, but at times, other materials. Boxes
    and other materials are stacked on the pallet, which is then movable by a forklift from one part of a
    factory to another, and then loaded onto trucks, etc.

TAM VS. TASM

In addition to the above, I would like to recommend an exercise to you. You may have heard of a TAM, *T-A-M* stands for <u>Total Addressable Market</u>. The *S* in TASM (sometimes called SAM) is the addition of the word: <u>Serviceable</u>.

▶ The **Total Market** is the big number of all people and money spent on products, services, and solutions similar to the one that you will be creating.

▶ The **Addressable Market** is the percentage of the Total to whom you can deliver a targeted meaningful message designed to inspire the customer to buy and use what you are offering.

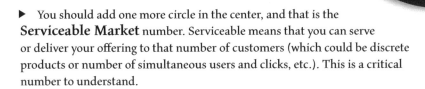

People will often draw a big circle and call it the Total and then draw a circle inside the big circle and call it the Addressable, and then declare a percentage of that number to represent the number of users or the amount of money that they hope to secure.

▶ You should add one more circle in the center, and that is the **Serviceable Market** number. Serviceable means that you can serve or deliver your offering to that number of customers (which could be discrete products or number of simultaneous users and clicks, etc.). This is a critical number to understand.

When you are presenting to a Board of Directors, or a CEO or CFO, or an investor, or to your team, the most relevant number is not the Total, it is the relationship and connection between the numbers that represent the Addressable and the Serviceable Markets. The amount of money that you will be investing in the Addressable correlates to the amount of money invested in the Serviceable.

Let's say that you spend so much in the Addressable that you have a higher conversion to cash (meaning paying customers) than you have capacity to serve; then you have either overinvested in the Addressable or underinvested in the Serviceable. What matters is that you "right size" the investment for both in a coordinated effort so that you convert to cash (achieve paying customers) at a comparable rate to the amount of product or capacity of the service that you have to offer.

If you were to build a TASM now, meaning a plan for your Total, Addressable, Serviceable Market, how big is the Total? (Don't anchor too much on this big number, as it matters but not as much as the next numbers.) How big is the Addressable Market? Who are the customers? Where are they? How will you deliver a meaningful message to them? At what cost? And how big is your Serviceable Market? That is, how much serviceable capacity do you anticipate needing to create so that you can profitably deliver to paying customers? Once you start measuring this way, you will have a better chance of impressing key influencers and decision makers because you know what you are doing.

> **ASSIGNMENT** Write at least one paragraph identifying WHO the target audience is for your offering and WHERE they are located. Then give some meaningful detail in at least one paragraph on HOW you will deliver your offering to them; be certain to account for special timing considerations that will impact adoption (this could be anything from budgeting cycles to known deadlines on their end to the impact of holidays in a market.) Then construct a TASM with numbers and details so that when you present you can explain the relationship between the investment made and how many people you addressed and how many you can serve. Explore and refine your questions.

TEAM AND EXECUTION

STEP 7

> "The right team and execution can make gold out of rubbish. The wrong team and execution will make rubbish out of gold."
> —Paul Kewene-Hite

Be inclusive and embrace diversity. Be an equal opportunity and equal pay for equal work employer. A critical mistake often made by first-time entrepreneurs is ignoring the "boring" execution details of what needs to be done to make the startup a reality. Thinking through and documenting these details is the equivalent of creating a recipe with a list of ingredients for the meal you want to prepare and eat. Execution modeling is a step-by-step inventory of what needs to be done so that your startup will become real. When you present to potential investors or potential team members, the right people will NEED to know that you know what must be done. If you went into a kitchen to cook a meal from raw ingredients, what is the order of operations that you would follow? What is the first activity that you need to do? What is the second activity? What is the third? Do the same thing for your startup. Inventory the activities that must be done in order. Be as specific and as detailed as possible.

Thinking through and writing out the above activities based on an inventory of what *must* be done is a good way to figure out whether or not you already have the team that you need, and who is missing and needs to be found and brought on board. Begin by listing all the activities that MUST be done. Put your name next to which of those activities you can credibly perform (not what you are willing to try but don't really know how to do). If there are others already committed to your startup, list their names next to those activities that they can credibly perform. Once that is done, you will see the gaps around must-do activities that have no names assigned to them. That tells you whom you need to find to complete your startup team. Those whom you need to find could be new hires as full-time employees (FTE) or part-time employees (PTE), or contract workers, etc.

One way to think about team and execution is to consider answers to the question "what does a clock do?" When you are explaining what you plan to do to create a new company, you'll need to describe *how* the clock will tell time, instead of just saying that it tells time. Imagine opening the face of a traditional clock to expose the clockworks showing the various moving parts: gears, springs, etc. It would be ideal if you could document and explain every detail, but at a minimum, be prepared to describe the basics of which mechanisms move and how they are connected to make the hands move, and in turn, tell time. Do that for the details—personnel and processes—of the company that you are working to build.

> **ASSIGNMENT** Inventory your top 20 (or more) mission-critical activities. Put names of committed team members next to each activity. The critical activities that have no name next to them tell you whom you need to recruit to help you. Write at least one paragraph on this section. Explore and refine your questions.

BUSINESS MODELING

STEP 8

Your business model is how you will make money (meaning revenue and more specifically, profit), as well as how you will otherwise finance and operate your company. When you are asked about your business model, the underlying question is how you will become a viable business and then stay profitable.

Your business model is the beating heart of your venture. Do not assume that how you will make revenue and profit[4] and otherwise finance your startup is obvious. When you are asked about your business model you need to have a better response than "we will sell what we make" (and raise investment capital). You need to be prepared with a robust response to questions about your business model.

Google's business model is an interesting example. I remember visiting Google's office when it was a startup. They had a monitor over the reception desk that showed every search that was happening real-time. I remember the tempo of it ... search (pause) search (pause) search, etc. I thought to myself "Wow, people are actually using it!" I sat in the lobby doing searches to watch them pop up on the monitor over the desk. Now there are more than 3.5 billion searches every day. People who use Google's search engine do not pay to perform a search. At Google, search is a vehicle that is leveraged to do much more than display results for the definition of a word or a website or a restaurant near you, and Google is much more than an Internet search company.

Google makes its money through Google AdWords, AdSense, Google Play store, Google Cloud, and more. Businesses pay Google to display their information in search results

---

4   Revenue is the money that you make from the sale of goods and services. Profit is the money that is left over after you make all of your payments, settle your debts, and in all ways account for your costs and expenses.

(AdWords). AdSense is interesting, because both Google and website publishers make a little money when an ad is placed by Google on a website and someone, somewhere on the planet, clicks on it. When an app is purchased on the Google Play store, Google makes a little money. Google does not make money on Android itself (the smart device operating system), interestingly, but it does make money on the ecosystem around it. An interesting feature of Google's business model is that, in addition to free searches, they have several offerings that do not generate revenue directly. As with search, these offerings create value in the Google brand by generating good will and loyalty. Take, as only one of dozens of possible examples, Google for Startups Accelerator (formerly Google's Launchpad Accelerator). Google for Startups Accelerator spends money to help startup companies around the world for free. It is an initiative that creates good will, healthy brand awareness and loyalty for Google; it also keeps Google current on what is happening with the best startups globally. I am an unpaid volunteer Anchor Mentor in the Google for Startups Accelerator, and there are hundreds of volunteers like me who work with Google to level the playing field for founders and startups around the world.

Here is a non-Internet example: How does BMW make money? Selling cars is the obvious response. They also make money on dealership franchises, parts, service and maintenance, leasing, rentals, and merchandise, among others.

Here is another: Star Wars has made more money on licensing and merchandise than on ticket sales for the movies themselves.

Here is another: "Razor and Blades" is a common expression in business. Companies will give away the handle of a razor used for shaving (even though it cost them money to design, engineer, and manufacture it) because there is more money to be made on selling the blades that attach to the end of the handle because the blades wear out and need to be replaced more frequently than the handle. An application of this expression would be a printer. Let's say, for example, that your offering is a 3D printer. You sell the printer for money (maybe at a discount so that people buy your printer over the competition); you then make additional revenue by selling the printer cartridges for your 3D printer. You could also sell a service contract to maintain the printer, and software to design what you print. Then software advertising might help you sell other 3D printer-related offerings.

When you think about the business you are starting, how do you plan to make money? Simple sales of what you are offering? Is there any other way? Maybe there could be other products or a service around the offering that you are selling? Is there a way to sell other products and services through your offering? Will you sell B2C (Business to Consumer, meaning you will sell and ship your offering directly from your business to your consumer), B2B (Business to Business), or B2G (Business to Government)? Include as much detail as you can.

ASSIGNMENT Articulate all the ways that you will make money (revenue and profit). Don't just say "sell product"—you need to be specific about how you will sell, and various ways that money will be made. Write at least one paragraph on this section. Explore and refine your questions.

FINANCIAL MODELING

> "Never, EVER, run out of cash!"
> —**Patrick Turner**, INSEAD Professor of Entrepreneurship

If you are just beginning the process to start a company, you probably don't have complete documents and data in a condition that will be helpful. As you build your company, you will also need to improve the condition of your data so that your future business has a financial model built on complete and accurate information.

If you can build a Cashflow from scratch, then you can explain the details when you are asked to defend the numbers during any meeting. When you present, have an updated copy of your Cashflow, and be prepared to explain the details to those who ask.

Work to frame a financial model going forward that progresses you from where you are to where you plan to go. Building a Cashflow (as well as an SG&A, P&L, Balance Sheet, along with Budgets for MDF/SDF, T&E/T&S, etc.) is fundamental for understanding your initiative. At this point you may not know what those words and acronyms mean, which is okay. You will, however, need to invest some effort in learning their meaning so that you can use them comfortably in sentences as well as comfortably answer questions about them when asked. The definitions are below.

In the business world it is very common for people to assume that other people will know how to build and read the numbers, so they invest very little study into it. Basic financial skills are very important for all people in business. Not everyone needs to be a Certified Public Accountant or Chartered Accountant but being able to build and read a Cashflow should be a required skill for all business professionals.

If an investor, board of directors, or shareholder calls you to a meeting to discuss your venture, grab an updated Cashflow on the way to the meeting. The other financial instruments such as a Profit and Loss (P&L), Balance Sheet, Sales General and Administrative (SG&A) etc., are also important but the Cashflow is the most critical. If you don't understand your cash position over time, you do not understand your business.

Good financial planning is key to persuading shareholders, the board, and leadership that you know what you are doing. If you don't (yet) know how to do it yourself, work side-by-side with a finance-professional to build complete financials. I say side-by-side so that you see how it is done, you fully understand the numbers, and can understand and explain the details. (If you can build a Cashflow from scratch then you can explain the details when you are asked to defend the numbers during any meeting.)

Here are a few overly simplified definitions of business words that you need to know:

▶ **Finance vs. Accounting**
Finance looks forward to what will happen.
Accounting looks back at what happened.

- ▸ **Payment vs. Expense**

  A <u>Payment</u> is when money leaves the company and is given to someone else.
  An <u>Expense</u> is the agreed responsibility to make a payment at some future date.

- ▸ **Revenue vs. Profit**

  <u>Revenue</u> is all money that comes into the company from sales.
  <u>Profit</u> is the money that is left over after you have paid all of your
  expenses and taxes.

- ▸ **Sources & Uses**

  <u>Source</u> is where you will get money.
  A <u>Use</u> is how the money will be spent.

- ▸ **Budget**

  A <u>Budget</u> is the amount of money (and time) that must be invested in order to do
  what must be done. Importantly budgeted amounts need to factor for how much
  money (and time) is actually available.[5]

- ▸ **Cashflow**

  A <u>Cashflow</u> is the financial detail of how a company is being operated; money
  coming in, all money measured impacts on debts and assets, and all money
  going out.[6]

- ▸ **Free Cashflow**

  <u>Free Cashflow</u> (not to be confused with the document that is called "a Cashflow")
  is the money that you have left over after all capital expenditures (aka CapEx,
  which is the money spent on fixed assets).

- ▸ **Working Capital**

  <u>Working Capital</u> = **Current Assets** minus **Current Liabilities**. <u>Assets</u> are tangible
  things that have value such as property, inventory, cash, etc. <u>Liabilities</u> are things
  that you need to pay such as debt, taxes, wages, rent, utilities, etc.

- ▸ **Professional Fees**

  <u>Professional Fees</u> are cash paid to professionals who are not your employees, such
  as lawyers, accountants, designers, engineers, etc.

- ▸ **CapEx vs OpEx**

  <u>CapEx</u> is Capital Expenditure, which is money spent on fixed assets.
  <u>OpEx</u> is Operating Expenditure, which is the money spent to operate the company.

---

5   Budgeting is incredibly valuable and essential for running your entrepreneurial venture and making
sure that you never run out of cash. Your budgets should be planned, reviewed, and updated
routinely as a team. Be sure to remind everyone that a budget is more than a plan for how much
money will be spent, it is a reconciliation of how much must be spent in order to accomplish your
plan compared to how much money there is to spend in the bank account. Monthly budgeting
meetings, accounting back a month, and financially planning forward a quarter are good practices.

6   This is a window into all money that comes in and leaves the company. (You should typically have
an 18 to 24-month Cashflow, with the next 13 weeks by week, and the rest of the months by month.)
Be sure to use mathematics rather than simply typing in numbers.

▶ Fixed Assets

Fixed Assets are physical things such as land, buildings, equipment, vehicles, etc.

▶ Burn Rate and Runway

Burn Rate is the amount of money that you spend in a month.
Runway is the number of months that you have until you are out of money.

▶ Break Even, and Profitability

Break Even is when the same amount of money comes in as goes out.
Profitability is when you have money left over after paying everything.

▶ Pro forma

Pro forma is Latin for "as a matter of form" or "for the sake of form" and is a word put on financials to show that the numbers are educated guesses or projections.

▶ T&E or T&S

T&S/T&E[7] is Travel & Subsistence or Travel & Expenses (occasionally referred to as Travel & Entertainment). This budget is for rental cars, trains, planes, hotels, lunches and dinners, etc. T&E is used in North American English and in North American influenced regions. T&S is used in British English and in British influenced regions.

▶ MDF and SPIF

MDF is an acronym for Market Development Fund and is the money that you spend to take your offering to market.
SPIF stands for Sales Promotion Incentive Fund and is a powerful tool for motivating the point of sale to inspire them to advocate for your offering over the competition (the seller and/or buyer). This could be, and is not limited to, a payment made to the salesperson or a discount/rebate offered to the customer.

> **ASSIGNMENT** Build a Cashflow. Do not assume that you will simply hire someone else to do it for you. Learn to build a Cashflow from a blank spreadsheet if you can; at a minimum, find someone on your team or work together as a team right now to build a basic Cashflow. Then write at least one paragraph on the details inside of the Cashflow, possibly including the details listed above. Explore and refine your questions. If you need to partner with a finance professional to help you, do it; but learn how to read financial documents, how to tell the stories of the numbers, and how to read along as others go through the numbers.

---

7   Watch this budget very carefully and put rules on all expenses and what can be claimed to make people responsible and hold people accountable. It happens at times that people (especially inside of large companies) game their expense reports so that they claim more money than they legitimately spend on real business. This line item can be value destructive when you are a fledgling venture that is carefully watching every dollar in the bank account.

FUNDABLE EVENT TIMELINES

Now that you have done your team and financial modeling, with your list of 20 or more mission-critical activities, you should put that list of activities on a timeline (for example 18 to 24 months). Creating a Gantt chart of mission-critical activities (highlighting milestones and fundable events) then harmonizing it with a Cashflow is good planning and good for presentations.

You can build your Gantt chart in a spreadsheet if you don't have project management software. What matters is that you can see the markers that represent the start and stop dates for each activity. On each bar you should name the activity as well as who is responsible along with the associated costs.

When you build a Cashflow you should then harmonize it with the Gantt chart to ensure that the activities and costs over the same months align month-by-month.

When you are building the timeline, with the completed Gantt on the top of the page and the Cashflow lined up below it, decision makers can quickly see that your financial and activities-based planning is complimentary in their construction.

The next thing that I suggest that you do is identify the **Milestones** (the moments in time when you complete an activity or task) on the Gantt chart. Then differentiate between which milestones simply mark the completion of a task and which milestones are actually evidence that you are right in what you intended, planned, and executed. (This could be a working prototype or a paying customer, etc. This is very different from finishing the writing for a business plan for example, which does not prove that you are right but just that you finished what you started.) The type of milestone that is evidence that you are right, is called a **Fundable Event** and it is very important for a few reasons.

▶ Evidence that you are right shows that the entrepreneurial venture is making progress!

▶ Evidence that you are right will be the proof that you need for continued funding and support from the company leadership and board.

▶ Evidence that you are right can be correlated to value creation (increasing value) and value capture (when the company is able to hold onto and make use of the value). Fundable events correlate to the increase in the value of what you are doing, and potentially increase the value of the company itself.

Investors and Boards and others who hold the keys to your future funding will be watching for the Fundable Events so that they can know that the work is progressing and that your corporate entrepreneurial venture is deserving of continued support.

When you have the Fundable Event Timeline planned out, and you regularly update it (you should update it at a minimum of once a week) then you and those who are supporting you can use it to keep track of progress and timings that might change over time.

Investors and Boards and other financial supporters might use the Fundable Event Timeline to plan when they will transfer resources and capital support to your initiative (just as an investor would do for a startup); when you hit your deliverables (the milestones and especially the fundable events) then you have a measurable defense for expecting ongoing support.

ASSIGNMENT Write at least one paragraph on this section. Explore and refine your questions. Create a Gantt chart identifying all of your activities (when each activity is intended to start and stop). Then put the Gantt chart and your Cashflow summary on the same page making sure that the months line up as shown in the following template (and on page 410). (You should have built a Cashflow in step 9.) Highlight the milestones that prove that you are right to call them Fundable Events; e.g., this is when the machine you are building actually works, it is when a stranger who has no connection to you purchases your product, etc. A fundable event is not when you simply finish what you started, such as writing a business plan or building a Cashflow with numbers that look good or designing a brochure that makes you happy, etc.

FUNDABLE
EVENT
TIMELINE

Cashflow Summary

	Month 1, Year 1	Month 2, Year 1	Month 3, Year 1	Month 4, Year 1	Month 5, Year 1	Month 6, Year 1	Month 7, Year 1	Month 8, Year 1	Month 9, Year 1	Month 10, Year 1	Month 11, Year 1	Month 12, Year 1
Opening Cash Balance												
Total CapEX												
Total OpEx												
Total Cash Out												
Total Cash In												
Closing Cash Balance												

Execution Timeline (Gantt Chart)

ACTIVITY	OWNER	ASSOCIATED COSTS US$	Month 1, Year 1	Month 2, Year 1	Month 3, Year 1	Month 4, Year 1	Month 5, Year 1	Month 6, Year 1	Month 7, Year 1	Month 8, Year 1	Month 9, Year 1	Month 10, Year 1	Month 11, Year 1	Month 12, Year 1

Note: Milestones mean that you finished what you started. Fundable Events are validation that you are right.

CAPITAL MODELING

You need to determine what capital will be required over time, and where that support will come from. Keep in mind that although capital is typically money, it might also be money equivalents (e.g., access to and use of buildings, equipment, etc.). Make sure to fully understand what capital is required to get your startup to the point where it can self-sustain, which is at break-even (meaning you are bringing in as much money as is going out), and profitability (which is when more money is coming in than is going out). Investors and shareholders will ask you what you need to take your startup from where you are now to the point of self-sufficiency; be prepared with an answer. It will be helpful to have a best case, base case, and worst case for your financials and capital requirements. If you can be successful with the worst case or base case numbers, then present those. Even though the best-case numbers look the most appealing, it is typically best to not present the best-case numbers since they are the most optimistic and therefore the most difficult to achieve.

When you think about the timing and costs associated with investment from others, you need to understand that money has the same three states as water: liquid, solid, and vapor.

▶ **Liquid**
This is when money is transportable, or otherwise in a state that it can be moved from one person or entity to another by either electronic transfer from one bank account to another, or from one person to another as some form of recognized currency. Example: When you have coins and bank notes in your pocket and use it to buy something at a store you are liquid, as your money is available for use. People will say "I'm not liquid at the moment." Which typically means "I have money, but I don't have access to it right now."

▶ **Solid**
This is when money is not available or for some reason, not liquid. The money might be in stocks or bonds, or otherwise invested into something that makes it not accessible, or portable, or moveable. But the idea is that it will expand as ice expands when water is frozen (because of interest or other successful growth by performance of the stock or investment or real estate, etc.). When an investor gives you money in exchange for equity (aka ownership) in your company, the idea is that their money will grow or expand (like ice) as you are successful as a company.

▶ **Vapor**
When ice is melted, a percentage of the ice becomes liquid (water) and a percentage is lost as vapor (e.g., steam). With money, the Vapor is any fee or charge or tax or disadvantageous exchange rate, etc., meaning there is some loss of value that could equal part, or potentially all of their money that was invested in a failed stock.

When an investor pledges to invest into your startup venture, they might be liquid in the moment and need to move quickly back into a solid before they incur taxes or other penalties on that money. Or they might need time to "liquidate" or otherwise liberate their money from other investments (stocks, bonds, real estate, etc.) so that they can give cash to you as an investment (either as a loan or as equity), which means that to invest in you they are going from a solid, to a liquid (with hopefully as little vapor as possible), then back into another solid that is ownership in your startup. The expectation is that their money will grow and expand during its time as a solid (equity ownership) with you, and at some future date in a few years they expect their investment back, plus more than they gave you in the first place.

Now that you have done a meaningful amount of work puzzling through your startup venture, you should know whether or not you need OPM (other people's money) to put fuel in the tank to run the engine of your new company. Do not raise investment capital unless you actually need it. If you can create and run your company without OPM, that could be a good thing. If you do need investment, it is best to build as much work as possible before selling an ownership percentage in your startup. If you have little value created, investors will take more ownership for less money. When you have more value created, investors will take less ownership for more money. Raise money if you need to, but there are a few things to keep in mind:

▶ **Smart Money vs. Dumb Money**

Not all money is equal. You may have heard the expressions *smart money* or *dumb money*. This has nothing to do with the relative intelligence of the investor, it has everything to do with whether or not they understand your industry, company, and what you are working to accomplish. If they understand you and can meaningfully help you then they are Smart Money in your deal. If they do not understand you and if they cannot meaningfully help you (other than by giving you money) then they are Dumb Money. Avoid Dumb Money.

▶ **Family and Friends**

(Sometimes called Family, Friends & Fools, the addition of *fools* is because people don't always understand what they are doing.) Your family and friends may not be legally eligible to give you money to start your company. Work with your lawyer before you take grandma's sock-drawer cash that she has been squirreling away for years, and don't let your brother take out a third mortgage on his house to fund you. If grandma and your brother are not qualified investors as far as the law is concerned, and if things go wrong and you lose their money and cannot pay them back, you might get in trouble. This goes for anyone who offers you money. Work with your lawyer to keep everything legitimate and legal.

▶ **Angels**

Wealthy individuals who legally qualify to put their money at risk without compromising themselves financially, are often referred to as Angels. Angels who pool their resources and invest together are called Super Angels. Angels and Supers have some advantages, such as speed to do investments and patience/time to invest in you. Be sure that you only work with Smart Money. Dumb Money is abundant, and it is dangerous; you don't want a Dumb Money investor second-guessing and doubting what you do. You need a Smart Money investor working with you productively side-by-side.

▶ **VC (Venture Capital)**

Professionally incorporated firms with (typically) larger amounts of capital than Angels (although some are feeling pressure from Super Angels). When you speak with a VC ask them where they are in the lifecycle of their fund. They will continue to develop "Deal Flow" even when they have no more money to invest. (Deal Flow is an inventory of opportunities to invest as evidence to their investors that they are succeeding as a fund.) Find Smart Money VC for your type of deal. As a startup, before you spend money that you don't have to fly to a VC to meet and discuss investment make sure that you are not Deal Flow for their weekly numbers, that they have the ability to invest, that they are Smart Money in your deal, and interview them to see if they have actually read your materials and that they "get" you.

▶ PE (Private Equity)

PE is the business term used to refer to investment funds that are organized around General Partners (GP) who run the fund and Limited Partners (LP) who are the financial backers and investors in the fund. PE typically buys and restructures companies that are not publicly traded on a stock exchange. PE is increasingly getting involved in smaller investment opportunities (such as startups).

There are many terms that you should understand, but here are three for starters:

▶ Pre or Post

Investors will ask you if the amount of money that you are raising in exchange for whatever percentage of ownership you are offering, is "pre" or "post." Pre is simply the value of the company before investment money comes in, while Post is the value of the company after investment money comes in. For example, if you are raising US$1 million and you are offering 33.3% Post, that means that you believe that your startup is worth US$3 million after their money is in the bank. This means that the Pre money valuation is US$2 million. Be prepared to defend these numbers. If you don't know the value (which is almost always the case), then tell the investor that you are willing to work with them to develop an accurate valuation. When investors ask you for an amount of money and a percentage of ownership, they are testing you to see if your thinking is in line with theirs. They will tell you what they think your startup is worth, how much money you need, and what percentage is, in their opinion, equal to that investment.

▶ LOI, MOU, and Term Sheets

An LOI is a Letter of Intent. An MOU is a Memorandum of Understanding. A Term Sheet is a document with an offer of investment and the intended terms and conditions. The investor creates and gives the LOI, MOU, and Term Sheet to the entrepreneur. (In the beginning of my career I made the mistake of giving a potential investor a term sheet that I had created. The investor thought it was humorous—he actually laughed at me. He also thought that my lack of experience and basic understanding of who gives the Term Sheet meant that I wasn't ready to receive one from him.) LOIs, MOUs, and Term Sheets are typically not legally binding; they are indications of the investor's thinking and what might happen; they are given to see if both sides of the conversation are aligned before any more time, money, and work is put into the deal to make an investment. The LOI and MOU typically come before the Term Sheet. Do not celebrate over an LOI, MOU, or Term Sheet. Once you accept a Term Sheet, the lawyers get involved to develop those terms into a shareholder agreement. Celebrate once the shareholders' agreement is signed and there is money in the bank.

▶ **Tranche is sometimes spelled "Traunch"**

In English we use <u>tranche</u> (sounds like: trawnch), the French word for *slice*, when talking about dividing up the money that you need into installments. Investors will typically tranche (slice up) the money that you are raising and tie each slice of money to you achieving what you say that you will do as a company. That US$1 million might be US$200,000 now to get you to that milestone in month eight that proves that you are on track, and then that will trigger then next US$200,000 (or whatever amount). Over time, you will eventually receive US$1 million (unless you have a discretionary term saying that if you overachieve your goals then you are not required to take later tranche ... work with a good lawyer to protect your future interests!).

READ *Mastering Private Equity*, Claudia Zeisberger, Michael Prahl, and Bowen White (2017)

ASSIGNMENT Write at least one paragraph on this section. Will you be raising money? How much will you raise in exchange for what percentage of equity (ownership in your company)? Have you identified an investor? When will you start the process? Explore and refine your questions.

STEP 12

LIQUIDITY AND EXITS

Investors almost always invest so that they can get out with more money than they put in. This may sound obvious but first-time entrepreneurs commonly make the mistake of messaging to investors that they plan on being in the startup for the rest of their lives, thinking that the investors will be moved by their absolute commitment. Investors cannot stay invested in your startup for the rest of your life; they will have a timeframe in mind for when they will need their money back. Keep in mind that an investor's exit from your startup does not necessarily mean the end of your company, it is simply a moment in time when that investor will no longer be invested.

Think of what an exit means from three perspectives: 1. the investor and shareholder, 2. the company itself, and 3. you and other founders. The investors will be trying to understand in the beginning, whether or not you will be a problem for them when they need to exit. When they ask about exit possibilities, give answers tailored to their best interest. It might be that the window of opportunity for the investor/shareholder's exit does not fit the best interest of the company or you and other Founders. For example, the company's best interest might be to never be merged or acquired by another company, or the company's potential might be best served if it were to be part of a bigger, more established company that has existing infrastructure, resources, and customers. Give careful thought to the answer before the question is asked.

FOUNDERITIS

> "Founders' attachment, overconfidence, and naïveté
> may be necessary to get new ventures up and running,
> but these emotions later create problems."
> —Noam Wasserman

READ "The Founder's Dilemma," Noam Wasserman, *Harvard Business Review* (HBR) (February 2008)

Founderitis is when a founder behaves in value destructive ways. Companies can be meaningfully harmed or even destroyed by the bad behavior of a founder. You need to take measures in the beginning when things are still good and healthy to protect everyone and everything from unforeseen value-destructive behavior in the future. Work with a good lawyer NOW on a rules-of-engagement agreement between the founders and shareholders to protect the company (and families of founders and shareholders) from what might go wrong in the future.

Founders who cause harm to the companies that they found and work to build are rarely as candid as American Apparel's founder Dov Charney who said, "My biggest weakness is me. I mean, lock me up already! It's obvious! Put me in a cage, I'll be fine. I'm my own worst enemy."[8]

You might find out too late that someone is value destructive. Again, take measures at the start when things are still early and being formed. Sit down with a qualified lawyer and document the rules for good conduct and what happens if one or more of the founders become value destructive. Hopefully you will never need to take action. Hopefully everyone will be rational and behave well.

Finding examples of well-known founders who harmed their successful companies is not that difficult. For every name brand person who fails their company, there are countless regular people who harmed their ventures (and those involved and around it) before they qualified for big press coverage.

> "We have met the enemy and he is us."
> From ***Pogo*** by Walt Kelly, who borrowed it from a 1970 Earth Day poster

---

8   Marketplace.org with Kai Ryssdal 20 January 2014, updated 27 March 2015 "American Apparel CEO Dov Charney on pushing boundaries and his biggest weakness"

There is reality in the humorous yet sad observation that no matter how well intentioned, we are very often our own worst enemy. Anticipate this reality and plan for what to do about it when (not if) our own behavior threatens to undo what good we are working to accomplish.

> **ASSIGNMENT** You and your co-founders (if you have them) need to put in writing what will happen if you or the partners become value destructive. Consider designating an arbiter or another independent, such as an independent senior industry expert or lawyer. This will need to be someone who agrees to function as an arbiter. Write at least one paragraph on this section. Explore and refine your questions.

BOARDS: ADVISORY AND GOVERNANCE

STEP 14

At the very beginning, you can organize a few people who are not legally affiliated with the company but are qualified to help guide you as you create and begin running your startup. This is called an advisory board. Advisors typically volunteer their time, but sometimes they ask for compensation.

> **HINT** If a person asks for money to give you advice when you need to protect what little money you have to run the startup, that person may not have the startup's best interests as a priority. If they want ownership in exchange for advice you should put them on a vesting schedule over time for a small percentage, and if they perform well over time, they earn the percentage.

Once the startup is showing signs of viability (that it will actually survive and hopefully thrive), then you should organize (constitute) a board of directors (in some jurisdictions this is called a board of governors). This is not the executive leadership (sometimes called an executive board), but it is responsible for the company as a whole. The CEO (Chief Executive Officer) reports to the chairman (chairperson) of the board of directors. The chairman is ideally an independent outsider (not the CEO, or an investor), so that they can be as objective as possible. It is ideal if the chairman has deep industry expertise. The board of directors, including the chairman, should be an uneven number so that there are no split votes. The founders and investors/shareholders would typically have an even number of seats. If you are a founder, be brave enough to put trusted non-employees and non-founders in your seats.

> **ASSIGNMENT** Identify up to four people (by name) who could serve as volunteers on your board of advisors. Make sure that these are people who understand what you are doing, understand the industry, and are accessible to you. Then identify an odd number of seats for

your board of directors (3, 5, 7, etc.). Identify a potential chairman of the board (e.g., ideally an independent senior industry expert to whom you have access). Write at least one paragraph on this section. Explore and refine your questions.

MARKETING, SALES, AND BUSINESS DEVELOPMENT

You may have noticed that the definitions and roles of <u>marketing</u> and <u>sales</u> and <u>business development</u> are not always the same from company to company. Sometimes marketing and sales is one integrated organization and other times they are separated, and sometimes they struggle to work together. Business development is sometimes part of marketing, sometimes part of sales, and other times it stands on its own.

I believe that one of the reasons why people sometimes struggle to differentiate between the three is because in the beginning of human beings exchanging what they had for what they needed the three were one integrated function. People wanted to exchange what they had for what other people had so they created marketplaces in town squares or villages and figured out how to transact with each other for goods and materials or money. Someone had grain to trade so they identified where would be the best place to engage people who needed grain (marketing), then they negotiated for permission to set up a stand in a good location with a market place from which they could exchange their grain with others (business development), then they actively negotiated with other to exchange the grain for other things (sales). Over time, people have artificially separated the three.

Stay flexible within the definitions; you will need to work with the definitions of the three as your company defines them.

For the purpose of this startup entrepreneurship training we will define the three neutrally, as follows:

▶ **Marketing**
The planning and research to discover where in the world the optimal customers are located and who those people are in that market; and the determination of how to capture the attention of paying customers with marketing activities like advertising, trade shows, press, etc.

▶ **Sales**
The activities that result in the exchange of the offering for money. This could be in person (traditional sales), or by taking credit card payments on a website, or in a mobile application (digital transactions).

▶ **Business development**
The securing of strategic relationships that open doors and remove barriers. For example, let's say that you are developing a device designed to help medical

patients better manage their pain during therapies. Business development (sometimes called "Biz Dev") would secure an agreement with a recognized medical research facility to perform a study to determine if your device actually does help people manage their pain during therapies.

You should identify the key activities that must be done for marketing, sales, and business development. If you already identified these activities in your team modeling and they are already reflected in your Gantt chart and fundable event timeline, then very well done! There is always more to do so you should continue to build the list of activities.

ASSIGNMENT Write at least one paragraph for marketing, another for sales, and another for business development. Give one or two specific examples of what you will do for marketing, one or two for sales, and one or two for business development. More than simply saying you will do it, SHOW what will be done and what will happen as a result. Do not write, "Do marketing." Give a detailed example, explaining why a specific type of marketing will be effective, and where, when, how, and by whom it will be done. Be prepared to be challenged on every detail that you write. Explore and refine your questions.

CALL TO ACTION OR THE ASK

In preparation for your presentations to potential lawyers, bankers, investors, strategic hires, and others, you need to identify the messages that will show key influencers and decision makers that you know what you are doing so that they will want to join you.

In business, the moment when you ask the listener for what you need from them is sometimes called a **Call to Action** or **The Ask** or **The Question**, but the intent of all three terms is the same.

Keep in mind that what is clear and motivates one listener may or may not be clear and motivate anyone else. Every person has their own requirements, mandates, needs, wants, hopes, stresses, pressures, and so on. Do your best to figure out what motivates the person to whom you are extending (what is often called "putting") The Ask or Call to Action.

For example, Steve Jobs (co-founder of Apple) asked John Sculley (the person who became CEO of Apple after Steve Jobs): "Do you want to sell sugared water for the rest of your life? Or do you want to come with me and change the world?" That Call to Action from Steve Jobs worked for John Sculley, but it might or might not have worked for anyone else. Steve Jobs did his homework on what motivated John Sculley and that specific Call to Action or Ask worked on him in that situation.

As another example, if you are presenting to an investor and you bias your presentation heavily toward revenue and profit but never mention shareholder value, they may not fund your startup if their top priority is shareholder value. Or it could be the other way around if their top priority is revenue and profit. You need to determine the critical motivations of your audience BEFORE you present the details and call them to action. Do not assume that your priorities or the primary benefits of your initiative are aligned with their priorities, or that you understand their priorities because to you this or that argument "makes sense."

Another thing to keep in mind is that if you are presenting to a group, everyone in that room is going to have their own biases and opinions. Figure out as much as you can about every influencer and decision maker who might be in the room during your presentation and call to action. It is okay to strategically lace messages throughout the presentation that speak to what each person in the room needs to hear; just be certain that all of those messages are truthful and consistent with what you are actually doing.

When you extend or put The Ask, depending on the culture and context, you can then briefly issue a call to action for each person in the room in the appropriate order of who matters most.

Sometimes, in some cultures, the messages in the body of the presentation are all that most need, and the formal ask would only be issued to the most relevant and important person in the room. So be sure that you know what is culturally appropriate before you enter the room to present.

> **ASSIGNMENT** Write at least one clear sentence for EACH person that you need to persuade to support your initiative. Never give the same pitch twice; what works for one person may or may not work for any other person. Explore and refine your questions.

EXECUTIVE SUMMARIES AND BUSINESS PLANS

> "Everyone has a plan 'til they get punched in the mouth."
> —**Mike Tyson**, former heavyweight boxing champion of the world

Hopefully you have been writing down all of your thoughts while going through each of the steps to this point. I have found great value in keeping track of all ideas or thoughts whether they seem relevant to me at the time or not.

You will need to complete a written executive summary (a document that takes the same amount of time to read as to drink a glass of water) that will help influencers and decision makers understand enough that they will 1. want to know more, and 2. be interested (or even excited) to support you and the initiative. A business plan is a long, more detailed executive summary.

▶ Executive Summary

An Executive Summary, not to be confused with a full Business Plan, is ideally two pages and no longer than three pages in length. It should have the most representative and most relevant details, which are explained in greater detail in the full business plan. Make sure that every word in the Executive Summary is relevant to persuade the reader that you know what you are doing to build and run the company. The Executive Summary should inspire the reader to ask you for more information.

▶ Business Plan

A Business Plan is a longer, more detailed document than an Executive Summary. A typical length for a business plan is 20–30 pages. When writing business plans you should bias the writing very heavily to execution detail; show what you will do, when, where, how, and why. State the problem, build out the execution detail around the solution to the problem, put some financials in so that the costs are understood, and call the reader to action. Use multiple proofreaders and listen to their feedback. Questions and comments give you insight into what is understandable and working (or not), so be grateful and never impatient with questions and comments.

(I once submitted a 30-page business plan to a government body, not realizing that they required a minimum of 100 pages because more pages demonstrated thorough and complete investigation and consideration. In the business world, a 100+ page business plan to an investor or leadership team might imply that you are overthinking or cannot succinctly say what you need to say.)

There is no single magic format or outline for business plans and executive summaries. You should write the details in a way that will flow most naturally and persuade the reader, while also providing a document that will help guide your running of the company.

The goal for an executive summary and business plan, along with all supportive financials, should be practical, meaning that you will actually use the documents as part of running your business. Stay flexible, move with what happens, and update your documentation regularly so that you are ready at a moment's notice to share and present. Do not get caught with a summary or plan that is out of date; that moment might be the game changer. Keep updating, practicing, learning, and adapting to change as you go forward.

> **ASSIGNMENT**   All of the topics explored in this framework can be used in your executive summary and business plan. Create your 2–3-page executive summary first in a separate document (name it uniquely and always save the date in the file name every time you update it). Once your executive summary is completed, save a copy of it as a different file (using "Save As … ") with the date in the file name in the same folder. Then, begin the work of meaningfully expanding the detail in each section until you have a 20–30-page full business plan.

PITCHING AND PRESENTATIONS

▶ Pitching

A pitch is a short format presentation. It should be quick, clear, and to the point. An elevator or lift pitch is typically no more than one or two minutes (the time it would take to get from one floor in a building to a few floors up). Quickly state your name, what you do for your company (this should take only a few seconds) and then get straight into the pitch. Your pitch should clearly state that there is an opportunity (a problem), something that can be done about the opportunity, what you are doing about it, and how the listener can be involved. Keep the pitch to the point and positive.

▶ Presentations

A presentation is a longer format pitch but has a similar structure.

> **HINT** Presentations tend to focus too much on the problem/ opportunity and have too little practical detail on what can be done and what you are actually doing (aka execution). It is true that the listener needs to believe that you are addressing an authentic problem (do not solve a non-problem, and do not be a solution looking for a problem to solve) but remember that the listener needs to believe that you know what you are doing (execution level detail). Explain the opportunity and give representative detail into what you are doing about that opportunity.

It is common for people not to practice their presentations in advance. People often work on their materials up to the moment before presenting and then walk into the room and start. This is a mistake. Practice your pitch and presentations before giving them. There is no substitute for practice. Make sure that the first time that you pitch, or present is during practice rather than in front of the person whom you need to persuade. You only get one chance at a first impression. In case you feel that practice will make you less spontaneous in the moment, keep in mind that practice will make you better in a moment. For example, professional athletes practice SO THAT they will be better able to be more powerfully and effectively spontaneous in a moment.

The opportunity to persuade a key influencer or decision maker might happen at any moment. The quick two-minute pitch is called an elevator pitch or lift pitch because you might be in an elevator or lift when you realize that you are standing next to a key influencer or decision maker. You then have the amount of time that it takes to go from the ground floor to when they exit the elevator or lift to plant a seed. Hopefully they will invite you to present to them based on the strength of that one short pitch.

I have successfully pitched in elevators/lifts, hallways/corridors, stairways, sidewalks, while crossing the street, while at a salad bar, standing in a line/queue, while on the phone, and sitting next to someone on a plane. The point is that you never know when the opportunity will present itself. Practice your pitch over and over until you can say it without thinking about it. And practice it on different people to make sure that it makes sense and is coherent.

Practice your pitching without slides or props or other visual support. If your pitch is reliant on a slide or a prop, you might find yourself fumbling with your phone or computer, trying to pull up whatever you need, and end up burning the seconds or minutes that you have to persuade the listener. Also keep in mind that you only have a handful of seconds to create a powerful first impression; if you know what you are talking about and can say it off the top of your head without notes or visual assistance, then all the better.

Full presentations can start with a quick two-minute pitch at the top, to snapshot the long story short and give the audience an idea of what you are doing. Then you can start the longer format presentation. The longer presentation can include slides and product demonstrations if you have them; just remember to tell the story in an order that makes sense. Practice, practice, practice. There is no substitute for practicing before you present. Then after you've presented, practice some more.

As to time management, let's say, for example, that you are given a 30-minute meeting to present. Do not prepare 30 minutes of presentations and slides and demonstrations. A good rule of thumb is to prepare presentations for half of the allotted time. So, in this example you would prepare 15 (or 20 maximum) minutes of a presentation, for a 30-minute meeting. Leave room for questions during the presentation as well as questions and answers at the end.

Here is a thumbnail EXAMPLE of how much time should be spent on each part of the presentation:

▶ **Intro** (~5% of the available time)
Don't apologize—it is a common opener, but it is a poor start. Be confident but never arrogant.

▶ **The Opportunity/Problem** (~25%)
Do not pander or exaggerate; be factual.

▶ **What options are possible** (~15%)
Give a few examples of options. Do not make the mistake of speaking poorly of any alternative to what you are recommending. Be factual.

▶ **What I am doing** (~45%)
Do not hold back any secret ingredient (aka silver bullet or game changer) during your presentation. It is a common problem that the presenter will save the big "wow" of their solution for a follow-up presentation. If the audience doesn't hear the wow in your first pitch, there may not be a second presentation.

▶ **How you can be involved** (~10%)
Do not tell them what they will do. Welcome them to the party and invite them to be involved.

Start on time and finish on time (or a little early). Going over time should only happen if the audience asks you to stay and explain more. Even then, be sensitive to being over time. It is typically better to leave when you are ahead while they want more and schedule a follow-up.

Do not feel nervous or upset about any questions that might be asked of you. Questions expose holes in your presentation and tell you what was not clear or understandable to the listener (no matter how clear you thought that you made the point). Questions also give you an indication of what matters to the person asking the question. Write down all the questions that you were asked, and the answers that you gave, and then use those notes as preparation for future meetings (and work on clearer presentations and better answers for the future).

> **ASSIGNMENT** Build the materials that you will need (e.g., 2–3-page executive summary, slides, etc.). Practice that 60-second pitch until you can say it without thinking. THEN start working on expanded detail versions of that pitch so that when people ask you to give them more you can do 60 seconds on this detail and 60 seconds on that detail. THEN work on a 30-minute expanded version of that pitch, which gives more meaningful insight and detail. Explore and refine your questions.

SAVE YOUR WORK, UPDATE IT REGULARLY, AND REFER TO IT OFTEN

Revisit all of the above work regularly. Remember to save your work regularly and keep backups on separate secure devices. Once a day, or at a minimum once a week on a routine day at a routine time, review and update details for all of the above work. The last time that out of date documents created a problem for me was when I was asked to send my current business plan to a meeting deciding the placement of millions of dollars (in the dot.com era) and I was not ready in the moment. Since that day I have always had current documents ready to send whenever a shareholder, investor, or board member asks. It always makes a good impression when you are ready to send freshly updated documents when asked.

Every time you update the document, save a unique version in a common reference folder on your computer. Use a consistent naming convention and update the name every time to include the date that you modified it (or some other intuitive system that others, not just you, will understand if they need to find information).

You never know when you will need to give someone a copy of your plan. You might be given advance warning, but sometimes the call is unexpected. Do not be caught off guard with an out of date version! Be prepared, and you will have nothing to fear.

ASSIGNMENT   Comb through your document. Save everything. If you write something and you aren't quite sure how it fits, either put the thought on the last empty page of the document or create a second document in the same folder just for thoughts that you aren't yet sure how to use. You do not want to find yourself in the situation where later on, you wish that you hadn't deleted that thought.

On future days when you open and edit the document, do a Save As and change the version date on the document so that it creates a new document that is saved in the same folder. It may happen that in the future you will want to refer to an earlier draft, and if anything happens to the file that you are working on that day, you can always go back to the most recent version rather than starting over.

Keep a backup somewhere other than on your computer. (You should regularly back up your entire hard drive.) If you are working on paper, you need to keep your binder safe and secure at all times. When you are able, you might have someone scan every page in the binder onto a file that you keep on a small portable computer stick for safekeeping. If you edit your document on a public computer, just make certain that you do not leave a copy of your document on the public hard drive.

Regularly update your writing, save copies, keep the dream alive, and work to make it real.

WHAT STARTUP CEOS
REALLY DO

Years ago, I was golfing with my two oldest (then little) children. Because they were too small to hit the ball very far, we played a scramble (meaning the three of us each hit a ball and then we all played from the best positioned, farthest hit ball ... which was always mine).

It was a leisurely round of golf. We laughed and talked as we went—it was a good day. At this particular golf course, each tee box featured a reasonably large stone that had an encouraging word carved into it. As we approached each stone the kids would read the word and ask me to define the word with an example. As we approached one large stone the word that was etched into it was "Courage." They asked me about the word,

and I said, "Courage is doing what must be done even though you are afraid." My then ~6-year-old daughter, Sasha, looked at me and without blinking said, "Oh, like you." She proceeded to give me examples of how she had seen me doing what needed to be done even when I didn't want to do it. Hearing her say it caused me to swell with emotion.

Around this same time, a friend was at our house visiting. We were chatting and he asked my kids if they knew what I did for a living. My then ~8-year-old son Joshua said, "My dad fixes broken things" and my daughter Sasha said, "Dad makes sure that other moms and dads can feed their kids." Their interpretation of what their entrepreneur

father did for a living was that I fixed broken things and worked to make sure that other moms and dads could feed their kids. I loved both answers.

The Reality

I have invested meaningful time with hundreds of startup CEOs over my career. In my experience, startup CEOs spend a significant amount of time puzzling and worrying. Puzzling and worrying at work, puzzling and worrying on the way to and way home from work, waking up in the middle of the night puzzling and worrying about schedules and deadlines, making sure they can make payroll, and more. It isn't part of any official job description (who would take the job?), but it is a reality for most. There might be a few who don't worry, but I have never met them.

Another reality is that the typical startup CEO (especially a first-time CEO) frets about what they don't know. They wonder where to turn when they need someone to talk to. A worry is that if you tell the board and shareholders that you aren't sure about something important then they might doubt, fire, and replace you ... if you tell your team, they might doubt you and worry about the startup and the viability of the future. I have had this particular conversation with countless CEOs in companies of all sizes around the world. Regardless of their nationality, level of education, domain expertise, etc., most CEOs worry. So, if this is how you feel, you are not alone.

The Actual Job Description

The #1 bona fide actual responsibility for the startup CEO from the shareholder and board's perspective is to make sure that there is money in the bank. (The CFO's #1 job is to spend that money wisely.) This might be money from investors, banks, grants, etc.; wherever the money comes from, the CEO's primary role is to find it and bring it home.

After that, there are the other responsibilities of:

▶ Making strategic presentations to the government (for support such as grants), banks (for all support that is available), potential investors, the press, influencers, etc.

▶ Working and communicating with shareholders (those who share in the ownership of the startup), the board of directors, as well as advisors. Keeping the shareholders and board informed is critical.

▶ Communicating with stakeholders (those who care about the success of the startup, including but not limited to lawyers and accountants).

▶ Ensuring that the optimal talent for the company (employees) are in the company

▶ Working and communicating with all employees, ensuring they are informed, productive, successful, and happy.

▶ Ensuring that the company is on the optimal path (strategy and execution) ... and then they focus on everything else.

Bottom-line, the startup CEO is the parent for the company.

How do you know who would make the best CEO for your startup? In my experience, the person who is most hungry to be the CEO typically will not be the best person for the role. I was once hired by a startup CEO to take over his job as CEO, and he then returned to his role leading engineering; he was an ideal startup CEO, and a world-class engineer. The George Washington effect is a good rule of thumb; Washington didn't want the job, others thrust the position upon him, which made him better at the role. He was one of the most famous and successful leaders in history. CEOs who are in it for the glory and title on their business card are easy to spot if you ask them about their priorities and the realities of being a startup CEO. You need to find a CEO who is courageous ... someone who will do what must be done, even though they are afraid.

SCIENCE &
TECHNOLOGY
ENTREPRENEURSHIP

"Chance favors the prepared mind."

—Louis Pasteur

I have learned that good business is more art than science. Specifically, applied art that uses the power tools of science to illuminate and provide essential insight to potential paths. This is also true for both management and leadership.

The following is an 18-step framework for Science and Technology Entrepreneurship training. The foundation of the framework is my personal experience and knowledge of what is expected from strategic others and what works in practice.

Scientists, engineers, technologists, business school students, and others have used this framework successfully to work with intellectual properties (IP) to both build new companies around the IP and build a viable business case around IP to position it for sale to other companies. This framework is not exhaustive but is designed to kick-start planning and execution to give you a path forward. The framework has been used to train teams around the world, across industries, and in structures of all sizes.

Before you start this framework: If you have not already done so, please go back to the page called **START HERE** at the beginning of the book and complete parts 1, 2, 3, and 4 of the Preparatory Frameworks. Once that is completed, come back to this page and move forward to the following:

STEP 1 **A Firm Foundation**

STEP 2 **The Offering Including an ORD**

STEP 3 **Storyboard**

STEP 4 **Team and Execution**

STEP 5 **Business Modeling**

STEP 6 **Financial Modeling**

STEP 7 **Fundable Event Timelines**

STEP 8 **Capital Modeling**

STEP 9 **Liquidity and Exits**

STEP 10 **Founderitis**

STEP 11 **Boards: Advisory and Governance**

STEP 12 **Marketing, Sales, and Business Development**

STEP 13 **Go to Market**

STEP 14 **The Big Play**

STEP 15 **Call to Action or The Ask**

STEP 16 **Executive Summaries and Business Plans**

STEP 17 **Pitching and Presentations**

STEP 18 **Save Your Work, Update It Regularly, and Refer to It Often**

The purpose of the framework is to help scientists, engineers, and technologists work to build viable companies around their IP. It can also be used to help non-scientists/engineers/technologists to work with scientists et al to develop businesses around the IP to an execution-ready condition so that they can: A. Persuade investors to invest, and B. Allow the individual and teams to actually launch an IP empowered startup. This framework can be taught in-person or via technology or worked on privately by an individual or team. The 18-step framework is as follows:

A FIRM FOUNDATION

Once you have decided to create a startup company around existing intellectual property (IP), an important first move is to seek qualified legal and accounting guidance. Among other important details you need qualified guidance on questions such as where to incorporate, where to operate, copyrights and patents, agreements between the founders on ownership of the company and the IP, and more.

You also need to work through Standard Operating Procedures (SOP) for all mission-critical activities including (but not limited to) all money that you spend on everything, as well as any and all money invested and spent by you and/or anyone else into and around the IP and your venture, and more. These are critical questions that people take for granted as they enthusiastically rush to create their company and to take an offering to market.

First focusing on the IP: The fact that you have existing IP means that right now, before you do anything else, the IP owner needs to work with a competent IP project professional (such as an IP lawyer or a reputable firm that focuses on patent filings) to put everything in proper order. Do not rely on the opinion of a family member or friend (unless they are an intellectual property lawyer) or on Internet searches to qualify as adequate understanding of how to protect your IP. If you are worried that you do not have the financial resources to pay for the services, then speak with the lawyer(s) and/or firm(s) to see if they can work with you on the costs and terms.

My father had two sayings that have stuck with me over the years: 1. "Buy the best and cry once," and 2. "Never buy fried chicken in a pizzeria." Interestingly, both apply in this lesson: 1. If you go cheap on your legal protection you will cry many times, not just the once that you would have cried when paying for the expensive lawyering, and 2. Work with someone who specializes in intellectual property protection rather than someone who is a different legal practice specialist who does not actually know IP law but is willing to help you with your IP questions. Go with the best IP protection lawyer and professional to whom you have access. You might cry about the upfront costs, but this will reduce the odds that you will cry later when you realize that your Internet search as a substitute for qualified legal counsel or budget counsel and advice has left your life's work exposed and vulnerable.

Where you incorporate will impact the taxes that you pay, access to support from the government (including grant money), and more. Where you operate will impact the cost of operating your company, your access to skilled employees, and more. Building a solid foundation when you start will save you trouble later when you realize that you should have incorporated in a different country or state, that you should have incorporated as a different type of legal entity, that you should have opened an office somewhere else, and now you need to move everything around, which may lose you money and key employees. Start with interviewing lawyers and accountants who understand the type of business you plan to create. Seek their counsel before you do anything.

Lawyers and accountants are extensions of your team. Keep them close and well informed and think of them as an integrated part of everything; do not make the common mistake of thinking of lawyers and accounts as "necessary evils," I know from experience that the right lawyers and accountants can protect you. The right team makes every opportunity better.

ASSIGNMENT If you already use the cloud to back up all of your work securely, that is excellent. If you regularly use software that keeps track of versions of your work, so that you never invest hours editing the wrong version of a document, that is superb. If, however, for any reason, you are not yet able to back-up in the cloud or you do not have access to software that keeps track of versions of your documents, you will need to do these things manually. If you are working on a computer, create a folder with a logical name that you will not forget. Put that folder in an obvious location on the computer (not a clever place, but a clear and easy to remember place), that will still be obvious to you tomorrow and the next day. Create a new document and save it in the folder that you just created. Name the file something easy to remember and give it today's date; then every day you edit it, save a version with that day's date so that you can tell the difference between files. Always work on the most recent date and version of the file. If you do not have a computer, buy a spiral binder with lined paper (or an equivalent that is available to you). Put your name and contact information on it and keep it in a safe place. Do all of your work in the document or binder.

ASSIGNMENT Identify a lawyer and accountant whom you can approach and with whom you can work. Identify where you will incorporate and where you plan to operate as a company (where you will have an office and employees). Write at least one paragraph on this section. Explore and refine your questions.

THE OFFERING
INCLUDING AN ORD

When you are producing a physical thing or a "widget" (whether it is electronics or a musical instrument or a serving of food or more), or software, or a service, you need to think about some combination of the following: Licensing, Pricing, Seats, Builds, Configurations, Distribution, Life Cycle, Manufacturing, Packaging, Maintenance, Forecasting, Procurement, Supply Chain, Inventory Control, and Portion Control.

It is possible that you developed your IP using an MRD (Market Requirements Document) and/or a PRD (Product Requirements Document). If so, that is good news as that work will ease your path forward.

Both an MRD and a PRD are very helpful for distinguishing what can be done from what must be done. Too many people just "do stuff," and then wonder why the end result doesn't look or perform as they had envisioned and why the market isn't responding to what they are offering. An MRD and PRD add structure to your development and deployment. It is important that the MRD and PRD are not just documents that you write; use them like road maps as you drive your opportunity. There are many different formats of MRD and PRD floating around in the world. Over the years I have developed my own version that works for me; I call it an ORD so that I can keep it clear in my own mind that it is my version of an MRD. You can use your own or mine, use whatever works best for you.

> **ASSIGNMENT** If you already have a completed Market Requirements Document (MRD) that is excellent news. Review and update it now and continue to do so on a regular basis. If you do not have an MRD (or if you aren't sure what that is) please do the work to complete an Offering Requirements Document (ORD) that is part of this system of frameworks (it is the next chapter). The ORD is a modified and adapted form of an MRD (Market Requirements Document). The ORD includes questions that need to be answered as part of this framework, so even if you have another version of an MRD that you have used, it may be helpful to review this ORD framework to ensure that you have answered all of the questions before progressing on to the next step.

STORYBOARD

If you have ever read a comic in a newspaper, or a graphic novel, or even picture-based instructions for assembling a toy or piece of furniture that is formatted as squares on a page filled with drawings that take you step-by-step through the story ... that is a story-board. (One of the early steps in movie making is also to storyboard.)

Use a storyboard to SHOW a compelling use-case for your product/service/platform (to the best of your ability) pictographically, so that others can better visualize what your science and technology will look and act like. Don't worry if you aren't an artist; just do your best. Draw the significant moments in the use of your product, service, or platform. Don't worry about showing action or movement, this is a snapshot of the meaningful transitional steps to show other people the basic idea of how the IP works. If you have a working version of your product/service/platform, you might use actual photographs in each frame.

I could not count how many times I've been in a meeting with a storyboard and the listener/audience has expressed appreciation for the way it enabled them to visualize the product and how it works or is used.

ASSIGNMENT Sketch (keep in mind that functional understanding is more important than making it pretty) or use photographs in a series on pieces of paper to make a rough storyboard. Use it to SHOW the app/service/platform (to the best of your ability) pictographically, so that others can better visualize what the product/service/platform looks like and performs. Think from the perspective of the things that must be done (i.e., activities), not job titles (i.e., functions).

Sample storyboard

Draw inside this square …		

TEAM AND EXECUTION

> "The right team and execution can
> make gold out of rubbish. The wrong team and
> execution will make rubbish out of gold."
> —Paul Kewene-Hite

Be inclusive and embrace diversity. Be an equal opportunity and equal pay for equal work employer. A critical mistake often made by first-time entrepreneurs is ignoring the "boring" execution details of what needs to be done to make the startup a reality. Thinking through and documenting these details is the equivalent of creating a recipe with a list of ingredients for the meal you want to prepare and eat. Execution modeling is a step-by-step inventory of what needs to be done so that your science and technology venture will become real. When you present to potential investors or potential team members, the right people will NEED to know that you know what must be done. If you went into a kitchen to cook a meal from raw ingredients, what is the order of operations that you would follow? What is the first activity that you need to do? What is the second activity? What is the third? Do the same thing for your startup. Inventory the activities that must be done in order. Be as specific and as detailed as possible.

Thinking through and writing out the above activities based an inventory of what *must* be done is a good way to figure out whether or not you already have the team that you need, and who is missing and needs to be found and brought on board. Begin by listing all the activities that MUST be done. Put your name next to which of those activities you can credibly perform (not what you are willing to try but don't really know how to do). If there are others already committed to your startup, list their names next to those activities that they can credibly perform. Once that is done, you will see the gaps around must-do activities that have no names assigned to them. That tells you whom you need to find to complete your startup team. Those whom you need to find could be new hires as full-time employees (FTE) or part-time employees (PTE), or contract workers, etc.

One way to think about team and execution is to consider answers to the question "what does a clock do?" ... When you are explaining what you plan to do to create a new company, you'll need to describe *how* the clock will tell time, instead of just saying that it tells time. Imagine opening the face of a traditional clock to expose the clockworks showing the gears, springs, and other moving parts. It would be ideal if you could document and explain every detail, but at a minimum, be prepared to describe the basics of which mechanisms move and how they are connected to make the hands move, and in turn, tell time. Do that for the details—personnel and processes—of the company that you are working to build.

ASSIGNMENT Inventory your top 20 (or more) mission-critical activities. Put names of committed team members next to each activity. The critical activities that have no name next to them tell you whom you need to recruit to help you. Write at least one paragraph on this section. Explore and refine your questions.

BUSINESS MODELING

Your business model is how you will make money (meaning revenue and more specifically, profit), as well as how you will otherwise finance and operate your company. When you are asked about your business model, the underlying question is how you will become a viable business and then stay profitable.

Your business model is the beating heart of your venture. Do not assume that how you will make revenue and profit[1] and otherwise finance your startup is obvious. When you are asked about your business model you need to have a better response than "we will sell what we make" (and raise investment capital). You need to be prepared with a robust response to questions about your business model.

Google's business model is an interesting example. I remember visiting Google's office when it was a startup. They had a monitor over the reception desk that showed every search that was happening real-time. I remember the tempo of it ... search (pause) search (pause) search. I thought to myself, "Wow, people are actually using it!" I sat in the lobby doing searches to watch the words that I typed in my own Google searches pop up on the monitor over the desk. Now there are more than 3.5 billion searches every day. People who use Google's search engine do not pay to perform a search. At Google, search is a vehicle that is leveraged to do much more than display results for the definition of a word or a website or a restaurant near you, and Google is much more than an Internet search company.

Google makes its money through Google AdWords, AdSense, Google Play store, Google Cloud, and more. Businesses pay Google to display their information in search results (AdWords). AdSense is interesting, because both Google and website publishers make a little money when an ad is placed by Google on a website and someone, somewhere on the planet, clicks on it. When an app is purchased on the Google Play store, Google makes a little money. Google does not make money on Android itself (the smart device operating system), interestingly, but it does make money on the ecosystem around it. An interesting feature of Google's business model is that, in addition to free searches, they have several offerings that do not generate revenue directly. As with search, these offerings create value in the Google brand by generating good will and loyalty. Take, as only one of dozens of possible examples, Google for Startups Accelerator (formerly Google's Launchpad Accelerator). Google for Startups Accelerator spends money to help startup companies around the world for free. It is an initiative that creates good will, healthy brand awareness and loyalty for Google; it also keeps Google current on what is happening with the best startups globally. I am an unpaid volunteer Anchor Mentor in the Google for Startups Accelerator, and there are hundreds of volunteers like me who work with Google to level the playing field for founders and startups around the world.

Here is a non-Internet example: How does BMW make money? Selling cars is the obvious response. They also make money on dealership franchises, parts, service and maintenance, leasing, rentals, and merchandise, among others.

---

1   Revenue is the money that you make from the sale of goods and services. Profit is the money that is left over after you make all of your payments, settle your debts, and in all ways account for your costs and expenses.

Here is another: Star Wars has made more money on licensing and merchandise than on ticket sales for the movies themselves.

Here is another: "Razor and Blades" is a common expression in business. Companies will give away the handle of a razor used for shaving (even though it cost them money to design, engineer, and manufacture it) because there is more money to be made on selling the blades that attach to the end of the razor handle because the blades wear out and need to be replaced more frequently than the handle. An application of this expression would be a printer. Let's say, for example, that your offering is a new type of 3D printer. Maybe you cannot afford to give the printer itself away but you can sell the printer at a discount so that people buy your printer over the competition; you then make additional revenue by selling the printer cartridges for your 3D printer. You could also sell a service contract to maintain the printer, and software to design what you print. Then software advertising might help you sell other 3D printer-related offerings.

When you think about the business you are starting, how do you plan to make money? Simple sales of what you are offering? Is there any other way? Maybe there could be other products or a service around the offering that you are selling? Is there a way to sell other products and services through your offering? Will you sell B2C (Business to Consumer, meaning you will sell and ship your offering directly from your business to your consumer), B2B (Business to Business), or B2G (Business to Government)? Include as much detail as you can.

> **ASSIGNMENT** Articulate all the ways that you will make money (revenue and profit). Don't just say "sell product"—you need to be specific about how you will sell, and various ways that money will be made. Write at least one paragraph on this section. Explore and refine your questions.

STEP 6

FINANCIAL MODELING

"Never, EVER, run out of cash!"
—**Patrick Turner**, INSEAD Professor of Entrepreneurship

If you are just beginning the process to start a company, you probably don't have complete documents and data in a condition that will be helpful. As you build your company, you will also need to improve the condition of your data so that your future business has a financial model built on complete and accurate information.

If you can build a Cashflow from scratch, then you can explain the details when you are asked to defend the numbers during any meeting. When you present, have an updated copy of your Cashflow, and be prepared to explain the details to those who ask.

Work to frame a financial model going forward that progresses you from where you are to where you plan to go. Building a Cashflow (as well as an SG&A, P&L, Balance Sheet, along with Budgets for MDF/SDF, T&E/T&S, etc.) is fundamental for understanding your initiative. At this point you may not know what those words and acronyms mean, which is okay. You will, however, need to invest some effort in learning their meaning so that you can use them comfortably in sentences as well as comfortably answer questions about them when asked. The definitions are below.

In the business world it is very common for people to assume that other people will know how to build and read the numbers, so they invest very little study into it. Basic financial skills are very important for all people in business. Not everyone needs to be a Certified Public Accountant or Chartered Accountant but being able to build and read a Cashflow should be a required skill for all business professionals.

If an investor, board of directors, or shareholder calls you to a meeting to discuss your venture, grab an updated Cashflow on the way to the meeting. The other financial instruments such as a Profit and Loss (P&L), Balance Sheet, Sales General and Administrative (SG&A) etc., are also important but the Cashflow is, in my experience, the most critical. If you don't understand your cash position over time, you do not understand your business.

Good financial planning is key to persuading shareholders, the board, and leadership that you know what you are doing. If you don't (yet) know how to do it yourself, work side-by-side with a finance-professional to build complete financials. I say side-by-side so that you see how it is done, you fully understand the numbers, and can understand and explain the details. (If you can build a Cashflow from scratch then you can explain the details when you are asked to defend the numbers during a meeting.)

Here are a few overly simplified definitions of business words that you need to know:

▶ **Finance vs. Accounting**
Finance looks forward to what will happen.
Accounting looks back at what happened.

▶ **Payment vs. Expense**
A Payment is when money leaves the company and is given to someone else.
An Expense is the agreed responsibility to make a payment at some future date.

▶ **Revenue vs. Profit**
Revenue is all money that comes into the company from sales.
Profit is the money that is left over after you have paid all of your expenses and taxes.

▶ **Sources & Uses**
Source is where you will get money.
A Use is how the money will be spent.

▶ **Budget**
A Budget is the amount of money (and time) that must be invested in order to do what must be done. Importantly budgeted amounts need to factor for how much money (and time) is actually available.[2]

▶ **Cashflow**
A Cashflow is the financial detail of how a company is being operated; money coming in, all money measured impacts on debts and assets, and all money going out.[3]

▶ **Free Cashflow**
Free Cashflow (not to be confused with the document that is called "a Cashflow") is the money that you have left over after all capital expenditures (aka CapEx, which is the money spent on fixed assets).

▶ **Working Capital**
Working Capital = **Current Assets** minus **Current Liabilities**. Assets are tangible things that have value such as property, inventory, cash, etc. Liabilities are things that you need to pay such as debt, taxes, wages, rent, utilities, etc.

▶ **Professional Fees**
Professional Fees are cash paid to professionals who are not your employees, such as lawyers, accountants, designers, engineers, etc.

▶ **CapEx vs OpEx**
CapEx is Capital Expenditure, which is money spent on fixed assets.
OpEx is Operating Expenditure, which is the money spent to operate the company.

▶ **Fixed Assets**
Fixed Assets are physical things such as land, buildings, equipment, vehicles, etc.

▶ **Burn Rate and Runway**
Burn Rate is the amount of money that you spend in a month.
Runway is the number of months that you have until you are out of money.

▶ **Break Even, and Profitability**
Break Even is when the same amount of money comes in as goes out.
Profitability is when you have money left over after paying everything.

▶ **Pro forma**
Pro forma is Latin for "as a matter of form" or "for the sake of form" and is a word put on financials to show that the numbers are educated guesses or projections.

---

2 Budgeting is incredibly valuable and essential for running your entrepreneurial venture and making sure that you never run out of cash. Your budgets should be planned, reviewed, and updated routinely as a team. Be sure to remind everyone that a budget is more than a plan for how much money will be spent, it is a reconciliation of how much must be spent in order to accomplish your plan compared to how much money there is to spend in the bank account. Monthly budgeting meetings, accounting back a month, and financially planning forward a quarter are good practices.

3 This is a window into all money that comes in and leaves the company. (You should typically have an 18 to 24-month Cashflow, with the next 13 weeks by week, and the rest of the months by month.) Be sure to use mathematics rather than simply typing in numbers.

▶ **T&E or T&S**

T&S/T&E[4] is <u>Travel & Subsistence</u> or <u>Travel & Expenses</u> (occasionally referred to as Travel & Entertainment). This budget is for rental cars, trains, planes, hotels, lunches and dinners, etc. T&E is used in North American English and in North American influenced regions. T&S is used in British English and in British influenced regions.

▶ **MDF and SPIF**

<u>MDF</u> is an acronym for Market Development Fund and is the money that you spend to take your offering to market.

<u>SPIF</u> stands for Sales Promotion Incentive Fund and is a powerful tool for motivating the point of sale to inspire them to advocate for your offering over the competition (the seller and/or buyer). This could be, and is not limited to, a payment made to the salesperson or a discount/rebate offered to the customer.

> **ASSIGNMENT** Build a Cashflow. Do not assume that you will simply hire someone else to do it for you. Learn to build a Cashflow from a blank spreadsheet if you can; at a minimum, find someone on your team or work together as a team right now to build a basic Cashflow. Then write at least one paragraph on the details inside of the Cashflow, possibly including the details listed above. Explore and refine your questions. If you need to partner with a finance professional to help you, do it; but learn how to read financial documents, how to tell the stories of the numbers, and how to read along as others go through the numbers.

FUNDABLE EVENT TIMELINES

Now that you have done your team and financial modeling, with your list of 20 or more mission-critical activities, you should put that list of activities on a timeline (for example 18 to 24 months). Creating a Gantt chart of mission-critical activities (highlighting milestones and fundable events) then harmonizing it with a Cashflow is good planning and good for presentations.

You can build your Gantt chart in a spreadsheet if you don't have project management software. What matters is that you can see the markers that represent the start and stop dates for each activity. On each bar you should name the activity as well as who is responsible along with the associated costs.

When you build a Cashflow you should then harmonize it with the Gantt chart to ensure that the activities and costs over the same months align month-by-month.

---

4   Watch this budget very carefully and put rules on all expenses and what can be claimed to make people responsible and hold people accountable. It happens at times that people (especially inside of large companies) game their expense reports so that they claim more money than they legitimately spend on real business. This line item can be value destructive when you are a fledgling venture that is carefully watching every dollar in the bank account.

When you are building the timeline, with the completed Gantt on the top of the page and the Cashflow lined up below it, decision makers can quickly see that your financial and activities-based planning is complimentary in their construction.

The next thing that I suggest that you do is identify the **Milestones** (the moments in time when you complete an activity or task) on the Gantt chart. Then differentiate between which milestones simply mark the completion of a task and which milestones are actually evidence that you are right in what you intended, planned, and executed. (This could be a working prototype or a paying customer, etc. This is very different from finishing the writing for a business plan for example, which does not prove that you are right but just that you finished what you started.) The type of milestone that is evidence that you are right, is called a **Fundable Event** and it is very important for a few reasons.

▶ Evidence that you are right shows that the entrepreneurial venture is making progress!

▶ Evidence that you are right will be the proof that you need for continued funding and support from the company leadership and board.

▶ Evidence that you are right can be correlated to value creation (increasing value) and value capture (when the company is able to hold onto and make use of the value). Fundable events correlate to the increase in the value of what you are doing, and potentially increase the value of the company itself.

Investors and Boards and others who hold the keys to your future funding will be watching for the Fundable Events so that they can know that the work is progressing and that your corporate entrepreneurial venture is deserving of continued support.

When you have the Fundable Event Timeline planned out, and you regularly update it (you should update it at a minimum of once a week) then you and those who are supporting you can use it to keep track of progress and timings that might change over time.

Investors and Boards and other financial supporters might use the Fundable Event Timeline to plan when they will transfer resources and capital support to your initiative (just as an investor would do for a startup); when you hit your deliverables (the milestones and especially the fundable events) then you have a measurable defense for expecting ongoing support.

ASSIGNMENT Write at least one paragraph on this section. Explore and refine your questions. Create a Gantt chart identifying all of your activities (when each activity is intended to start and stop). Then put the Gantt chart and your Cashflow summary on the same page making sure that the months line up as shown in the following template (and on page 410). (You should have built a Cashflow in step 6.) Highlight the milestones that prove that you are right to call them Fundable Events; e.g., this is when the machine you are building actually works, it is when a stranger who has no connection to you purchases your product, etc. A fundable event is not when you simply finish what you started, such as writing a business plan or building a Cashflow with numbers that look good or designing a brochure that makes you happy, etc.

Cashflow Summary

	Month 1, Year 1	Month 2, Year 1	Month 3, Year 1	Month 4, Year 1	Month 5, Year 1	Month 6, Year 1	Month 7, Year 1	Month 8, Year 1	Month 9, Year 1	Month 10, Year 1	Month 11, Year 1	Month 12, Year 1
Opening Cash Balance												
Total CapEX												
Total OpEx												
Total Cash Out												
Total Cash In												
Closing Cash Balance												

Execution Timeline (Gantt Chart)

ACTIVITY	OWNER	ASSOCIATED COSTS US$	Month 1, Year 1	Month 2, Year 1	Month 3, Year 1	Month 4, Year 1	Month 5, Year 1	Month 6, Year 1	Month 7, Year 1	Month 8, Year 1	Month 9, Year 1	Month 10, Year 1	Month 11, Year 1	Month 12, Year 1

Note: Milestones mean that you finished what you started. Fundable Events are validation that you are right.

CAPITAL MODELING

STEP 8

You need to determine what capital will be required over time, and where that support will come from. Keep in mind that although capital is typically money, it might also be money equivalents (e.g., access to and use of buildings, equipment, etc.). Make sure to fully understand what capital is required to get your startup to the point where it can self-sustain, which is at break-even (meaning you are bringing in as much money as is going out), and profitability (which is when more money is coming in than is going out). Investors and shareholders will ask you what you need to take your startup from where you are now to the point of self-sufficiency; be prepared with an answer. It will be helpful to have a best case, base case, and worst case for your financials and capital requirements. If you can be successful with the worst case or base case numbers, then present those. Even though the best-case numbers look the most appealing, it is typically best to not present the best-case numbers since they are the most optimistic and therefore the most difficult to achieve.

When you think about the timing and costs associated with investment from others, you need to understand that money has the same three states as water: liquid, solid, and vapor.

▶ **Liquid**
This is when money is transportable, or otherwise in a state that it can be moved from one person or entity to another by either electronic transfer from one bank

account to another, or from one person to another as some form of recognized currency. Example: When you have coins and bank notes in your pocket and use it to buy something at a store you are <u>liquid</u>, as your money is available for use. People will say "I'm not liquid at the moment." Which typically means "I have money, but I don't have access to it right now."

▸ Solid

This is when money is not available or for some reason, not liquid. The money might be in stocks or bonds, or otherwise invested into something that makes it not accessible, or portable, or moveable. But the idea is that it will expand as ice expands when water is frozen (because of interest or other successful growth by performance of the stock or investment or real estate, etc.). When an investor gives you money in exchange for equity (aka ownership) in your company, the idea is that their money will grow or expand (like ice) as you are successful as a company.

▸ Vapor

When ice is melted, a percentage of the ice becomes liquid (water) and a percentage is lost as vapor (e.g., steam). With money, the <u>Vapor</u> is any fee or charge or tax or disadvantageous exchange rate, etc., meaning there is some loss of value that could equal part, or potentially all of their money that was invested in a failed stock.

When an investor pledges to invest into your startup venture, they might be liquid in the moment and need to move quickly back into a solid before they incur taxes or other penalties on that money. Or they might need time to "liquidate" or otherwise liberate their money from other investments (stocks, bonds, real estate, etc.) so that they can give cash to you as an investment (either as a loan or as equity), which means that to invest in you they are going from a solid, to a liquid (with hopefully as little vapor as possible), then back into another solid that is ownership in your startup. The expectation is that their money will grow and expand during its time as a solid (equity ownership) with you, and at some future date in a few years they expect their investment back, plus more than they gave you in the first place.

Now that you have done a meaningful amount of work puzzling through your startup venture, you should know whether or not you need OPM (other people's money) to put fuel in the tank to run the engine of your new company. Do not raise investment capital unless you actually need it. If you can create and run your company without OPM, that could be a good thing. If you do need investment, it is best to build as much work as possible before selling an ownership percentage in your startup. If you have little value created, investors will take more ownership for less money. When you have more value created, investors will take less ownership for more money. Raise money if you need to, but there are a few things to keep in mind:

▸ Smart Money vs. Dumb Money

Not all money is equal. You may have heard the expressions *smart money* or *dumb money*. This has nothing to do with the relative intelligence of the investor, it has everything to do with whether or not they understand your industry, company, and what you are working to accomplish. If they understand you and can meaningfully help you then they are <u>Smart Money</u> in your deal. If they do not understand you and if they cannot meaningfully help you (other than by giving you money) then they are <u>Dumb Money</u>. Avoid Dumb Money.

▶ Family and Friends
(Sometimes called <u>Family, Friends & Fools</u>, the addition of *fools* is because people don't always understand what they are doing.) Your family and friends may not be legally eligible to give you money to start your company. Work with your lawyer before you take grandma's sock-drawer cash that she has been squirreling away for years, and don't let your brother take out a third mortgage on his house to fund you. If grandma and your brother are not qualified investors as far as the law is concerned, and if things go wrong and you lose their money and cannot pay them back, you might get in trouble. This goes for anyone who offers you money. Work with your lawyer to keep everything legitimate and legal.

▶ Angels
Wealthy individuals who legally qualify to put their money at risk without compromising themselves financially, are often referred to as <u>Angels</u>. Angels who pool their resources and invest together are called <u>Super Angels</u>. Angels and Supers have some advantages, such as speed to do investments and patience/time to invest in you. Be sure that you only work with Smart Money. Dumb Money is abundant, and it is dangerous; you don't want a Dumb Money investor second-guessing and doubting what you do. You need a Smart Money investor working with you productively side-by-side.

▶ VC (Venture Capital)
Professionally incorporated firms with (typically) larger amounts of capital than Angels (although some are feeling pressure from Super Angels). When you speak with a <u>VC</u> ask them where they are in the lifecycle of their fund. They will continue to develop "Deal Flow" even when they have no more money to invest. (<u>Deal Flow</u> is an inventory of opportunities to invest as evidence to their investors that they are succeeding as a fund.) Find Smart Money VC for your type of deal. As a startup, before you spend money that you don't have to fly to a VC to meet and discuss investment make sure that you are not Deal Flow for their weekly numbers, that they have the ability to invest, that they are Smart Money in your deal, and interview them to see if they have actually read your materials and that they "get" you.

▶ PE (Private Equity)
<u>PE</u> is the business term used to refer to investment funds that are organized around General Partners (GP) who run the fund and Limited Partners (LP) who are the financial backers and investors in the fund. PE typically buys and restructures companies that are not publicly traded on a stock exchange. PE is increasingly getting involved in smaller investment opportunities (such as startups).

There are many terms that you should understand, but here are three for starters:

▶ Pre or Post
Investors will ask you if the amount of money that you are raising in exchange for whatever percentage of ownership you are offering, is "pre" or "post." <u>Pre</u> is simply the value of the company before investment money comes in, while <u>Post</u>

is the value of the company after investment money comes in. For example, if you are raising US$1 million and you are offering 33.3% Post, that means that you believe that your startup is worth US$3 million after their money is in the bank. This means that the Pre money valuation is US$2 million. Be prepared to defend these numbers. If you don't know the value (which is almost always the case), then tell the investor that you are willing to work with them to develop an accurate valuation. When investors ask you for an amount of money and a percentage of ownership, they are testing you to see if your thinking is in line with theirs. They will tell you what they think your startup is worth, how much money you need, and what percentage is, in their opinion, equal to that investment.

▶ LOI, MOU, and Term Sheets

An LOI is a Letter of Intent. An MOU is a Memorandum of Understanding. A Term Sheet is a document with an offer of investment and the intended terms and conditions. The investor creates and gives the LOI, MOU, and Term Sheet to the entrepreneur. (In the beginning of my career I made the mistake of giving a potential investor a term sheet that I had created. The investor thought it was humorous—he actually laughed at me. He also thought that my lack of experience and basic understanding of who gives the Term Sheet meant that I wasn't ready to receive one from him.) LOIs, MOUs, and Term Sheets are typically not legally binding; they are indications of the investor's thinking and what might happen; they are given to see if both sides of the conversation are aligned before any more time, money, and work is put into the deal to make an investment. The LOI and MOU typically come before the Term Sheet. Do not celebrate over an LOI, MOU, or Term Sheet. Once you accept a Term Sheet, the lawyers get involved to develop those terms into a shareholder agreement. Celebrate once the shareholders' agreement is signed and there is money in the bank.

▶ Tranche is sometimes spelled "Traunch"

In English we use tranche (sounds like: trawnch), the French word for *slice*, when talking about dividing up the money that you need into installments. Investors will typically tranche (slice up) the money that you are raising and tie each slice of money to you achieving what you say that you will do as a company. That US$1 million might be US$200,000 now to get you to that milestone in month eight that proves that you are on track, and then that will trigger then next US$200,000 (or whatever amount). Over time, you will eventually receive US$1 million (unless you have a discretionary term saying that if you overachieve your goals then you are not required to take later tranche ... work with a good lawyer to protect your future interests!).

Read *Mastering Private Equity*, Claudia Zeisberger, Michael Prahl, and Bowen White (2017)

ASSIGNMENT Write at least one paragraph on this section. Will you be raising money? How much will you raise in exchange for what percentage of equity (ownership in your company)? Have you identified an investor? When will you start the process? Explore and refine your questions

LIQUIDITY AND EXITS

One of the paths forward that you need to carefully consider for yourself and with your team, is whether it will be optimal to build a company around your IP and run with it yourself, or to let a bigger company with mature infrastructure run with it.

Investors almost always invest so that they can get out with more money than they put in. This may sound obvious, but first-time entrepreneurs commonly make the mistake of messaging to investors that they plan on being in the startup for the rest of their lives, thinking that the investors will be moved by their absolute commitment. Investors cannot stay invested in your startup for the rest of your life; they will have a timeframe in mind for when they will need their money back. Keep in mind that an investor's exit from your startup does not necessarily mean the end of your company, it is simply a moment in time when that investor will no longer be invested.

Think of an exit from three perspectives: 1. the investor and shareholder, 2. the company itself, and 3. you and other founders. The investors will be trying to understand in the beginning, whether or not you will be a problem for them when they need to exit. When they ask about exit possibilities, give answers that bias to their best interest. It might be that the window of opportunity for the investor/shareholder's exit does not fit the best interest of the company or you, along with other Founders. For example, the company's best interest might be to never be merged or acquired by another company, or the company's potential might be best served if it were to be part of a bigger, more established company that has existing infrastructure, resources, and customers. Give careful thought to the answer before the question is asked.

ASSIGNMENT Write at least one paragraph on this section from each of the three perspectives: 1. The investor and shareholder, 2. The company, and 3. The founders. Explore and refine your questions.

FOUNDERITIS

> "Founders' attachment, overconfidence, and naïveté may be necessary to get new ventures up and running, but these emotions later create problems."
> —**Noam Wasserman**

READ "The Founder's Dilemma," Noam Wasserman, *Harvard Business Review* (HBR) (February 2008)

Founderitis is when a founder behaves in value destructive ways. Companies can be meaningfully harmed or even destroyed by the bad behavior of a founder. You need to take measures in the beginning when things are still good and healthy to protect everyone and everything from unforeseen value-destructive behavior in the future. Work with a good lawyer NOW on a rules-of-engagement agreement between the founders and shareholders to protect the company (and families of founders and shareholders) from what might go wrong in the future.

Founders who cause harm to the companies that they found and work to build are rarely as candid as American Apparel's founder Dov Charney who told Marketplace in 2014, "My biggest weakness is me. I mean, lock me up already! It's obvious! Put me in a cage, I'll be fine. I'm my own worst enemy."[5]

You might find out too late that someone is value destructive. Again, take measures at the start when things are still early and being formed. Sit down with a qualified lawyer and document the rules for good conduct and what happens if one or more of the founders become value destructive. Hopefully you will never need to take action. Hopefully everyone will be rational and behave well.

Finding examples of well-known founders who harmed their successful companies is not that difficult. For every name brand person who fails their company, there are countless regular people who harmed their ventures (and those involved and around it) before they qualified for big press coverage.

> "We have met the enemy and he is us."
> From ***Pogo*** by Walt Kelly, who borrowed it from a 1970 Earth Day poster

There is reality in the humorous yet sad observation that no matter how well intentioned, we are very often our own worst enemy. Anticipate this reality and plan for what to do about it when (not if) our own behavior threatens to undo what good we are working to accomplish.

---

5   Marketplace.org with Kai Ryssdal 20 January 2014, updated 27 March 2015 "American Apparel CEO Dov Charney on pushing boundaries and his biggest weakness"

BOARDS:
ADVISORY AND GOVERNANCE

At the very beginning, you can organize a few people who are not legally affiliated with the company but are qualified to help guide you as you create and begin running your startup. This is called an Advisory Board. Advisors typically volunteer their time, but sometimes they ask for compensation.

> **HINT** If a person asks for money to give you advice when you need to protect what little money you have to run the startup, that person may not have the startup's best interests as a priority. If they want ownership in exchange for advice you should put them on a vesting schedule over time for a small percentage, and if they perform well over time, they earn the percentage.

Once the startup is showing signs of viability (that it will actually survive and hopefully thrive), then you should organize (constitute) a board of directors (in some jurisdictions this is called a board of governors). This is not the executive leadership (sometimes called an executive board), but it is responsible for the company as a whole. The CEO (Chief Executive Officer) reports to the chairman (chairperson) of the board of directors. The chairman is ideally an independent outsider (not the CEO, or an investor), so that they can be as objective as possible. It is ideal if the chairman has deep industry expertise. The board of directors, including the chairman, should be an uneven number so that there are no split votes. The founders and investors/shareholders would typically have an even number of seats. If you are a founder, be brave enough to put trusted non-employees and non-founders in your seats.

ASSIGNMENT Identify up to four people (by name) who could serve as volunteers on your board of advisers. Make sure that these are people who understand what you are doing, they understand the industry, and you have access to them. Then identify an odd number of seats for your board of directors (3, 5, 7, etc.). Identify a potential chairman of the board (e.g., ideally an independent senior industry expert to whom you have access). Write at least one paragraph on this section. Explore and refine your questions.

MARKETING, SALES, AND BUSINESS DEVELOPMENT

You may have noticed that the definitions and roles of <u>marketing</u> and <u>sales</u> and <u>business development</u> are not always the same from company to company. Sometimes marketing and sales is one integrated organization and other times they are separated, and sometimes they struggle to work together. Business development is sometimes part of marketing, sometimes part of sales, and other times it stands on its own.

I believe that one of the reasons why people sometimes struggle to differentiate between the three is because in the beginning the three were one integrated function. People wanted to exchange what they had for what other people had so they created marketplaces in town squares or villages and figured out how to transact with each other for goods and materials or money. Over time, people have artificially separated the three.

We will need to stay flexible within the definitions; you will need to work with the definitions of the three as your company defines them.

For the purpose of this startup entrepreneurship training, we will define the three, neutrally, as follows:

▶ **Marketing**
The research and planning of where in the world the optimal customers are located and who those people are in that market. Then determining the means by which to capture the attention of paying customers (via the sundry activities that we typically associate with marketing, such as advertising, trade shows, press, etc.)

▶ **Sales**
The activities that result in the exchange of the offering for money. This could be in person (traditional sales), or through to taking credit cards on a website or inside a mobile application (digital transactions).

▶ **Business development**
The securing of strategic relationships that open doors and remove barriers. For example, let's say that you are developing a device designed to help medical patients better manage their pain during therapies. Business development (sometimes called "Biz Dev") would secure an agreement with a recognized medical research facility to perform a study to determine if your device actually does help people manage their pain during therapies.

You should identify the key activities that must be done for marketing, sales, and business development. If you already identified these activities in your team modeling and they are already reflected in your Gantt chart and fundable event timeline then very well done! There is always more to do so you should continue to build the list of activities.

GO TO MARKET

You need to plan how to deliver your offering to the target customer and market (whether it is internal to your company or external). Where, when, how, and to whom the offering will be delivered should be detailed to a meaningful degree.

It is often helpful to think backward from the hands of the customer. How did the offering make it into their hands so that they can start using it? Then take one step at a time back to where you are now. Will you be manufacturing a physical product? Will it be software that is downloaded from the cloud or used at-will via a web browser and delivered from a cloud-based server (including the delivery of installers and plug-ins)? Is it a service that will be delivered over the cloud or in person? Think through all of the moving parts as if you were building the clockworks inside of a mechanical watch.

Let me give you a high-level example that begins with the goal and works backwards. In the business world, this is commonly called "Reverse Engineering"—taking a process or product apart to see how it was built so that you can build the same thing without starting from scratch. Of course, this timeline is for example only and will differ for every product and market as every delivery involves unique considerations that must be factored into planning.

Let's say that your startup will be designing, engineering, manufacturing, and then delivering a physical electronic device to the market. (I'll use a physical product that needs to be manufactured as an example, because it tends to be more complicated than engineering and delivering software.) Let's further assume that there are seasonality considerations for your target market.

1. **Product in stores (online as well as brick-and-mortar)**
   Let's say that you need to have the product in stores (online and in physical locations) by November (for example), so that you can hit the big selling season for your product in late November through late-December.

2. **Pallets[6] of finished goods shipping to distribution, fulfillment, and stores**
   Which means that you need to have pallets of boxes of your physical product in distribution by October so that it can be delivered to stores in October and November.

3. **Active manufacturing**
   Which means that you should be actively manufacturing by August or no later than September so that you can begin shipping in September to hit distribution in October.

4. **Raw materials to manufacturing**
   Which means that you need to have all raw materials, casts, tools, and manufacturing BOMs (Bill of Materials) and specifications, etc. to the manufacturer by August, but ideally in July for manufacture in August.

5. **Testing complete**
   Which means that you need to have the product finalized and tested and ready for manufacturing no later than July.

6. **Active Beta and Alpha testing along with bug regression and fixes**
   Which means that you should have been in beta testing no later than May, and alpha testing (for example) as early as February or March, giving your team time for bug regression and fixes. This is also the time that you should be ordering all of the raw materials to make sure that they arrive at the manufacturer's facility on time.

7. **Technical Specifications and other engineering completed**
   The freeze on modifications to all technical specifications for the product should happen by February, with engineering and design completed by that time.

8. **Research and Development (R&D)**
   You need to work with engineering to ensure that you have time to complete that work between now and January-February, which also means working with Marketing and all other internal parties to ensure that the device that you are making is correctly planned and aligned with all relevant expectations.

9. **Marketing and Sales Activities well in advance**
   Then you have considerations for all marketing and sales activities. You need to advertise to stores and distribution so that they can order the product and have it in stores in time, and that needs to be done far in advance. You also need to plan when you will advertise to the customer, so that they are motivated to buy once the product is in stores and online.

---

6   A pallet is a type of low profile platform typically made of wood, but at times, other materials. Boxes and other materials are stacked on the pallet, which is then movable by a forklift from one part of a factory to another, and then loaded onto trucks, etc.

In addition to the above, I would like to recommend an exercise to you. You may have heard of a TAM, *T-A-M* stands for <u>Total Addressable Market</u>. The *S* in TASM (sometimes called SAM) is the addition of the word: <u>Serviceable</u>.

▶ The **Total Market** is the big number of all people and money spent on products, services, and solutions similar to the one that you will be creating.

▶ The **Addressable Market** is the percentage of the Total to whom you can deliver a targeted meaningful message designed to inspire the customer to buy and use what you are offering.

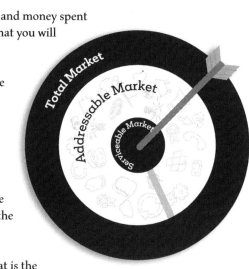

People will often draw a big circle and call it the Total and then draw a circle inside the big circle and call it the Addressable, and then declare a percentage of that number to represent the number of users or the amount of money that they hope to secure.

▶ You should add one more circle in the center, and that is the **Serviceable Market** number. Serviceable means that you can serve or deliver your offering to that number of customers (which could be discrete products or number of simultaneous users and clicks, etc.). This is a critical number to understand.

When you are presenting to a Board of Directors, or a CEO or CFO, or an investor, or to your team, the most relevant number is not the Total, it is the relationship and connection between the numbers that represent the Addressable and the Serviceable Markets. The amount of money that you will be investing in the Addressable correlates to the amount of money invested in the Serviceable.

Let's say that you spend so much in the Addressable that you have a higher conversion to cash (meaning paying customers) than you have capacity to serve; then you have either overinvested in the Addressable or underinvested in the Serviceable. What matters is that you "right size" the investment for both in a coordinated effort so that you convert to cash (achieve paying customers) at a comparable rate to the amount of product or capacity of the service that you have to offer.

If you were to build a TASM now, meaning a plan for your Total, Addressable, Serviceable Market, how big is the Total? (Don't anchor too much on this big number, as it matters but not as much as the next numbers.) How big is the Addressable Market? Who are the customers? Where are they? How will you deliver a meaningful message to them? At what cost? And how big is your Serviceable Market? That is, how much serviceable capacity do you anticipate needing to create so that you can profitably deliver to paying customers? Once you start measuring this way, you will have a better chance of impressing key influencers and decision makers because you know what you are doing.

THE BIG PLAY

You have now evolved this first IP to the point that you need to answer the question of whether or not this IP is the sole purpose of your new company or whether or not there will be more. Investors, shareholders, Boards of Directors/Governors, and your team will need to understand A. Is your startup a one-trick pony, meaning will your company ever do more than whatever you have decided to do as a first offering (e.g., product, service, solution?). B. How the first offering (and the hopeful follow-on offerings that you are lining up) fits into a bigger opportunity for the company, shareholders, and stakeholders.

For example, let's say that you have identified the need for digital disruption of the traditional forecasting, procurement, supply chain, and inventory management in your company. Let's say that you intend to create a new software development unit that will create custom software that will serve the needs of the business operations and finance units in the company, so that they can use your custom software to optimize the company's forecasting, procurement, supply chain, and inventory controls. You should think for a moment about the bigger play for the software as well as the initiative. What impacts will there be on various parts of the business beyond the specific scope of the proposed work? What will be the impact on the value of the company, if any? Will there be any other follow-on opportunities that could result from this work (assuming all goes well with it)? For example, could this software then be sold as a product to other companies or would it be more valuable if preserved exclusively in-house?

Think for a moment about companies such as McDonalds, Amazon, and Tesla. What is the bigger play for those companies? Even though the average person thinks of McDonalds as a fast food restaurant, it is actually a real estate company that has realized significant wealth from controlling and creatively deploying their real estate holdings. It is important to note that real estate being a part of the value creation and value capture at McDonalds was not part of their beginning—it came later, thanks to Corporate Entrepreneurship.

Next, most people think that Amazon is an e-commerce retailer on the Internet that sells books, electronic devices, and more. Thanks to Corporate Entrepreneurship however, Amazon is a company that does much more then e-commerce of books and consumer electronics; Amazon as a company controls a meaningful percentage of the transactions in the cloud, thanks to Amazon Web Services (AWS).

Next, consider Tesla. Most people think of Tesla as a maker of high-end electric cars. But thanks to Corporate Entrepreneurship, Tesla is becoming a power company that produces various products from the shingles on roof tops harvesting solar energy to power stations that you install in your garage to power your house and your car.

So the question for you at this point is: What is the bigger picture for your company in light of your entrepreneurial engagement right now? You may be working on a specific solution or product or service, but what is the potential bigger impact on the company? Clarifying and defining your intention up front will help you as you go. This may change and evolve as you go, and that is normal.

> **ASSIGNMENT** Write at least one paragraph on this section. Think, what is the bigger play for what you are working to accomplish? How does this tree (your initiative) more fully complete the forest, or potentially elevate what is now a stand of trees to become a fully-fledged forest? If you cannot explain how what you plan to do creates and captures increased value beyond the scope or your project itself, then your initiative might stop here. Explore and refine your questions.

CALL TO ACTION OR THE ASK

In preparation for your presentations to potential lawyers, bankers, investors, strategic hires, and others, you need to identify the message(s) that will inspire key influencers and decision makers that you know what you are doing so that they will want to join you.

In business, the moment when you ask the listener for what you need from them is sometimes called a **Call to Action** or **The Ask** or **The Question**, but the intent of all three terms is the same.

Keep in mind that what is clear and motivates one listener may or may not be clear and motivate anyone else. Every person has their own requirements, mandates, needs, wants, hopes, stresses, pressures, and so on. Do your best to figure out what motivates the person to whom you are extending (what is often called "putting") The Ask or Call to Action.

For example, Steve Jobs (co-founder of Apple) asked John Sculley (the person who became CEO of Apple after Steve Jobs): "Do you want to sell sugared water for the rest of your life? Or do you want to come with me and change the world?" That Call to Action from Steve Jobs worked for John Sculley, but it might or might not have worked for anyone else. Steve Jobs did his homework on what motivated John Sculley and that specific Call to Action or Ask worked on him in that situation.

As another example, if you are presenting to an investor and you bias your presentation heavily toward revenue and profit but never mention shareholder value, they may not fund your startup if their priorities are shareholder value. Or it could be the other way around if their top priority is revenue and profit. You need to puzzle through and figure out the critical motivations of your audience BEFORE you present the details and call them to action. Do not assume that your priorities or the primary benefits of your initiative are aligned with their priorities, or that you understand their priorities because to you this or that argument "makes sense."

Another thing to keep in mind is that if you are presenting to a group, everyone in that room is going to have their own biases and opinions. Figure out as much as you can about every influencer and decision maker who might be in the room during your presentation and Call to Action. It is okay to strategically lace messages throughout the presentation that speak to what each person in the room needs to hear; just be certain that all of those messages are truthful and consistent with what you are actually doing.

When you extend or put The Ask, depending on the culture and context, you can then briefly issue a call to action for each person in the room in the appropriate order of who matters most.

Sometimes, in some cultures, the messages in the body of the presentation are all that most need, and the formal Ask would only be issued to the most relevant and important person in the room. So be sure that you know what is most appropriate before you enter the room to present.

ASSIGNMENT Write at least one clean sentence for EACH person that you need to persuade to support your initiative. Never give the same pitch twice; what works for one person may or may not work for any other person. Explore and refine your questions.

EXECUTIVE SUMMARIES AND BUSINESS PLANS

> "Everyone has a plan 'til they get punched in the mouth."
> —**Mike Tyson**, former heavyweight boxing champion of the world

Hopefully you have been writing down all of your thoughts while going through each of the steps to this point. I have found great value in keeping track of all ideas or thoughts whether they seem relevant to me at the time or not.

You will need to complete a written <u>executive summary</u> (a document that takes the same amount of time to read as to drink a glass of water) that will help influencers and decision makers understand enough that they will 1. want to know more, and 2. be interested (or even excited) to support you and the initiative. A <u>business plan</u> is a long, more detailed executive summary.

▶ Executive Summary

An Executive Summary, not to be confused with a full Business Plan, is ideally two pages and no longer than three pages in length. It should have the most representative and most relevant details, which are explained in greater detail in the full business plan. Make sure that every word in the Executive Summary is relevant to persuade the reader that you know what you are doing to build and run the company. The Executive Summary should inspire the reader to ask you for more information.

▶ Business Plan

A Business Plan is a longer, more detailed document than an Executive Summary. A typical length for a business plan is 20–30 pages. When writing business plans you should bias the writing very heavily to execution detail; show what you will do, when, where, how, and why. State the problem, build out the execution detail around the solution to the problem, put some financials in so that the costs are understood, and call the reader to action. Use multiple proofreaders and listen to their feedback. Questions and comments give you insight into what is understandable and working (or not), so be grateful and never impatient with questions and comments.

(I once submitted a 30-page business plan to a government body, not realizing that they required a minimum of 100 pages because more pages demonstrated thorough and complete investigation and consideration. In the business world, a 100+ page business plan to an investor or leadership team might imply that you are overthinking or cannot succinctly say what you need to say.)

There is no single magic format or outline for business plans and executive summaries. You should write the details in a way that will flow most naturally and persuade the reader, while also providing a document that will help guide your running of the company.

The goal for an executive summary and business plan, along with all supportive financials, should be to use it as practice. Stay flexible, move with what happens, and update your documentation regularly so that you are ready at a moment's notice to share and present. Do not get caught with a summary or plan that is out of date; that moment might be the game changer. Keep updating, practicing, learning, and adapting to change as you go forward.

> **ASSIGNMENT** All of the topics explored in this framework can be used in your executive summary and business plan. Create your 2–3-page executive summary first in a separate document (name it uniquely and always save the date in the file name every time you update it). Once your executive summary is completed, save a copy of it as a different file (using "Save As … ") with the date in the file name in the same folder. Then, begin the work of meaningfully expanding the detail in each section until you have a 20–30-page full business plan.

PITCHING AND PRESENTATIONS

▶ Pitching

A pitch is a short format presentation. It should be quick, clear, and to the point. An elevator or lift pitch is typically no more than one or two minutes (the time it would take to get from one floor in a building to a few floors up). Quickly state your name, what you do for your company (this should take only a few seconds) and then get straight into the pitch. Your pitch should clearly state that there is an opportunity (a problem), something that can be done about the opportunity, what you are doing about it, and how the listener can be involved. Keep the pitch to the point and positive.

▶ Presentations

A presentation is a longer format pitch but has a similar structure.

> **HINT** Presentations tend to focus too much on the problem/opportunity and have too little practical detail on what can be done and what you are actually doing (aka execution). It is true that the listener needs to believe that you are addressing an authentic problem (do not solve a non-problem, and do not be a solution looking for a problem to solve) but remember that the listener needs to believe that you know what you are doing (execution level detail). Explain the opportunity and give representative detail into what you are doing about that opportunity.

It is common for people not to practice their presentations in advance. People often work on their materials up to the moment before presenting and then walk into the room and start. This is a mistake. Practice your pitch and presentations before giving them. There is no substitute for practice. Make sure that the first time that you pitch, or present is during practice rather than in front of the person whom you need to persuade. You only get one chance at a first impression. In case you feel that practice will make you less spontaneous in the moment, keep in mind that practice will make you better in a moment. For example, professional athletes practice SO THAT they will be better able to be more powerfully and effectively spontaneous in a moment.

The opportunity to persuade a key influencer or decision maker might happen at any moment. The quick two-minute pitch is called an elevator pitch or lift pitch because you might be in an elevator or lift when you realize that you are standing next to a key influencer or decision maker. You then have the amount of time that it takes to go from the ground floor to when they exit the elevator or lift to plant a seed. Hopefully they will invite you to present to them based on the strength of that one short pitch.

I have successfully pitched in elevators/lifts, hallways/corridors, stairways, sidewalks, while crossing the street, while at a salad bar, standing in a line/queue, while on the phone, and sitting next to someone on a plane. The point is that you never know when the opportunity will present itself. Practice your pitch over and over until you can say it without thinking about it. And practice it on different people to make sure that it makes sense and is coherent.

Practice your pitching without slides or props or other visual support. You never know when, where, or how you will be pitching. If your pitch is reliant on a slide or a prop, you might find yourself fumbling with your phone or computer, trying to pull up whatever you need, and end up burning the seconds or minutes that you have to persuade the listener. Also keep in mind that you only have a handful of seconds to create a powerful first impression; if you know what you are talking about and can say it off the top of your head without notes or visual assistance, then all the better.

If you have technology that can be quickly and effortlessly shown, then do it; just be aware that if it doesn't work then that is what the listener will remember.

Full presentations can start with a quick two-minute pitch at the top, to snapshot the long story short and give the audience an idea of what you are doing. Then you can start the longer format presentation. The longer presentation can include slides and product demonstrations if you have them; just remember to tell the story in an order that makes sense. Practice, practice, practice. There is no substitute for practicing before you present. Then after you've presented, practice some more.

As to time management, let's say, for example, that you are given a 30-minute meeting to present. Do not prepare 30 minutes of presentations and slides and demonstrations. A good rule of thumb is to prepare presentations for half of the allotted time. So, in this example you would prepare 15 (or 20 maximum) minutes of a presentation, for a 30-minute meeting. Leave room for questions during the presentation as well as questions and answers at the end.

Here is a thumbnail EXAMPLE of how much time should be spent on each part of the presentation:

▶ **Intro** (~5% of the available time)
Don't apologize—it is a common opener, but it is a poor start. Be confident but never arrogant.

▶ **The Opportunity/Problem** (~25%)
Do not pander or exaggerate; be factual.

▶ What options are possible (~15%)

Give a few examples of options. Do not make the mistake of speaking poorly of any alternative to what you are recommending. Be factual.

▶ What I am doing (~45%)

Do not hold back any secret ingredient (aka silver bullet or game changer) during your presentation. It is a common problem that the presenter will save the big "wow" of their solution for a follow-up presentation. If the audience doesn't hear the wow in your first pitch, there may not be a second presentation.

▶ How you can be involved (~10%)

Do not tell them what they will do. Welcome them to the party and invite them to be involved.

Start on time and finish on time (or a little early). Going over time should only happen if the audience asks you to stay and explain more. Even then, be sensitive to being over time. It is typically better to leave when you are ahead while they want more and schedule a follow-up.

Do not feel nervous or upset about any questions that might be asked of you. Questions expose holes in your presentation and tell you what was not clear or understandable to the listener (no matter how clear you thought that you made the point). Questions also give you an indication of what matters to the person asking the question. Write down all the questions that you were asked, and the answers that you gave, and then use those notes as preparation for future meetings (and work on clearer presentations and better answers for the future).

> **ASSIGNMENT** Build the materials that you will need (e.g., 2–3-page executive summary, slides, etc.). Practice that 60-second pitch until you can say it without thinking. THEN start working on expanded detail versions of that pitch so that when people ask you to give them more you can do 60 seconds on this detail and 60 seconds on that detail. THEN work on a 30-minute expanded version of that pitch, which gives more meaningful insight and detail. Explore and refine your questions.

SAVE YOUR WORK, UPDATE IT REGULARLY, AND REFER TO IT OFTEN

Revisit all of the above work regularly. Remember to save your work regularly and keep backups on separate secure devices. Once a day, or at a minimum once a week on a routine day at a routine time, review and update details for all of the above work. The last time that out of date documents created a problem for me was when I was asked to send my current business plan to a meeting deciding the placement of millions of dollars (in the dot.com era) and I was not ready in the moment. Since that day I have always had current documents ready to send whenever a shareholder, investor, or board member asks. It always makes a good impression when you are ready to send freshly updated documents when asked.

Every time you update the document, save a unique version in a common reference folder on your computer. Use a consistent naming convention and update the name every time to include the date that you modified it (or some other intuitive system that others, not just you, will understand if they need to find information).

You never know when you will need to give someone a copy of your plan. You might be given advance warning, but sometimes the call is unexpected. Do not be caught off guard with an out of date version! Be prepared, and you will have nothing to fear.

ASSIGNMENT Comb through your document. Save everything. If you write something and you aren't quite sure how it fits, either put the thought on the last empty page of the document or create a second document in the same folder just for thoughts that you aren't yet sure how to use. You do not want to find yourself in the situation where later on, you wish that you hadn't deleted that thought.

On future days when you open and edit the document, do a Save As and change the version date on the document so that it creates a new document that is saved in the same folder. It may happen that in the future you will want to refer to an earlier draft, and if anything happens to the file that you are working on that day, you can always go back to the most recent version rather than starting over.

Keep a backup somewhere other than on your computer. (You should regularly back up your entire hard drive.) If you are working on paper, you need to keep your binder safe and secure at all times. When you are able, you might have someone scan every page in the binder onto a file that you keep on a small portable computer stick for safekeeping. If you edit your document on a public computer, just make certain that you do not leave a copy of your document on the public hard drive.

Regularly update your writing, save copies, keep the dream alive, and work to make it real.

DISRUPTIVE INNOVATION AND BLUE OCEANS

Disruptive Innovation

In 1997, Harvard Business School (HBS) Professor Clayton Christensen revolutionized the way the business world thought about everything with his very practical and insightful theory of Disruptive Innovation. Disruptive Innovation has been called the most influential business idea of the 21st century.

For years, I misunderstood the meaning of Disruptive Innovation. I made the mistake of oversimplifying the theory to the point of thinking that anything innovative that disrupted anything else was Disruptive Innovation. Not so.

READ THE ARTICLE "What Is Disruptive Innovation?," Clayton Christensen, *Harvard Business Review* (HBR) (December 2015)

If what you are offering can achieve a low-end foothold and *then* disrupt the incumbent, then it is Disruptive Innovation. For example, selling a book over the Internet is Disruptive Innovation because it costs less than selling a book in a store. Then selling a digital book on a tablet is Disruptive Innovation because it (typically) costs less than a book that is printed on paper.

READ THE BOOK *The Innovator's Dilemma*, Clayton Christensen (1997)
The entire Innovation series with Clay Christensen is worth reading.

The Disruptive Innovation Model

This diagram contrasts product *performance trajectories* (the dashed lines showing how products or services improve over time) with customer demand trajectories (the dotted gray lines showing customers' willingness to pay for performance). As incumbent companies introduce higher-quality products or services (upper dashed line) to satisfy the high end of the market (where profitability is highest), they overshoot the needs of low-end customers and many mainstream customers. This leaves an opening for entrants to find footholds in the less-profitable segments that incumbents are neglecting. Entrants on a disruptive trajectory (lower dashed line) improve the performance of their offerings and move upmarket (where profitability is highest for them, too) and challenge the dominance of the incumbents.

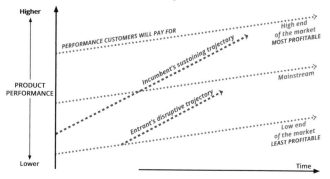

SOURCE CLAYTON M. CHRISTENSEN, MICHAEL RAYNOR, AND RORY MCDONALD FROM "WHAT IS DISRUPTIVE INNOVATION?" DECEMBER 2015.

©HBR.ORG

A Bridge Between the Disruptive Innovation and Blue Ocean ...

If what you are offering costs the same or more, even if you are competing with an incumbent and working to disrupt them, then you are not engaging in Disruptive Innovation.

If, for example, you are reimagining and repositioning how:

- ▶ My car is being shared with and used by other people
- ▶ I will use other people's cars
- ▶ My car is being used as a type of taxi so that I can make money with it
- ▶ Other people pick me up in their cars like a taxi

... but the advantage to any of the above is less the cost and more the convenience and approach to people in the market who need transportation ... then you are swimming in the waters of Blue Ocean.

Blue Ocean

In 2004, INSEAD Professors W. Chan Kim and Renée Mauborgne shifted the way the business world thought about congestion and competitiveness in markets (Red Oceans), and how to adapt and shift approaches to create opportunities in new markets (Blue Oceans).

I had my "Aha!" moment around Blue Ocean Strategy when I heard Professor Mauborgne speak in Dubai at a conference. For the first time, I thought "Oh, that is what Blue Ocean means! I like it." Then I actually read the books rather than guessing at what Blue Ocean Strategy meant from how I heard people talk about it. Go to the source.

READ THE ARTICLE "Blue Ocean Strategy," W. Chan Kim and Renée Mauborgne *Harvard Business Review* (HBR) (October 2004)

READ THE BOOK *Blue Ocean Strategy,* W. Chan Kim and Renée Mauborgne (2004)

The classic example of Blue Ocean Strategy is a traditional circus vs. Cirque du Soleil. A traditional circus focuses on sensational moments with clowns, animals, and side-shows, etc. targeting kids who bring their parents. Cirque du Soleil focuses on telling a story with acrobats targeting adults who sometimes bring kids. Cirque du Soleil is not less expensive than a traditional circus; Cirque du Soleil is actually more expensive. Both are a "circus" but they approach different markets (Oceans), rather than competing head-to-head for the same share of the same wallet.

Are you Blue Ocean or Disruptive Innovation?

Is your entrepreneurial initiative doing what others are doing? Are you coming in at the low-end and attacking the market position of a more expensive and more established player? Or are you not less expensive but creating a new approach to a newly redefined market?

I have heard people argue that one is better than the other, but I think they are both good, just different. Some companies will Blue Ocean their offering and prove what they are doing, and then refine their offering, processes, and costs so that they can then position for a Disruptive Innovation play.

Both Disruptive Innovation and Blue Oceans are worthy pursuits. Understand the differences and similarities, then push forward on the path to engage Disruptive Innovation and/or into the Blue Oceans of new market opportunities.

SOFTWARE
DEVELOPMENT

"Computers themselves, and software yet to be developed,
will revolutionize the way we learn."

—Steve Jobs

"Software innovation, like almost every other kind
of innovation, requires the ability to collaborate and
share ideas with other people, and
to sit down and talk with customers and get
their feedback and understand their needs."

—Bill Gates

The following is a 17-step framework for Software Development as Entrepreneurship training that I have created over my career. The foundation of the framework is my personal experience and knowledge of what is expected from strategic others[1], and what works in practice. People of all education levels around the world have used this framework successfully to plan the development of their software ideas. This framework is not exhaustive but is designed to kick-start planning and execution to give you a path forward.

Before you start this framework: If you have not already done so, please go back to the page called START HERE at the beginning of the book and complete parts 1, 2, 3, and 4 of the Preparatory Frameworks. Once that is completed, come back to this page and move forward to the following:

PREAMBLE **Write Everything Down**

STEP 1 **A Firm Foundation**

STEP 2 **What Is Software? What About Enterprise? Consumer? App? AI/ML?**

STEP 3 **The Offering Including an ORD**

STEP 4 **Storyboarding and Wireframing**

STEP 5 **Execution and Team Modeling**

STEP 6 **Business Modeling**

STEP 7 **Financial Modeling**

STEP 8 **Execution and Fundable Event Timelines**

STEP 9 **Capital Modeling**

STEP 10 **Liquidity and Exits**

STEP 11 **Founderitis**

STEP 12 **Marketing, Sales, and Business Development**

STEP 13 **The Big Play**

STEP 14 **Call to Action or The Ask**

STEP 15 **Executive Summaries and Business Plans**

STEP 16 **Presentations (Pitching and Longer Format)**

STEP 17 **Save Your Work, Update It Regularly, and Refer to It Often**

---

1   By "strategic others" I mean anyone who matters to what you are working to accomplish. These people might be investors, bankers, lawyers, boards of directors, shareholders, executives, workers, unions, the press, suppliers, customers, the government, etc.

The purpose of the framework is to help anyone with an idea for a software application to plan the application in some detail. With this work, you should be able to approach software developers (unless you are a developer already), creatives who will build the graphic elements, user interface designers, and strategic others such as investors.

WRITE EVERYTHING DOWN

It is common that people have a bright idea, then they think and dream about it (most likely talking themselves out of it), but never write down the details. Then they forget. At the time the idea seemed so obvious, so clearly brilliant but an hour later, or the next morning ... it is gone. Get into the habit of writing down all of your bright ideas.

Once you have an idea for some software that you believe needs to exist, the first thing that you should do is write down all of your thoughts about it. Don't worry about the structure of the writing yet; write down everything that you can think of that you want the software to do. If writing does not work for you then record yourself talking; if you can't do that then draw pictures; if you can't do that then ask someone to help you with one of the options. Once you've documented your thoughts, get started with the 17-step framework and refer to your documented thoughts as you go. Do not delete any of your thoughts, drawings, or recordings. Use all of it as a reference as you work. Special note: Stay flexible around the central idea. Things will be evolving and moving around. Keep track of the details.

I chose the quote from the Princess Bride at the top of this framework very deliberately. Over the years I have seen many people with bright ideas waving their hands in meetings with engineers and creatives trying to explain what they are thinking but ultimately verbalizing a jumble of words around their thoughts. They draw on paper and the white board, explaining this and that, erasing and rewriting, using jazz hands, and then believing that surely everyone in the room must now picture the same thing in their respective minds and understanding. When you do this (and people do it all the time) with a team of engineers, do not be surprised when tens of thousands of dollars later you are required to pay for a piece of software that does not look like or do what you thought it would look like and do.

How you write down and explain your thinking matters.

Let's get started.

A FIRM FOUNDATION

It may be that your idea will become actual software that you and other people use. You might sell it or you might build a startup company around it. You might be able to do it all by yourself, and you might need help. As you will see during the 17 steps of the framework, there is more to consider than the software idea itself.

If you want to create a company around the software then you will need qualified legal guidance on questions such as where to incorporate, where to operate, copyrights and patents, agreements between the founders on ownership of the company (and the intellectual property (IP) if any can be legally claimed), Standard Operating Procedures (SOP) for all mission-critical activities including (but not limited to) all money that you spend on everything, as well as any and all money invested and spent by you and/or anyone else in and around the IP and your venture, and more. These are critical questions that people take for granted as they enthusiastically rush to create their software and maybe a company around it.

If you hope to make money from your software, or if your plan to invest your money into the development of it, or if you will need other people's money (OPM) to develop it, you are going to need an accountant to be involved.

Lawyers and accountants are extensions of your team. Keep them close and well informed and think of them as integrated parts of everything; do not make the common mistake of thinking of lawyers and accounts as "necessary evils." The right team makes every opportunity better.

There are other extended team members that will likely be needed unless you are an expert at all forms and levels of software engineering, user interface design, creative development of all graphic and visual details, sales and marketing, distribution, and more.

ASSIGNMENT If you already use the cloud to back up all of your work securely, that is excellent. If you regularly use software that keeps track of versions of your work, so that you never invest hours editing the wrong version of a document, that is superb. If, however, for any reason, you are not yet able to back-up in the cloud or you do not have access to software that keeps track of versions of your documents, you will need to do these things manually. If you are working on a computer, create a folder with a logical name that you will not forget. Put that folder in an obvious location on the computer (not a clever place, but a clear and easy to remember place), that will still be obvious to you tomorrow and the next day. Create a new document and save it in the folder that you just created. Name the file something easy to remember and give it today's date; then every day you edit it, save a version with that day's date so that you can tell the difference between files. Always work on the most recent date and version of the file. If you do not have a computer, buy a spiral binder with lined paper (or an equivalent that is available to you). Put your name and contact information on it and keep it in a safe place. Do all of your work in the document or binder.

ASSIGNMENT Identify a lawyer and accountant whom you can approach, and with whom you can work. Identify where you will incorporate and where you plan to operate as a company (where you will have an office and employees). Write at least one paragraph on this section. Explore and refine your questions.

STEP 2

WHAT IS SOFTWARE?
WHAT IS ENTERPRISE? CONSUMER?
APP? AI/ML? ETC.?

▶ **Software**

Physical machines are controlled by one of two things: 1. Humans, 2. Software.

Software might be as simple as turning on a light when a sensor detects a sound or movement, or as complex as navigating a rocket to and landing on a distant planet. Software that you benefit from but never see is very likely all around you; for example, the internet and everything on it, traffic and street lights, satellites orbiting the earth broadcasting TV and movies as well as providing GPS/SatNav information to your phone or navigation system in your car, and much more. Ranging from governments to whole city infrastructures to your car and TV, software makes the modern world run.

▶ **Enterprise**

Enterprise is software that will be used by large organizations (companies and/or governments), or to perform very complex tasks.

▶ **Consumer vs. Prosumer vs. Professional**

It could be that the Consumer (sometimes called the "home edition") of software is used at work, but the general guidelines can be described as follows:

Consumer: The point-and-click simplified features version to be used by non-professionals at home.

Prosumer: This is the version for an advanced amateur or professional at home—more feature-rich than the consumer version but more affordable than the full professional version of the software that they use at work. (Prosumer is a portmanteau of Professional and Consumer.)

Professional: The most feature-rich and powerful version, the step above Professional is Enterprise; the biggest difference may be features but is typically the number of users.

▶ App

App is actually a contraction (short version of the word) *Application* but has made its way into languages around the world as its own word, meaning software that you can interact with on a portable device. There was a time when the only software on a telephone made telephone calls. Then software on a phone allowed you to send a text-based message from one phone to another. At that time, an App was software on a computer. Then with the rise of *Smart Devices* such as phones and tablets, etc., an App became the software on the device that allowed you to use your phone or tablet as everything from a game-playing device to a productivity tool. Many non-English languages use the word *App* without knowing its association with the original word *Application* they just say "App" or "A-P-P" because that is what interactive software on a Smart Device is called.

If you are targeting some type of App on a Smart Device then you need to think about things such as whether it will be a **Native App** or a **Web App**. In basic terms, the difference is the following:

Native App: Designed to reside in the storage of the device itself and run on the device's operating system. Native Apps are typically more robust and feature-rich in their abilities, but they are more complex and typically more expensive to build and maintain. Depending on the device, you might need to do a validation test on every version of the operating system across devices, even if they use what sounds like a common operating system (each build of the operating system might be subtly or meaningfully different on each device).

Web App: A small app that is actually a type of Web browser that displays content that is on the Internet so that you can interact with it via your Smart Device. Web Apps are typically less robust and feature-rich, but simpler and less expensive to build and maintain. (If you have an App that does not work when your device is not connected to the Internet then it might be a Web App; unless it is a native app that relies on sending and receiving information from the Internet.)

▶ SaaS

Software as a Service (sometimes called on-demand-software) is software that resides on a server on the Internet, and you access it via software on your computer or device (it is a *Client and Server* solution). SaaS is typically subscription based or otherwise licensed for access and use.

▶ Client and Server

In the world of software, there are two basic sides of most solutions.

The Client is the software that you use on your device to access data somewhere else. A metaphor that might help is a person sitting in a restaurant for a meal. They do not go into the kitchen to deliver the food order or to prepare their own meal, they place the order and consume food, then they pay for it, and are on their way.

The <u>Server</u> is the supplier of the Client software's requests. Continuing with the metaphor of the restaurant, the "server" works with the client to take their order and then goes back to the kitchen to place the order and then returns the food from the kitchen to the Client's table. The Server is both the waiter and the cook in the kitchen; two in one.

▶ AI/ML

AI is an acronym for **Artificial Intelligence** and ML is an acronym for **Machine Learning**.

<u>AI</u>: When people think of AI they typically imagine either: 1. Machines that can think for themselves just like humans do (which is not yet possible), 2. Software that runs machines and mimics certain processes traditionally performed by humans. (Such as opening a door when you approach it or recognizing patterns in an x-ray to identify disease.)

AI can, at times, be better than humans at tasks like rapid deep computational mathematics, pattern recognition, or running a task without the need for breaks to eat, rest, feed an addiction, or sleep). AI can also be worse than humans at tasks like interpreting what data implies and how it can be used or laterally applied, critical thinking, strategic thinking, creativity, imagination, and empathy.

<u>ML</u>: Machine Learning simply means software that can learn and improve over time. An example of this would be a Natural Language Chat-Bot on a company's website. As more people interact with the non-natural person via chat, it learns as humans type responses into it, and over time, it becomes better at answering questions.

Some people and companies (such as Google) only use the acronym *ML* or the words *Machine Learning* when referring to either *AI* or *ML*.

There are uncountable other definitions in the world of software that would be helpful to know and understand. If what you are doing does not fit any of the above, keep working on your idea, doing your best, then when you are finished with this work and you show it to a qualified software professional, they will be able to help you understand what else they need from you in order to more fully understand about what you are working to build.

ASSIGNMENT Write at least one paragraph on this section. Explore and refine your questions around what type of software you are planning. Be specific so that you and others will understand as precisely as possible what you intend for this software. These details will have significant implications on cost and time.

THE OFFERING, INCLUDING AN ORD

When you are planning your software (whether it is an App or something more intricate and expansive), you need to think about some combination of the following: Licensing, Pricing, Seats, Builds, Configurations, Distribution, Life Cycle, Production, Packaging (not just physical materials, but positioning, and creative visuals), Maintenance, etc.

Both an MRD (Market Requirements Document) and a PRD (Product Requirements Document) are very helpful to reconciling what *can* be done with what *needs* to be done. Too many people just "do stuff" and then wonder why the software doesn't look or perform as they had envisioned, and why the market isn't responding to what they are offering. An MRD and a PRD are structure to your development and deployment. It is important that the MRD and PRD are not just documents that you write; use them like road maps as you drive your opportunity.

At this point, please do the work to complete an **Offering Requirements Document (ORD)**[2] that is part of my system of frameworks. The ORD is a modified and adapted form of an MRD (Market Requirements Document). The ORD includes questions that need to be answered as part of this framework, so even if you have another version of an MRD that you have used, please review this ORD framework to ensure that you have answered all of the questions before progressing on to Step 4:

> **ASSIGNMENT** If you already have a completed Market Requirements Document (MRD), that is excellent news. Review and update it now and continue to do so on a regular basis. If you do not have an MRD (or if you aren't sure what that is), please do the work to complete an Offering Requirements Document (ORD) for Software Development that is part of this system of frameworks (it is the next chapter). The ORD is a modified and adapted form of an MRD (Market Requirements Document). The ORD includes questions that need to be answered as part of this framework, so even if you have another version of an MRD that you have used it may be helpful to review this ORD framework to ensure that you have answered all of the questions before progressing on to the next step.

---

2   In Old and Middle English "ord" was the point of the spear, the beginning of the weapon, as well as the vanguard.

STORYBOARDING AND WIREFRAMING

▶ Storyboarding

If you have ever read a comic in a newspaper, or a graphic novel in a book, or even picture-based instructions for assembling a toy or piece of furniture that is formatted as squares on a page filled with drawings that take you step-by-step through the story ... that is a storyboard. (One of the advance steps in movie making is also to storyboard.)

Use a storyboard to SHOW a compelling use-case for your product/service/platform (to the best of your ability) pictographically, so that others can better visualize what it will look and act like. Don't worry if you aren't an artist; just do your best. Draw the significant moments in the use of your product, service, or platform. Don't worry about showing action or movement, this is a snapshot of the meaningful transitional steps to show other people the basic idea of how the IP works. If you have a working version of your product/service/platform, you might use actual photographs in each frame.

I could not count how many times I've been in a meeting with a storyboard and the listener/audience has expressed appreciation for the way it enabled them to visualize the product and how it works or is used.

▶ Wireframing

Imagine a piece of paper that has a life-sized outline of a blank phone screen or computer monitor. If you were to copy every button, graphic, and line of text from the screen onto that paper, where would everything be located? How big, what color, and what font type would the text be? How large and what shape and color are the buttons? What would happen when you click on a button or type text and submit? What are all of the possible things that could happen?

Early in my career working in software companies, we would take a stack of paper and draw every screen, number every button, and then put an index explaining each numbered button's function. This stack of paper would be spread out on conference room tables, then the graphic artists and software engineers would come into the room and we would walk them through every screen, every click, and what would happen with every click, until they understood exactly what we needed them to build. The graphic artists would then create every graphic element for the user interface, and the software engineers would connect everything together so that button actually performed the action that we had imagined during our planning meetings. If what we dreamed would happen was not technologically possible (which was often the case), then we worked side-by-side with the engineers to figure out what was possible.

These days, there are software tools that will let you draw, sketch, and puzzle through your graphic user interface (GUI) placing buttons, text, and other elements on the proxy phone, tablet, or computer screen. It is like modeling in clay before building the actual full-size car or truck. If you have access to a wireframing tool, use it; if you don't, you might get a ream of blank paper and draw out the functions on that; you might get a correctly sized blank mobile phone screen or a standard rectangle representing a computer screen, and print out a dozen or so pages that you can start drawing on to see how the user interface might look.

ASSIGNMENT Create a storyboard showing how the software will be used, and then make a wireframe of the application itself. Sketch (keep in mind that functional understanding is more important than making it pretty), or use photographs in a series on pieces of paper. This is where you SHOW the app/service/platform (to the best of your ability) pictographically so that others can better visualize what the product/service/platform looks like and how it performs. Think from the perspective of the things that must be done (i.e., activities), not job titles (i.e., functions).

Sample storyboard

Draw inside this square ...

Sample smart device outline for manual wireframing

TEAM AND EXECUTION

> "The right team and execution can
> make gold out of rubbish. The wrong team and
> execution will make rubbish out of gold."
> —Paul Kewene-Hite

Be inclusive and embrace diversity. Be an equal opportunity and equal pay for equal work employer. A critical mistake made by first time entrepreneurs is ignoring the "boring" execution details of what needs to be done to make the idea a reality. Performing an activities-based inventory of what *must* be done is a good way to figure out whether or not you already have the team that you need, and who is missing and needs to be found and brought on board your team to make your idea into software. Begin by inventorying what activities MUST be done and then put your name next to which of those activities you can credibly perform (not what you are willing to try but don't really know how to do).

Here is a partial sample inventory to get you started:

1. Complete the ORD for Software Development.

2. Interview lawyers and accountants about what can and needs to be done.

3. Identify and interview User Interface (UI) designers.

4. Identify and interview Creatives (e.g., graphic artists) who can design the graphical elements for the UI.

5. Identify and interview Software Engineers who can do the work to build the software.

6. Identify and interview potential investors and bankers who can help finance the work to make my idea real software.

If you went into a kitchen to cook a meal from raw ingredients, what is the order of operations that you would follow? What is the first activity that you need to do? What is the second activity? What is the third? Do the same thing for your startup. Inventory the activities that must be done in order. Be as specific and as detailed as possible.

Here's a way to think about team and execution: When you are explaining what you plan to do to create a new company, it is not unlike explaining *how* a clock tells time not just that it tells time. Imagine opening the face of a traditional clock to expose the clockworks showing the gears, springs, and other moving parts. It would be ideal if you could document and explain every detail, but at a minimum, be prepared to give representative detail on what mechanisms move and how to make the hands move, and in turn, tell time. Do that for the details of the software that you are working to build.

BUSINESS MODELING

STEP 6

Your business model is how you will make money (meaning revenue and more specifically, profit), as well as how you will otherwise finance and operate your company. When you are asked about your business model, the underlying question is how you will become and then stay a viable business.

Your business model is the beating heart of your venture. Do not assume that how you will make revenue and profit[3] and otherwise finance your startup is obvious. When you are asked about your business model you need to have a better response than "we will sell what we make" (and raise investment capital). You need to be prepared with a robust response to questions about your business model.

Google's business model is an interesting example. I remember visiting Google's office when it was a startup. They had a monitor over the reception desk that showed every search that was happening real-time. I remember the tempo of it ... search (pause) search (pause) search. I thought to myself "Wow, people are actually using it." I sat in the lobby doing searches to watch them pop up on the monitor over the desk. As of now, there are more than 3.5 billion searches every day. People who use Google's search engine do not pay to perform their search. At Google, search is a vehicle that is leveraged to do much more than display results for the definition of a word or a website or a restaurant near you, and Google is much more than an Internet search company.

Google makes its money through Google AdWords, AdSense, Google Play store, Google Cloud, and more. Businesses pay Google to display their information in search results (AdWords). AdSense is interesting, because both Google and website publishers make a little money when an ad is placed by Google on a website and someone, somewhere on the planet, clicks on it. When an app is purchased on the Google Play store, Google makes a little money. Google does not make money on Android itself (the smart device operating system), interestingly, but it does make money on the ecosystem around it. An interesting feature of Google's business model is that, in addition to free searches, they have several offerings that do not generate revenue directly. As with search, these offerings create value in the Google brand by generating good will and loyalty. Take, as only one of dozens of possible examples, Google for Startups Accelerator (formerly Google's Launchpad Accelerator). Google for Startups Accelerator spends money to help startup companies

---

3   Revenue is the money that you make from the sale of goods and services. Profit is the money that is left over after you make all of your payments, settle your debts, and in all ways account for your costs and expenses.

around the world for free. It is an initiative that creates good will, healthy brand awareness and loyalty for Google; it also keeps Google current on what is happening with the best startups globally. I am an unpaid volunteer Anchor Mentor in the Google for Startups Accelerator, and there are hundreds of volunteers like me who work with Google to level the playing field for founders and startups around the world.

Here is a non-Internet example: How does BMW make money? Selling cars is the obvious response. They also make money on dealership franchises, parts, service and maintenance, leasing, rentals, and merchandise, among others.

Here is another: Star Wars has made more money on licensing and merchandise than on ticket sales for the movies themselves.

Here is another: "Razor and Blades" is a common expression in business. Companies will give away the handle of a razor used for shaving (even though it cost them money to design, engineer, and manufacture it) because there is more money to be made on selling the blades that attach to the end of the handle because the blades wear out and need to be replaced more frequently than the handle. An application of this expression would be a printer. Let's say, for example, that your offering is a 3D printer. You sell the printer for money (maybe at a discount so that people buy your printer over the competition); you then make additional revenue by selling the printer cartridges for your 3D printer. You could also sell a service contract to maintain the printer, and software to design what you print. Then software advertising might help you sell other 3D printer-related offerings.

In software, you have several options to consider. Will your software be installed on personal computers and smart devices? Will it be accessed via a web browser but never be installed on a computer or device? If it is installed on a computer, will you charge the user a single fee once or will they pay by use or time (e.g., a monthly fee)? The more traditional model of payment is that the user gives you money in exchange for a license to use the software (e.g., single user, multi-user, site license, etc.). Increasingly, users subscribe and pay overtime for access such as the SaaS model (SaaS means Software as a Service).

A common razor and blades-ish model is to either give away the software for free or for a small one-time fee, and then push opportunities to make purchases while using the software. The user can decide to make the purchases or not, but they are potentially limited when they do not make the purchases.

"Freemium" is a portmanteau of the words free and premium. This is when you allow a user to download a basic version of your software for free, giving them a limited or restricted feature set that is sufficient to function. The free version should be compelling enough that the user will want to pay to unlock the full, feature-rich version of the software.

When you think about the business you are starting, how will you make money? Simple sales of what you are offering? Is there any other way? Maybe there could be other products or a service around the offering that you are selling? Is there a way to sell other products and services through your offering? Will you sell B2C (Business to Consumer, meaning you will sell and ship your offering directly from your business to your consumer), B2B (Business to Business), or B2G (Business to Government)? Some detail would be helpful.

FINANCIAL MODELING

STEP 7

> "Never, EVER, run out of cash!"
> —**Patrick Turner**, INSEAD Professor of Entrepreneurship

Even though you might be building software and not thinking (yet) about building a company around the software, you MUST think about money (even if you are a zillionaire with seemingly endless resources). Good financial modeling is good business.

If you can build a Cashflow from scratch, then you can explain the details when you are asked to defend the numbers during any meeting. When you present, have an updated copy of your Cashflow, and be prepared to explain the details to those who ask.

Work to frame a financial model going forward that progresses you from where you are to where you plan to go. Building a Cashflow (as well as an SG&A, P&L, Balance Sheet, along with Budgets for MDF/SDF, T&E/T&S, etc.) is fundamental for understanding your initiative. At this point you may not know what those words and acronyms mean, which is okay. You will, however, need to invest some effort in learning their meaning so that you can use them comfortably in sentences as well as comfortably answer questions about them when asked. The definitions are below.

In the business world it is very common for people to assume that other people will know how to build and read the numbers, so they invest very little study into it. Basic financial skills are very important for all people in business. Not everyone needs to be a Certified Public Accountant or Chartered Accountant but being able to build and read a Cashflow should be a required skill for all business professionals.

If an investor, board of directors, or shareholder calls you to a meeting to discuss your venture, grab an updated Cashflow on the way to the meeting. The other financial instruments such as a Profit and Loss (P&L), Balance Sheet, Sales General and Administrative (SG&A) etc., are also important but the Cashflow is the most critical. If you don't understand your cash position over time, you do not understand your business.

Good financial planning is key to persuading shareholders, the board, and leadership that you know what you are doing. If you don't (yet) know how to do it yourself, work side-by-side with a finance-professional to build complete financials. I say side-by-side so that you see how it is done, you fully understand the numbers, and can understand and explain the details. (If you can build a Cashflow from scratch then you can explain the details when you are asked to defend the numbers during any meeting.)

Here are a few overly simplified definitions of business words that you need to know:

▶ **Finance vs. Accounting**
Finance looks forward to what will happen.
Accounting looks back at what happened.

▶ **Payment vs. Expense**
A Payment is when money leaves the company and is given to someone else.
An Expense is the agreed responsibility to make a payment at some future date.

▶ **Revenue vs. Profit**
Revenue is all money that comes into the company from sales.
Profit is the money that is left over after you have paid all of your expenses and taxes.

▶ **Sources & Uses**
Source is where you will get money.
A Use is how the money will be spent.

▶ **Budget**
A Budget is the amount of money (and time) that must be invested in order to do what must be done. Importantly budgeted amounts need to factor for how much money (and time) is actually available.[4]

▶ **Cashflow**
A Cashflow is the financial detail of how a company is being operated; money coming in, all money measured impacts on debts and assets, and all money going out.[5]

▶ **Free Cashflow**
Free Cashflow (not to be confused with the document that is called "a Cashflow") is the money that you have left over after all capital expenditures (aka CapEx, which is the money spent on fixed assets).

▶ **Working Capital**
Working Capital = **Current Assets** minus **Current Liabilities**. Assets are tangible things that have value such as property, inventory, cash, etc. Liabilities are things that you need to pay such as debt, taxes, wages, rent, utilities, etc.

▶ **Professional Fees**
Professional Fees are cash paid to professionals who are not your employees, such as lawyers, accountants, designers, engineers, etc.

---

4   Budgeting is incredibly valuable and essential for running your entrepreneurial venture and making sure that you never run out of cash. Your budgets should be planned, reviewed, and updated routinely as a team. Be sure to remind everyone that a budget is more than a plan for how much money will be spent, it is a reconciliation of how much must be spent in order to accomplish your plan compared to how much money there is to spend in the bank account. Monthly budgeting meetings, accounting back a month, and financially planning forward a quarter are good practices.

5   This is a window into all money that comes in and leaves the company. (You should typically have an 18 to 24-month Cashflow, with the next 13 weeks by week, and the rest of the months by month.) Be sure to use mathematics rather than simply typing in numbers.

- ▶ **CapEx vs OpEx**

  CapEx is Capital Expenditure, which is money spent on fixed assets.
  OpEx is Operating Expenditure, which is the money spent to operate the company.

- ▶ **Fixed Assets**

  Fixed Assets are physical things such as land, buildings, equipment, vehicles, etc.

- ▶ **Burn Rate and Runway**

  Burn Rate is the amount of money that you spend in a month.
  Runway is the number of months that you have until you are out of money.

- ▶ **Break Even, and Profitability**

  Break Even is when the same amount of money comes in as goes out.
  Profitability is when you have money left over after paying everything.

- ▶ **Pro forma**

  Pro forma is Latin for "as a matter of form" or "for the sake of form" and is a word
  put on financials to show that the numbers are educated guesses or projections.

- ▶ **T&E or T&S**

  T&S/T&E[6] is Travel & Subsistence or Travel & Expenses (occasionally referred
  to as Travel & Entertainment). This budget is for rental cars, trains, planes,
  hotels, lunches and dinners, etc. T&E is used in North American English and in
  North American influenced regions. T&S is used in British English and in British
  influenced regions.

- ▶ **MDF and SPIF**

  MDF is an acronym for Market Development Fund and is the money that you
  spend to take your offering to market.
  SPIF stands for Sales Promotion Incentive Fund and is a powerful tool for
  motivating the point of sale to inspire them to advocate for your offering over
  the competition (the seller and/or buyer). This could be, and is not limited to, a
  payment made to the salesperson or a discount/rebate offered to the customer.

> **ASSIGNMENT** Build a Cashflow. Do not assume that you will simply hire someone else to do
> it for you. Learn to build a Cashflow from a blank spreadsheet if you can; at a minimum, find
> someone on your team or work together as a team right now to build a basic Cashflow. Then
> write at least one paragraph on the details inside of the Cashflow, possibly including the
> details listed above. Explore and refine your questions. If you need to partner with a finance
> professional to help you, do it; but learn how to read financial documents, how to tell the
> stories of the numbers, and how to read along as others go through the numbers.

---

6 Watch this budget very carefully and put rules on all expenses and what can be claimed to make
   people responsible and hold people accountable. It happens at times that people (especially
   inside of large companies) game their expense reports so that they claim more money than they
   legitimately spend on real business. This line item can be value destructive when you are a fledgling
   venture that is carefully watching every dollar in the bank account.

EXECUTION AND
FUNDABLE EVENT TIMELINES

Now that you have done your team and financial modeling, with your list of 20 or more mission-critical activities, you should put that list of activities on a time line (for example 18 to 24 months). Creating a Gantt chart of mission-critical activities (highlighting milestones and fundable events) then harmonizing it with a Cashflow is good planning and good for presentations.

You can build your Gantt chart in a spreadsheet if you don't have project management software. What matters is that you can see the markers that represent the start and stop dates for each activity. On each bar you should name the activity as well as who is responsible along with the associated costs.

When you build a Cashflow you should then harmonize it with the Gantt chart to ensure that the activities and costs over the same months align month-by-month.

When you are building the timeline, with the completed Gantt on the top of the page and the Cashflow lined up below it, decision makers can quickly see that your financial and activities-based planning is complimentary in their construction.

The next thing that I suggest that you do is identify the **Milestones** (the moments in time when you complete an activity or task) on the Gantt chart. Then differentiate between which milestones simply mark the completion of a task and which milestones are actually evidence that you are right in what you intended, planned, and executed. (This could be a working prototype or a paying customer, etc. This is very different from finishing the writing for a business plan for example, which does not prove that you are right but just that you finished what you started.) The type of milestone that is evidence that you are right, is called a **Fundable Event** and it is very important for a few reasons.

▶ Evidence that you are right shows that the entrepreneurial venture is making progress!

▶ Evidence that you are right will be the proof that you need for continued funding and support from the company leadership and board.

▶ Evidence that you are right can be correlated to value creation (increasing value) and value capture (when the company is able to hold onto and make use of the value). Fundable events correlate to the increase in the value of what you are doing, and potentially increase the value of the company itself.

Investors and boards and others who hold the keys to your future funding will be watching for the Fundable Events so that they can know that the work is progressing and that your corporate entrepreneurial venture is deserving of continued support.

When you have the Fundable Event Timeline planned out, and you regularly update it (you should update it at a minimum of once a week) then you and those who are supporting you can use it to keep track of progress and timings that might change over time.

Investors and boards and other financial supporters might use the Fundable Event Timeline to plan when they will transfer resources and capital support to your initiative (just as an investor would do for a startup); when you hit your deliverables (the milestones and especially the fundable events) then you have a measurable defense for expecting ongoing support.

> **ASSIGNMENT** Write at least one paragraph on this section. Explore and refine your questions. Create a Gantt chart identifying all of your activities (when each activity is intended to start and stop). Then put the Gantt chart and your Cashflow summary on the same page making sure that the months line up as shown in the following template (and on page 410). (You should have built a Cashflow in step 7.) Highlight the milestones that prove that you are right to call them Fundable Events; e.g., this is when the machine you are building actually works, it is when a stranger who has no connection to you purchases your product, etc. A fundable event is not when you simply finish what you started, such as writing a business plan or building a Cashflow with numbers that look good or designing a brochure that makes you happy, etc.

FUNDABLE
EVENT
TIMELINE

Cashflow Summary

	Month 1, Year 1	Month 2, Year 1	Month 3, Year 1	Month 4, Year 1	Month 5, Year 1	Month 6, Year 1	Month 7, Year 1	Month 8, Year 1	Month 9, Year 1	Month 10, Year 1	Month 11, Year 1	Month 12, Year 1
Opening Cash Balance												
Total CapEX												
Total OpEx												
Total Cash Out												
Total Cash In												
Closing Cash Balance												

Execution Timeline (Gantt Chart)

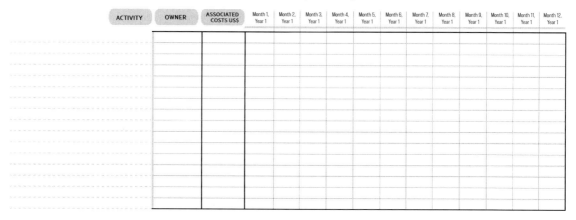

ACTIVITY	OWNER	ASSOCIATED COSTS US$	Month 1, Year 1	Month 2, Year 1	Month 3, Year 1	Month 4, Year 1	Month 5, Year 1	Month 6, Year 1	Month 7, Year 1	Month 8, Year 1	Month 9, Year 1	Month 10, Year 1	Month 11, Year 1	Month 12, Year 1

Note: Milestones mean that you finished what you started. Fundable Events are validation that you are right.

CAPITAL MODELING

Making software takes time and money. Depending on the complexity, you might need more resources (e.g., equipment and people). You should determine how much money you need and where that money will come from.

You need to determine what capital will be required over time, and where that support will come from. Keep in mind that although capital is typically money, it might also be money equivalents (e.g., access to and use of buildings, equipment, etc.). Make sure to fully understand what capital is required to get your startup to the point where it can self-sustain, which is at break-even (meaning you are bringing in as much money as is going out), and profitability (which is when more money is coming in than is going out). Investors and shareholders will ask you what you need to take your startup from where you are now to the point of self-sufficiency; be prepared with an answer. It will be helpful to have a best case, base case, and worst case for your financials and capital requirements. If you can be successful with the worst case or base case numbers, then present those. Even though the best-case numbers look the most appealing, it is typically best to not present the best-case numbers since they are the most optimistic and therefore the most difficult to achieve.

When you think about the timing and costs associated with investment from others, you need to understand that money has the same three states as water: liquid, solid, and vapor.

▶ Liquid

This is when money is transportable, or otherwise in a state that it can be moved from one person or entity to another by either electronic transfer from one bank account to another, or from one person to another as some form of recognized currency. Example: When you have coins and bank notes in your pocket and use it to buy something at a store you are <u>liquid</u>, as your money is available for use. People will say "I'm not liquid at the moment." Which typically means "I have money, but I don't have access to it right now."

▶ Solid

This is when money is not available or for some reason, not liquid. The money might be in stocks or bonds, or otherwise invested into something that makes it not accessible, or portable, or moveable. But the idea is that it will expand as ice expands when water is frozen (because of interest or other successful growth by performance of the stock or investment or real estate, etc.). When an investor gives you money in exchange for equity (aka ownership) in your company, the idea is that their money will grow or expand (like ice) as you are successful as a company.

▶ Vapor

When ice is melted, a percentage of the ice becomes liquid (water) and a percentage is lost as vapor (e.g., steam). With money, the <u>Vapor</u> is any fee or charge or tax or disadvantageous exchange rate, etc., meaning there is some loss of value that could equal part, or potentially all of their money that was invested in a failed stock.

When an investor pledges to invest into your startup venture, they might be liquid in the moment and need to move quickly back into a solid before they incur taxes or other penalties on that money. Or they might need time to "liquidate" or otherwise liberate their money from other investments (stocks, bonds, real estate, etc.) so that they can give cash to you as an investment (either as a loan or as equity), which means that to invest in you they are going from a solid, to a liquid (with hopefully as little vapor as possible), then back into another solid that is ownership in your startup. The expectation is that their money will grow and expand during its time as a solid (equity ownership) with you, and at some future date in a few years they expect their investment back, plus more than they gave you in the first place.

> **ASSIGNMENT** Write at least one paragraph on this section. Explore and refine your questions. Will you be raising money? How much will you raise in exchange for what percentage of equity (ownership in your company)? Have you identified an investor? When will you start the process?

STEP 10

LIQUIDITY AND EXITS

This is where you think about the far other side end result for your software. Will you simply keep investing in progressively newer updated versions of the software indefinitely? Or will there be a point when you sell it to a company or another person or simply stop working on it? All software eventually becomes outmoded, or at a minimum, unable to operate on progressively newer hardware and machines. You need to anticipate now what you will do then.

Investors almost always invest so that they can get out with more money than they put in. This may sound obvious but first-time entrepreneurs commonly make the mistake of messaging to investors that they plan on being in the startup for the rest of their lives, thinking that the investors will be moved by their absolute commitment. Investors cannot stay invested in your startup for the rest of your life; they will have a timeframe in mind for when they will need their money back. Keep in mind that an investor's exit from your startup does not necessarily mean the end of your company, it is simply a moment in time when that investor will no longer be invested.

Think of an exit from three perspectives: 1. the investor and shareholder, 2. the company itself, and 3. you and other founders. The investors will be trying to understand in the beginning whether or not you will be a problem for them when they need to exit. When they ask about exit possibilities, give answers that bias to their best interest. It might be that the window of opportunity for the investor/shareholder's exit does not fit the best interest of the company or you, along with other Founders. For example, the company's best interest might be to never be merged or acquired by another company, or the company's potential might be best served if it were to be part of a bigger, more established company that has existing infrastructure, resources, and customers. Give careful thought to the answer before the question is asked.

ASSIGNMENT Write at least one paragraph on this section from each of the three perspectives: 1. The investor and shareholder, 2. The company, and 3. The founders. Explore and refine your questions.

FOUNDERITIS

> "Founders' attachment, overconfidence, and naïveté may be necessary to get new ventures up and running, but these emotions later create problems."
> —Noam Wasserman

READ "The Founder's Dilemma," Noam Wasserman, *Harvard Business Review* (HBR) (February 2008)

Founderitis is when a founder behaves in value destructive ways. Companies can be meaningfully harmed or even destroyed by the bad behavior of a founder. You need to take measures in the beginning when things are still good and healthy to protect everyone and everything from unforeseen value-destructive behavior in the future. Work with a good lawyer NOW on a rules-of-engagement agreement between the founders and shareholders to protect the company (and families of founders and shareholders) from what might go wrong in the future.

Founders who cause harm to the companies that they found and work to build are rarely as candid as American Apparel's founder Dov Charney who told Marketplace in 2014, "My biggest weakness is me. I mean, lock me up already! It's obvious! Put me in a cage, I'll be fine. I'm my own worst enemy."[7]

You might find out too late that someone is value destructive. Again, take measures at the start when things are still early and being formed. Sit down with a qualified lawyer and document the rules for good conduct and what happens if one or more of the founders become value destructive. Hopefully you will never need to take action. Hopefully everyone will be rational and behave well.

Finding examples of well-known founders who harmed their successful companies is not that difficult. For every name brand person who fails their company, there are countless regular people who harmed their ventures (and those involved and around it) before they qualified for big press coverage.

---

7   Marketplace.org with Kai Ryssdal 20 January 2014, updated 27 March 2015 "American Apparel CEO Dov Charney on pushing boundaries and his biggest weakness"

There is reality in the humorous yet sad observation that no matter how well intentioned, we are very often our own worst enemy. Anticipate this reality and plan for what to do about it when (not if) our own behavior threatens to undo what good we are working to accomplish.

> **ASSIGNMENT** You and your co-founders (if you have them) need to put in writing what will happen if you or the partners become value destructive. Consider designating an arbiter or another independent, such as an independent senior industry expert or lawyer. This will need to be someone who agrees to function as an arbiter. Write at least one paragraph on this section. Explore and refine your questions.

STEP 12

MARKETING, SALES, AND BUSINESS DEVELOPMENT

You may have noticed that the definitions and roles of <u>marketing</u> and <u>sales</u> and <u>business development</u> are not always the same from company to company. Sometimes marketing and sales is one integrated organization and other times they are separated, and sometimes they struggle to work together. Business development is sometimes part of marketing, sometimes part of sales, and other times it stands on its own.

I believe that one of the reasons why people sometimes struggle to differentiate between the three is because in the beginning the three were one integrated function. People wanted to exchange what they had for what other people had so they created market places in town squares or villages and figured out how to transact with each other for goods and materials or money. Over time, people have artificially separated the three.

We will need to stay flexible within the definitions; you will need to work with the definitions of the three as your company defines them.

For the purpose of this startup entrepreneurship training we will define the three neutrally, as follows:

▶ **Marketing**
The research and planning of where in the world the optimal customers are located and who those people are in that market. Then determining the means by which to capture the attention of paying customers (via the sundry activities that we typically associate with marketing, such as advertising, trade shows, press, etc.)

▶ **Sales**

The activities that result in the exchange of the offering for money. This could be in person (traditional sales), or through to taking credit cards on a website or inside a mobile application (digital transactions).

▶ **Business development**

The securing of strategic relationships that open doors and remove barriers. For example, let's say that you are developing a device designed to help medical patients better manage their pain during therapies. Business development (sometimes called "Biz Dev") would secure an agreement with a recognized medical research facility to perform a study to determine if your device actually does help people manage their pain during therapies.

You should identify the key activities that must be done for marketing, sales, and business development. If you already identified these activities in your team modeling and they are already reflected in your Gantt chart and fundable event timeline then very well done! There is always more to do so you should continue to build the list of activities.

> **ASSIGNMENT** Write at least one paragraph for marketing, another for sales, and another for business development. Give one or two specific examples of what you will do for marketing, one or two for sales, and one or two for business development. More than simply saying you will do it, SHOW what will be done and what will happen as a result. Do not write, "Do marketing." Give a detailed example of why what specific type of marketing will be done where, when, how, and by whom. Be prepared to be challenged on every detail that you write. Explore and refine your questions.

THE BIG PLAY

You have now evolved your software to the point that you need to answer the question of whether or not the software is being developed for itself or if its purpose is bigger than the software itself. Investors, shareholders, Boards of Directors/Governors, and your team will need to understand A. Is your startup a one-trick pony, meaning will your company ever do more than whatever you have decided to do as a first offering (e.g., product, service, solution?). B. How the first offering (and the hopeful follow-on offerings that you are lining up) fits into a bigger opportunity for the company, shareholders, and stakeholders.

For example, let's say that you have identified the need for digital disruption of the traditional forecasting, procurement, supply chain, and inventory management in your company. Let's say that you intend to create a new software development unit that will create custom software that will serve the needs of the business operations and finance units in the company, so that they can use your custom software to optimize the company's forecasting, procurement, supply chain, and inventory controls. You should think for a moment about the bigger play for the software as well as the initiative. What impacts will there be on various parts of the business beyond the specific scope of the proposed work? What will be the impact on the value of the company, if any? Will there be any other follow-on opportunities that could result from this work (assuming all goes well with it)? For example, could this software then be sold as a product to other companies or would it be more valuable if preserved exclusively in-house?

Think for a moment about companies such as McDonalds, Amazon, and Tesla. What is the bigger play for those companies? Even though the average person thinks of McDonalds as a fast food restaurant, it is actually a real estate company that has realized significant wealth from controlling and creatively deploying their real estate holdings. It is important to note that real estate being a part of the value creation and value capture at McDonalds was not part of their beginning—it came later, thanks to Corporate Entrepreneurship.

Next, most people think that Amazon is an e-commerce retailer on the Internet that sells books, electronic devices, and more. Thanks to Corporate Entrepreneurship however, Amazon is a company that does much more then e-commerce of books and consumer electronics; Amazon as a company controls a meaningful percentage of the transactions in the cloud, thanks to Amazon Web Services (AWS).

Next, consider Tesla. Most people think of Tesla as a maker of high-end electric cars. But thanks to Corporate Entrepreneurship, Tesla is becoming a power company that produces various products from the shingles on roof tops harvesting solar energy to power stations that you install in your garage to power your house and your car.

So the question for you at this point is: What is the bigger picture for your company in light of your entrepreneurial engagement right now? You may be working on a specific solution or product or service, but what is the potential bigger impact on the company? Clarifying and defining your intention up front will help you as you go. This may change and evolve as you go, and that is normal.

ASSIGNMENT Write at least one paragraph on this section. Think, what is the bigger play for what you are working to accomplish? How does this tree (your initiative) more fully complete the forest, or potentially elevate what is now a stand of trees to become a fully-fledged forest? If you cannot explain how what you plan to do creates and captures increased value beyond the scope or your project itself, then your initiative might stop here. Explore and refine your questions.

CALL TO ACTION OR THE ASK

In preparation for your presentations to potential software engineers, graphic artists, and potentially those who you need to help you with your software development initiative that will inspire key influencers and decision makers that you know what you are doing so that they will want to join you.

In business, the moment when you ask the listener for what you need from them is sometimes called a **Call to Action** or **The Ask** or **The Question**, but the intent of all three terms is the same.

Keep in mind that what is clear and motivates one listener may or may not be clear and motivate anyone else. Every person has their own requirements, mandates, needs, wants, hopes, stresses, pressures, and so on. Do your best to figure out what motivates the person to whom you are extending (what is often called "putting") The Ask or Call to Action.

For example, Steve Jobs (co-founder of Apple) asked John Sculley (the person who became CEO of Apple after Steve Jobs): "Do you want to sell sugared water for the rest of your life? Or do you want to come with me and change the world?" That call to action from Steve Jobs worked for John Sculley, but it might or might not have worked for anyone else. Steve Jobs did his homework on what motivated John Sculley and that specific Call to Action or Ask worked on him in that situation.

As another example, if you are presenting to an investor and you bias your presentation heavily toward revenue and profit but never mention shareholder value they may not fund your startup if their priorities are shareholder value. Or it could be the other way around if their top priority is revenue and profit. You need to puzzle through and figure out the critical motivations of your audience BEFORE you present the details and call them to action. Do not assume that your priorities or the primary benefits of your initiative are aligned with their priorities, or that you understand their priorities because to you this or that argument "makes sense."

Another thing to keep in mind is that if you are presenting to a group, everyone in that room is going to have their own biases and opinions. Figure out as much as you can about every influencer and decision maker who might be in the room during your presentation and Call to Action. It is okay to strategically lace messages throughout the presentation that speak to what each person in the room needs to hear; just be certain that all of those messages are truthful and consistent with what you are actually doing.

When you extend or put The Ask, depending on the culture and context, you can then briefly issue a call to action for each person in the room in the appropriate order of who matters most.

Sometimes, in some cultures, the messages in the body of the presentation are all that most need, and the formal Ask would only be issued to the most relevant and important person in the room. So be sure that you know what is most appropriate before you enter the room to present.

EXECUTIVE SUMMARIES AND BUSINESS PLANS

"Everyone has a plan 'til they get punched in the mouth."
—**Mike Tyson,** former heavyweight boxing champion of the world

Hopefully you have been writing down all of your thoughts while going through each of the steps to this point. I have found great value in keeping track of all ideas or thoughts whether they seem relevant to me at the time or not.

You will need to complete a written executive summary (a document that takes the same amount of time to read as to drink a glass of water) that will help influencers and decision makers understand enough that they will 1. want to know more, and 2. be interested (or even excited) to support you and the initiative. A business plan is a long, more detailed executive summary.

▶ Executive Summary

An Executive Summary, not to be confused with a full Business Plan, is ideally two pages and no longer than three pages in length. It should have the most representative and most relevant details, which are explained in greater detail in the full business plan. Make sure that every word in the Executive Summary is relevant to persuade the reader that you know what you are doing to build and run the company. The Executive Summary should inspire the reader to ask you for more information.

▶ Business Plan

A Business Plan is a longer, more detailed document than an Executive Summary. A typical length for a business plan is 20–30 pages. When writing business plans you should bias the writing very heavily to execution detail; show what you will do, when, where, how, and why. State the problem, build out the execution detail around the solution to the problem, put some financials in so that the costs are understood, and call the reader to action. Use multiple proofreaders and listen to their feedback. Questions and comments give you insight into what is understandable and working (or not), so be grateful and never impatient with questions and comments.

(I once submitted a 30-page business plan to a government body, not realizing that they required a minimum of 100 pages because more pages demonstrated thorough and complete investigation and consideration. In the business world, a 100+ page business plan to an investor or leadership team might imply that you are overthinking or cannot succinctly say what you need to say.)

There is no single magic format or outline for business plans and executive summaries. You should write the details in a way that will flow most naturally and persuade the reader, while also providing a document that will help guide your running of the company.

The goal for an executive summary and business plan, along with all supportive financials, should be to use it as practice. Stay flexible, move with what happens, and update your documentation regularly so that you are ready at a moment's notice to share and present. Do not get caught with a summary or plan that is out of date; that moment might be the game changer. Keep updating, practicing, learning, and adapting to change as you go forward.

> **ASSIGNMENT** All of the topics explored in this framework can be used in your executive summary and business plan. Create your 2–3-page executive summary first in a separate document (name it uniquely and always save the date in the file name every time you update it). Once your executive summary is completed, save a copy of it as a different file (using "Save As ... ") with the date in the file name in the same folder. Then, begin the work of meaningfully expanding the detail in each section until you have a 20–30-page full business plan.

PITCHING AND PRESENTATIONS

▶ Pitching

A pitch is a short format presentation. It should be quick, clear, and to the point. An elevator or lift pitch is typically no more than one or two minutes (the time it would take to get from one floor in a building to a few floors up). Quickly state your name, what you do for your company (this should take only a few seconds) and then get straight into the pitch. Your pitch should clearly state that there is an opportunity (a problem), something that can be done about the opportunity, what you are doing about it, and how the listener can be involved. Keep the pitch to the point and positive.

▶ Presentations

A presentation is a longer format pitch but has a similar structure.

> **HINT** Presentations tend to focus too much on the problem/ opportunity and have too little practical detail on what can be done and what you are actually doing (aka execution). It is true that the listener needs to believe that you are addressing an authentic problem (do not solve a non-problem, and do not be a solution looking for a problem to solve) but remember that the listener needs to believe that you know what you are doing (execution level detail). Explain the opportunity and give representative detail into what you are doing about that opportunity.

It is common for people not to practice their presentations in advance. People often work on their materials up to the moment before presenting and then walk into the room and start. This is a mistake. Practice your pitch and presentations before giving them. There is no substitute for practice. Make sure that the first time that you pitch, or present is during practice rather than in front of the person whom you need to persuade. You only get one chance at a first impression. In case you feel that practice will make you less spontaneous in the moment, keep in mind that practice will make you better in a moment. For example, professional athletes practice SO THAT they will be better able to be more powerfully and effectively spontaneous in a moment.

The opportunity to persuade a key influencer or decision maker might happen at any moment. The quick two-minute pitch is called an elevator pitch or lift pitch because you might be in an elevator or lift when you realize that you are standing next to a key influencer or decision maker. You then have the amount of time that it takes to go from the ground floor to when they exit the elevator or lift to plant a seed. Hopefully they will invite you to present to them based on the strength of that one short pitch.

I have successfully pitched in elevators/lifts, hallways/corridors, stairways, sidewalks, while crossing the street, while at a salad bar, standing in a line/queue, while on the phone, and sitting next to someone on a plane. The point is that you never know when the opportunity will present itself. Practice your pitch over and over until you can say it without thinking about it. And practice it on different people to make sure that it makes sense and is coherent.

Practice your pitching without slides or props or other visual support. You never know when, where, or how you will be pitching. If your pitch is reliant on a slide or a prop, you might find yourself fumbling with your phone or computer, trying to pull up whatever you need, and end up burning the seconds or minutes that you have to persuade the listener. Also keep in mind that you only have a handful of seconds to create a powerful first impression; if you know what you are talking about and can say it off the top of your head without notes or visual assistance, then all the better.

If you have technology that can be quickly and effortlessly shown, then do it; just be aware that if it doesn't work then that is what the listener will remember.

Full presentations can start with a quick two-minute pitch at the top, to snapshot the long story short and give the audience an idea of what you are doing. Then you can start the longer format presentation. The longer presentation can include slides and product demonstrations if you have them; just remember to tell the story in an order that makes sense. Practice, practice, practice. There is no substitute for practicing before you present. Then after you've presented, practice some more.

As to time management, let's say, for example, that you are given a 30-minute meeting to present. Do not prepare 30 minutes of presentations and slides and demonstrations. A good rule of thumb is to prepare presentations for half of the allotted time. So, in this example you would prepare 15 (or 20 maximum) minutes of a presentation, for a 30-minute meeting. Leave room for questions during the presentation as well as questions and answers at the end.

Here is a thumbnail EXAMPLE of how much time should be spent on each part of the presentation:

▶ **Intro** (~5% of the available time)
Don't apologize—it is a common opener, but it is a poor start. Be confident but never arrogant.

▶ **The Opportunity/Problem** (~25%)
Do not pander or exaggerate; be factual.

▶ **What options are possible** (~15%)
Give a few examples of options. Do not make the mistake of speaking poorly of any alternative to what you are recommending. Be factual.

▶ **What I am doing** (~45%)
Do not hold back any secret ingredient (aka silver bullet or game changer) during your presentation. It is a common problem that the presenter will save the big "wow" of their solution for a follow-up presentation. If the audience doesn't hear the wow in your first pitch, there may not be a second presentation.

▶ **How you can be involved** (~10%)
Do not tell them what they will do. Welcome them to the party and invite them to be involved.

Start on time and finish on time (or a little early). Going over time should only happen if the audience asks you to stay and explain more. Even then, be sensitive to being over time. It is typically better to leave when you are ahead while they want more and schedule a follow-up.

Do not feel nervous or upset about any questions that might be asked of you. Questions expose holes in your presentation and tell you what was not clear or understandable to the listener (no matter how clear you thought that you made the point). Questions also give you an indication of what matters to the person asking the question. Write down all the questions that you were asked, and the answers that you gave, and then use those notes as preparation for future meetings (and work on clearer presentations and better answers for the future).

> **ASSIGNMENT** Build the materials that you will need (e.g., 2–3-page executive summary, slides, etc.). Practice that 60-second pitch until you can say it without thinking. THEN start working on expanded detail versions of that pitch so that when people ask you to give them more you can do 60 seconds on this detail and 60 seconds on that detail. THEN work on a 30-minute expanded version of that pitch, which gives more meaningful insight and detail. Explore and refine your questions.

SAVE YOUR WORK, UPDATE IT REGULARLY, AND REFER TO IT OFTEN

Revisit all of the above work regularly. Remember to save your work regularly and keep backups on separate secure devices. Once a day, or at a minimum once a week on a routine day at a routine time, review and update details for all of the above work. The last time that out of date documents created a problem for me was when I was asked to send my current business plan to a meeting deciding the placement of millions of dollars (in the dot.com era) and I was not ready in the moment. Since that day I have always had current documents ready to send whenever a shareholder, investor, or board member asks. It always makes a good impression when you are ready to send freshly updated documents when asked.

Every time you update the document, save a unique version in a common reference folder on your computer. Use a consistent naming convention and update the name every time to include the date that you modified it (or some other intuitive system that others, not just you, will understand if they need to find information).

You never know when you will need to give someone a copy of your plan. You might be given advance warning, but sometimes the call is unexpected. Do not be caught off guard with an out of date version! Be prepared, and you will have nothing to fear.

ASSIGNMENT Comb through your document. Save everything. If you write something and you aren't quite sure how it fits, either put the thought on the last empty page of the document or create a second document in the same folder just for thoughts that you aren't yet sure how to use. You do not want to find yourself in the situation where later on, you wish that you hadn't deleted that thought.

On future days when you open and edit the document, do a Save As and change the version date on the document so that it creates a new document that is saved in the same folder. It may happen that in the future you will want to refer to an earlier draft, and if anything happens to the file that you are working on that day, you can always go back to the most recent version rather than starting over.

Keep a backup somewhere other than on your computer. (You should regularly back up your entire hard drive.) If you are working on paper, you need to keep your binder safe and secure at all times. When you are able, you might have someone scan every page in the binder onto a file that you keep on a small portable computer stick for safekeeping. If you edit your document on a public computer, just make certain that you do not leave a copy of your document on the public hard drive.

Regularly update your writing, save copies, keep the dream alive, and work to make it real.

WHO IS AN ENTREPRENEUR?

In my teaching, I work to dispel the myth that entrepreneurs are exclusively 20-somethings in the Silicon Valley, building technology startups.

Anyone who has ever had insufficient time, incomplete information, inadequate resources, and a deadline looming, has needed to work like an entrepreneur to figure things out, get things done, and meet their deadline.

When people ask me to explain entrepreneurship, my immediate thought is often the science fiction characters Captain Kirk and Chief Engineer Montgomery Scott (aka Scotty) on Star Trek. Countless times, the engines were offline, weapons were down, an enemy had the upper hand, and Captain Kirk would urgently ask Scotty how long until weapons and engines would be back up. Scotty would give an estimate of time, and Kirk would give him a fraction of that time, telling him to make it happen, then Scotty would work miracles to bring everything back online within seconds of certain destruction to save the day. Time and again, Captain Kirk and Scotty succeeded by thinking and working like entrepreneurs.

Entrepreneurship is ancient, it has been happening since the beginning of time. It is the work to understand what berries to eat and which will make you sick. Entrepreneurship

was used in the successful hunting of mammoth. Entrepreneurship is the historic practice of growing food to eat, as well as exchanging things you have for things you need. Entrepreneurs are farmers/ranchers, artists, barbers, scientists, lawyers, hot-dog vendors in NYC, politicians, and children picking through garbage in the developing world to find recyclables that they are able to trade for food or money. Entrepreneurs are mothers in the developing world rolling old magazines into necklaces, a developer of homes for the elderly in the countryside, an after-school tutor in a busy city, someone improvising a taxi out of a homemade cart made out of scraps that they attached to a 40 year old bicycle, and more.

The French word *entrepreneur* means builder. When we lived in Paris, we hired entrepreneurs to install our kitchen. Entrepreneurs would build a tool shed in the garden. If ever you are in Paris, look at the cornerstone of certain old buildings, and you will see the word ENTREPRENEUR and a date next to the name of the person responsible for the construction of that building.

One of my favorite examples of the collision of old and new entrepreneurship, is a man in China from whom I have purchased fresh fruit several times. He has a dilapidated cart, and he picks his own fruit along the side of the road, then sells it by the side of the road in the city. He knows fruit, and the quality is always superb. You don't pay him with cash, he holds up a mobile phone showing a QR (Quick Response) code and you scan it with your mobile phone and money transfers from your Alipay account to his Alipay account (not a bank account, he is one of the estimated >1.7 billion unbanked people in the world). His Alipay account is how he pays all of his bills and feeds his family.

Everyone from teenagers to the elderly can take control of their own entrepreneurial dream and do something creative with their life and career. Too many people feel lost and unsure. They lack confidence in their own potential and capacities. I know from experience that an open mind, open heart, and a willingness to work are the keys to success as an entrepreneur. If you can add education (training and coaching) to the mix with an open heart, mind, and willingness to work, then you will be on a path that could make your entrepreneurial ambitions a reality.

I have personally trained thousands of people around the world, rich and poor, educated and illiterate, from Nigeria to Tokyo, and I have witnessed people moving from a standstill to success with the power of their own ideas and willingness to work. Their successes are theirs. I was simply a guide, using one or more of these frameworks for a moment, suggesting adjustments to their thinking, approaches, and trajectories.

Your entrepreneurial path might be in Startups, Corporate Initiatives, Government Initiatives, Science and Technology, Software, Acquisitions, Turnarounds, Social Impact, Lifestyle, Personal Reinvention ... and more.

Explore. Embrace a path. Fulfill your potential.

No matter your past, age, gender, economics, education, or any other demographics, you can be an entrepreneur. Other than the principles and laws that govern the universe, you yourself are all that stands in the way of what is possible. Open the door and confidently walk through as the entrepreneur you were born to be. Yes, I mean you.

CORPORATE, FAMILY ENTERPRISE, SCHOOL, AND GOVERNMENT
ENTREPRENEURSHIP

"There is nothing so useless as doing efficiently that which
should not be done at all."

—Peter Drucker

This framework has been used successfully around the world in corporations, family enterprises, schools, and governments. For simplicity I will only use the words "Corporate Entrepreneurship," although the framework applies equally well to entrepreneurship in family businesses, educational institutions (schools), and governments.

The following is a 19-step framework for Corporate Entrepreneurship training that I have created over my career. The foundation of the framework is my personal experience and knowledge of what is expected from strategic others[1] and what works in practice. This framework is not exhaustive but is designed to kick-start your planning and execution to give you a clearer path forward. This framework has been used successfully to build new initiatives and train teams around the world, across industries, and in structures of all sizes.

The purpose of the framework is to help individuals, teams, and organizations plan entrepreneurial initiatives inside of any type of existing organization (which is typically called "Corporate Entrepreneurship" but is sometimes called "Intrapreneurship"). This framework will help employees structure their ideas into an execution-ready condition so that they can:

1. Persuade their organization's leadership to sign off on their initiative

2. Persuade their organization's leadership to give financial and resource support

3. Allow the individual and teams to actually launch their initiative within the organization.

> "Early in the process of developing your idea, seek out others who can be involved. You might find three or four others who share your vision or who are working on related ideas inside the company. Their perspectives might expand what you can see and will give the idea compelling dimension. Get others on board early, so that they share in a sense of ownership and responsibility for the idea."
> —Sami Kizilbash

If we were working through this framework together in person, I would suggest doing the 19 steps to clarify your own perspective on the idea and then seek out others in the organization as Sami suggests above. This approach will prepare you for the questions that others will ask you about your idea. Then together you would work through the 19 steps again with the expanded perspectives of the others. You could also seek out others first, and then work as a team on the 19 steps.

This framework can be taught in-person or via technology or worked on privately by an individual or team.

---

1 By "strategic others" I mean anyone who matters to what you are working to accomplish. These people might be investors, bankers, lawyers, boards of directors, shareholders, executives, workers, unions, the press, suppliers, customers, the government, etc.

Before you start this framework: If you have not already done so, please go back to the page called START HERE at the beginning of the book and complete parts 1, 2, 3, and 4 of the Preparatory Frameworks. Once that is completed, come back to this page and move forward to the following:

STEP 1 **Why**

STEP 2 **What**

STEP 3 **The Big Play**

STEP 4 **The Offering**

STEP 5 **Value Proposition, Unique Selling Proposition (USP), or Why-to-Buy**

STEP 6 **Go to Market**

STEP 7 **Team and Execution**

STEP 8 **Fundable Event Timeline**

STEP 9 **Marketing, Sales, and Business Development**

STEP 10 **Financial Modeling**

STEP 11 **Capital Modeling**

STEP 12 **Corporate Development**

STEP 13 **Barriers and Roadblocks**

STEP 14 **The Ideal Internal Champion(s)**

STEP 15 **Decision Makers: CEO, CFO, Boards, Strategic Others**

STEP 16 **Call to Action**

STEP 17 **Executive Summaries and Business Plans**

STEP 18 **Pitching and Presentations**

STEP 19 **Save Your Work, Update It Regularly, and Refer to It Often**

The 19-step framework is as follows:

WHY

Before investing time and resources into an entrepreneurial opportunity inside the company, you need to establish and clarify your motivations for engaging it. Strategic influencers and decision makers are likely to ask you why you want to do what you are doing; the question may come from the Board of Directors, the CEO, the CFO or others inside the company, or from strategic partners, investors, the government, and others outside the company. Be ready with a good answer. If you cannot answer why you are doing (or want to do) what you are doing, it will weaken your position and could result in you not getting the support that you need.

A good clear response to the **why** is even more important than a good response to who will do what, when, where, and how they will do it.

Never give an answer that implies that you are engaging entrepreneurship because you are bored, or you don't like your job, or it sounds interesting, or you want to give it a try, or you need some excitement in your work life, or you have always wanted to be an entrepreneur, or you want to be an entrepreneur while you have the security of a paycheck to rely on, and so on. Your answer must focus on the benefit to the company and on how the entrepreneurial initiative will create and capture shareholder value; if what you want to do does not make the company better in some measurable and meaningful way or it does not create and capture more value for shareholders, then it will be difficult to get the support that you need.

Consider who in the company might feel either excited by or threatened by your initiative. For example, if there is another group in the company that could be disrupted by your initiative, you will need to plan your messages around that disruptive impact very carefully. Your current boss might feel threatened that you're working on an entrepreneurial initiative internally, which could lead to your current boss not supporting and actively trying to block your initiative. Or it could be that your boss needs more information and better information so that they can think of ways that they can help you.

The answer to "why," could be that you have identified an opportunity to disrupt the company itself before others outside disrupt the company in a way that is beyond the company's direct control. Or it could be that you have identified a critical weakness in the company that you know how to make strong, or possibly there is an existing business unit or team that is struggling, and you see a way to turn it around. Be prepared to give clear explanations of the situation and the potential impacts.

The point is that you need to consider and formulate clear and trust-based reasons for why your venture is needed and understand how to message and position your reasons in a way that will lower the barriers and clear the pathway forward.

Think in simple, clear sentences that could be explained in greater detail. Lead with the simple messages and be prepared to answer with detail when the time comes.

ASSIGNMENT If you already use the cloud to back up all of your work securely, that is excellent. If you regularly use software that keeps track of versions of your work, so that you never invest hours editing the wrong version of a document, that is superb. If, however, for any reason, you are not yet able to back-up in the cloud or you do not have access to software that keeps track of versions of your documents, you will need to do these things manually. If you are working on a computer, create a folder with a logical name that you will not forget. Put that folder in an obvious location on the computer (not a clever place, but a clear and easy to remember place), that will still be obvious to you tomorrow and the next day. Create a new document and save it in the folder that you just created. Name the file something easy to remember and give it today's date; then every day you edit it, save a version with that day's date so that you can tell the difference between files. Always work on the most recent date and version of the file. If you do not have a computer, buy a spiral binder with lined paper (or an equivalent that is available to you). Put your name and contact information on it and keep it in a safe place. Do all of your work in the document or binder.

ASSIGNMENT Write at least one paragraph on this section. "Why" is a critical question. Start by writing out your current thinking on why the initiative that you have in mind matters. Then as you work to create and build the details for the initiative, continually refine your thinking on the question of why. Keep the question in mind as you go and be prepared to address it with confidence when the time comes. Be prepared, you might be challenged as to "why" for every step in this framework so keep this vital question in mind every step of the way.

STEP 2

WHAT

There are, of course, many ways that you can think about <u>what</u> you will be doing entrepreneurially inside the company. I would like you to identify what the entrepreneurial initiative will do and accomplish, and whether it will require inventing, innovating, renovating, or revolutionizing inside the company.

For our purposes, I want you to think about invention, innovation, renovation, and revolution as ways of defining what you will do. Here are some definitions:

Invention ▶ Uncommon. This is when you work to achieve what has never been before. This can be done but it is comparatively rare, and it is often the most expensive in both cost and time.

Innovation ▶ Common. This is when you take an existing thing and materially change, modify, adapt, and reposition it into a new and improved thing. The key here is that innovation is done to something that already exists. This is significantly more common than invention and typically less expensive in both cost and time. Importantly, innovation does not necessarily stay positioned where it is at the moment; part of the innovation is that it might be repositioned and/or relocated.

Renovation ▶ Common. Renovation makes material modifications and adaptations to something that already exists, but it differs from innovation in two respects: 1. The renovated thing is typically intended to stay positioned where it already is, and 2. The primary goal is to uplift and refresh the thing so that it can be revived and stay relevant.

Revolution ▶ Uncommon. This is when you engage (maybe even fight against) the way that things are to effect significant change from the status quo, so that things can become what they should be. Revolution commonly requires invention as well as innovation, and the renovation of many things rather than effecting change to only one specific thing.

Nothing ▶ *This fifth option is the most common.* Most companies do more of the same, even when they know that they need to change. Doing something just to be doing something, or because you can, is also not good enough, and might be value destructive rather than value creative. Do not break something that is working and should not be changed. Think about this carefully; this question circles back to question #1: WHY are you doing whatever it is that you plan to do?

At the beginning of your explanation of what you hope to do and accomplish, I suggest that you first identify whether (and why) you intend to invent, innovate, renovate, or revolutionize, (or leave whatever it is as is) inside the company.

Next, in the context of that declared intention, you need to give some detail about the thing itself that you intend to work on and accomplish. Create as much definition to what it currently is and what it can and should become (it is helpful if you can connect it back to the why).

Keep in mind that the what will likely evolve over time, and that is normal. You will be experimenting and exploring, trying different approaches, possibly pivoting once or more, until you find the right combination to open the lock on this opportunity.

> **ASSIGNMENT** Write at least one paragraph in your own words about what you plan to do. Then identify whether or not this work will require invention of something new, an innovation or renovation of an existing thing, or a revolution to overthrow something. Explore and refine your questions.

THE BIG PLAY

STEP 3

Beyond the creation and performance of your entrepreneurial initiative itself, it is important to identify the far-reaching impacts of the entrepreneurial initiative on the company. For example, what is the intended and potential impact on shareholder value?

The board, executives, and strategic others will want to know what your entrepreneurial work inside the company will achieve from a bigger perspective than the specific work that you are hoping to accomplish.

For example, let's say that you have identified the need for digital disruption of the traditional forecasting, procurement, supply chain, and inventory management in your company. Let's say that you intend to create a new software development unit that will create custom software that will serve the needs of the business operations and finance units in the company, so that they can use your custom software to optimize the company's forecasting, procurement, supply chain, and inventory controls. You should think for a moment about the bigger play for the software as well as the initiative. What impacts will there be on various parts of the business beyond the specific scope of the proposed work? What will be the impact on the value of the company, if any? Will there be any other follow-on opportunities that could result from this work (assuming all goes well with it)? For example, could this software then be sold as a product to other companies or would it be more valuable if preserved exclusively in-house?

Think for a moment about companies such as McDonalds, Amazon, and Tesla. What is the bigger play for those companies? Even though the average person thinks of McDonalds as a fast food restaurant, it is actually a real estate company that has realized significant wealth from controlling and creatively deploying their real estate holdings. It is important to note that real estate being a part of the value creation and value capture at McDonalds was not part of their beginning—it came later, thanks to Corporate Entrepreneurship.

Next, most people think that Amazon is an e-commerce retailer on the Internet that sells books, electronic devices, and more. Thanks to Corporate Entrepreneurship however, Amazon is a company that does much more then e-commerce of books and consumer electronics; Amazon as a company controls a meaningful percentage of the transactions in the cloud, thanks to Amazon Web Services (AWS).

Next, consider Tesla. Most people think of Tesla as a maker of high-end electric cars. But thanks to Corporate Entrepreneurship, Tesla is becoming a power company that produces various products from the shingles on roof tops harvesting solar energy to power stations that you install in your garage to power your house and your car.

So the question for you at this point is: What is the bigger picture for your company in light of your entrepreneurial engagement right now? You may be working on a specific solution or product or service, but what is the potential bigger impact on the company? Clarifying and defining your intention up front will help you as you go. This may change and evolve as you go, and that is normal.

ASSIGNMENT Write at least one paragraph on this section. Think, what is the bigger play for what you are working to accomplish? How does this tree (your initiative) more fully complete the forest, or potentially elevate what is now a stand of trees to become a fully-fledged forest? If you cannot explain how what you plan to do creates and captures increased value beyond the scope or your project itself, then your initiative might stop here. Explore and refine your questions.

OFFER MODELING

A company that is known for its corporate entrepreneurship as well as the invention and innovation of its "offerings" is 3M (the makers of home, office, and industrial products). 3M was founded in 1902 and the three Ms that originally composed the name of the company were the Minnesota Mining and Manufacturing company. The original idea for the company was to mine for a mineral called corundum that they planned to use for making sandpaper[2] along with other uses. It turned out that corundum was too poor in quality for use in sandpaper. Thus, 3M's first pivot was to abandon mining and to use other commercially available raw materials for their sandpaper. From sandpaper, 3M went on to explore and build other products. It took 3M fourteen years from its founding (until 1916) to become financially stable. 3M now employs around 90,000 people worldwide and has revenues of $30 billion. Today 3M is best known for products like Post-It Notes and Scotch tape, ACE bandages, scouring pads and more; 3M manufactures and sells over 55,000 products—there are over 1,000 types of Post-It products alone. All of which is a far cry from the original idea of mining. The lesson here is that success is possible, even if not with your original idea. It took focused and deliberate corporate entrepreneurship when the company was struggling to make the difficult decision to stop mining and to focus on a completely different offering to very different customers. But their early corporate entrepreneurship efforts proved to be successful; they reinvented the company when the original idea did not work, and they are now a large and successful company that continues to evolve through corporate entrepreneurship over a hundred years later.

A pivot may be a simple recalibration and mild course correction, or it might require more extreme measures. A corporate entrepreneur identifies what is what is working and what is not and then puzzles through what needs to be done.

At this point you need to define in some meaningful detail what it is that you are building and offering, and to whom it is being offered. The user of your offering might be inside or outside the company, and you should specify which. But focus on the features and benefits, with special emphasis on the standards and differentiators. A standard is a common or typical feature; it may also be something that is required by the industry, regulators, government, company, or customer. A differentiator is an uncommon feature; you want it to be unique and compelling rather than simply non-standard and potentially undesirable. If what you offer is purely different and ignores industry standards a customer may not be able to engage your offering.

Entrepreneurs and companies far too often engineer and build products and solutions without planning out why they are doing what they are doing, only to realize after a significant investment of time and money that they should have been more detailed and specific in their planning. Give some meaningful forward thinking to what you believe your product or service is actually offering. You should consider authoring a full Market Requirements Document (MRD), which is a comprehensive inventory of what will go into the product or service, complete with explanations and research showing why. If you are working on software, or science and technology, you might consider using one of the

---

2   Sandpaper is a heavy paper with granules or coarse material (such as sand) glued to the paper that is used in carpentry to make rough surfaces smooth

Offering Requirements Document (ORD) frameworks in this workbook as it is a type of MRD.

As part of the ORD or MRD you would also create a SWOT (an S-W-O-T which stands for Strengths, Weaknesses, Opportunities, and Threats). This important document will help you practically and productively inventory what you have that is already strong that can be leveraged; what is weak and needs attention and how it can become strong; what is a threat and how it can be neutralized and converted into an asset and therefore a strength. All of these are opportunities to be meaningfully engaged. Think about a SWOT in actionable terms; what is done and what can be done? Also think of a SWOT both inside and outside the company (so a "Cross SWOT").

You need to think in core messages that matter most.

For example, what are the standards for a product like yours and what are the key differentiators? A standard could be a feature or benefit that most other competing products or services offer, but also think about what feature or benefit is actually required by the target customer (whether they are inside or outside of the company). Sometimes, entrepreneurs don't personally use, like, or agree with, certain features, so they leave them out. This is a risk that you might take because you believe that you are right (and you might even be right) but doing so might alienate or simply block your potential customer if they commonly use or have a mandate for that feature. It might be that your customer simply cannot buy or use a product that does not have a standard feature, even if everyone agrees that it is useless. So be careful.

> **HINT** Do not make the mistake of messaging the differentiated features and benefits too heavily. The familiar comforts decision makers. Sometimes, standard features that are outdated or outmoded are still required for acceptance or purchase. Do your research to determine if this is the case for your target audience. Then show that what you are offering is equal to how things are currently done, and then how you will differentiate and evolve how things are done.

So, ask yourself honestly which features in your offering are essential and which are not. Then ask which features are differentiated and desirable? Just because you include a special new feature does not mean that customers will find it desirable and use it.

Think of it this way: a standard makes it possible for your intended customer to consider your offering, THEN the differentiator motivates the customer to go with your offering instead of the competition. But that differentiated feature needs to solve an identifiable and recognizable pain. So, focusing on your future customer's pain; what does your customer need from you to make their pain go away?

Right now, give some clear definition to your offering. What are the features that are standards and what is differentiated? How does it work?

STEP 5

VALUE PROPOSITION, UNIQUE SELLING PROPOSITION (USP), OR WHY-TO-BUY

Now that you have inventoried the features and benefits, you need a simple-to-understand statement of who will care about it and why (e.g., shareholders, Board of Directors, employees, customers, suppliers, etc.) You might need multiple statements of value; do not assume that one statement fits all purposes, each stakeholder may have a unique perspective on what about what you are doing is valuable to them.

So, establishing the value of the offering to intended beneficiaries (i.e., most critically, the company itself, but also any customers and users) is key. Why would someone buy it? Especially, why should they do what you want them to do rather than doing nothing differently? From a corporate entrepreneurship perspective you need to think about value, USP, and why-to-buy from several perspectives: the shareholders, the company's leadership who will sign off on your initiative and allocate resources to make it happen, as well as your target customer.

Establishing the value of the offering to the intended beneficiaries is key (i.e., most critically to your own company itself but also for your target customers and users). Why would someone buy and/or use what you are offering?

This is another opportunity to think in the context of standards and differentiators. People have standard motivations to buy, such as needing a product or service or solution that actually works as advertised and as suits their needs. But they are also motivated by the values around the offering that are different and set your offering apart from any other offerings.

When putting together and puzzling through the value of the offering and why anyone would buy it, think about their specific requirements and pain points.

For example, as to the value proposition for your own company itself: Answer the question of how this offering increases the value of the company. Does it enhance your brand or does it conflict or detract from the brand? If so, how? Does the offering create and capture shareholder value? If so, how? Will it make processes more efficient and/or effective? If so, how?

As another example, regarding the value proposition for your target customer (whether inside or outside of the company): As a base line, does your offering satisfy their fundamental needs and requirements? Once that is established (hopefully easily and quickly), start thinking about their motivations. Are they motivated at all? (Keep in mind that the most common competition is "nothing," meaning the user does nothing to change what they are currently doing.) If they are motivated to change, what is behind that motivation? Everyone has a drive that is separate and distinct from the thing that they are buying. For example, they might have a leadership or management problem, or a workflow problem, or a budget or cash problem, or they are losing market share, etc. There is something that is causing your customer to be frustrated or stressed or to lose sleep. You need to figure out what that is so that you can address it.

As an example, when I worked at a technology company we were presenting for a significant contract worth millions of dollars. We figured out that a primary motivation was around the fact that they had a unified global P&L anchored on a single currency and they needed to purchase in that single currency everywhere in the world. We figured out how to make it possible for the client to buy in their single currency anywhere in the world, and that very heavily biased them toward buying our technology. It was less the features and benefits of the technology itself that mattered. As long as the technology met the basic technical specifications, it was how they bought the technology that differentiated our offering and motivated them to buy from our company versus the other companies that presented to them at the same time.

So what you need to do right now is to think about two value propositions:

1. For your own company and what is the value that your initiative will deliver to your company?

2. For your primary target customer/user. What is their primary motivation and therefore the top three most compelling values that you are offering them?

ASSIGNMENT Write at least one sentence but no more than three sentences for each target audience on this section. Your value proposition or why-to-buy statement needs to be easy to say in 30 seconds and easy for your audience to remember. You are creating the hook. Your goal is for your target audience to say, "Wow, you can do that? Tell me more!" Explore and refine your questions. (Special note: This will change and evolve as you do the work in the rest of this framework. Check back routinely to make sure that this proposition is still relevant, and make updates as needed.)

GO TO MARKET

You need to think about and plan around delivering your offering to the target customer and market (whether it is internal to your company or external). Where, to whom, how, and when the offering will be delivered should be detailed to a meaningful degree.

It is often helpful to think backward from the hands of the customer. How did the offering make it into their hands so that they can start using it? Then take one step at a time back to where you are now. Will you be manufacturing a physical product? Will it be software that is downloaded from the cloud or used at-will via a web browser and delivered from a cloud-based server (including the delivery of installers and plug-ins)? Is it a service that will be delivered over the cloud or in person? You need to think through all of the moving parts as if you were building the clockworks inside of a mechanical watch.

Let me give you a high level example. Now this timeline is for example only and will differ for every product and market as every delivery is unique and has its own considerations to factor. Let's say that your corporate entrepreneurial initiative will be designing, engineering, manufacturing, and then delivering a physical electronic device to the market. (I'll use a physical product that needs to be manufactured as an example, because it tends to be more complicated than engineering and delivering software.) Let's further assume that there are seasonality considerations for your target market.

1. **Product in stores (online as well as brick-and-mortar)**
   Let's say that you need to have the product in stores (online and in physical locations) by November (for example), so that you can hit the big selling season for your product in late November through late-December.

2. **Pallets[3] of finished goods shipping to distribution, fulfillment, and stores**
   Which means that you need to have pallets of boxes of your physical product in distribution by October so that it can be delivered to stores in October and November.

3. **Active manufacturing**
   Which means that you should be actively manufacturing by August or no later than September so that you can begin shipping in September to hit distribution in October.

4. **Raw materials to manufacturing**
   Which means that you need to have all raw materials, casts, tools, and manufacturing BOMs (Bill of Materials) and specifications, etc. to the manufacturer by August, but ideally in July for manufacture in August.

---

3   A pallet is a type of low profile platform typically made of wood, but at times, other materials. Boxes and other materials are stacked on the pallet, which is then movable by a forklift from one part of a factory to another, and then loaded onto trucks, etc.

5. **Testing complete**
   Which means that you need to have the product finalized and tested and ready for manufacturing no later than July.

6. **Active Beta and Alpha testing along with bug regression and fixes**
   Which means that you should have been in beta testing no later than May, and alpha testing (for example) as early as February or March, giving your team time for bug regression and fixes. This is also the time that you should be ordering all of the raw materials to make sure that they arrive at the manufacturer's facility on time.

7. **Technical Specifications and other engineering completed**
   The freeze on modifications to all technical specifications for the product should happen by February, with engineering and design completed by that time.

8. **Research and Development (R&D)**
   You need to work with engineering to ensure that you have time to complete that work between now and January-February, which also means working with Marketing and all other internal parties to ensure that the device that you are making is correctly planned and aligned with all relevant expectations.

9. **Marketing and Sales Activities well in advance**
   Then you have considerations for all marketing and sales activities. You need to advertise to stores and distribution so that they can order the product and have it in stores in time, and that needs to be done far in advance. You also need to plan when you will advertise to the customer, so that they are motivated to buy once the product is in stores and online.

TAM VS. TASM

In addition to the above, I would like to recommend an exercise to you. You may have heard of a TAM, *T-A-M* stands for <u>Total Addressable Market</u>. The *S* in TASM (sometimes called SAM) is the addition of the word: <u>Serviceable</u>.

▶ The **Total Market** is the big number of all people and money spent on products, services, and solutions similar to the one that you will be creating.

▶ The **Addressable Market** is the percentage of the Total to whom you can deliver a targeted meaningful message designed to inspire the customer to buy and use what you are offering.

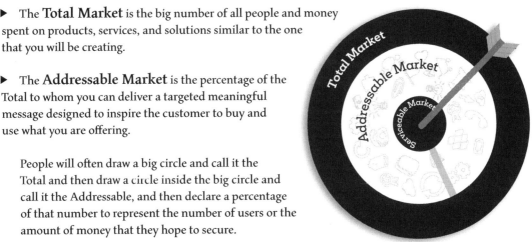

People will often draw a big circle and call it the Total and then draw a circle inside the big circle and call it the Addressable, and then declare a percentage of that number to represent the number of users or the amount of money that they hope to secure.

▶ You should add one more circle in the center, and that is the **Serviceable Market** number. Serviceable means that you can serve or deliver your offering to that number of customers (which could be discrete products or number of simultaneous users and clicks, etc.). This is a critical number to understand.

When you are presenting to a Board of Directors, or a CEO or CFO, or an investor, or to your team, the most relevant number is not the Total, it is the relationship and connection between the numbers that represent the Addressable and the Serviceable Markets. The amount of money that you will be investing in the Addressable correlates to the amount of money invested in the Serviceable.

Let's say that you spend so much in the Addressable that you have a higher conversion to cash (meaning paying customers) than you have capacity to serve; then you have either overinvested in the Addressable or underinvested in the Serviceable. What matters is that you "right size" the investment for both in a coordinated effort so that you convert to cash (achieve paying customers) at a comparable rate to the amount of product or capacity of the service that you have to offer.

If you were to build a TASM now, meaning a plan for your Total, Addressable, Serviceable Market, how big is the Total? (Don't anchor too much on this big number, as it matters but not as much as the next numbers.) How big is the Addressable Market? Who are the customers? Where are they? How will you put a meaningful message to them? At what cost? And how big is your Serviceable Market? Meaning how much serviceable capacity do you anticipate needing to create so that you can profitably deliver to paying customers? Once you start measuring this way, you will have a better chance of impressing key influencers and decision makers because you know what you are doing.

ASSIGNMENT Write at least one paragraph identifying WHO the target audience is for your offering and WHERE they are located. Then give some meaningful detail in at least one paragraph on HOW you will deliver your offering to them; be certain to factor for special timing considerations that will impact adoption (e.g., this could be anything ranging from budgeting cycles to known deadlines on their end to the impact of holidays in a market.) Then construct a TASM with numbers and details so that when you present you can explain the relationship between the investment made and how many of any given thing can be accomplished. Explore and refine your questions.

TEAM AND EXECUTION

> "The right team and execution can
> make gold out of rubbish. The wrong team and
> execution will make rubbish out of gold."
> —Paul Kewene-Hite

Be inclusive and embrace diversity. Be an equal opportunity and equal pay for equal work employer.

Performing an activities-based analysis of what must be done is a good way to figure out whether or not you already have the team that you need, and who is missing from the team. Those who you need to find and add to the team could be via secondment[4], contract, FTE/PTE, etc.

It is a chronic behavior in the corporate world that people draw boxes in a classic hierarchy and put job titles in the boxes and then start plugging in names. This type of job title/function-based planning is typical of most businesses, but it doesn't help you or a decision maker know whether or not you have the right people on your team and who you might need to hire in order to perform the activities necessary to succeed in your corporate entrepreneurial endeavor inside the company.

If, rather than drawing boxes with job titles, you listed the mission-critical activities that must be accomplished in order for your entrepreneurial venture to succeed, you would be on a more productive path to configuring a coherent team. Once you have listed, say the top 20 mission-critical activities (but you should be able to list many more as there is always much to do!), start writing names next to each activity.

I would like to take a moment to dispel a popular myth about entrepreneurship. Entrepreneurs love to talk about how they do everything themselves, saying that they are "chief cook and bottle washer," meaning they do absolutely everything themselves. I have done this myself, but you need to understand that to an investor or Board of Directors or CEO, this type of heroic do-everything-myself talk might not sound positive but could sound an alarm that there is risk and unhealthy exposure around you. Rather than falling into the trap of "I need to do everything myself" thinking, you need to think like a professional chef with a kitchen staff in a five-star restaurant that understands the order of activities and ingredients where everyone works together.

So, you need to know what must be done and who can engage and succeed at the performance of each activity with a high level of professionalism.

If, after you have listed your top 20 mission-critical do-or-die activities, and you have put your hand on your heart when you have put each name of a team member next to a task that they are already professionally qualified to perform, then look at two things:

---

4   Secondment is a temporary transfer or loan of an employee from one department to another, or one company to another.

1. The **overlaps**

2. The **gaps**

The overlaps tell you if you have people on your team with highly duplicated skills and abilities. It could be that you need many people with those particular skills. That is for you to decide.

The gaps tell you who is missing so that you can go find them. In those gaps you need to decide if that is a one-time thing that needs to be done (and how long it will take) or if it is something that will always be a need (or will take a long time to accomplish). This will indicate whether or not you should work to bring someone internally via secondment[5] to your team, or if you need to work to hire a FTE (full-time employee) or a PTE (part-time employee), or a contractor who comes in to do a specific work project and then leaves. All of which will, of course, have cost implications but it needs to be puzzled through and figured out.

> **ASSIGNMENT** Write at least one paragraph explaining who is on your team and why they are the right people to make this initiative a reality. Build your inventory of mission-critical activities with names of each team member next to those activities that they can credibly accomplish (be prepared to be challenged on each Assignment; if they cannot perform that work at a professional level, do not name them to do it.) Identify who is currently missing from the team, what they will need to accomplish by when, and what you are doing to find them and bring them onboard. Explore and refine your questions.

FUNDABLE EVENT TIMELINE
STEP 8

Now that you have done your team modeling, with your list of 20 or more mission-critical activities, you should put that list of activities on a time line (for example 18 to 24 months). Creating a Gantt chart of mission-critical activities (highlighting milestones and fundable events) then harmonizing it with a Cashflow is good planning and good for presentations.

You can build your Gantt chart in a spreadsheet if you don't have project management software. What matters is that you can see the bars that represent the start and stop dates for each activity. On each bar you should name the activity as well as who is responsible along with the associated costs.

When you build a Cashflow you should then harmonize it with the Gantt chart to ensure that the activities and costs over the same months align month-by-month.

---

5   Secondment is a temporary transfer or loan of an employee from one department to another, or one company to another.

When you are building the timeline, with the completed Gantt on the top of the page and the Cashflow lined up below it, decision makers can quickly see that your financial and activities-based planning is complimentary in their construction.

The next thing that I suggest that you do is identify the **Milestones** (the moments in time when you complete an activity or task) on the Gantt chart. Then differentiate between which milestones simply mark the completion of a task and which milestones are actually evidence that you are right in what you intended, planned, and executed. (This could be a working prototype or a paying customer, etc. This is very different from finishing the writing for a business plan for example, which does not prove that you are right but just that you finished what you started.) The type of milestone that is evidence that you are right, is called a **Fundable Event** and it is very important for a few reasons.

▶ Evidence that you are right shows that the entrepreneurial venture is making progress!

▶ Evidence that you are right will be the proof that you need for continued funding and support from the company leadership and board.

▶ Evidence that you are right can be correlated to value creation (increasing value) and value capture (when the company is able to hold onto and make use of the value). Fundable events correlate to the increase in the value of what you are doing, and potentially increase the value of the company itself.

Investors and boards and others who hold the keys to your future funding will be watching for the Fundable Events so that they can know that the work is progressing and that your corporate entrepreneurial venture is deserving of continued support.

When you have the Fundable Event Timeline planned out, and you regularly update it (you should update it at a minimum of once a week) then you and those who are supporting you can use it to keep track of progress and timings that might change over time.

Investors and boards and other financial supporters might use the Fundable Event Timeline to plan when they will transfer resources and capital support to your initiative (just as an investor would do for a startup); when you hit your deliverables (the milestones and especially the fundable events) then you have a measurable defense for expecting ongoing support.

FUNDABLE EVENT TIMELINE

Cashflow Summary

	Month 1, Year 1	Month 2, Year 1	Month 3, Year 1	Month 4, Year 1	Month 5, Year 1	Month 6, Year 1	Month 7, Year 1	Month 8, Year 1	Month 9, Year 1	Month 10, Year 1	Month 11, Year 1	Month 12, Year 1
Opening Cash Balance												
Total CapEX												
Total OpEx												
Total Cash Out												
Total Cash In												
Closing Cash Balance												

Execution Timeline (Gantt Chart)

ACTIVITY	OWNER	ASSOCIATED COSTS US$	Month 1, Year 1	Month 2, Year 1	Month 3, Year 1	Month 4, Year 1	Month 5, Year 1	Month 6, Year 1	Month 7, Year 1	Month 8, Year 1	Month 9, Year 1	Month 10, Year 1	Month 11, Year 1	Month 12, Year 1

Note: Milestones mean that you finished what you started. Fundable Events are validation that you are right.

STEP 9

MARKETING, SALES, AND BUSINESS DEVELOPMENT

You may have noticed that the definitions and roles of marketing and sales and business development are not always the same from company to company. Sometimes marketing and sales is one integrated organization and other times they are separated, and sometimes they struggle to work together. Business development is sometimes part of marketing, sometimes part of sales, and other times it stands on its own.

I believe that one of the reasons why people sometimes struggle to differentiate between the three is because in the beginning the three were one integrated function. People wanted to exchange what they had for what other people had so they created market places in town squares or villages and figured out how to transact with each other for goods and materials or money. Over time, people have artificially separated the three.

We will need to stay flexible within the definitions; you will need to work with the definitions of the three as your company defines them. For the purpose of this corporate entrepreneurship training we will define the three neutrally, as follows:

▶ Marketing

The research and planning of where in the world the optimal customers are located and who those people are in that market. Then determining the means by which to capture the attention of paying customers (via the sundry activities that we typically associate with marketing, such as advertising, trade shows, press, etc.)

▶ Sales

The activities that result in the exchange of the offering for money. This could be in person (traditional sales), or through to taking credit cards on a website or inside a mobile application (digital transactions).

▶ Business development

The securing of strategic relationships that open doors and remove barriers. For example, let's say that you are developing a device designed to help medical patients better manage their pain during therapies. Business development (sometimes called "Biz Dev") would secure an agreement with a recognized medical research facility to perform a study to determine if your device actually does help people manage their pain during therapies.

You should identify the key activities that must be done for marketing, sales, and business development. If you already identified these activities in your team modeling and they are already reflected in your Gantt chart and fundable event timeline then very well done! There is always more to do so you should continue to build the list of activities.

> **ASSIGNMENT** Write at least one paragraph for marketing, another for sales, and another for business development. Give one or two specific examples of what you will do for marketing, one or two for sales, and one or two for business development. More than simply saying you will do it, SHOW what will be done and what will happen as a result. Do not write, "Do marketing." Give a detailed example of why what specific type of marketing will be done where, when, how, and by whom. Be prepared to be challenged on every detail that you write. Explore and refine your questions.

FINANCIAL MODELING

STEP 10

> "Never, EVER, run out of cash!"
> —**Patrick Turner**, INSEAD Professor of Entrepreneurship

Work to frame a financial model going forward that progresses you from where you are to where you plan to go. Building a Cashflow (as well as an SG&A, P&L, Balance Sheet, along with Budgets for MDF/SDF, T&E/T&S, etc.) is fundamental for understanding your initiative. At this point you may not know what those words and acronyms mean, which is okay. You will, however, need to invest some effort in learning their meaning so that you can use them comfortably in sentences as well as comfortably answer questions about them when asked. I will give you definitions soon.

In the business world it is very common for people to assume that other people will know how to build and read the numbers, so they invest very little study into it. Basic financial skills are very important for all people in business. Not everyone needs to be a Certified Public Accountant or Chartered Accountant but being able to build and read a Cashflow should be a required skill for all business professionals.

If an investor, board of directors, or shareholder calls you to a meeting to discuss your venture, grab an updated Cashflow on the way to the meeting. The other financial instruments such as a Profit and Loss (P&L), Balance Sheet, Sales General and Administrative (SG&A) etc., are also important but the Cashflow is the most critical. If you don't understand your cash position over time, you do not understand your business.

Good financial planning is key to persuading shareholders, the board, and leadership that you know what you are doing. If you don't (yet) know how to do it yourself, work side-by-side with a finance-professional to build complete financials. I say side-by-side so that you see how it is done, you fully understand the numbers, and can understand and explain the details. (If you can build a Cashflow from scratch then you can explain the details when you are asked to defend the numbers during any meeting.)

Here are a few overly simplified definitions of business words that you need to know:

▶ **Finance vs. Accounting**
Finance looks forward to what will happen.
Accounting looks back at what happened.

▶ **Payment vs. Expense**
A Payment is when money leaves the company and is given to someone else.
An Expense is the agreed responsibility to make a payment at some future date.

▶ **Revenue vs. Profit**
Revenue is all money that comes into the company from sales.
Profit is the money that is left over after you have paid all of your expenses and taxes.

▶ **Sources & Uses**
Source is where you will get money.
A Use is how the money will be spent.

▶ **Budget**

A Budget is the amount of money (and time) that must be invested in order to do what must be done. Importantly budgeted amounts need to factor for how much money (and time) is actually available.[6]

▶ **Cashflow**

A Cashflow is the financial detail of how a company is being operated; money coming in, all money measured impacts on debts and assets, and all money going out.[7]

▶ **Free Cashflow**

Free Cashflow (not to be confused with the document that is called "a Cashflow") is the money that you have left over after all capital expenditures (aka CapEx, which is the money spent on fixed assets).

▶ **Working Capital**

Working Capital = **Current Assets** minus **Current Liabilities**. Assets are tangible things that have value such as property, inventory, cash, etc. Liabilities are things that you need to pay such as debt, taxes, wages, rent, utilities, etc.

▶ **Professional Fees**

Professional Fees are cash paid to professionals who are not your employees, such as lawyers, accountants, designers, engineers, etc.

▶ **CapEx vs OpEx**

CapEx is Capital Expenditure, which is money spent on fixed assets.
OpEx is Operating Expenditure, which is the money spent to operate the company.

▶ **Fixed Assets**

Fixed Assets are physical things such as land, buildings, equipment, vehicles, etc.

▶ **Burn Rate and Runway**

Burn Rate is the amount of money that you spend in a month.
Runway is the number of months that you have until you are out of money.

▶ **Break Even, and Profitability**

Break Even is when the same amount of money comes in as goes out.
Profitability is when you have money left over after paying everything.

▶ **Pro forma**

Pro forma is Latin for "as a matter of form" or "for the sake of form" and is a word put on financials to show that the numbers are educated guesses or projections.

---

6   Budgeting is incredibly valuable and essential for running your entrepreneurial venture and making sure that you never run out of cash. Your budgets should be planned, reviewed, and updated routinely as a team. Be sure to remind everyone that a budget is more than a plan for how much money will be spent, it is a reconciliation of how much must be spent in order to accomplish your plan compared to how much money there is to spend in the bank account. Monthly budgeting meetings, accounting back a month, and financially planning forward a quarter are good practices.

7   This is a window into all money that comes in and leaves the company. (You should typically have an 18 to 24-month Cashflow, with the next 13 weeks by week, and the rest of the months by month.) Be sure to use mathematics rather than simply typing in numbers.

- **T&E or T&S**

  T&S/T&E[8] is <u>Travel & Subsistence</u> or <u>Travel & Expenses</u> (occasionally referred to as Travel & Entertainment). This budget is for rental cars, trains, planes, hotels, lunches and dinners, etc. T&E is used in North American English and in North American influenced regions. T&S is used in British English and in British influenced regions.

- **MDF and SPIF**

  <u>MDF</u> is an acronym for Market Development Fund and is the money that you spend to take your offering to market.

  <u>SPIF</u> stands for Sales Promotion Incentive Fund and is a powerful tool for motivating the point of sale to inspire them to advocate for your offering over the competition (the seller and/or buyer). This could be, and is not limited to, a payment made to the salesperson or a discount/rebate offered to the customer.

> **ASSIGNMENT** Build a Cashflow. Do not assume that you will simply hire someone else to do it for you. Learn to build a Cashflow from a blank spreadsheet if you can; at a minimum, find someone on your team or work together as a team right now to build a basic Cashflow. Then write at least one paragraph on the details inside of the Cashflow, possibly including the details listed above. Explore and refine your questions. If you need to partner with a finance professional to help you, do it; but learn how to read financial documents, how to tell the stories of the numbers, and how to read along as others go through the numbers.

CAPITAL MODELING

You need to determine what capital will be required to fuel your corporate entrepreneurial initiative, and from where that support will come.

You now have enough thought invested into your idea that you should know what it will cost to engage your corporate entrepreneurial initiative inside the company. The question is from where will you receive the capital to run it?

The foundational questions around capital are related to sources and uses. Sources are from where the capital comes and uses are how you deploy that capital.

You have at least two key uses:

---

8   Watch this budget very carefully and put rules on all expenses and what can be claimed to make people responsible and hold people accountable. It happens at times that people (especially inside of large companies) game their expense reports so that they claim more money than they legitimately spend on real business. This line item can be value destructive when you are a fledgling venture that is carefully watching every dollar in the bank account.

1. Cash money considerations

You need to pay salaries, taxes, insurance, legal fees, and potentially many other things in your SG&A (Sales, General, and Administrative) planning. How much money will you need to cover your expenses for the first year? What about the second year and so on? From where will you receive those funds?

2. Potential non-cash considerations

What office space will you use? Will the company let you use company offices without charge, or will there be an associated fee? What about desks, chairs, computers, phones, Internet, etc.? If you cannot use company assets and need to invest in your own, that moves all of these considerations back to the cash money considerations.

Is your team all in the same area or are you scattered around the world? If you are scattered, then you might need to arrange for an office space for each person individually (which is just more negotiations than a single space for everyone). Then you will need to communicate as well as you can, as often as you can. This becomes costly in time, effort, and potentially in real money terms.

As to the potential sources of capital, consider the following options:

▶ **The company**

Capital support from the company will require a conversation with budget owners. Depending on the size of your company, this might be as high as the CEO and CFO, but it might also be a vice president or senior manager who has a budget that they can allocate to your initiative.

You will need to factor for budget cycles, and whether or not a P&L owner or a person responsible for a budget has the ability and the interest in pledging and transferring capital to you. In these conversations always remember that if a pledge is not written, it might happen, but there is no guarantee. A good rule of thumb is that if it isn't written it isn't real.

You will need to speak with the finance department to clarify the protocols for creating a new initiative in the company.

The motivations for the company to invest in your venture are typically around value creation and value capture more than revenue and profitability, but that largely depends on the motivations of the person who will be supporting you and your venture. They might have a revenue and profitability mandate, so it could be very important to them. Be sure to do your due diligence before presenting to them so that you know their position before positioning what you are doing and why they should want to be involved.

▶ **Government support**

There could be grants and other money (such as loans) available from local or national governments for the type of work that you are doing. You might research funding available from sources ranging from the local mayor's office to national levels to see what might be possible.

The motivations for government support are typically around job creation and economic growth. So, when you are presenting, be ready with information geared around jobs and economic impact.

▶ **External Investors**
It is less common for external investors to become involved in putting money into ventures within a company, but it does happen.

When an external investor is involved, you will need to be ready with information about their return on investment.

If your internal venture will not generate revenue or profit, but remain a cost center perpetually, then you will require ongoing capital support. This is possible if the value created and captured for the company is significant enough to warrant the capital support.

But if your venture will generate revenue and profit, your funding and support will need to take you through to the key milestones of first revenue, break-even, and profitability. Please note that even though **first revenue** happens once (when someone other than yourselves gives you money for your offering), **break-even** implies more than a moment in time, but when roughly as much revenue is coming in as the money that you are spending month-on-month. **Profit** also implies more than a single moment in time, but when you consistently/regularly have money left over after you have spent all money that you need to spend month-on-month.

Sources of capital will want to know that you have invested time and thought into what it will take to make your corporate entrepreneurial venture successful. The numbers don't need to be perfect (they rarely are exactly right), but you need to demonstrate that you have thought through all of the possibilities for what is needed.

ASSIGNMENT Keeping the above in mind, write at least one paragraph on what capital will be required for your initiative. Give some meaningful detail in defense of the numbers and amounts. Prepare to be challenged on the details. Explore and refine your questions.

STEP 12

CORPORATE DEVELOPMENT

At this point, you have modeled enough of your entrepreneurial initiative to be able to determine whether or not it would be more efficient and effective to build internally or to acquire an existing external venture that can be plugged in and adapted to the company.

The CEO is typically the driver for corporate development, but there may be a department or group in the company responsible for planning and executing strategies designed to achieve company objectives. This could include recruitment, strategic alliances, mergers and acquisitions, disposition of company assets, developing or phasing out markets and products, the development and disposition of intellectual properties, and more. The internal venture that you are working on will impact corporate development in one way or another, so you need to be aware and plan your message and approach on the topic.

Building your own new venture inside of the company may be a very exciting prospect, but there might be another company or asset outside of the company that could be acquired and plugged into the company. Acquiring an asset and fitting it into the company might be faster and/or less complicated (and painful), and/or less capital intensive than inventing or innovating or renovating inside. But it might be slower, or more complicated, or more capital intensive. You need to model it to know.

The point is that you should anticipate the moment in your presentation to the company when someone in a position of power asks you the question of why you are building inside rather than acquiring an existing asset. Have a well-considered answer ready.

Part of the consideration could be that the company has a mandate or budget to acquire, while there is no mandate or budget to build internally, or vice versa. It could be that there is direction from the board of directors or the C-Suite to do more of one or the other.

The push to build or acquire will be driven in large part by the impact on the value to the company, and whatever will have the greatest impact on shareholder value.

There are many different types of acquisitions that might work (it doesn't need to be an entire company that is acquired and brought inside), it could be an asset acquisition that may or may not include people. Dealing with mergers and acquisitions is an equally exciting form of corporate entrepreneurship that poses its own challenges and opportunities.

If you have done a competitive analysis, and you have been honest in your evaluation of what is already happening in the industry and market, then you should know which companies, products, services, and solutions are active in the space, along with their value. Have a recommendation ready for what the other players mean, how your company might consider engaging, and a recommendation for what you think is in the ultimate best interest of your company (not what is best for you personally, no matter how much you would rather pursue one path or another).

ASSIGNMENT Write at least one paragraph from the perspective of the CEO on what should be done. This is where you would make your stand as to whether this initiative should be performed by the organization, or if an external business should be merged or acquired and plugged into the organization, or other options. Do not make the mistake of writing this from a perspective that is not sympathetic to the CEO's mandate from the board and shareholders; demonstrate that you understand the CEO's position. Explore and refine your questions.

BARRIERS AND ROADBLOCKS

Anticipating and identifying the threats to success is very important. More than simply pointing at the potential barriers, identify what will be done about them. Be as honest and as clear-minded as possible about what might be in your way and what might be working to undermine your initiative. Work with your champion (you'll identify this person in Step 14) to identify and plan for overcoming barriers to your initiative.

Inside the company, the barriers and roadblocks might be as fundamental as a lack of resources and funding. Another might be a lack of authorization to pursue the work. Others inside the company might be threatened by the work that you propose to do or are doing. It could be that they are actively working to stop your progress and success due to internal organizational politics. Whatever the motivations or reasons, you need to identify what is happening and have a plan for how to deal with it.

Outside the company, there will also be challenges and competitive pressures, but this is normal business. You will need to have answers prepared in advance of presentations and discussions about what you see and plan to do about the challenges and competitive pressures.

Keep in mind that when people say that there are no challenges to what they are doing, that implies that either 1. They are naïve and fooling themselves, 2. What they are doing is of little value if it doesn't threaten anyone or the status quo, or 3. They aren't trying hard enough so they are not meeting any resistance. Change and disruption sometimes makes others unhappy; anticipate who will be unhappy about what you are doing so that you can prepare and get ahead of what they might do in response. Resistance is not necessarily a negative or bad thing; it might mean that they are on the right path.

> **ASSIGNMENT** It is vital that you understand what might harm you and otherwise get in your way. Create a list. Very importantly you must identify not only that the barrier exists, but what you will do about each. This will be very sensitive information, especially if it is regarding a person, so do not distribute this information. As soon as you click send on an email or click print you need to expect that the information is public information and the person in question will see a copy of it. Write at least one paragraph on this section. Explore and refine your questions.

THE IDEAL INTERNAL CHAMPION(S)

You will need to identify the people in the company who will be the most effective and powerful allies and champions for your entrepreneurial venture.

Contrary to popular myth, entrepreneurship is rarely done alone. Lifestyle entrepreneurs might primarily work alone, but there is almost always a time when they need others to be involved. Even when a person is building a startup company in their garage, there will be a point when they will need others to do things that they cannot do for themselves. This is especially true in corporate entrepreneurship; when you are engaging an internal opportunity, you most certainly will need others for a multitude of reasons.

A powerful advocate and champion could mean the difference between an early collapse of your initiative and long-term success. Things might take longer than expected, critical expenditures might be more expensive than planned for, there might be technological roadblocks, you might need to pivot and adjust your planning and execution, and many other unforeseen challenges might arise that will require extra patience and calm recalculations and engagement. A powerful and patient internal champion could make all of the difference for you and your initiative inside the company.

Keep in mind that just because someone has a powerful-sounding job title does not mean that they are the best person to clear the path for you and your internal venture. You need someone who has a strong reputation, who has a credible voice in high level meetings, who has an ability to advocate your position on your behalf, who can open doors and remove roadblocks and barriers in your path, and who understands what you are working to accomplish.

Do your research and identify a person or two as the ideal champions for you. Ideally, this person is already someone who knows and trusts you and your abilities. If you do not know the person whom you've identified, figure out who you know who does know them. Someone who knows and trusts you, who can advocate to a powerful champion on your behalf, might be your best introduction. If, however, you do not know anyone close enough to an ideal potential champion to make an introduction, you will need to do it yourself.

When approaching a potential champion, you need to make sure that you are ready with your presentation and materials. Plan everything, print two copies of everything that you need to give them and have an electronic ("soft") copy available for them to easily access. Then contact their personal assistant to make an appointment. I know from experience that the meeting might take a great deal of time and possibly many persistent gentle requests before you are given a 10–15-minute meeting. Have a simple, clear purpose for the meeting stated so that the assistant and the potential champion can make a decision about why they should accept the meeting request. I also know from experience that sometimes you think that it will take time to make the meeting, but one can happen very quickly, which is why you should be ready to present when you ask for the meeting. Continue working on your entrepreneurial initiative while you work to secure the support of a champion.

ASSIGNMENT Write at least one paragraph identifying who in the top leadership would be your ideal champion. Bring them onboard before you give any presentation naming them. Be certain that they will actually support you and not work to block you or change their stated position during your presentation to unveil your initiative (a written statement of support would be helpful to avoid potentially awkward or embarrassing moments in presentations). Explore and refine your questions.

DECISION MAKERS:
CEO, CFO, BOARDS, STRATEGIC OTHERS

Next, identify who can and will influence your corporate entrepreneurial venture, and who has the power to sign off on it. Keep in mind that not everyone who takes a meeting with you about your initiative can influence or make a decision.

Depending on the size and structure of your organization, the board of directors, the CEO, or the CFO might be the right people, but they might be too high up in the organization. The right person who can make decisions could be in the middle of the company structure; you will need to figure that out for yourself.

The bottom line for what you need is:

1. **Authorization** to undertake the work to engage your entrepreneurial initiative. Some companies have tight controls on authority while others are comparatively relaxed.

2. **Ownership** to actually do the work. Some companies are very strict about who is responsible and who can do what inside the company. Make sure you know whether your ownership includes the authority to actually do the work.

The people whom you need to identify and engage, with the help of your champion, are:

1. **Influencers** who have the ear of decision makers and can advocate on your behalf.

2. **Decision Makers** who have signature authority and can make things happen for you.

If you have direct access to decision makers, engage them. Decision makers will often seek the counsel and advice of their trusted influencers, so chances are that you will eventually present to them as well (if you haven't already done so before presenting to the decision maker).

A cautionary note is that you need to engage your champion in planning whom to approach and when. It is important that you don't create political challenges and difficulties when your initiative is young, and you haven't had time to build strength and evidence of your value to the company.

At this point, focus on identifying key influencers and decision makers as well as planning the optimal time to approach them.

> **ASSIGNMENT** Write at least one paragraph inventorying what authorizations and ownerships are needed to make your initiative successful. Then identify the influencers and decision makers that you need to bring onto your side to make your initiative a reality. Explore and refine your questions.

CALL TO ACTION

In preparation for your presentations you need to identify the message(s) that will inspire key influencers and decision makers to do what must be done for the initiative.

In business, the moment when you ask the listener for what you need from them is sometimes called a **Call to Action** or **The Ask** or **The Question**, but the intent of all three terms is the same.

Keep in mind that what is clear and motivates one listener may or may not be clear and motivate anyone else. Every person has their own requirements, mandates, needs, wants, hopes, stresses, pressures, and so on. Do your best to figure out what motivates the person to whom you are extending (what is often called "putting") The Ask or Call to Action.

For example, Steve Jobs (co-founder of Apple) asked John Sculley (the person who became CEO of Apple after Steve Jobs): "Do you want to sell sugared water for the rest of your life? Or do you want to come with me and change the world?" That call to action from Steve Jobs worked for John Sculley, but it might or might not have worked for anyone else. That specific Call to Action or Ask worked in that situation.

As another example, if you are presenting to a Board of Directors and you bias your presentation heavily toward revenue and profit but never mention shareholder value they may not endorse and fund your initiative if their mandate is shareholder value. Or it could be the other way around if their top priority is revenue and profit. You need to puzzle through and figure out the critical motivations of your audience BEFORE you present the details and call them to action. Do not assume that your priorities or the primary benefits of your initiative are aligned with their priorities, or that you understand their priorities because to you this or that argument "makes sense."

Another thing to keep in mind is that if you are presenting to a group, everyone in that room is going to have their own biases and opinions. Figure out as much as you can about every influencer and decision maker who might be in the room during your presentation and Call to Action. It is okay to strategically lace messages throughout the presentation that speak to what each person in the room needs to hear; just be certain that all of those messages are truthful and consistent with what you are actually doing.

When you extend or put The Ask, depending on the culture and context, you can then briefly issue a call to action for each person in the room in the appropriate order of who matters most.

Sometimes, in some cultures, the messages in the body of the presentation are all that most need, and the formal Ask would only be issued to the most relevant and important person in the room. So be sure that you know what is most appropriate before you enter the room to present.

STEP 17

EXECUTIVE SUMMARIES AND BUSINESS PLANS

"Everyone has a plan 'til they get punched in the mouth."
—**Mike Tyson,** former heavyweight boxing champion of the world

Hopefully you have been writing down all of your thoughts while going through each of the steps to this point. I have found great value in keeping track of all ideas or thoughts whether they seem relevant to me at the time or not.

You will need to complete a written executive summary (a document that takes the same amount of time to read as to drink a glass of water) that will help influencers and decision makers understand enough that they will 1. want to know more, and 2. be interested (or even excited) to support you and the initiative. A business plan is a long, more detailed executive summary.

▶ Executive Summary

An Executive Summary, not to be confused with a full Business Plan, is ideally two pages and no longer than three pages in length. It should have the most representative and most relevant details, which are explained in greater detail in the full business plan. Make sure that every word in the Executive Summary is relevant to persuade the reader that you know what you are doing to build and run the company. The Executive Summary should inspire the reader to ask you for more information.

▶ Business Plan

A Business Plan is a longer, more detailed document than an Executive Summary. A typical length for a business plan is 20–30 pages. When writing business plans you should bias the writing very heavily to execution detail; show what you will do, when, where, how, and why. State the problem, build out the execution detail around the solution to the problem, put some financials in so that the costs are understood, and call the reader to action. Use multiple proofreaders and listen to their feedback. Questions and comments give you insight into what is understandable and working (or not), so be grateful and never impatient with questions and comments.

(I once submitted a 30-page business plan to a government body, not realizing that they required a minimum of 100 pages because more pages demonstrated thorough and complete investigation and consideration. In the business world, a 100+ page business plan to an investor or leadership team might imply that you are overthinking or cannot succinctly say what you need to say.)

There is no single magic format or outline for business plans and executive summaries. You should write the details in a way that will flow most naturally and persuade the reader, while also providing a document that will help guide your running of the company.

The goal for an executive summary and business plan, along with all supportive financials, should be to use it as practice. Stay flexible, move with what happens, and update your documentation regularly so that you are ready at a moment's notice to share and present. Do not get caught with a summary or plan that is out of date; that moment might be the game changer. Keep updating, practicing, learning, and adapting to change as you go forward.

> **ASSIGNMENT** All of the topics explored in this framework can be used in your executive summary and business plan. Create your 2–3-page executive summary first in a separate document (name it uniquely and always save the date in the file name every time you update it). Once your executive summary is completed, save a copy of it as a different file (using "Save As … ") with the date in the file name in the same folder. Then, begin the work of meaningfully expanding the detail in each section until you have a 20–30-page full business plan.

PITCHING AND PRESENTATIONS

▶ Pitching

A pitch is a short format presentation. It should be quick, clear, and to the point. An elevator or lift pitch is typically no more than one or two minutes (the time it would take to get from one floor in a building to a few floors up). Quickly state your name, what you do for your company (this should take only a few seconds) and then get straight into the pitch. Your pitch should clearly state that there is an opportunity (a problem), something that can be done about the opportunity, what you are doing about it, and how the listener can be involved. Keep the pitch to the point and positive.

▶ Presentations

A presentation is a longer format pitch but has a similar structure.

> **HINT** Presentations tend to focus too much on the problem/ opportunity and have too little practical detail on what can be done and what you are actually doing (aka execution). It is true that the listener needs to believe that you are addressing an authentic problem (do not solve a non-problem, and do not be a solution looking for a problem to solve) but remember that the listener needs to believe that you know what you are doing (execution level detail). Explain the opportunity and give representative detail into what you are doing about that opportunity.

It is common for people not to practice their presentations in advance. People often work on their materials up to the moment before presenting and then walk into the room and start. This is a mistake. Practice your pitch and presentations before giving them. There is no substitute for practice. Make sure that the first time that you pitch, or present is during practice rather than in front of the person whom you need to persuade. You only get one chance at a first impression. In case you feel that practice will make you less spontaneous in the moment, keep in mind that practice will make you better in a moment. For example, professional athletes practice SO THAT they will be better able to be more powerfully and effectively spontaneous in a moment.

The opportunity to persuade a key influencer or decision maker might happen at any moment. The quick two-minute pitch is called an elevator pitch or lift pitch because you might be in an elevator or lift when you realize that you are standing next to a key influencer or decision maker. You then have the amount of time that it takes to go from the ground floor to when they exit the elevator or lift to plant a seed. Hopefully they will invite you to present to them based on the strength of that one short pitch.

I have successfully pitched in elevators/lifts, hallways/corridors, stairways, sidewalks, while crossing the street, while at a salad bar, standing in a line/queue, while on the phone, and sitting next to someone on a plane. The point is that you never know when the opportunity will present itself. Practice your pitch over and over until you can say it without thinking about it. And practice it on different people to make sure that it makes sense and is coherent.

Practice your pitching without slides or props or other visual support. You never know when, where, or how you will be pitching. If your pitch is reliant on a slide or a prop, you might find yourself fumbling with your phone or computer, trying to pull up whatever you need, and end up burning the seconds or minutes that you have to persuade the listener. Also keep in mind that you only have a handful of seconds to create a powerful first impression; if you know what you are talking about and can say it off the top of your head without notes or visual assistance, then all the better.

If you have technology that can be quickly and effortlessly shown, then do it; just be aware that if it doesn't work then that is what the listener will remember.

Full presentations can start with a quick two-minute pitch at the top, to snapshot the long story short and give the audience an idea of what you are doing. Then you can start the longer format presentation. The longer presentation can include slides and product demonstrations if you have them; just remember to tell the story in an order that makes sense. Practice, practice, practice. There is no substitute for practicing before you present. Then after you've presented, practice some more.

As to time management, let's say, for example, that you are given a 30-minute meeting to present. Do not prepare 30 minutes of presentations and slides and demonstrations. A good rule of thumb is to prepare presentations for half of the allotted time. So, in this example you would prepare 15 (or 20 maximum) minutes of a presentation, for a 30-minute meeting. Leave room for questions during the presentation as well as questions and answers at the end.

Here is a thumbnail EXAMPLE of how much time should be spent on each part of the presentation:

▶ **Intro** (~5% of the available time)
Don't apologize—it is a common opener, but it is a poor start. Be confident but never arrogant.

▶ **The Opportunity/Problem** (~25%)
Do not pander or exaggerate; be factual.

▶ **What options are possible** (~15%)
Give a few examples of options. Do not make the mistake of speaking poorly of any alternative to what you are recommending. Be factual.

▶ **What I am doing** (~45%)
Do not hold back any secret ingredient (aka silver bullet or game changer) during your presentation. It is a common problem that the presenter will save the big "wow" of their solution for a follow-up presentation. If the audience doesn't hear the wow in your first pitch, there may not be a second presentation.

▶ **How you can be involved** (~10%)
Do not tell them what they will do. Welcome them to the party and invite them to be involved.

Start on time and finish on time (or a little early). Going over time should only happen if the audience asks you to stay and explain more. Even then, be sensitive to being over time. It is typically better to leave when you are ahead while they want more and schedule a follow-up.

Do not feel nervous or upset about any questions that might be asked of you. Questions expose holes in your presentation and tell you what was not clear or understandable to the listener (no matter how clear you thought that you made the point). Questions also give you an indication of what matters to the person asking the question. Write down all the questions that you were asked, and the answers that you gave, and then use those notes as preparation for future meetings (and work on clearer presentations and better answers for the future).

> **ASSIGNMENT** Build the materials that you will need (e.g., 2–3-page executive summary, slides, etc.). Practice that 60-second pitch until you can say it without thinking. THEN start working on expanded detail versions of that pitch so that when people ask you to give them more you can do 60 seconds on this detail and 60 seconds on that detail. THEN work on a 30-minute expanded version of that pitch, which gives more meaningful insight and detail. Explore and refine your questions.

SAVE YOUR WORK, UPDATE IT REGULARLY, AND REFER TO IT OFTEN

Revisit all of the above work regularly. Remember to save your work regularly and keep backups on separate secure devices. Once a day, or at a minimum once a week on a routine day at a routine time, review and update details for all of the above work. The last time that out of date documents created a problem for me was when I was asked to send my current business plan to a meeting deciding the placement of millions of dollars (in the dot.com era) and I was not ready in the moment. Since that day I have always had current documents ready to send whenever a shareholder, investor, or board member asks. It always makes a good impression when you are ready to send freshly updated documents when asked.

Every time you update the document, save a unique version in a common reference folder on your computer. Use a consistent naming convention and update the name every time to include the date that you modified it (or some other intuitive system that others, not just you, will understand if they need to find information).

You never know when you will need to give someone a copy of your plan. You might be given advance warning, but sometimes the call is unexpected. Do not be caught off guard with an out of date version! Be prepared, and you will have nothing to fear

ASSIGNMENT Comb through your document. Save everything. If you write something and you aren't quite sure how it fits, either put the thought on the last empty page of the document or create a second document in the same folder just for thoughts that you aren't yet sure how to use. You do not want to find yourself in the situation where later on, you wish that you hadn't deleted that thought.

On future days when you open and edit the document, do a Save As and change the version date on the document so that it creates a new document that is saved in the same folder. It may happen that in the future you will want to refer to an earlier draft, and if anything happens to the file that you are working on that day, you can always go back to the most recent version rather than starting over.

Keep a backup somewhere other than on your computer. (You should regularly back up your entire hard drive.) If you are working on paper, you need to keep your binder safe and secure at all times. When you are able, you might have someone scan every page in the binder onto a file that you keep on a small portable computer stick for safekeeping. If you edit your document on a public computer, just make certain that you do not leave a copy of your document on the public hard drive.

Regularly update your writing, save copies, keep the dream alive, and work to make it real.

SCALING ATOMS TO BITS

Atoms are physical things (including everything from machines to humans). Bits are non-physical things that are storable (most commonly, software).[1]

Scale is when a small thing becomes big(ger) in the transition from the ability to serve one, to serving a few, to serving many. Scaling a business can be intimidating to think about, and the work required can be daunting to say the least.

Scale matters, and scaling a business typically generates value creative advantages for a business. However, things tend to break when a company tries to scale before the people, processes, and vital systems in the company are strong enough and prepared to scale.

---

1   I've heard people argue that human thinking counts as Bits pointing at the new frontier of brain implants, and the theoretic future potential Whole Brain Emulation (WBE). It is my opinion, as of this writing, that human thought and thinking does not count as Bits.

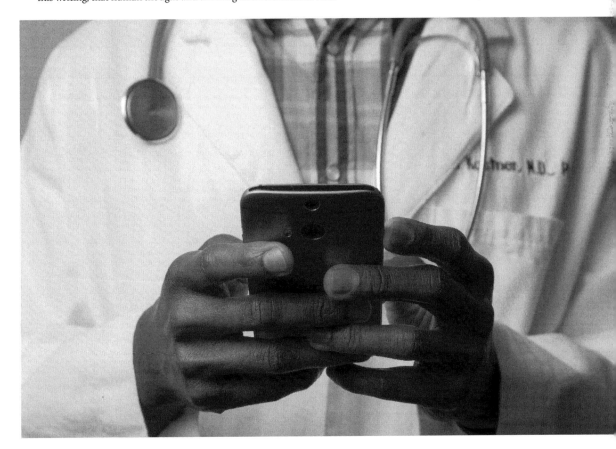

Efficient vs Effective

Efficient has to do with *how* you do something, effective has to do with *what* happens when you do something. Efficiency is very scale-friendly, but be careful, because what is efficient at scale may not be as effective as it was before you scaled and may not be as effective as you need it to be.

Take, for example, a person who wants to sell wood carvings. Consider a master wood carver who listens to the personal story of their customer for whom they are carving. The carver then works to incorporate the customer's personal story into their carving; the carver then follows the themes from the story as well as the grain of the wood to carefully and lovingly produce a masterpiece. A machine would have been more efficient. It could be argued that when using the right software and machines a quality carving could have been accomplished in a fraction of the time for less cost. What is more, thousands of carvings could be made in the same time as the master wood carver did their one work by hand. Then it could be argued that the one hand carved piece being made by hand and one of a kind makes it more valuable. If your goal is one heirloom piece, then the "inefficiencies" of the master carver creating it by hand has a more relevant effect. If, however, the goal is mass production of quality wood carvings, then the efficiencies of software and machines will have the desired effect of acceptable quality, in less time, at a lower cost. Knowing what matters more in your specific case is important.

> "What is effective is not always efficient, and what is efficient is not always effective. Sometimes you choose to be less efficient in order to be more effective."
> —Steven J. Hite,
> EdD Harvard University,
> BYU emeritus professor of Educational Leadership and Foundations,
> Founder and CEO of TRUE Africa

With the above in mind, here are a few steps to take you through questions around what atoms might be more effective as bits:

STEP 1 How things are now

Make an objective inventory of the mission-critical activities that, as of today, make your business run. Create two lists, one for the existing atoms and one for existing bits.

Take these frameworks for example. When I deliver the training in person, that is atomic or atoms-based activity. This workbook is still atoms when printed, but it becomes bits when delivered as an eBook. When the frameworks are made into audio and video files, shared on a website, or delivered other ways via the Internet, the frameworks are also bits.

STEP 2 What Atoms should become Bits?

Some atoms are more effective as atoms, while some are better as bits. But it also depends on the use case (how people use it). From the perspective of receiving personalized training, coaching, and feedback in the moment, these frameworks are better as atoms (meaning in person) when compared to being delivered as bits. But from the perspective of being able to take your own pace and time, being able to repeat and review, the frameworks are better as bits. The pages of a book (atoms as paper but bits as an eBook), videos, and audio files (bits) don't get tired of being revisited and repeated over and over, and the work in a book or online can be done anytime day or night. Machine learning, natural language processing, and the most effective chat bots are not yet as good as a live instructor, but they are improving at breakneck speed. In time, a virtual trainer might meet the needs of most people.

STEP 3 How step 2 will make you more agile

Now that you have the above lists about what atoms you have and which should stay as atoms and which might be equally effective as bits, you need to gather facts that can inform your actions. Create a story for the activities in #1 and #2 above and include an impact assessment. For example, how would the conversion from atoms to bits:

A. Make the business more efficient.

B. Make the business more effective.

C. Make the business more agile and flexible.

D. Impact the bottom and top line of the company.

E. Create and capture shareholder value.

Items A, B & C above correlate directly to the impact on scale. When enough of what you do as a company is bits-based, then technological scale is more achievable. All items combined become the argument to your investors, shareholders, board, and leadership team for support to keep your atoms as atoms and/or to make your atoms into bits.

In the example of these frameworks, the atoms of in-person training scale poorly, the atoms of printed books scale better than humans, but the eBook and bits of Internet delivery scale well. It becomes a question of tolerances; effective is best (of course), but less effective is more desirable than no effect.

STEP 4 Factoring for Friction

Contact creates friction. In business, every time a person needs to do something to make a transaction happen it creates friction, which slows things down and increases costs in time and potentially money. There are two basic types of friction in business: Process and People. An aspiration in business is a frictionless transaction (or as close to frictionless as you can manage). This means as few touches or clicks (simpler transactions and interactions) as possible.

Back to these frameworks, in-person training (atoms) is high-friction but high value. Independent reading of the physical book (atoms) or eBook (bits)—self-paced training—is less friction than you would experience if you logged into a website to watch videos and do work online, which is higher friction than books and eBooks. The online training could be less friction or higher friction than in face-to-face in-person training, depending on how you look at it. Even high repeated friction online would be classified as tireless process friction, while an equivalent frequency of repeated questions day and night (if even possible) in-person, would be very tiring people friction.

As a final thought

Let software, machines, and computers do the things that they do better than people and refocus people to do the things that they do better than machines. When the bits and atoms are optimized and balanced in your business, you will be better positioned to scale.

ACQUISITIONS
(AKA BUYING
A COMPANY)

"A person often meets his destiny on the road
he took to avoid it."

—A French Proverb attributed to **Jean de La Fontaine**

You want to be an entrepreneur but you "don't have an idea" and maybe you don't want all of the uncertainty around starting something from nothing, so the idea of hitting the ground running with something that already exists sounds more in line with your interests. Acquiring someone else's existing company is a great way to jump into the life of an entrepreneur. The day after you buy the company, you will have products, employees, customers, suppliers, and more.

The following is a 24-step framework for Acquisition as Entrepreneurship training that I have created over my career. The foundation of the framework is my personal experience and knowledge of what is expected from strategic others[1] and what works in practice. This framework is not exhaustive but is designed to kick-start planning and execution to give you a path forward. The framework can be used to train teams around the world, across industries, and in structures of all sizes.

The purpose of the framework is to help plan and execute the acquisition of an existing company. This framework will help you think through a plan so that you can 1. Persuade shareholders, the board, and other leadership to support your interest in buying a company, 2. Persuade strategic others to give financial and resource support, and 3. Allow the individual and teams to actually buy a company. This framework can be taught in-person or via technology or worked on privately by an individual or team. The 24-step framework is as follows:

Before you start this framework: If you have not already done so, please go back to the page called START HERE at the beginning of the book and complete parts 1, 2, 3, and 4 of the Preparatory Frameworks. Once that is completed, come back to this page and move forward to the following:

PREAMBLE **What Is an Acquisition?**

STEP 1 **Other People's Money (OPM)**

STEP 2 **Search Funds**

STEP 3 **How Do I Find a Company to Buy?**

STEP 4 **Team and Execution**

STEP 5 **Lawyers, Bankers, Accountants, and Finance Professionals**

---

1   By "strategic others" I mean anyone who matters to what you are working to accomplish. These people might be investors, bankers, lawyers, boards of directors, shareholders, executives, workers, unions, the press, suppliers, customers, the government, etc.

WHAT IS AN ACQUISITION?

Acquisition (noun) 1. The act of acquiring something, 2. Something acquired or gained

Acquire (verb) 1. To get as one's own, to come into possession or control of often by unspecified means, to come to have as a new or added characteristic, trait, or ability (as by sustained effort or natural selection)

At times the definition of a word does not help us understand it. "Acquisition is the act of acquiring." Then acquiring is "to come into possession or control of often by unspecified means." The "unspecified means" are precisely the purpose of this framework.

Mergers & Acquisitions (M&A) are commonly said in the same breath and often sound like "M-n-A" said quickly. The two are related but there are differences.

▶ Acquisitions

An acquisition is when a person or group of persons purchases a company. An acquisition happens most commonly so that the acquirer(s) can own and operate the company. Sometimes, however, an acquisition happens specifically to liquidate part or all of the acquired company, especially if the value of the parts is greater than the value of the company as a whole. The assets (aka anything that has value) are purchased, or the stock or shares[2] of the company are purchased. If you acquire the assets only you might be able to seperate out and not take over the liabilities (for example debt).

▶ Mergers

A merger is when two companies are joined together, typically by "Company A" assimilating and taking over "Company B" which then blends into Company A so that both become part of a single expanded enterprise. Sometimes Company A is a newly created company. All assets and liabilities will typically transfer from the seller to the buyer. Company A will at times keep specific parts of Company B that are of greatest value and then liquidate the rest. It also sometimes happens that Company B is merged into Company A so that Company B can be eliminated. Mergers offer a special set of challenges and opportunities, including difficulties with the two sets of employees learning to work together (sometimes corporate cultures struggle to blend), duplication of roles (e.g., two CFOs, two VPs of Sales, etc.) product duplication, and more. Branding can also be complicated: In the year 2000 when X.com merged with Confinity, they changed the merged company name to Paypal, which was the name of one of Confinity's products. When United Airlines and Continental Airlines merged in 2010, they kept the name United and the logo from Continental.

For our purposes we will use the word acquisition to mean both mergers and acquisitions. We will also assume that the purpose of an acquisition is to run the acquired company.

The first two steps in this acquisition framework are groundwork for anything you do in life and business, then Step 3 is when we get into the work to acquire something.

Let's get started.

> **ASSIGNMENT** If you already use the cloud to back up all of your work securely, that is excellent. If you regularly use software that keeps track of versions of your work, so that you never invest hours editing the wrong version of a document, that is superb. If, however, for any reason, you are not yet able to back-up in the cloud or you do not have access to software that keeps track of versions of your documents, you will need to do these things manually. If you are working on a computer, create a folder with a logical name that you will not forget. Put that folder in an obvious location on the computer (not a clever place, but a clear and easy to remember place), that will still be obvious to you tomorrow and the next day. Create a new document and save it in the folder that you just created. Name the file something easy to remember and give it today's date; then every day you edit it, save a version with that day's date so that you can tell the difference between files. Always work on the most recent date and version of the file. If you do not have a computer, buy a spiral binder with lined paper (or an equivalent that is available to you). Put your name and contact information on it and keep it in a safe place. Do all of your work in the document or binder.

---

2   "Stock" (also known as "equity") means ownership. "Shares" are units of stock and are certificates which make you a shareholder.

STEP 1

OTHER PEOPLE'S MONEY (OPM)

If you have your own money and you want to use it to buy a company, that's fantastic. That dramatically simplifies everything.

Most people, however, do not have enough money to buy a company. Even if you have your own money, there are advantages (and disadvantages) to using other people's money (OPM).

To simplify the options, I will mention the three types of OPM: seller-financing, lending institutions, and investors.

▶ **Seller-financing**

A seller might be willing to become your lender. You would sign an agreement that in exchange for taking ownership of their company you will make payments to them over time, the way that you would make regular payments on a loan from a bank or other lending institution. This is sometimes called a Seller's Note. Depending on where the company and seller are located, there might be tax and other advantages to the seller for financing your acquisition of their company. Seller financing can simplify the transaction if there is no third party (e.g., an investor or a lending institution) who supplies the money for you to make the purchase. Seller financing might also be combined with investor and/or other debt financing. A key to seller-financing working is that you can actually make your payments and not default. Carefully forecast and plan before entering into the arrangement. Work with good lawyers and finance professionals. Look at the base-case and worst-case forecasts and planning[3]; if you are confident that you can make the payments then you might be in a good position for this type of arrangement. Also look carefully at the terms and conditions for what happens in the event of missed payments and defaults.

▶ **Lending Institutions**

Debt can be a powerful tool for people who know what they are doing. Debt can be destructive to people who do not know what they are doing. A cautionary note is that most people (even those who think that they are good at managing debt) are not skilled at managing debt. Just because a bank or other lending institution is willing to loan you the money does not mean that you will be good at servicing that debt and should take it. Before you take a loan, very carefully forecast and plan into the future. Work with good lawyers and finance professionals before

---

3   Do not make the mistake of embracing the best-case, or most optimistic view, of the future. If you can still succeed in the base-case or worst-case, there are still no guarantees, but the odds of success are better.

agreeing to any debt-based financing. If good planning indicates that the conservative base-case or worst-case scenarios still position you to make payments, and service the debt, then consider it.

▶ **Investors**

A cautionary note regarding investors is that not all investors are equal. Different investors will give you different terms and conditions on an investment to buy a company with you. Sometimes the terms will be fair to you, and sometimes they will be decidedly unfair to you (the terms will rarely favor you and at the disadvantage of the investor). Other people's money (OPM) can be good, and it can be destructive. Learn to know the difference.

▶ **Dumb Money vs. Smart Money**

This has less to do with actual intelligence than with whether or not the investor understands the type of business, industry, and what you will be working to accomplish. If the investor has deep practical understanding and expertise in this type of company and industry and they are aligned with what you hope to achieve, then they are Smart Money in your deal. If they do not understand this type of company, they have limited or no experience in the industry, and they are not aligned with what you are working to accomplish, then they are Dumb Money in your deal. Importantly, investors who are Smart Money in one deal may be Dumb Money in another deal. The best, most trustworthy investors will tell you when they are Dumb Money in your deal; someone who is honest enough to admit when they are Dumb Money might be able to recommend to you who would be Smart Money in your opportunity.

▶ **Value Destructive Money vs. Value Constructive Money**

Sometimes an investor looks ideal on paper (e.g., they have the right domain expertise) but once invested they are more harmful than helpful. They are pushy, overstepping and directive, they call you all times of day and night, the frequency and nature of their calls start to feel like harassment, and they get in your way. It happens. This behavior is value destructive. You need people who are positive, insightful and helpful, who give you space to work and can jump in to help as needed, and who call during business hours unless it is an actual emergency; these people are value constructive.

Before you get into a relationship you need to call on references (including people you know about but the person you are considering partnering with possibly did not tell you about) to see how other people experienced working with the investor. Structure your interviews so that you can compare notes fairly and evenly across all those whom you call. Remember that if you are advanced enough in the conversation to call on a reference, it means that you like what you hear and you plan to do a deal once everything checks out. Be professional and polite during the calls. Don't go seeking dirt and secrets. Ask things such as "What is your experience working with investor X?" "Would you take investment from them again if you had multiple offers from other investors offering equal terms?" "Would you recommend to a family member or friend that they take investment from them?" Listen for what they don't say as much as what they do say. For example, if they simply confirm the relationship but don't say anything positive or they evade your question, their silence may be implying that they were not happy with the relationship. Write down every answer and compare the notes to your notes from other calls. Do not share your notes with anyone else whom you call for a reference. Do not breach any confidences and do not get into any negative messaging about anyone to anyone. Only seek information.

When you align with smart and value constructive money you are in a powerful position to embrace the acquisition opportunity.

An important note: OPM is likely to want you to invest your own money. (This is sometimes called "throwing in" or "skin in the game," but it is simply your investment in the opportunity.) You putting your own money into the investment is a way for the investors to believe that you are authentically invested in the opportunity and that you won't run too easily for any reason once the deal is done. The amount that you put in as joint investment does not need to equal an investor's investment; it does, however, need to be an amount that is meaningful to you. If you are driving a nice car and asking for OPM, those investors might suggest that you sell that nice car and take the bus so that you can put that car money into the venture. If you are living on the couch of a friend's apartment and already taking the bus and eating every other day because you simply have no money (but they still believe that you are capable of successfully running the to be acquired company) then whatever you have or might have in the future is what they might ask of you as skin in the game. (For example, an investor might ask you to invest x% of your future income, etc.)

> **ASSIGNMENT** Do your research and find the optimal OPM with at least four backup options. Inventory why each is Smart Money and Value Creative Money in your deal. Write at least one paragraph on this section. Explore and refine your questions.

	STEP 2
## SEARCH FUNDS	

The traditional order of things when working to buy a company is to:

1. Find the company that you want to buy
2. Work to line up the investors, lawyers, bankers, etc. to help you buy the company

A Search Fund is the reverse order, which means that you would:

1. Work to line up the investors, lawyers, bankers, etc. to help you buy a company
2. Work to find the company that you want to buy

The traditional method puts you at risk of losing out on the company that you want to buy while you work to line up the funding, banking, lawyers, etc. With a search fund, you are ready to go when you find the company that you want to purchase and operate.

A way to think about the two options is the typical route of first finding a house that you want to buy and then working to line up the financing, working with lawyers and bankers et al which might mean that you lose out on the new home. The other way to go about it would be to first line up the financing, bankers, and lawyers, so that when you find your new home you will be ready to make an offer without delay.

The traditional model of finding a company to buy and then figuring out how to buy it is a very old model. The search fund model is generally accepted as having been originated by Professor H. Irving Grousbeck in 1984 at Stanford University's Graduate School of Business (GSB). Search funds have been successful over the years, but it is still a less common approach to acquisitions. The search fund model has been significantly refined and elevated by Timothy Bovard who put his INSEAD MBA to good use, successfully acquiring companies after graduation. Then as an Adjunct Professor of Entrepreneurship at INSEAD he taught a wildly popular course called Realizing Entrepreneurial Potential (REP) on how to search for and acquire a company. Timothy is the founder and CEO of the Search Fund Accelerator in Boston and New Orleans USA.

ASSIGNMENT If you do not yet have a company identified to buy, you should consider a search fund. Write at least one paragraph about whether or not a Search Fund is for you. Explore and refine your questions. If you already have a company in mind to purchase, then inventory the investors, lawyers, and bankers with whom you will work. If you do not already have those relationships, list those whom you plan to approach. Do not list only one investor, one lawyer, one banker etc.; list several and prioritize them. Then work on how and when to approach them, including thinking of who you know who might make an introduction and, if you have no one to make the introduction, how you will introduce yourself. Complete this framework before approaching them so that you will have something to show them when you knock on their door.

STEP 3

HOW DO I FIND A COMPANY TO BUY?

Engaging the power of networking is key. By networking, I mean more than simply knowing people, linking to them via social media, being part of the same alumni group and club, etc. You should proactively engage the people whom you know (and who they, in turn, know) to find out what they know about the type of company that you are seeking to acquire.

Next, you might be surprised by the responses you will receive if you knock on a door and ask if a company is available for acquisition. A reasonable rule of thumb is that if you don't ask, you won't know. I have experience with students of mine who have been warmly embraced when knocking on doors. Several have successfully acquired companies that they found by doing advance research and critical thinking and *then* knocking on the door to ask. Be prepared with a proposal and a potential path forward before you knock on the door.

Keep in mind that in most jurisdictions, a CEO is obliged to put all written offers of acquisition to the shareholders and board with their recommendation to accept or decline the offer. If the company that you are interested in acquiring does not have shareholders or a board of directors, you might simply speak with the owner(s) to determine their interest. If there is a company that you admire, you might reach out to them. You never know what they will say until you ask. Sometimes the best time to offer is before the owners have decided that it is time to sell.

In 1979, entrepreneur Victor Kiam bought the company Remington Products in a leveraged buyout. He ran Remington as CEO and made a fortune from it. In the 1980s, he became famous around the world for the phrase "I liked the shaver so much, I bought the company." In 1988, Kiam bought the American football team, the New England Patriots, for similar reasons.

What industry excites you? What company do you admire? What products do you use and love? These questions might lead you to a list of candidate companies to approach. Also keep your heart, mind, and ears open; an industry and company opportunity that you would have never imagined might pop up and surprise you. Several years ago, I was working with a student who found his way to a rebar bending company that showed real promise as an acquisition. He had never thought of rebar bending as an exciting prospect, but the more he looked into it, the more compelling it proved to be.

ASSIGNMENT Record whether or not you have already identified a company to acquire. If you already have the company identified, inventory why it is a good acquisition target; be sure to be honest about potential weaknesses and threats in the opportunity. Write at least one paragraph on this section. Explore and refine your questions.

STEP 4

TEAM AND EXECUTION

"The right team and execution can make gold out of rubbish. The wrong team and execution will make rubbish out of gold."
—Paul Kewene-Hite

Be inclusive and embrace diversity. Be an equal opportunity and equal pay for equal work employer. Your team and the team's execution are absolutely vital to the success of first finding, acquiring, and then operating a company successfully.

Performing an activities-based analysis of what *must* be done, is a good way to figure out whether or not you already have the team that you need, and who is missing and needs to be found and brought on board.

Begin by inventorying what activities MUST be done and then put your name next to which of those activities you can credibly perform (not what you are willing to try but don't really know how to do). Then list the names of the others in the company who are best qualified and best suited to perform those activities. Note that I did not say write the names of the people who are currently in those jobs and/or currently assigned to perform those activities, but who is best suited to perform the activities.

Once done, you will see at least two things:

1. The **gaps** around the must-do activities that have no name assigned to it

2. When you **overlay** who is in which current job and Assignment, you will better see what changes might need to be made

Those who you need to find could be people you know or people you need to find. If you have the luxury of working from inside of a company that is looking to buy another company, those people might be acquired by secondment, permanent transfer, new hires as full-time employees (FTE) or part-time employees (PTE), contract workers, etc.

A way to think about team and execution: When you are explaining what you plan to do to create a new company, it is not unlike explaining *how* a clock tells time, not just *that* it tells time. Imagine opening the face of a traditional clock to expose the clockworks showing the gears, springs, and other moving parts. It would be ideal if you could document and explain every detail, but at a minimum, be prepared to give representative detail on what mechanisms move and how to make the hands move, and in turn, tell time. Do that for the details of the company that you are working to acquire.

> **ASSIGNMENT** Inventory your top 20 (or more) mission critical activities. Put names of committed team members next to each activity. The critical activities that have no name next to them tell you whom you need to recruit to help you. Write at least one paragraph on this section. Explore and refine your questions.

STEP 5

LAWYERS, BANKERS, ACCOUNTANTS, AND FINANCE PROFESSIONALS

> "Good lawyers and advisors are expensive.
> Bad lawyers and advisors can cost you everything."
> —Douglas Rosefsky

Competent legal, banking, accounting, and financial advice is vital. There are at least two sets of lawyers, bankers, accountants, and finance professionals to factor. Those who will help you acquire a company and those who work for the company you will acquire. (There are other teams, such as those who work with your investor. You will likely be interacting with them in the process as well.)

You will need your own team for your work to acquire a company. Once you acquire the company you would decide which lawyers, accounts, and finance professionals to use going forward.

Part of that process would be accomplished when your acquisitions team performs a review of business records for the company. If you uncover problems, that tells you at least two things, 1. What action needs to be taken by the company as a condition for your acquisition or what you will need to deal with post acquisition, and 2. If the current team in the company created those problems you don't want.

During the acquisition process, you will interface with the company's current legal counsel, bankers, accountants, and finance people. If you are happy with the quality of work that they are providing you, then once you acquire the company you might embrace them as part of your team going forward. If changes need to be made, then carefully plan the transition. If there are no lawyers, bankers, accountants, or finance professionals in place, then you need to seek out those professionals and bring them onto your team.

For all of the grief given to lawyers and accountants, if you are in legal difficulty or have an accounting problem, you will need good lawyers and accountants to help you sort out the problems.

My dad always said, "Buy the best and cry once." This, in my opinion, applies to the professional fees charged by the best lawyers and accountants. Partner with the best. Their professional fees might be high, but you do not want to find yourself in a compromised position because you used bargain basement lawyers and accountants.

Keep in mind that lawyers, bankers, accountants, and finance professionals who are experts at acquisitions and/or mergers are the key. It is a common mistake to hire a "good lawyer" or "good accountant" who does their best but they do not have deep expertise and understanding around how acquisitions and mergers work.

A helpful way to think about lawyers is similar in that they will work to protect you from what might happen in the future, as well as defend you regarding what happened in the past. Your lawyers should be doing more than reading and generating contracts for you.

As to the difference between accounting and finance being commonly misunderstood, just remember that finance looks at what should happen in the future, while accounting looks at what did happen in the past. Your accountants and finance professionals should be doing more than creating spreadsheets for you. Your bankers should be doing more than opening a current or checking account for you.

The right people open doors that might otherwise be closed to you or that you might not even know about.

Regarding your acquisition, one of the questions that you should validate is whether or not the legal, accounting, and financial structure of the business is as it should be. Good lawyers, accountants, and finance professionals can help you with these questions. One example, that is not obvious, is whether the business is incorporated and/or operating in the optimal place(s) in the world. It might be necessary to move the incorporation or operation elsewhere in the world to save it. Consider all overhead costs, taxes, potential support from the government, etc.

Work with legal as well as finance and accounting professionals to help you explore the salient value, impactful questions.

> **ASSIGNMENT** Identify the lawyers and accountants with whom you will work. If you already have a relationship with them, explain the details of those relationships. If you do not yet have the relationship, then you need to make a plan to develop it. Write at least one paragraph on this section. Explore and refine your questions.

DUE DILIGENCE (DD)

Due diligence (DD) is when you investigate the details of the company to make certain (to the best of your ability) that the company is as advertised and that there are no details that you cannot see that will become a problem.

Do your own DD. Do not take any DD given to you by the seller who may have hired a big firm to create their exciting and persuasive documentation. Anything that you receive from the seller is designed to sell you the company. You need an independent 3rd party to show you the details inside the opportunity. Bring in your own people to ensure that the company is 1. what you are being told it is, and 2. what you need it to be.

This is not unlike having a mechanic whom you trust inspect a car before you buy it.

> **HINT** As you run your own company keep a copy of all legal documentation (keep every original document as well as a copy in a second location) in a binder or a folder on your computer. This is everything and the kitchen sink, for example: All contracts (with anyone for anything), regularly updated financials, tax filings, banking information, leases, asset registries, and a thousand other details. Your lawyer can help you with the details that are most relevant for your type of company and industry. Whenever a new thing happens, update the binder or folder. This compilation of all vital documents will be convenient in shareholder and board meetings, as well as when the time comes to sell your company. Most people are not this organized, and it takes them time to pull all vital documentation together. When you are doing DD on a company that you want to buy, you need to factor for the time that it will take a typically unorganized company to give you the information that you need from them to make a decision.

STEP 7

CHAMPIONS AND CANARIES IN THE COAL MINE

While you are performing your DD, one of the things that you need to pay careful attention to is who (inside the company that you might acquire) will be able to help you do what must be done once you take over the company.

Of the many types of help that you will need, I would like to focus on two here: champions and canaries in the coal mine.

▶ **Champions**

Look for individuals who can be effective and powerful allies as you work to take over the business. This is a person (or people) with credibility, power, and influence inside the organization. They can clear paths, open doors, and protect your initiatives to give them time and resources necessary to succeed.

▶ **Canaries in the coal mine**

Before electronic equipment that could warn you if there was an odorless and colorless gas in the mine that would kill you, miners would take happy but delicate singing birds into the mines. If the bird continued to sing happily, they knew that all was well but if the bird died they knew to clear out and get to the surface. In groups of humans, including at work, there is typically a person whom everyone watches to see if they are happy about the company. If they are worried and leave, then others are more likely to do the same. So it is helpful to identify the person or people whom others in the company watch and listen to. Keep those people informed and on board, and the wider group is more likely to stay on board as well. One way to identify a canary is to listen for names that repeat positively in conversations, especially when people need help or insight into the company.

ASSIGNMENT If you know the names of the people you need to bring onto your side, explain whom they are and what you plan to do to keep them informed and happy. If you do not know who they are then you need to explore how to find them, and get to work. Write at least one paragraph on this section. Explore and refine your questions.

NEGOTIATIONS AND AGREEMENTS

▶ **Negotiations**

READ Get your hands on the workbook *Value Negotiation: How to Finally Get the Win-Win Right,* Horacio Falcão (2010)

Do not negotiate alone. Role-play with trusted people who are on your side before negotiating for real. Be prepared and professional, use critical thinking and problem solving, employ value-creative execution, build trust. Remember that one of the greatest powers you can exercise is the ability to walk away; be prepared and willing to walk.

The purchase price is commonly pursued as the most critical point to negotiate. As important as the purchase price is, you need to be certain that the company that you purchase, regardless of the purchase price, is in a condition capable of surviving, and that nothing in the deal or company will result in you getting into trouble just because you bought it. I have seen people buy companies for an excellent price only to find big angry problems in the company once they acquire it. You can negotiate skillfully to buy a car for $1, but if the car is dangerous to drive and is so far gone that it will cost more to repair than to buy a new car, you wasted your time and a dollar.

Tackle the angry bear that is threatening your family before you shoo rabbits out of the garden. Put out the fire in the kitchen before you negotiate a new color for the ugly walls.

I tell them to not negotiate their irritations, but it is very difficult not to scratch an itch. It might sound obvious, but you need to prioritize those things that can harm you, the life-threatening things. Think of it as prioritizing heart surgery over a paper cut. Paper cuts are painful and irritating in the best of times, but if you put your time and attention into the paper cut and ignore the heart surgery that is needed then your health and life may be compromised (then that paper cut and all time and effort that you invested into it will be irrelevant). It might sound obvious, but I know from experience that people will try to heal the little things to get them out of the way because they seem easier, but you need to address the big difficult things first.

For example: The environmental report being incomplete, there being questions about toxic materials dumping and environmental compliance, and the factory having banned materials in the walls near workers, etc. is more critical to address than your salary once the acquisition is completed. You might have the paycheck that you want along with a lawsuit that bankrupts the company. Even the purchase price of the company is less important than the critical details that could land you in trouble after the acquisition; buying a company for one dollar and then finding yourself in deep trouble with the law (for example) because of something you missed while focusing on the purchase price is a bad deal.

Those who can prioritize accurately, and take deliberate action according to those priorities, tend to win.

▶ Agreements

Term sheets, shareholders' agreement, sale and purchase agreements, tax covenants, and more.

Work with a lawyer. to examine every detail in the deal ranging from the most exciting to the most boring. A classic blunder is to focus on the irritations and exciting things. As much as you need to minimize irritations, and as nice as it is to have exciting details to anticipate, you first need to make sure that nothing in the deal will get you in trouble with the banks or the law, or anyone in between. Again, work with a lawyer who understands this type of acquisition to cross every t and dot every i in the details.

ASSIGNMENT Explore the details of what you need and what you are willing to concede. Write at least one paragraph on this section. Explore and refine your questions.

STEP 9

Ts & Cs AS WELL AS REPS AND WARRANTIES

Get a lawyer involved in the details of the contracts. Even if you are a lawyer, you need another objective set of eyes on the details. You also need to read every word, and you need to understand what those words mean. Do not just leave the reading, and understanding, to the lawyers. Have your lawyers explain to you anything that you do not understand.

Pay careful attention to the **terms and conditions (Ts & Cs)**. You need to read through every detail to make sure you understand. Do this with your lawyer if need be, or less expensively, ask them specific questions about anything you don't understand. It will be your signature on the document, so you need to understand what you are signing.

"You make your money on the signature" is an expression that I have heard throughout my career. It means that when you sign a contract, that piece of paper determines whether or not you will make the money that you think you will in the future. I know from personal experience that you might slave and toil over time, only to realize too late that you are not getting what you thought you would receive out of your deal. I have friends who have worked for years to build value in a company, only to realize on selling their company that they would receive much less than expected (and in one case nothing) because of the Ts & Cs that they did not fully understand on documents they signed years previously.

The **Representations and Warranties (Reps and Warranties)** are especially important. It is important to treat "Representations and Warranties" as a complete term rather than two separate terms because it could change the interpretation and legal handling when treated separately. The bottom line is that Reps and Warranties are when the seller tells you everything that they can (or are willing to) about the company that you are buying and what they are offering to do about it (if anything).

As with Ts & Cs, the Reps and Warranties may bite you in the future if you don't under-stand the meaning and implications of every detail before you buy the company. You need to do your own discovery (due diligence or DD), and then compare that to the Reps and Warranties to make sure that everything lines up Do not simply take what they offer you, be prepared to negotiate based on critical thinking.

I would like to repeat this point to make sure the point is not lost or underappreciated: The due diligence (DD) that *you* perform is important in the context of disclosures made by the seller. You need to make certain that everything that they report to you matches everything that you find.

In the context of your DD, the warranties that are made in the context of the representa-tions become extremely important. Work with your lawyers to make certain that the war-ranties are adequate to protect you once the acquisition is complete. If a building is part of the acquisition, make sure that all environmental surveys and audits are completed and reflected in the paperwork before you sign. Ensure that all taxes, retirement contributions, salaries, debts, obligations to unions, loans and other debts, etc. are documented and paid in full before you sign. If you take on any unpaid balances and debts, make absolutely cer-tain that you fully understand ALL of the implications and responsibilities.

> **ASSIGNMENT** Inventory the potential threats inside all Ts & Cs as well as the Reps & Warran-ties. Do not make the mistake of paying too much attention to irritations, but focus on things that could equal legal trouble or other value destructive details. Write at least one paragraph on this section. Explore and refine your questions.

STEP 10

RESPONSIBILITIES AND AUTHORIZATIONS

You need to inventory all mission critical activities in the business. Then write the name of the person responsible for each activity. Then write the name of the person who has authority to make decisions for that activity. If the name of the responsible person is not the same as the person with authority over it, you need to understand why and what rules of engagement and protocols are formalized around the two. Being responsible with no real authority can be frustrating for the responsible person. If the responsibility and authority is in line with the best interest of the business and it is both effective and efficient, then all is well. If there are no rules of engagement or protocols, and/or if the dynamic is not effec-tive or efficient at an appropriate level, you need to build those rules and protocols. Make certain that mission critical activities have a responsible and authorized person assigned to make them happen. Clear the paths for those activities so that red-tape and processes don't restrict or negatively impact their performance. Focus on the value creative effect of the rules and protocols rather than the politics or efficiency.

> "What is effective is not always efficient, and what is efficient is not always effective. Sometimes you choose to be less efficient in order to be more effective."
> —**Steven J. Hite,** EdD Harvard University, BYU emeritus professor of Educational Leadership and Foundations, Founder and CEO of TRUE Africa

SPECIAL NOTE The words efficient and effective are the same word in some languages. In English, the two words are causally connected but different. Simply stated: Efficient refers to how something is done. Effective refers to what happens as a result of what is done. Sometimes, a process can be made so efficient that it compromises the effect, then to have the desired effect, you need to allow some degree of inefficiency. It is both art and science.

ASSIGNMENT Identify mission-critical processes, who should be responsible and who has what authority, and whether they operate with the necessary level of efficiencies to have the needed effects on the business. Write at least one paragraph on this section. Explore and refine your questions.

MEASURES AND CONTROLS

It is vital that you work to understand what you can control, what you cannot control but you can influence, and what you can neither control nor influence.

Take the inventory from Step 4 above, and score it two ways:

1. **Priorities**

    Those who can prioritize accurately and then take action according to their priorities tend to succeed ahead of those who do not. Most people just do stuff and then wonder why so little progress was made on the things that matter most.

2. **Control, Influence, or Neither**

    Write a "C" for what is actually in the responsible person's control, an "I" for what the responsible person can influence but not control, and then an "N" for what is outside of the responsible person's control and influence. Then do the same for the person who has authorization (if they are a different person). (Important note: The only thing that anyone can control is his or her own thoughts and actions.)

As one important example of a common business function that needs to be controlled as a first order of business during a new acquisition, consider all payments that leave the company. Inventory all of the ways that payments are made ranging from cash, checks/cheques, wires/bank transfers, standing orders (or whatever your bank and country call an instruction at the bank to transfer a specified amount of money from your account to someone else's bank account on a specified recurring date), and so on through to who has what signature authority on the company bank account(s). Also routinely review all wiring instructions with those who receive those transfers; sample three different people inside the recipient organization to make certain that the account information that you have is the legitimate account of the correct person or company. (This is an anti-fraud measure.) Then regularly review all of these payment measures to ensure that you know how even the smallest amount of money leaves the company.

If you do not control your cash, you are not in control of your business.

> **ASSIGNMENT** List and prioritize all measures and controls in the company that you are working to acquire. Write at least one paragraph on this section. Explore and refine your questions.

INVENTORIES

STEP 12

Beyond what you can see in a balance sheet and asset list, you need to build a comprehensive inventory of all assets and their disposition, including land, buildings, furnishings and equipment, raw materials, works-in-progress, finished goods inventories, and more. Make sure that the asset lists are up to date and detailed; for example, not just that you have a building, but the condition of it, the fair market value, any encumbrances, possible uses, what can potentially be done with it, etc.

If you have any raw materials, you need to inventory viable and non-viable materials, including what is essential for normal business operation and for non-essential or outdated materials, potential liquidation options, and values.

Then comes a more difficult type of inventory, which is an evaluation of products, product lines, and their profitability and value to the business. Next, list business units and initiatives, and their impact on the value of the business. Then list working teams, production lines, etc. and their value to the business. That will get you into an inventory of essential and non-essential personnel, FTE (Full Time Employees), PTE (Part Time Employees), contractors, temporary workers, and so on. You will need to consider what products, processes, and personnel to keep, and why. Think and plan long term, then take action near term.

> **ASSIGNMENT** If you have any inventories, you need to explain the condition/disposition of all of them, and what you plan to do with them. Write at least one paragraph on this section. Explore and refine your questions.

STABILIZATION, RETURN TO BREAK EVEN, AND RETURN TO PROFITABILITY

It could be that you are acquiring a stable company. Perform your due diligence, assess the situation and risks, and then move forward.

If the company is not stable, or if you think it is stable but then experience instability there could still be a path forward, it just requires a different mode of work and operations.

If an elite athlete was in an accident and is now fighting for his or her life, your first priority should be ensuring that they live, before you try to get them back into their sport. In business, people will commonly push a failing company to perform before they first work to understand what is broken and failing, performing necessary repairs to stabilize it, and ensuring a return to good health. Thus, the first order of business is to work out what is hurt inside the body of the failing business unit or company. Think and take action like a trauma surgeon working to find everything that is threatening the life of their patient. Perform repairs to every *vital* broken process, and ensure that it stabilizes and starts functioning again.

Once the company is stable, take action to return it to normal functioning. For our athlete, this would be normal everyday living without pain or complications from their injuries. In business, this is when you operate normally and make as much money as you spend (also known as "break-even").

After basic functioning is established, our athlete can start planning and taking action to return to elite performance levels in their sport. The same goes for your business unit and company.

When you try to force a sick body or a broken company to do more than it is able based on the realities of its condition, you might make the situation worse. Heal, then return with strength.

The first year of a turnaround should focus on stabilization. If you can stabilize sooner, then all the better. The second year should be a return to break-even (which is when you have as much money coming in as is going out). If you can break-even sooner, that would be good. Then the third year would be a return to profitability (which is when you have cash in the bank left after you pay all of your payables.) If you can achieve sustainable profitability sooner, that will be welcome news. It is typically better to conservatively plan and then overachieve key performance indicators (KPIs), than to aggressively plan and come up short.

ASSIGNMENT Write some meaningful detail for your plan going forward. Inventory the broken processes and prioritize them by their value and necessity to the business, so that you can fix the most critical broken things first. Write at least one paragraph on this section. Explore and refine your questions.

FINANCIAL MODELING

"Never, EVER, run out of cash!"
—**Patrick Turner**, INSEAD Professor of Entrepreneurship

When acquiring a company, it is common to have incomplete and flawed information. You will need to work to frame a financial model going forward that progresses you from the current state of things to a version of the business in the future that has complete and accurate information.

If you can build a Cashflow from scratch, then you can explain the details when you are asked to defend the numbers during any meeting. When you present, have an updated copy of your Cashflow, and be prepared to explain the details to those who ask.

Work to frame a financial model going forward that progresses you from where you are to where you plan to go. Building a Cashflow (as well as an SG&A, P&L, Balance Sheet, along with Budgets for MDF/SDF, T&E/T&S, etc.) is fundamental for understanding your initiative. At this point you may not know what those words and acronyms mean, which is okay. You will, however, need to invest some effort in learning their meaning so that you can use them comfortably in sentences as well as comfortably answer questions about them when asked. The definitions are below.

In the business world it is very common for people to assume that other people will know how to build and read the numbers, so they invest very little study into it. Basic financial skills are very important for all people in business. Not everyone needs to be a Certified Public Accountant or Chartered Accountant but being able to build and read a Cashflow should be a required skill for all business professionals.

If an investor, board of directors, or shareholder calls you to a meeting to discuss your venture, grab an updated Cashflow on the way to the meeting. The other financial instruments such as a Profit and Loss (P&L), Balance Sheet, Sales General and Administrative (SG&A) etc., are also important but the Cashflow is the most critical. If you don't understand your cash position over time, you do not understand your business.

Good financial planning is key to persuading shareholders, the board, and leadership that you know what you are doing. If you don't (yet) know how to do it yourself, work side-by-side with a finance-professional to build complete financials. I say side-by-side so that you see how it is done, you fully understand the numbers, and can understand and explain the details. (If you can build a Cashflow from scratch then you can explain the details when you are asked to defend the numbers during any meeting.)

Here are a few overly simplified definitions of business words that you need to know:

▶ **Finance vs. Accounting**
Finance looks forward to what will happen.
Accounting looks back at what happened.

▶ **Payment vs. Expense**

A Payment is when money leaves the company and is given to someone else.
An Expense is the agreed responsibility to make a payment at some future date.

▶ **Revenue vs. Profit**

Revenue is all money that comes into the company from sales.
Profit is the money that is left over after you have paid all of your
expenses and taxes.

▶ **Sources & Uses**

Source is where you will get money.
A Use is how the money will be spent.

▶ **Budget**

A Budget is the amount of money (and time) that must be invested in order to do
what must be done. Importantly budgeted amounts need to factor for how much
money (and time) is actually available.[4]

▶ **Cashflow**

A Cashflow is the financial detail of how a company is being operated; money
coming in, all money measured impacts on debts and assets, and all money
going out.[5]

▶ **Free Cashflow**

Free Cashflow (not to be confused with the document that is called "a Cashflow")
is the money that you have left over after all capital expenditures (aka CapEx,
which is the money spent on fixed assets).

▶ **Working Capital**

Working Capital = **Current Assets** minus **Current Liabilities**. Assets are tangible
things that have value such as property, inventory, cash, etc. Liabilities are things
that you need to pay such as debt, taxes, wages, rent, utilities, etc.

▶ **Professional Fees**

Professional Fees are cash paid to professionals who are not your employees, such
as lawyers, accountants, designers, engineers, etc.

▶ **CapEx vs OpEx**

CapEx is Capital Expenditure, which is money spent on fixed assets.
OpEx is Operating Expenditure, which is the money spent to operate the company.

---

4   Budgeting is incredibly valuable and essential for running your entrepreneurial venture and making
    sure that you never run out of cash. Your budgets should be planned, reviewed, and updated
    routinely as a team. Be sure to remind everyone that a budget is more than a plan for how much
    money will be spent, it is a reconciliation of how much must be spent in order to accomplish your
    plan compared to how much money there is to spend in the bank account. Monthly budgeting
    meetings, accounting back a month, and financially planning forward a quarter are good practices.

5   This is a window into all money that comes in and leaves the company. (You should typically have
    an 18 to 24-month Cashflow, with the next 13 weeks by week, and the rest of the months by month.)
    Be sure to use mathematics rather than simply typing in numbers.

- ▶ **Fixed Assets**

  Fixed Assets are physical things such as land, buildings, equipment, vehicles, etc.

- ▶ **Burn Rate and Runway**

  Burn Rate is the amount of money that you spend in a month.

  Runway is the number of months that you have until you are out of money.

- ▶ **Break Even, and Profitability**

  Break Even is when the same amount of money comes in as goes out.

  Profitability is when you have money left over after paying everything.

- ▶ **Pro forma**

  Pro forma is Latin for "as a matter of form" or "for the sake of form" and is a word put on financials to show that the numbers are educated guesses or projections.

- ▶ **T&E or T&S**

  T&S/T&E[6] is Travel & Subsistence or Travel & Expenses (occasionally referred to as Travel & Entertainment). This budget is for rental cars, trains, planes, hotels, lunches and dinners, etc. T&E is used in North American English and in North American influenced regions. T&S is used in British English and in British influenced regions.

- ▶ **MDF and SPIF**

  MDF is an acronym for Market Development Fund and is the money that you spend to take your offering to market.

  SPIF stands for Sales Promotion Incentive Fund and is a powerful tool for motivating the point of sale to inspire them to advocate for your offering over the competition (the seller and/or buyer). This could be, and is not limited to, a payment made to the salesperson or a discount/rebate offered to the customer.

> **ASSIGNMENT** Build a Cashflow. Do not assume that you will simply hire someone else to do it for you. Learn to build a Cashflow from a blank spreadsheet if you can; at a minimum, find someone on your team or work together as a team right now to build a basic Cashflow. Then write at least one paragraph on the details inside of the Cashflow, possibly including the details listed above. Explore and refine your questions. If you need to partner with a finance professional to help you, do it; but learn how to read financial documents, how to tell the stories of the numbers, and how to read along as others go through the numbers.

---

6   Watch this budget very carefully and put rules on all expenses and what can be claimed to make people responsible and hold people accountable. It happens at times that people (especially inside of large companies) game their expense reports so that they claim more money than they legitimately spend on real business. This line item can be value destructive when you are a fledgling venture that is carefully watching every dollar in the bank account.

FUNDABLE EVENT TIMELINE

Now that you have done your team and financial modeling, with your list of 20 or more mission-critical activities, you should put that list of activities on a timeline (for example 18 to 24 months). Creating a Gantt chart of mission-critical activities (highlighting milestones and fundable events) then harmonizing it with a Cashflow is good planning and good for presentations.

You can build your Gantt chart in a spreadsheet if you don't have project management software. What matters is that you can see the bars that represent the start and stop dates for each activity. On each bar you should name the activity as well as who is responsible along with the associated costs.

When you build a Cashflow you should then harmonize it with the Gantt chart to ensure that the activities and costs over the same months align month-by-month.

When you are building the timeline, with the completed Gantt on the top of the page and the Cashflow lined up below it, decision makers can quickly see that your financial and activities-based planning is complimentary in their construction.

The next thing that I suggest that you do is identify the **Milestones** (the moments in time when you complete an activity or task) on the Gantt chart. Then differentiate between which milestones simply mark the completion of a task and which milestones are actually evidence that you are right in what you intended, planned, and executed. (This could be a working prototype or a paying customer, etc. This is very different from finishing the writing for a business plan for example, which does not prove that you are right but just that you finished what you started.) The type of milestone that is evidence that you are right, is called a **Fundable Event** and it is very important for a few reasons.

▶ Evidence that you are right shows that the entrepreneurial venture is making progress!

▶ Evidence that you are right will be the proof that you need for continued funding and support from the company leadership and board.

▶ Evidence that you are right can be correlated to value creation (increasing value) and value capture (when the company is able to hold onto and make use of the value). Fundable events correlate to the increase in the value of what you are doing, and potentially increase the value of the company itself.

Investors and boards and others who hold the keys to your future funding will be watching for the Fundable Events so that they can know that the work is progressing and that your corporate entrepreneurial venture is deserving of continued support.

When you have the Fundable Event Timeline planned out, and you regularly update it (you should update it at a minimum of once a week) then you and those who are supporting you can use it to keep track of progress and timings that might change over time.

Investors and boards and other financial supporters might use the Fundable Event Timeline to plan when they will transfer resources and capital support to your initiative (just as an investor would do for a startup); when you hit your deliverables (the milestones and especially the fundable events) then you have a measurable defense for expecting ongoing support.

ASSIGNMENT Write at least one paragraph on this section. Explore and refine your questions. Create a Gantt chart identifying all of your activities (when each activity is intended to start and stop). Then put the Gantt chart and your Cashflow summary on the same page making sure that the months line up as shown in the following template (and on page 410). (You should have built a Cashflow in step 14.) Highlight the milestones that prove that you are right to call them Fundable Events; e.g., this is when the machine you are building actually works, it is when a stranger who has no connection to you purchases your product, etc. A fundable event is not when you simply finish what you started, such as writing a business plan or building a Cashflow with numbers that look good or designing a brochure that makes you happy, etc.

TEMPLATE

FUNDABLE
EVENT
TIMELINE

Cashflow Summary

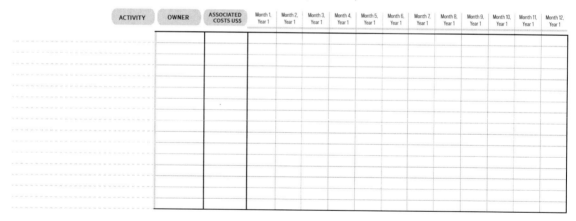

	Month 1, Year 1	Month 2, Year 1	Month 3, Year 1	Month 4, Year 1	Month 5, Year 1	Month 6, Year 1	Month 7, Year 1	Month 8, Year 1	Month 9, Year 1	Month 10, Year 1	Month 11, Year 1	Month 12, Year 1
Opening Cash Balance												
Total CapEX												
Total OpEx												
Total Cash Out												
Total Cash In												
Closing Cash Balance												

Execution Timeline (Gantt Chart)

ACTIVITY	OWNER	ASSOCIATED COSTS US$	Month 1, Year 1	Month 2, Year 1	Month 3, Year 1	Month 4, Year 1	Month 5, Year 1	Month 6, Year 1	Month 7, Year 1	Month 8, Year 1	Month 9, Year 1	Month 10, Year 1	Month 11, Year 1	Month 12, Year 1

Note: Milestones mean that you finished what you started. Fundable Events are validation that you are right.

SUPPLIERS AND CUSTOMERS

Review all agreements, especially the terms and conditions (aka the Ts & Cs), but also the relevance of the relationship with the business. The payment terms, with both suppliers and customers, are vital and need to be evaluated (and potentially modified). Also consider the concentration of customers; evaluate whether the company is overly reliant on specific customers and then the condition of those relationships over the last three years and today. Evaluate the performance of all relationships in the context of their profitability and value creation and preservation for the company. Meet key suppliers and customers as both opportunities to say hello and to gather data (as critical thinking). Be prepared and professional. Be careful not to make any promises or agreements until you fully understand the impact of those promises and agreements on the company's ability to stabilize and return to profitability. Also review the relevance of inefficiencies in the suppliers; for example, you might have a specialty supplier that is essential for a specific product or process. If you eliminate that specialty supplier because you think it is inefficient, you might break an essential process in the company. Review all causal relationships before making decisions.

ASSIGNMENT Make sure that you identify every supplier and customer; comb through the books. You will need to make decisions about each of them; get copies of all agreements and reports on historical performance. Prioritize who is a must-keep and who might need to be transitioned. Speak with the existing team before making any decisions and before you make contact with the suppliers and customers. Know what you need from each, and plan for them before any conversations. Write at least one paragraph on this section. Explore and refine your questions.

BARRIERS AND ROADBLOCKS

Anticipating and identifying the threats to success is very important. More than simply pointing at the potential barriers, identify what will be done about them. Be as honest and as clear minded as possible about what might be in your way and what might be working to undermine your work to turnaround the business.

Work with your champion(s) to identify and plan for overcoming barriers. Anticipating and identifying the threats to your turnaround's success is very important. More than simply pointing at the potential barriers and roadblocks, it is important that you identify what will be done about them.

Inside the company, the barriers and roadblocks might be as fundamental as lack of resources and funding. Another might be lack of authorization to pursue the work. Whatever the motivations or reasons, you need to identify what is happening and have a plan for how to deal with any and all of it.

"We have met the enemy and he is us." From the comic strip Pogo by Walt Kelly, who borrowed it from a 1970 Earth Day poster. There is reality in the humorous yet sad observation that, no matter how well intentioned, we are very often our own worst enemy. Anticipate this reality and plan for what to do about it when (not if) our own behavior threatens to undo what good we are working to accomplish.

Outside the company, there will be challenges and competitive pressures, but this is normal business. You will need to have answers prepared in advance of presentations and discussions about what you see and plan to do about it.

Keep in mind that when people say that there are no challenges to what they are doing, that implies that either 1. They are naïve and fooling themselves, 2. What they are doing is of little value if it doesn't threaten anyone or the status quo, 3. They aren't trying hard enough if they are not meeting any resistance. Change and disruption sometimes makes others unhappy; anticipate who will be unhappy about what you are doing so that you can prepare and get ahead of what they might do in response. So resistance is not necessarily a negative or bad thing; it might mean that they are on the right path.

> **ASSIGNMENT** It is vital that you understand what might harm you and otherwise get in your way. Create a list. Very importantly, you must identify not only that the barriers exist but what you will do about each. This will be very sensitive information, especially if it is regarding a person, so do not distribute this information. As soon as you click send on an email or click print, you need to expect that the information is public domain info and the person in question will see a copy of it. Write at least one paragraph on this section. Explore and refine your questions.

CAPITAL MODELING

You now have enough thought invested into your intention to buy a company that you now need to determine what capital will be required to fuel your acquisition (both the acquisition itself and the operating of the company once acquired).

Then, you need to determine from where that capital will come. Capital is most commonly money but could be other non-cash assets (e.g. buildings, equipment, etc.) A foundational question around capital that will be asked of you is: What are your Sources and Uses? Sources are from where the capital comes and Uses are how you deploy that capital.

You have at least two key Uses:

1. **Cash money considerations**
   You need to pay salaries, taxes, insurance, legal fees, and potentially many other things in your SG&A (Sales, General, and Administrative) planning. How much

money will you need to cover your expenses for the first year? What about the second year and so on? From where will you receive those funds?

2. Potential Non-Cash considerations

What office space will you use? Will the company let you use company offices without charge, or will there be an associated fee? What about desks, chairs, computers, phones, Internet, etc.? If you cannot use company assets and need to invest in your own, that moves all of these considerations back to the Cash money considerations.

Is your team all in the same area or are you scattered around the world? If you are scattered, then you might need to arrange for an office space for each person individually (which is just more negotiations than a single space for everyone). Then you will need to communicate as best you can, as often as you can. This becomes costly in time, effort, and potentially in real money terms.

As to the potential Sources of capital, consider the following options:

▶ **The company**

The company that you are working to acquire might be in debt and you might be expected to service those debts. The company may be debt free. It might have revenue, it may be profitable, it might have cash reserves in the bank. You will need to clearly understand and be prepared to explain the company's cash situation and the implications on the acquisition and running of the company.

▶ **Government support**

There could be grants and other money (such as loans) available from local or national governments for the type of work that you are doing. You might explore conversations ranging from the local mayor's office to national levels to see what might be possible.

The motivations for government are typically around job creation and economic growth. So when you are presenting, be ready with information geared around the current jobs in the company (especially if you plan on firing workers or creating new jobs) and all reasonable potential impact on economies.

▶ **External investors**

Unless you have your own money to buy a company, other people's money (OPM) is going to be vital to making your acquisition possible.

When an external investor is involved, you will need to be ready with the information around their return on investment.

If the company you intend to acquire is not currently profitable, or may not be profitable in the near future, you need to be 100% honest about this reality and have a plan for what you will do about it. If your venture is generating revenue but not profit, your funding and support will need to take you through to the key milestones of break-even and profitability. Please note that break-even implies more than a moment in time; it implies when roughly as much revenue is regularly coming in as the money that you are spending month-on-month. Profit also implies more than a single moment in time, but when you consistently/regularly have money left over after you have spent all money that you need to spend month-on-month.

Sources of capital will want to know that you have invested time and thought into what it will take to make your corporate entrepreneurial venture successful. The numbers don't need to be perfect (they rarely are exactly right), but you need to demonstrate that you have thought through all of the possibilities for what is needed.

Next, when you think about the timing and costs associated with investment from others, you need to understand that money has the same three states as water: liquid, solid, and vapor.

▶ Liquid
This is when money is transportable, or otherwise in a state that it can be moved from one person or entity to another by either electronic transfer from one bank account to another, or from one person to another as some form of recognized currency. Example: When you have coins and bank notes in your pocket and use it to buy something at a store you are liquid, as your money is available for use. People will say "I'm not liquid at the moment." Which typically means "I have money, but I don't have access to it right now."

▶ Solid
This is when money is not available or for some reason, not liquid. The money might be in stocks or bonds, or otherwise invested into something that makes it not accessible, or portable, or moveable. But the idea is that it will expand as ice expands when water is frozen (because of interest or other successful growth by performance of the stock or investment or real estate, etc.). When an investor gives you money in exchange for equity (aka ownership) in your company, the idea is that their money will grow or expand (like ice) as you are successful as a company.

▶ Vapor
When ice is melted, a percentage of the ice becomes liquid (water) and a percentage is lost as vapor (e.g., steam). With money, the Vapor is any fee or charge or tax or disadvantageous exchange rate, etc., meaning there is some loss of value that could equal part, or potentially all of their money that was invested in a failed stock.

When an investor pledges to invest into your acquisition, they might be liquid in the moment and need to move quickly back into a solid before they incur taxes or other penalties on that money. Or they might need time to "liquidate" or otherwise liberate their money from other investments (stocks, bonds, real estate, etc.) so that they can give cash to you as an investment (either as a loan or as equity), which means that to invest in you they are going from a solid, to a liquid (with hopefully as little vapor as possible), then back into another solid that is ownership in the company that you are buying. The expectation is that their money will grow and expand during its time as a solid (equity ownership) with you, and at some future date in a few years they expect their investment back, plus more than they gave you in the first place.

Now that you have done a meaningful amount of work puzzling through your acquisition, you should know whether or not you need OPM (other people's money) to put fuel in the tank to run the engine of your new company. Do not raise investment capital unless you actually need it. If you can create and run your company without OPM, that could be a good thing. If you do need investment, it is best to build as much work as possible before selling an ownership percentage in your startup. If you have little value created, investors will take more ownership for less money. When you have more value created, investors will take less ownership for more money. Raise money if you need to, but there are a few things to keep in mind:

▶ Smart Money vs. Dumb Money

Not all money is equal. You may have heard the expressions *smart money* or *dumb money*. This has nothing to do with the relative intelligence of the investor, it has everything to do with whether or not they understand your industry, company, and what you are working to accomplish. If they understand you and can meaningfully help you then they are Smart Money in your deal. If they do not understand you and if they cannot meaningfully help you (other than by giving you money) then they are Dumb Money. Avoid Dumb Money.

▶ Family and Friends

(Sometimes called Family, Friends & Fools, the addition of *fools* is because people don't always understand what they are doing.) Your family and friends may not be legally eligible to give you money to start your company. Work with your lawyer before you take grandma's sock-drawer cash that she has been squirreling away for years, and don't let your brother take out a third mortgage on his house to fund you. If grandma and your brother are not qualified investors as far as the law is concerned, and if things go wrong and you lose their money and cannot pay them back, you might get in trouble. This goes for anyone who offers you money. Work with your lawyer to keep everything legitimate and legal.

▶ Angels

Wealthy individuals who legally qualify to put their money at risk without compromising themselves financially, are often referred to as Angels. Angels who pool their resources and invest together are called Super Angels. Angels and Supers have some advantages, such as speed to do investments and patience/ time to invest in you. Be sure that you only work with Smart Money. Dumb Money is abundant, and it is dangerous; you don't want a Dumb Money investor second-guessing and doubting what you do. You need a Smart Money investor working with you productively side-by-side.

▶ VC (Venture Capital)

Professionally incorporated firms with (typically) larger amounts of capital than Angels (although some are feeling pressure from Super Angels). When you speak with a VC ask them where they are in the lifecycle of their fund. They will continue to develop "Deal Flow" even when they have no more money to invest. (Deal Flow is an inventory of opportunities to invest as evidence to their investors that they are succeeding as a fund.) Find Smart Money VC for your type of deal. As a startup, before you spend money that you don't have to fly to a VC to meet and discuss investment make sure that you are not Deal Flow for their weekly numbers, that they have the ability to invest, that they are Smart Money in your deal, and interview them to see if they have actually read your materials and that they "get" you.

▶ PE (Private Equity)

PE is the business term used to refer to investment funds that are organized around General Partners (GP) who run the fund and Limited Partners (LP) who are the financial backers and investors in the fund. PE typically buys and restructures companies that are not publicly traded on a stock exchange. PE is increasingly getting involved in smaller investment opportunities (such as startups). When you are working to acquire a company, you are most likely looking for a PE partner.

There are many terms that you should understand, but here are three for starters:

▶ Pre or Post

Investors will ask you if the amount of money that you are raising in exchange for whatever percentage of ownership you are offering, is "pre" or "post." Pre is simply the value of the company before investment money comes in, while Post is the value of the company after investment money comes in. For example, if you are raising US$1 million and you are offering 33.3% Post, that means that you believe that your startup is worth US$3 million after their money is in the bank. This means that the Pre money valuation is US$2 million. Be prepared to defend these numbers. If you don't know the value (which is almost always the case), then tell the investor that you are willing to work with them to develop an accurate valuation. When investors ask you for an amount of money and a percentage of ownership, they are testing you to see if your thinking is in line with theirs. They will tell you what they think your startup is worth, how much money you need, and what percentage is, in their opinion, equal to that investment.

▶ LOI, MOU, and Term Sheets

An LOI is a Letter of Intent. An MOU is a Memorandum of Understanding. A Term Sheet is a document with an offer of investment and the intended terms and conditions. The investor creates and gives the LOI, MOU, and Term Sheet to the entrepreneur. (In the beginning of my career I made the mistake of giving a potential investor a term sheet that I had created. The investor thought it was humorous—he actually laughed at me. He also thought that my lack of experience and basic understanding of who gives the Term Sheet meant that I wasn't ready to receive one from him.) LOIs, MOUs, and Term Sheets are typically not legally binding; they are indications of the investor's thinking and what might happen; they are given to see if both sides of the conversation are aligned before any more time, money, and work is put into the deal to make an investment. The LOI and MOU typically come before the Term Sheet. Do not celebrate over an LOI, MOU, or Term Sheet. Once you accept a Term Sheet, the lawyers get involved to develop those terms into a shareholder agreement. Celebrate once the shareholders' agreement is signed and there is money in the bank.

▶ Tranche is sometimes spelled "Traunch"

In English we use tranche (sounds like: trawnch), the French word for *slice*, when talking about dividing up the money that you need into installments. Investors will typically tranche (slice up) the money that you are raising and tie each slice of money to you achieving what you say that you will do as a company. That US$1 million might be US$200,000 now to get you to that milestone in month eight that proves that you are on track, and then that will trigger then next US$200,000 (or whatever amount). Over time, you will eventually receive US$1 million (unless you have a discretionary term saying that if you overachieve your goals then you are not required to take later tranche ... work with a good lawyer to protect your future interests!). Be very careful of tranching when you are acquiring a company ... you need to structure the deal and the investment in a way that the capital lines up with all party's expectations and timeframes.

> **Read** *Mastering Private Equity*, Claudia Zeisberger, Michael Prahl, and Bowen White (2017)

> **ASSIGNMENT** Write at least one paragraph on this section. Explore and refine your questions. Will you be raising money? How much will you raise in exchange for what percentage of equity (ownership in your company)? Have you identified an investor? When will you start the process?

DECISION MAKERS, BOARDS, AND SHAREHOLDERS

If you have all decision-making responsibility and authority, that dramatically simplifies things. But if you don't, then you need to identify who can and will influence, and who has the power to sign off on the decisions that you need to make to turnaround the business. Keep in mind that not everyone who takes a meeting with you about your initiative can influence or make a decision.

The bottom line for what you need is:

1. **Authorization** to undertake the work to make your decisions happen.

2. **Ownership or Responsibility** to actually do the work.

The people whom you need to identify and engage, with the help of your champion, are:

1. **Influencers** who have the ear of decision makers and can advocate on your behalf.

2. **Decision Makers** who have signature authority and can make things happen for you.

If you are the decision maker, then move forward. If you are not the decision maker but you have direct access to decision makers, then engage them. Decision makers will often seek the counsel and advice of their trusted influencers, so chances are that you will eventually present to them as well (if you already haven't before presenting to the decision maker).

CORPORATE DEVELOPMENT

The CEO is typically the driver for corporate development, but there may be a department or group in the company responsible for planning and executing strategies designed to achieve company objectives. This could include recruitment, strategic alliances, mergers and acquisitions, disposition of company assets, developing or phasing out markets and products, the development and disposition of intellectual properties, and more. Taking this into consideration, the internal venture that you are working on will impact Corporate Development in one way or another, so you need to be aware and plan your message and approach on the topic.

There are at least two approaches to corporate development that you need to consider:

1. The company's current CEO's corporate development agenda and work
2. The post-acquisition CEO's corporate development agenda and work to be engaged

The two approaches above may be compatible or very divergent. Understand both scenarios.

What Corporate Entrepreneurship initiatives exist inside the company that you are working to acquire? Are they successful? Should they be preserved and continued? What initiatives will be pursued post acquisition?

All Corporate Development work gears around:

1. The performance of the company
2. The impact on the value of the company and shareholder value

Have a recommendation ready for potential investors, bankers, teams, etc., as to what is being done and needs to be done.

EXECUTIVE SUMMARIES AND BUSINESS PLANS

"Everyone has a plan 'til they get punched in the mouth."
—Mike Tyson, former heavyweight boxing champion of the world

Hopefully, you have been writing down all of your thoughts while going through each of the steps to this point. I have found great value in keeping track of all ideas or thoughts whether they seem relevant to me at the time or not.

You will need to complete a written <u>executive summary</u> (a document that takes the same amount of time to read as to drink a glass of water) that will help influencers and decision makers understand enough that they will 1. want to know more, and 2. be interested (or even excited) to support you and the initiative. A <u>business plan</u> is a long, more detailed executive summary.

▶ Executive Summary

An Executive Summary, not to be confused with a full Business Plan, is ideally two pages and no longer than three pages in length. It should have the most representative and most relevant details, which are explained in greater detail in the full business plan. Make sure that every word in the Executive Summary is relevant to persuade the reader that you know what you are doing to build and run the company. The Executive Summary should inspire the reader to ask you for more information.

▶ Business Plan

A Business Plan is a longer, more detailed document than an Executive Summary. A typical length for a business plan is 20–30 pages. When writing business plans you should bias the writing very heavily to execution detail; show what you will do, when, where, how, and why. State the problem, build out the execution detail around the solution to the problem, put some financials in so that the costs are understood, and call the reader to action. Use multiple proofreaders and listen to their feedback. Questions and comments give you insight into what is understandable and working (or not), so be grateful and never impatient with questions and comments.

(I once submitted a 30-page business plan to a government body, not realizing that they required a minimum of 100 pages because more pages demonstrated thorough and complete investigation and consideration. In the business world, a 100+ page business plan to an investor or leadership team might imply that you are overthinking or cannot succinctly say what you need to say.)

There is no single magic format or outline for business plans and executive summaries. You should write the details in a way that will flow most naturally and persuade the reader, while also providing a document that will help guide your running of the company.

The goal for an executive summary and business plan, along with all supportive financials, should be to use it as practice. Stay flexible, move with what happens, and update your documentation regularly so that you are ready at a moment's notice to share and present. Do not get caught with a summary or plan that is out of date; that moment might be the game changer. Keep updating, practicing, learning, and adapting to change as you go forward.

> **ASSIGNMENT** All of the topics explored in this framework can be used in your executive summary and business plan. Create your 2–3-page executive summary first in a separate document (name it uniquely and always save the date in the file name every time you update it). Once your executive summary is completed, save a copy of it as a different file (using "Save As … ") with the date in the file name in the same folder. Then, begin the work of meaningfully expanding the detail in each section until you have a 20–30-page full business plan.

PITCHING AND PRESENTATIONS

Practice until you are polished with your presentations. Write down what you will say, memorize everything so that you are not reading off of paper or slides while you present. Practice your presentations to friends and family and your team. Practice in the mirror. Record yourself on camera, then watch yourself and learn from what you see. Then practice more.

▶ Pitching

A pitch is a short format presentation. It should be quick, clear, and to the point. An elevator or lift pitch is typically no more than one or two minutes (the time it would take to get from one floor in a building to a few floors up). Quickly state your name, what you do for your company (this should take only a few seconds) and then get straight into the pitch. Your pitch should clearly state that there is an opportunity (a problem), something that can be done about the opportunity, what you are doing about it, and how the listener can be involved. Keep the pitch to the point and positive.

▶ Presentation

A presentation is a longer format pitch but has a similar structure.

> **HINT** Presentations tend to focus too much on the problem/opportunity and have too little practical detail on what can be done and what you are actually doing (aka execution). It is true that the listener needs to believe that you are addressing an authentic problem (do not solve a non-problem, and do not be a solution looking for a problem to solve) but remember that the listener needs to believe that you know what you are doing (execution level detail). Explain the opportunity and give representative detail into what you are doing about that opportunity.

It is common for people not to practice their presentations in advance. People often work on their materials up to the moment before presenting and then walk into the room and start. This is a mistake. Practice your pitch and presentations before giving them. There is no substitute for practice. Make sure that the first time that you pitch, or present is during practice rather than in front of the person whom you need to persuade. You only get one chance at a first impression. In case you feel that practice will make you less spontaneous in the moment, keep in mind that practice will make you better in a moment. For example, professional athletes practice SO THAT they will be better able to be more powerfully and effectively spontaneous in a moment.

The opportunity to persuade a key influencer or decision maker might happen at any moment. The quick two-minute pitch is called an elevator pitch or lift pitch because you might be in an elevator or lift when you realize that you are standing next to a key influencer or decision maker. You then have the amount of time that it takes to go from the ground floor to when they exit the elevator or lift to plant a seed. Hopefully they will invite you to present to them based on the strength of that one short pitch.

I have successfully pitched in elevators/lifts, hallways/corridors, stairways, sidewalks, while crossing the street, while at a salad bar, standing in a line/queue, while on the phone, and sitting next to someone on a plane. The point is that you never know when the opportunity will present itself. Practice your pitch over and over until you can say it without thinking about it. And practice it on different people to make sure that it makes sense and is coherent.

Practice your pitching without slides or props or other visual support. You never know when, where, or how you will be pitching. If your pitch is reliant on a slide or a prop, you might find yourself fumbling with your phone or computer, trying to pull up whatever you need, and end up burning the seconds or minutes that you have to persuade the listener. Also keep in mind that you only have a handful of seconds to create a powerful first impression; if you know what you are talking about and can say it off the top of your head without notes or visual assistance, then all the better.

If you have technology that can be quickly and effortlessly shown, then do it; just be aware that if it doesn't work then that is what the listener will remember.

Full presentations can start with a quick two-minute pitch at the top, to snapshot the long story short and give the audience an idea of what you are doing. Then you can start the longer format presentation. The longer presentation can include slides and product demonstrations if you have them; just remember to tell the story in an order that makes sense. Practice, practice, practice. There is no substitute for practicing before you present. Then after you've presented, practice some more.

As to time management, let's say, for example, that you are given a 30-minute meeting to present. Do not prepare 30 minutes of presentations and slides and demonstrations. A good rule of thumb is to prepare presentations for half of the allotted time. So, in this example you would prepare 15 (or 20 maximum) minutes of a presentation, for a 30-minute meeting. Leave room for questions during the presentation as well as questions and answers at the end.

▶ **Intro** (~5% of the available time)
Don't apologize—it is a common opener, but it is a poor start. Be confident but never arrogant.

▶ **The Opportunity/Problem** (~25%)

Do not pander or exaggerate; be factual.

▶ **What options are possible** (~15%)

Give a few examples of options. Do not make the mistake of speaking poorly of any alternative to what you are recommending. Be factual.

▶ **What I am doing** (~45%)

Do not hold back any secret ingredient (aka silver bullet or game changer) during your presentation. It is a common problem that the presenter will save the big "wow" of their solution for a follow-up presentation. If the audience doesn't hear the wow in your first pitch, there may not be a second presentation.

▶ **How you can be involved** (~10%)

Do not tell them what they will do. Welcome them to the party and invite them to be involved.

Start on time and finish on time (or a little early). Going over time should only happen if the audience asks you to stay and explain more. Even then, be sensitive to being over time. It is typically better to leave when you are ahead while they want more and schedule a follow-up.

Do not feel nervous or upset about any questions that might be asked of you. Questions expose holes in your presentation and tell you what was not clear or understandable to the listener (no matter how clear you thought that you made the point). Questions also give you an indication of what matters to the person asking the question. Write down all the questions that you were asked, and the answers that you gave, and then use those notes as preparation for future meetings (and work on clearer presentations and better answers for the future).

ASSIGNMENT Build the materials that you will need (e.g., 2–3-page executive summary, slides, etc.). Practice that 60-second pitch until you can say it without thinking. THEN start working on expanded detail versions of that pitch so that when people ask you to give them more you can do 60 seconds on this detail and 60 seconds on that detail. THEN work on a 30-minute expanded version of that pitch, which gives more meaningful insight and detail. Explore and refine your questions.

YOUR FIRST DAY, FIRST QUARTER, AND FIRST THREE YEARS

▶ **Day 1**

When you arrive on your first day, have a plan, and prepare to put it into action. When you walk in the door that first day, the people who are already in the company will be eager (and anxious) to see what you do.

Will you have a town hall meeting with everyone? Is that wise? Is it even logistically possible? What would you say? Are you prepared for tough questions (e.g., "will people lose their jobs?")? Are their unions in the company that you need to meet? If so, do you understand the current agreement(s) and negotiation cycles? Will you meet with key leaders? Will you move your office onto the floor with other workers or stay behind a closable door? The point is that you need to think things through *before* that first day. Don't show up without a plan that everyone on your new leadership team clearly understands. Then be prepared to stay flexible around that plan because your first day (week, month, quarter) will very likely not go according to plan. Be organized, and then do as Bruce Lee suggests "Be water my friend." Move in and around everything, understanding and measuring the shape of everything that you encounter.

▶ **Q1**

I have heard many people advocate big changes early in the tenure of new leadership. It is my experience that during the first two or three months you do not yet know enough to take drastic measures. You need a little time to gather your base of facts about what is really happening in the company. Remember that critical thinking is the gathering of facts that inform your opinions and plans around what you then do. Think critically, invest the work and time, before you act.

A cautionary note: Big surprises will typically show up in your first quarter.[7] During your first quarter in the company, turn over every rock in the company. Be prepared ... if there are any dead bodies or flesh-eating zombies, you will likely find them in this period. Dead bodies are those things that you thought were viable but it turns out they are not (e.g., bad relationships with customers, accounts receivables that you thought were viable but turn out to be dead and will be written off, poor intellectual property protection, etc.) Flesh-eating zombies are those things that actively work to cause ongoing harm (e.g., lawsuits, environmental problems, protests or strikes by workers, etc.)

My mother always said, "The true test of a person is not how they behave when things are good." Anyone can behave well during the good times; it is how they act when things are not good that shows their true character.

▶ **Y1–3**

Your first year's objective is to stabilize. If the company is already stable, then your goal is to not destabilize it.

---

7   In business we typically divide years into halves and quarters. The first six months is called H1 or the first half, and the second six months is H2 or the second half. The first three months is Q1 or the first quarter, then each following set of three months is the second, third, and fourth quarters or Q2, Q3, and Q4.

Your second year's objective is to achieve break-even. If the company is already breaking-even, then your goal is to not operate into a deficit.

Your third year's objective is to achieve profitability. If the company is already profitable then your goal is to keep it that way.

Growth is your objective in the third year. Work with your shareholders, board, and leadership team to ensure that your plans for the future of the company are consistent with their willingness to support you and what you plan to do going forward.

ASSIGNMENT Write at least one paragraph for each year and what you plan to accomplish. Think in the context of strategy and tactics. Explore and refine your questions.

STEP 24

SAVE YOUR WORK, UPDATE IT REGULARLY, AND REFER TO IT OFTEN

Revisit all of the above work regularly. Remember to save your work regularly and keep backups on separate secure devices. Once a day, or at a minimum once a week on a routine day at a routine time, review and update details for all of the above work. The last time that out of date documents created a problem for me was when I was asked to send my current business plan to a meeting deciding the placement of millions of dollars (in the dot.com era) and I was not ready in the moment. Since that day I have always had current documents ready to send whenever a shareholder, investor, or board member asks. It always makes a good impression when you are ready to send freshly updated documents when asked.

Every time you update the document, save a unique version in a common reference folder on your computer. Use a consistent naming convention and update the name every time to include the date that you modified it (or some other intuitive system that others, not just you, will understand if they need to find information).

You never know when you will need to give someone a copy of your plan. You might be given advance warning, but sometimes the call is unexpected. Do not be caught off guard with an out of date version! Be prepared, and you will have nothing to fear.

ASSIGNMENT Comb through your document. Save everything. If you write something and you aren't quite sure how it fits, either put the thought on the last empty page of the document or create a second document in the same folder just for thoughts that you aren't yet sure how to use. You do not want to find yourself in the situation where later on, you wish that you hadn't deleted that thought.

On future days when you open and edit the document, do a Save As and change the version date on the document so that it creates a new document that is saved in the same folder. It may happen that in the future you will want to refer to an earlier draft, and if anything happens to the file that you are working on that day, you can always go back to the most recent version rather than starting over.

Keep a backup somewhere other than on your computer. (You should regularly back up your entire hard drive.) If you are working on paper, you need to keep your binder safe and secure at all times. When you are able, you might have someone scan every page in the binder onto a file that you keep on a small portable computer stick for safekeeping. If you edit your document on a public computer, just make certain that you do not leave a copy of your document on the public hard drive.

Regularly update your writing, save copies, keep the dream alive, and work to make it real.

Stella Geneva Thomas Wilson

EVERY STORM PASSES

My maternal grandmother, Stella Geneva Thomas Wilson, was born in rural America in 1891. She was so small at birth that she slept in a shoebox. During the cold nights, they put the shoebox on the open door of the potbellied stove to keep her warm.

As an adult, at her full height, she was not half as tall as me. She had a step stool that she stood on to reach the countertop to cook and wash the dishes. When she was around 13 years old, she was taken out of school so that she could cook and clean for sick family members and others who needed help. In her 30s, when she was a mother of small children, she went back to a small one room schoolhouse to earn her 8th grade diploma; she wanted to show her children by example that a person finishing his or her education is important. (In the USA, 8th grade is around 13–14 years old.) She was charismatic, smart, grounded, spiritual, had a beautiful soprano singing voice, was a magnificent cook, and is one of my all-time favorite people.

I loved staying at her home and would happily go whenever I was able. Before the sun was up, she would wash the clothes and the floors, then do all of the cooking for the day. Every morning I would wake up to the smell of coffee percolating in the kitchen for my aunt; I think this is why I am comforted by the smell of coffee even though I don't drink it.

My Grandma was finished with the day's chores by the time the sun came up. Every morning she would stand on her footstool at the kitchen sink facing east to watch the sun rise over the mountains of Utah (USA). She would drink "two tall glasses of warm water" because it was good for your constitution. I would stand next to her watching the sunrise. It didn't matter the season, if the weather was peaceful or stormy; every morning was beautiful to her.

One particular morning, there was a terrible storm lashing wind and rain, pounding her little white house. She stood there calmly marveling at the new day. I said to her "Grandma, how can you be happy about this horrible weather? Look at the rain and wind and mess outside!"

She put her hand on mine and gave it a squeeze saying: "Ah Pauly. Don't be too worried about storms. In the vastness of the universe, our little planet and especially this storm in our little corner of this earth are smaller than the tip of a pin. Even more importantly, the sun is still shining completely unbothered by this storm. Every storm passes, you'll see."

I think about this when I am in life and business situations with storms and difficulties raging.

She spoke the truth. I know from experience that every storm does, in fact, pass.

TURNAROUNDS

"We cannot solve our problems with the same
kind of thinking we used when we created them."

—Albert Einstein

Years ago, I was investing my days at a struggling company, working to save it. During one of my first days in the company I was doing interviews with individuals and teams to assess the situation, and a middle manager said to me, "I know we are broken in too many ways to count. But rather than addressing the problems it feels like we are just driving around and not going anywhere in particular. As we drive, we are all sitting in the car looking out the window at the failing parts of our business. 'There is one—that isn't working. Yep, neither is that. Oh, look over there—surprise, surprise there is another.' A few times I've shaken my boss trying to point something out, but he is nonresponsive at this point. The drive goes on and on and we never get out to do anything about any of it. Now all of the tires are flat, the rubber is ripping off the rims, and pretty soon we'll be driving on bare rims and we aren't getting out to fix even the tires. The CEO is driving the car, and the other 'leaders' are sitting with him in the front seat looking shell-shocked. The rest of us have sort of given up thinking that we can fix any of it, there is just too much to fix, so we just keep driving around pretending we can't hear the scraping of the rims on the road. I suppose we are just waiting for the car to run out of fuel. It will be interesting to see whether we just sit in the car even after we stop moving entirely. When does someone show up to tell us to get out of the car? Is that you?"

The following is a 12-step framework for Turnaround Entrepreneurship training that I have created over the course of my career. The foundation of the framework is my personal experience and knowledge of what is expected from strategic others[1] and what works in practice. All types of organizations ranging from for-profit companies, non-profit entities, and governments, can use this framework to evaluate and address the challenges that they face inside of their organizations. This framework is not exhaustive but is designed to kick-start planning and execution to give you a path forward. The framework can be used to train teams around the world, across industries, and in structures of all sizes.

---

1   By "strategic others" I mean anyone who matters to what you are working to accomplish. These people might be investors, bankers, lawyers, boards of directors, shareholders, executives, workers, unions, the press, suppliers, customers, the government, etc.

Before you start this framework: If you have not already done so, please go back to the page called <u>START HERE</u> at the beginning of the book and complete parts 1, 2, 3, and 4 of the Preparatory Frameworks. Once that is completed, come back to this page and move forward to the following:

PREAMBLE **What Matters Most**

STEP 1 **Goals: Stabilization, Return to Break Even, and Return to Profitability**

STEP 2 **First Meetings: A. Lawyers, B. Chairman, C. Banks, D. Your Team**

STEP 3 **Champions and Canaries in the Coal Mine**

STEP 4 **Barriers and Roadblocks**

STEP 5 **Suppliers and Customers**

STEP 6 **Inventories**

STEP 7 **Financial Modeling**

STEP 8 **Fundable Event Timeline**

STEP 9 **Capital Modeling**

STEP 10 **Invention, Innovation, Renovation, and Revolution**

STEP 11 **Presentations**

STEP 12 **Save Your Work, Update It Regularly, and Refer to It Often**

The purpose of the framework is to help plan and execute the turnaround of a struggling or failing initiative, business unit within an organization, or a company. This framework will help those in a company to structure an execution-ready plan so that they can: 1. Persuade shareholders, the board, and other leadership to support their work to turnaround the company, 2. Persuade their organization's leadership to give financial and resource support, and 3. Allow the individual and teams to actually work the turnaround. This framework can be taught in-person or via technology or worked on privately by an individual or team. The 12-step framework is as follows:

PREAMBLE

WHAT MATTERS MOST

In my experience, individual heroics are a poor indicator of winningness over time, while individuals who practice and collaborate as a unified team do tend to win over time.

One form of heroics that might win in a moment but not over time is when a worker or leader stresses themselves to a breaking point. Take care of yourself. Your physical, mental, spiritual, and emotional health matters. Get enough sleep. Take time to exercise. Eat well. If you need someone to talk to, don't "tough it out" or "suck it up" or "be a man" (I know women who have suffered from this flawed mindset as well). Think of it in the context of the instructions that are given at the beginning of flights everywhere in the world, put the oxygen mask on yourself before assisting others. I am not the only person to have asked a flight attendant about the reasoning for the instruction. She told me "You won't be of any help to anyone when you are passed out because you don't have oxygen."

A healthy, well rested, well fed person will be more help to you than a sleep deprived, undernourished person. If your situation is dire enough, bring in healthy foods and fresh fruit and designate a safe and secure resting area.

Be inclusive and embrace diversity. Be an equal opportunity and equal pay for equal work employer. Importantly, create a psychologically safe[2] work environment.

ASSIGNMENT Create a plan for yourself and your team: when you will arrive, take breaks, eat meals, exercise/go for walks, and go home, sleep, and create psychological safety in your workplace.

GOALS: STABILIZATION, RETURN TO BREAK EVEN, AND RETURN TO PROFITABILITY

Calibrate your expectations.

> "I skate to where the puck is going to be, not where it has been."
> —National Hockey League all-time great **Wayne Gretzky**

If an elite athlete was in a life threatening accident during the Olympics and is now fighting for his or her life, your first priority should be ensuring that they live; *not* trying to get them back into the Olympics ASAP. In business, people will often push a failing company to perform, thinking that performance will fix the broken things rather than first working to understand what is broken and failing, performing necessary repairs to stabilize it, and ensuring a return to good health. Thus the first order of business should be to work out what is hurt inside the body of the failing business unit or company. Think and take action like a trauma surgeon working to find everything that is threatening the life of their

---

2   Psychological Safety is when individuals bring their authentic best selves to a situation. They show their real opinions and ideas because they feel safe doing so. Google maintains that Psychological Safety is the #1 factor in successful teams: https://rework.withgoogle.com/blog/five-keys-to-a-successful-google-team

READ *Fearless Organizations: Creating Psychological Safety in the Workplace for Learning, Innovation, and Growth,* Amy Edmondson

patient. Perform repairs to every vital broken thing, ensure that it stabilizes and starts functioning again.

Once the company is stable, take action to return it to normal functioning. For our athlete, this would be normal everyday living without pain or complications from the accident. In business, this is when you normally operate and make as much money as you spend (aka "break even").

Then our athlete can start planning and taking action to return to elite performance levels in their sport, and the same for your business unit and company.

When you try to force a sick body or a broken company to do more than it is able based on the realities of its condition, you might make the situation worse. Heal, then return with strength.

The first year of a turnaround should focus on stabilization. If you can stabilize sooner, all the better. The second year should be a return to break even (which is when you have as much money coming in as is going out). If you can break even sooner, all the better. Then the third year would be a return to profitability (which is when you have cash left in the bank after you pay all of your payables). If you can achieve sustainable profitability sooner, that will be welcome news. It is typically better to plan conservatively and then overachieve key performance indicators (KPIs), than to plan aggressively and come up short.

A note regarding your first three months of a turnaround: It is my experience that during the first two or three months you do not yet know enough to take drastic measures (such as firing employees and other "rightsizing" activities). You need a little time to gather your base of facts about what is really happening in the company. Remember that critical thinking is the gathering of facts that inform your opinions and plans around what you then do. Think critically, invest the work and time, before you act.

On the topic of firing people: In my teaching and work to turnaround struggling organizations, it is common for managers to start circling names of people to fire early in the process. Terminating someone's employment "For Cause" (meaning you can prove that they did something to violate their employment contract) is difficult. Firing good employees to save the organization, employees who are hardworking and loyal, is a miserable task. Think about all of your options very carefully, and do not be cavalier about the options and what you decide to do. Fully explore the possibilities, along with the causal effects, before you start circling names. Your actions will impact people's lives. If you do take the action, don't just cut them loose, help them think through their options and potential paths forward. Make introductions and connections as you are able. Don't just close the door, open doors for them if you can.

> **ASSIGNMENT**   Right now, you should establish for yourself that you are going to focus on stabilizing the company and how long that might take. The Board and Shareholders will likely have strong opinions about the timing. The same goes for a return to break even and then profitability. Work out your priorities and anticipated timing, then arrange a meeting with your Chairman.

FIRST MEETINGS:
1. LAWYERS, 2. CHAIRMAN,
3. BANKS, 4. YOUR TEAM

1. Lawyers

Establish contact with the current company lawyers. Meet ASAP to get their take on the company and to understand their position, relationship, and insight into the state of play at the company. Make changes if necessary. You need good corporate lawyers on your side who are ready and able to help as needed.

> **ASSIGNMENT** Treat your lawyer like a member of your team. The current lawyer might not be the right person or firm; you need to make this evaluation and make any necessary changes. Make sure that the lawyer and their firm are aligned with the objectives that you have agreed to with the Chairman of the Board.

2. The Chairman[3] of the Board and the Board of Directors

If the company that you acquire is small, you might be the chairman. You might consider bringing onboard an independent person who is expert in the industry to be the chairman. The board and chairman are vital to the success of the company, they are critical members of your team.

Keep the board, and the chairman if they are not you, fully informed and start with establishing alignment on the current state of play and the work that you are doing. You do not want the chairman or board to be caught off guard or surprised by anything that happens or anything that you are planning.

If you are not the chairman, I recommend setting up a regular update session with the chairman to make sure that you have alignment. This includes implications and impacts on Corporate Development[4].

The chairman will decide when there will be meetings to update the whole board.

> **ASSIGNMENT** Work with your chairman of the board to set up regular meetings. Seek alignment on what needs to be done, how, and by when. Ensure that you (and everyone in your organization) are clear on responsibilities and authorizations.

---

3   I am opting to use the word Chairman to mean the CEO's boss and leader of the Board of Directors regardless of any demographic details of the person who holds that responsibility.

4   Corporate Development is the big picture from the CEO, Board, and shareholder's perspective. It is when everything that you now know (as Critical Thinking) informs the CEO, Board, and Shareholders as to what is to be done, such as whether to invest in the necessary measures, or to take other actions (such as liquidation) to fulfill the responsibilities of the shareholders, company, stakeholders such as employees, all debtors, etc.

3. Banks

You need to get control of your cash and every detail that impacts your cash immediately. This means getting visibility on every detail at every bank account.

You need eyes on every detail of every facility at every bank. Make appointments ASAP to visit every bank and financial institution of any kind that is associated with the company. Make sure that you have all identification and paperwork proving that you have the right to access the account, Together with whoever in the company is responsible for the relationships, physically visit the bank(s), and financial institutions if possible (if not physically possible, call them on the phone and speak with a human being).

You need to inventory every penny owed by the company and every penny owed to the company.

If you do not control your cash, you are not in control of your business. If you control your cash, you are unlikely to run out of cash.

> "The first thing to do is to get control of cash. Then you have a chance of buying time while demonstrating control which is crucial when negotiating with potential sources. But if you never get control of cash in the first place and then run out, the company is dead." —Douglas Rosefsky

As a first step to get control of your cash, go to your bank right now and get eyes on your account(s). Don't just look at your bank statement to see transactions and balances. You need to see every rule and instruction on your account so that you can see every way that money leaves your account(s). Review signature cards (authorizations on the account, and who can sign for what and at which levels), account for all check books, review standing orders for automatic payments, review everything and check it all three times.

You might need to stop all payments temporarily by giving the instruction to turn everything off and then deliberately turn things back on one at a time. If you do this, the first things to turn back on would be mission critical payments such as paying employees. Open lines of communication with utilities and tax authorities; do not just stop paying them, but dialogue and plan together. Negotiate with suppliers, if need be, to delay payments. Do not panic them; carefully message everything (consider having your lawyer check all correspondence related to finances). Do not shoot off emails or calls signaling that your company is in trouble ... be diplomatic and tactful.

Before you turn payments back on, check every detail to make sure that they are correct. For example, verify everyone's pay line by line to make sure that each person is paid the correct amount. Check all account numbers and amounts for payments to suppliers. Comb through everything.

Special note: Do not miss a paycheck to employees; most people are counting the seconds until their pay hits their hands ... if you delay pay by a day you might create messes for them in their lives that will distract them at work and you do not want distracted and worried workers.

ASSIGNMENT Don't assume that those who are currently working in finance and accounting are the right people for the job. Sit down with each of them to discuss what is happening and how each of them make healthy and productive change possible in your business. Make sure that each person is aligned with the objectives that you have agreed to with the chairman of the board. Agree on the work that each will perform to ensure that all business processes and records are in order. Have each report any discrepancies to you.

ASSIGNMENT You need to see every possible way that money leaves the company. Update signature cards, update who has what authorizations with banks, review and update who authorizes or makes any payments of any kind inside or on behalf of the company. Update and review who places or agrees to any orders or purchasing of any type at every level in the company. Get control of the money; control the cash, and you will control the company.

4. Your Team

The broken things that need fixing in the company might be caused by people or by non-people (e.g., equipment, systems, processes and protocols, etc.)

> **HINT** People are the most difficult part of business. If you have the right people, you have a better chance of getting everything else right in your business.

> "The right team and execution can make gold out of rubbish. The wrong team and execution will make rubbish out of gold."
> —Paul Kewene-Hite

Be inclusive and embrace diversity. Be an equal opportunity and equal pay for equal work employer.

If you do not have an HR professional whom you trust in the company, you might seriously consider finding someone to work with you ASAP. Engage your professional network to find someone who is skilled at turnarounds and restructuring. Call their references to check before engaging them. You might be fortunate to already have an HR professional in house who is a clear thinker who understands your objectives and who knows everyone in the organization. Making sure the HR leader is the right person is a good step toward reviewing the rest of the organization to make sure that everyone is in the right position.

Do the same for the leader of Operations (this includes everything from physical facilities to equipment and technology).

Do the same for Accounting and Finance. Ensure that all policies and procedures are clear and working properly.

Do not assume that all is well with any of your departments and people just because they tell you that all is well. Years ago, I was working a turnaround, and the AP/AR (Accounts Payable and Accounts Receivable) person assured me that everything was working perfectly and according to "best practices." I asked her to give me a few detailed examples of her work, and it was immediately clear that she was paying everyone and everything immediately (to keep everyone happy), and she was rarely calling anyone who owed the company money because she did not want anyone to be unhappy about her call to collect money.

These behaviors were not company policy; they were what she considered to be the "best practice" because everyone was "happy." We found her another role in the organization where she could be happy making people happy in a customer care role, and we put a new person in the AR role and a new person in the AP role. The cash situation in the company began to improve very quickly. This is only one example of the level of detail that you need to explore into the people and processes of the company to see what is working, what is not, and why they are or are not working.

You need to find out what your team can see, what they are doing, and how they are feeling. Establish a structured interview and a method of gathering responses. Make it efficient. Be professional, kind, and sensitive to the challenges that teams, and team members may be facing. Warmth in the process will (in my experience) increase the effectiveness of it. You need to structure the interactions so that you can inventory and measure the problems (what is being done or not done), so that you can plan a path forward.

Sit down with each top leader, and then, depending on how big your organization is, you might visit with all or a representative sample of the workforce.

It is critical that you see as much of what is happening as possible, and it is equally critical that people believe that they are being heard and that something meaningful will result from the exercise.

ASSIGNMENT Create a structured interview that is no more than one page long (ideally no longer than 10 questions). If you are able, use technology to administer questions and then gather and analyze the data. Ideally this would be a blended delivery, with people sitting together to discuss things rather than potentially grumbling and frustrated people unhappily clicking buttons or ignoring what might be perceived as a cold and impersonal survey. Put as much humanity into the process as possible. Once you have the results, organize the feedback into a prioritized action plan. Then take action.

It is imperative that you understand how things are done in your company, what is working, and what is not. Of the mission critical activities, who is responsible for what? Who has what authorizations? What are the measures and controls?

If you are a typical company, you probably do not have good documentation, and many processes and protocols are higgledy-piggledy (meaning confused, disordered, haphazard). Now is the time to give clarity and structure to all mission-critical activities.

As you work to understand what activities are being done, what activities are not done but need to be done, how they are done, and what is working or not working, keep in mind that the effect of an activity matters more than the efficiency.

> "What is effective is not always efficient, and what is efficient is not always effective. Sometimes you choose to be less efficient in order to be more effective."
> —**Steven J. Hite,** EdD Harvard University, BYU emeritus professor of Educational Leadership and Foundations, Founder and CEO of TRUE Africa

The words efficient and effective are the same word in some languages. In English, the two words are causally connected but different. Simply stated: Efficient refers to how something is done. Effective refers to what happens as a result of what is done.

> **ASSIGNMENT** Inventory all mission-critical activities in the business. Write the name of the person responsible for each activity, then write the name of the person who has authority to make decisions for that activity. If the name of the responsible person is not the same as the person with authority, you need to understand why and what rules of engagement and protocols are formalized around the two. Being responsible with no real authority can be frustrating for the responsible person. If the responsibility and authority are in line with the best interest of the business and both effective and efficient, then all is well. If there are no rules of engagement or protocols, and/or if it is neither effective nor efficient then you need to build those rules and protocols. Do not make the mistake of leaving mission-critical activities without definition, and do not make the equally damaging mistake of over-engineering the rules and protocols to the point that the activity has a limited chance at success. Focus on the value creative effect of the rules and protocols, rather than the politics or efficiency.

It is vital that you work to understand what you can control, what you cannot control but you can influence, and what you can neither control nor influence.

> **HINT** As to where to start looking for mission-critical activities that are not working: 1. Where things have stopped and are not moving, 2. Where there is commotion (where there is smoke, there is fire), and 3. Look carefully at any area or people who are saying nothing or saying that they don't need help.

Take the inventory above and score it two ways:

1. Priorities
Those who can prioritize accurately and then take action according to their priorities tend to succeed ahead of those who do not. Most people just do stuff and then wonder why so little progress was made on the things that matter most.

2. Control, Influence, or Neither
Write a "C" for what is actually in the responsible person's control, an "I" for what the responsible person can influence but not control, and then an "N" for what is outside of the responsible person's control and influence. Then do the same for the person who has authorization (if they are a different person). (Important note: The only thing that anyone can actually control is his or her own thoughts and actions.)

▶ Then name the person who is responsible and who has authority over it. Make sure the people listed are qualified for the task. If you do not have a qualified person for that activity, then leave the name blank.

Once you have done this you will see the gaps around the mission critical activities with no associated names. This tells you who needs to be found and brought onto the team.

CHAMPIONS AND CANARIES IN THE COAL MINE

Quickly identify two types of people inside the company who can help with the situation: champions and canaries in the coal mine

▶ Champions

Look for individuals who can be effective and powerful allies as you work to take over the business. This is a person (or people) with credibility, power, and influence inside the organization. They can clear the paths, open doors, and protect your initiatives to give them time and resources necessary to succeed. A savvy champion can help you clear barriers and roadblocks.

Keep in mind that your leadership team and your employees are also your champions in a broader, yet very practical, sense of the word. Create a vision and a fact-based strategic, financial and operational plan with your leadership team that can then be used to convince the larger employee base regarding the path forward. Have a detailed plan for 18 months to two years; incorporate milestones and then measure performance to that plan (making necessary adjustments) over time.

▶ Canaries in the coal mine

Before electronic equipment that could warn you if there was an odorless and colorless gas in the mine that would kill you, miners would take happy but delicate singing birds into the mines. If the bird continued to sing happily, they knew that all was well but if the bird died, they knew to clear out and get to the surface. In groups of humans, including at work, there is typically a person whom everyone watches to see if they are happy about the company. If they are worried and leave, then others are more likely to do the same. So, it is helpful to identify the person or people whom others in the company watch and listen. Keep those people informed and on board, and the wider group is more likely to stay on board as well. One way to identify a canary is to listen for names that repeat positively in conversations, especially when people need help or insight into the company.

You will most likely not have the confidence of your champions and canaries on day one. This goes for everyone in the ecosystem from customers and suppliers, to employees and unions. Demonstrate from day one that confidence in you is warranted. Nurture the relationships, communicate transparently, do what you say you will do. Prove that trust in you is warranted.

ASSIGNMENT If you know the names of the people you need to bring onto your side, explain whom they are and what you plan to do to keep them informed and happy. If you do not know who they are then you need to explore how to find them and get to work. Write at least one paragraph on this section. Explore and refine your questions.

BARRIERS AND ROADBLOCKS

Anticipating and identifying the threats to success is very important. More than simply pointing at the potential barriers, identify what will be done about them. Be as honest and as clear-minded as possible about what might be in your way and what might be working to undermine your initiative. Work with your champion to identify and plan for overcoming barriers to your initiative.

Inside the company, the barriers and roadblocks might be as fundamental as a lack of resources and funding. Another might be a lack of authorization to pursue the work. Others inside the company might be threatened by the work that you propose to do or are doing. It could be that they are actively working to stop your progress and success for political reasons. Whatever the motivations or reasons, you need to identify what is happening and have a plan for how to deal with it.

Outside the company, there will also be challenges and competitive pressures, but this is normal business. You will need to have answers prepared in advance of presentations and discussions about what you see and plan to do about the challenges and competitive pressures.

Keep in mind that when people say that there are no challenges to what they are doing, that implies that either 1. They are naïve and fooling themselves, 2. What they are doing is of little value if it doesn't threaten anyone or the status quo, 3. They aren't trying hard enough if they are not meeting any resistance. Change and disruption sometimes makes others unhappy; anticipate who will be unhappy about what you are doing so that you can prepare and get ahead of what they might do in response. So resistance is not necessarily a negative or bad thing; it might mean that they are on the right path.

> **ASSIGNMENT** It is vital that you understand what might harm you and otherwise get in your way. Create a list. Very importantly, you must identify not only that the barriers exist, but what you will do about each. This will be very sensitive information, especially if it is regarding a person, so do not distribute this information. As soon as you click send on an email or click print you need to expect that the information is public domain info and the person in question will see a copy of it. Write at least one paragraph on this section. Explore and refine your questions.

SUPPLIERS AND CUSTOMERS

Review all agreements, especially the terms and conditions (aka the Ts & Cs) but also the relevance of the relationship with the business. Evaluate the performance of all relationships in the context of their profitability and value creation and preservation for the company. Meet key suppliers and customers as both opportunities to say hello and to gather data (as critical thinking). Be prepared and professional. Be careful not to make any promises or agreements until you fully understand the impact of those promises and agreements on the company's ability to stabilize and return to profitability.

Keep in mind that big suppliers and customers will have more capacity to work with you, but they are less motivated. Small customers and suppliers will have less practical ability to be flexible with you but they are more motivated. Do not exploit the motivations of small players; I have known customers and suppliers who have gone bankrupt trying to work with bigger players who have forced flexibility into the terms that favored the bigger player. Be sympathetic to the little player, especially when you are in a difficult situation yourself. Negotiate with the bigger customers and suppliers first. Understand their motivations and how you might help each other.

> **ASSIGNMENT** Work to understand the contracted terms, track records (good and bad on both sides of the relationship) and how essential each customer and supplier is to your business BEFORE meeting with them. Then meet with customers and suppliers in order of their importance to your company. Know what you need from them BEFORE you meet with them.

INVENTORIES

STEP 6

Beyond what you can see in a balance sheet and an asset list, you need to build a comprehensive inventory of all assets and their disposition, including land, buildings, furnishings and equipment, and more. Make sure that the asset list is up to date and detailed; for example, don't just say that you have a building, but describe the condition of it, the fair market value, any encumbrances, possible uses, what can potentially be done with it, etc.

If you have any raw materials, you need to inventory all viable and non-viable materials, including what is essential for normal business operation and for non-essential or outdated materials that you might be able to liquidate.

Then comes a more difficult type of inventory, which is an evaluation of products and product lines, and their profitability and value to the business, then business units and initiatives and their impact on the value of the business, then working teams, production lines, etc. and their value to the business. That will get you into an inventory of essential and non-essential personnel, FTE (Full Time Employee), PTE (Part Time Employee), contractors, temporary workers, and so on. You will need to consider what to keep and why. Think and plan long-term, then take action near term.

FINANCIAL MODELING

> "Never, EVER, run out of cash!"
> —**Patrick Turner**, INSEAD Professor of Entrepreneurship

Because you are working to turn around a struggling business, it is unlikely that you will have documents and data in a condition that will be helpful or complete. While turning around a struggling company you need to make peace with incomplete and flawed information. You will need to work to frame a financial model going forward that progresses you from the current state of imperfection to a version of the business in the future that has complete and accurate information.

If you can build a Cashflow from scratch, then you can explain the details when you are asked to defend the numbers during any meeting. When you present, have an updated copy of your Cashflow, and be prepared to explain the details to those who ask.

Work to frame a financial model going forward that progresses you from where you are to where you plan to go. Building a Cashflow (as well as an SG&A, P&L, Balance Sheet, along with Budgets for MDF/SDF, T&E/T&S, etc.) is fundamental for understanding your initiative. At this point you may not know what those words and acronyms mean, which is okay. You will, however, need to invest some effort in learning their meaning so that you can use them comfortably in sentences as well as comfortably answer questions about them when asked. The definitions are below.

In the business world it is very common for people to assume that other people will know how to build and read the numbers, so they invest very little study into it. Basic financial skills are very important for all people in business. Not everyone needs to be a Certified Public Accountant or Chartered Accountant but being able to build and read a Cashflow should be a required skill for all business professionals.

If an investor, board of directors, or shareholder calls you to a meeting to discuss your venture, grab an updated Cashflow on the way to the meeting. The other financial instruments such as a Profit and Loss (P&L), Balance Sheet, Sales General and Administrative (SG&A) etc., are also important but the Cashflow is the most critical. If you don't understand your cash position over time, you do not understand your business.

Good financial planning is key to persuading shareholders, the board, and leadership that you know what you are doing. If you don't (yet) know how to do it yourself, work side-by-side with a finance-professional to build complete financials. I say side-by-side so that you see how it is done, you fully understand the numbers, and can understand and explain the details. (If you can build a Cashflow from scratch then you can explain the details when you are asked to defend the numbers during any meeting.)

Here are a few overly simplified definitions of business words that you need to know:

▶ **Finance vs. Accounting**
Finance looks forward to what will happen.
Accounting looks back at what happened.

▶ **Payment vs. Expense**
A Payment is when money leaves the company and is given to someone else.
An Expense is the agreed responsibility to make a payment at some future date.

▶ **Revenue vs. Profit**
Revenue is all money that comes into the company from sales.
Profit is the money that is left over after you have paid all of your expenses and taxes.

▶ **Sources & Uses**
Source is where you will get money.
A Use is how the money will be spent.

▶ **Budget**
A Budget is the amount of money (and time) that must be invested in order to do what must be done. Importantly budgeted amounts need to factor for how much money (and time) is actually available.[5]

▶ **Cashflow**
A Cashflow is the financial detail of how a company is being operated; money coming in, all money measured impacts on debts and assets, and all money going out.[6]

▶ **Free Cashflow**
Free Cashflow (not to be confused with the document that is called "a Cashflow") is the money that you have left over after all capital expenditures (aka CapEx, which is the money spent on fixed assets).

▶ **Working Capital**
Working Capital = **Current Assets** minus **Current Liabilities**. Assets are tangible things that have value such as property, inventory, cash, etc. Liabilities are things that you need to pay such as debt, taxes, wages, rent, utilities, etc.

---

5   Budgeting is incredibly valuable and essential for running your entrepreneurial venture and making sure that you never run out of cash. Your budgets should be planned, reviewed, and updated routinely as a team. Be sure to remind everyone that a budget is more than a plan for how much money will be spent, it is a reconciliation of how much must be spent in order to accomplish your plan compared to how much money there is to spend in the bank account. Monthly budgeting meetings, accounting back a month, and financially planning forward a quarter are good practices.

6   This is a window into all money that comes in and leaves the company. (You should typically have an 18 to 24-month Cashflow, with the next 13 weeks by week, and the rest of the months by month.) Be sure to use mathematics rather than simply typing in numbers.

▶ Professional Fees

Professional Fees are cash paid to professionals who are not your employees, such as lawyers, accountants, designers, engineers, etc.

▶ CapEx vs OpEx

CapEx is Capital Expenditure, which is money spent on fixed assets.
OpEx is Operating Expenditure, which is the money spent to operate the company.

▶ Fixed Assets

Fixed Assets are physical things such as land, buildings, equipment, vehicles, etc.

▶ Burn Rate and Runway

Burn Rate is the amount of money that you spend in a month.
Runway is the number of months that you have until you are out of money.

▶ Break Even, and Profitability

Break Even is when the same amount of money comes in as goes out.
Profitability is when you have money left over after paying everything.

▶ Pro forma

Pro forma is Latin for "as a matter of form" or "for the sake of form" and is a word put on financials to show that the numbers are educated guesses or projections.

▶ T&E or T&S

T&S/T&E[7] is Travel & Subsistence or Travel & Expenses (occasionally referred to as Travel & Entertainment). This budget is for rental cars, trains, planes, hotels, lunches and dinners, etc. T&E is used in North American English and in North American influenced regions. T&S is used in British English and in British influenced regions.

▶ MDF and SPIF

MDF is an acronym for Market Development Fund and is the money that you spend to take your offering to market.
SPIF stands for Sales Promotion Incentive Fund and is a powerful tool for motivating the point of sale to inspire them to advocate for your offering over the competition (the seller and/or buyer). This could be, and is not limited to, a payment made to the salesperson or a discount/rebate offered to the customer.

> **ASSIGNMENT** Build a Cashflow. Do not assume that you will simply hire someone else to do it for you. Learn to build a Cashflow from a blank spreadsheet if you can; at a minimum, find someone on your team or work together as a team right now to build a basic Cashflow. Then write at least one paragraph on the details inside of the Cashflow, possibly including the

---

7 Watch this budget very carefully and put rules on all expenses and what can be claimed to make people responsible and hold people accountable. It happens at times that people (especially inside of large companies) game their expense reports so that they claim more money than they legitimately spend on real business. This line item can be value destructive when you are a fledgling venture that is carefully watching every dollar in the bank account.

details listed above. Explore and refine your questions. If you need to partner with a finance professional to help you, do it; but learn how to read financial documents, how to tell the stories of the numbers, and how to read along as others go through the numbers.

FUNDABLE EVENT TIMELINE

As a companion to the Cashflow as well as an inventory of mission-critical activities, create a Gantt chart of those activities (highlighting milestones and fundable events) then harmonize it with a Cashflow.

You can build your Gantt chart in a spreadsheet if you don't have project management software. What matters is that you can see the bars that represent the start and stop dates for each activity. On each bar you should name the activity as well as who is responsible along with the associated costs.

When you build a Cashflow you should then harmonize it with the Gantt chart to ensure that the activities and costs over the same months align month-by-month.

When you are building the timeline with the completed Gantt on the top of the page and the Cashflow lined up below it, decision makers can quickly see that your financial and activities-based planning is complimentary in their construction.

The next thing that I suggest that you do is identify the **Milestones** (the moments in time when you complete an activity or task) on the Gantt chart. Then differentiate between which milestones simply mark the completion of a task and which milestones are actually evidence that you are right in what you intended, planned, and executed. (This could be a working prototype or a paying customer, etc. This is very different from finishing the writing for a business plan for example, which does not prove that you are right but just that you finished what you started.) The type of milestone that is evidence that you are right, is called a **Fundable Event** and it is very important for a few reasons.

▶ Evidence that you are right shows that the entrepreneurial venture is making progress!

▶ Evidence that you are right will be the proof that you need for continued funding and support from the company leadership and board.

▶ Evidence that you are right can be correlated to value creation (increasing value) and value capture (when the company is able to hold on to and make use of the value). Fundable events correlate to the increase in the value of what you are doing, and potentially increase the value of the company itself.

Investors and boards and others who hold the keys to your future funding will be watching for the Fundable Events so that they can know that the work is progressing and that your corporate entrepreneurial venture is deserving of continued support.

When you have the Fundable Event Timeline planned out, and you regularly update it (you should update it at a minimum of once a week), you and those who are supporting you can use it to keep track of progress and timings that might change over time.

Investors and boards and other financial supporters might use the Fundable Event Timeline to plan when they will transfer resources and capital support to your initiative (just as an investor would do for a startup); when you hit your deliverables (the milestones and especially the fundable events), you have a measurable defense for expecting ongoing support.

ASSIGNMENT Write at least one paragraph on this section. Explore and refine your questions. Create a Gantt chart identifying all of your activities (when each activity is intended to start and stop). Then put the Gantt chart and your Cashflow summary on the same page making sure that the months line up as shown in the following template (and on page 410). (You should have built a Cashflow in step 7.) Highlight the milestones that prove that you are right to call them Fundable Events. This is when the machine you are building actually works; it is when a stranger who has no connection to you purchases your product, etc. A fundable event is not when you simply finish what you started, such as writing a business plan or building a Cashflow with numbers that look good or designing a brochure that makes you happy, etc.

TEMPLATE

FUNDABLE
EVENT
TIMELINE

Cashflow Summary

	Month 1, Year 1	Month 2, Year 1	Month 3, Year 1	Month 4, Year 1	Month 5, Year 1	Month 6, Year 1	Month 7, Year 1	Month 8, Year 1	Month 9, Year 1	Month 10, Year 1	Month 11, Year 1	Month 12, Year 1
Opening Cash Balance												
Total CapEX												
Total OpEx												
Total Cash Out												
Total Cash In												
Closing Cash Balance												

Execution Timeline (Gantt Chart)

ACTIVITY	OWNER	ASSOCIATED COSTS US$	Month 1, Year 1	Month 2, Year 1	Month 3, Year 1	Month 4, Year 1	Month 5, Year 1	Month 6, Year 1	Month 7, Year 1	Month 8, Year 1	Month 9, Year 1	Month 10, Year 1	Month 11, Year 1	Month 12, Year 1

Note: Milestones mean that you finished what you started. Fundable Events are validation that you are right.

CAPITAL MODELING

You need to determine what capital will be required to fuel your turnaround, and from where that support will come.

You now have enough thought invested that you should know what it will cost to do it. The question is: where will you receive the capital if your revenue is insufficient?

A foundational question around capital is Sources and Uses. Sources are from where the capital comes and Uses are how you deploy that capital.

You have at least two key Uses:

1. **Cash money considerations**
   You need to pay salaries, taxes, insurance, legal fees, and potentially many other things in your SG&A (Sales, General, and Administrative) planning. How much money will you need to cover your expenses for the first year? What about the second year and so on? From where will you receive those funds?

2. **Potential Non-Cash considerations**
   What office space will you use? Will the company let you use company offices without charge, or will there be an associated fee? What about desks, chairs, computers, phones, Internet, etc.? If you cannot use company assets and need to invest in your own, that moves all of these considerations back to the Cash money considerations.

   Is your team all in the same area or are you scattered around the world? If you are scattered, then you might need to arrange for an office space for each person individually (which is just more negotiations than a single space for everyone). Then you will need to communicate as best you can, as often as you can. This becomes costly in time, effort, and potentially, in real money terms.

As to the potential Sources of capital, consider the following options:

▶ **The company**
   Does the company have money to invest in its own turnaround and recovery?

▶ **Government support**
   There could be grants and other money (such as loans) available from local or national governments for the type of work that you are doing. You might explore conversations ranging from the local mayor's office to national levels to see what might be possible.

   The motivations for government are typically around job creation and economic growth. So when you are presenting, be ready with information geared around jobs and economic impact.

- **External investors**

  Will you need to seek help from external investors? Will you seek their involvement as debt or equity (ownership in the company)? Work with the Chairman on the details of whether this is the optimal path forward.

- **Banks**

  It is easier to get a loan when you don't need it. But it might be possible to work with a bank to give you a line or credit or some other facility.

Important note: Be very careful with debt. Most people are not good with debt and end up in more trouble because of it. If you have a solid plan for servicing the debt, then speak with the Chairman and seek a loan if there is no other path forward.

Sources of capital will want to know that you have invested time and thought into what it will take to make your corporate entrepreneurial venture successful. The numbers don't need to be perfect (they rarely are exactly right), but you need to demonstrate that you have thought through all of the possibilities for what is needed.

ASSIGNMENT Keeping the above in mind, write at least one paragraph on what capital will be required for your turnaround. Give some meaningful detail in defense of the numbers and amounts. Prepare to be challenged on the details. Explore and refine your questions.

STEP 10

INVENTION, INNOVATION, RENOVATION, AND REVOLUTION

It will be helpful for you to decide which of the following is needed by your company:

Invention ▶ Uncommon. This is when you work to achieve what has never been before. This can be done but it is comparatively rare, and it is often the most expensive in both cost and time.

Innovation ▶ Common. This is when you take an existing thing and materially change, modify, adapt, and reposition it into a new and improved thing. The key here is that innovation is done to something that already exists. This is significantly more common than invention and typically less expensive in both cost and time. Importantly, innovation does not necessarily stay positioned where it is at the moment; part of the innovation is that it might be repositioned and/or relocated.

Renovation ▶ Common. Renovation makes material modifications and adaptations to something that already exists, but it differs from innovation in two respects: 1. The renovated thing is typically intended to stay positioned where it already is, and 2. The primary goal is to uplift and refresh the thing so that it can be revived and stay relevant.

Revolution ▸ Uncommon. This is when you engage (maybe even fight against) the way that things are to effect significant change from the status quo, so that things can become what they should be. Revolution commonly requires invention as well as innovation, and the renovation of many things rather than effecting change to only one specific thing.

Nothing ▸ *This fifth option is the most common.* Most companies do more of the same, even when they know that they need to change. Doing something just to be doing something, or because you can, is also not good enough, and might be value destructive rather than value creative. Do not break something that is working and should not be changed. Think about this carefully; this question circles back to question #1: WHY are you doing whatever it is that you plan to do?

Most people do not work to effect change in their turnaround. You might.

ASSIGNMENT Write at least one paragraph in your own words about what you plan to do. Then identify whether or not this work will require invention of something new, an innovation or renovation of an existing thing, or a revolution to overthrow something. Explore and refine your questions.

PITCHING AND PRESENTATIONS

You will be giving presentations often as you work to turnaround your company. Presenting to your team(s), the Board, banks, etc.

Practice until you are polished with your presentations. Write down what you will say, memorize everything so that you are not reading off of paper or slides while you present. Practice your presentations to friends and family and your team. Practice in the mirror. Record yourself on camera, then watch yourself and learn from what you see. Then practice more.

▸ Pitching

A pitch is a short format presentation. It should be quick, clear, and to the point. An elevator or lift pitch is typically no more than one or two minutes (the time it would take to get from one floor in a building to a few floors up). Quickly state your name, what you do for your company (this should take only a few seconds) and then get straight into the pitch. Your pitch should clearly state that there is an opportunity (a problem), something that can be done about the opportunity, what you are doing about it, and how the listener can be involved. Keep the pitch to the point and positive.

▶ Presentations

A presentation is a longer format pitch but has a similar structure.

> **HINT** Presentations tend to focus too much on the problem/opportunity and have too little practical detail on what can be done and what you are actually doing (aka execution). It is true that the listener needs to believe that you are addressing an authentic problem (do not solve a non-problem, and do not be a solution looking for a problem to solve) but remember that the listener needs to believe that you know what you are doing (execution level detail). Explain the opportunity and give representative detail into what you are doing about that opportunity.

It is common for people not to practice their presentations in advance. People often work on their materials up to the moment before presenting and then walk into the room and start. This is a mistake. Practice your pitch and presentations before giving them. There is no substitute for practice. Make sure that the first time that you pitch, or present is during practice rather than in front of the person whom you need to persuade. You only get one chance at a first impression. In case you feel that practice will make you less spontaneous in the moment, keep in mind that practice will make you better in a moment. For example, professional athletes practice SO THAT they will be better able to be more powerfully and effectively spontaneous in a moment.

The opportunity to persuade a key influencer or decision maker might happen at any moment. The quick two-minute pitch is called an elevator pitch or lift pitch because you might be in an elevator or lift when you realize that you are standing next to a key influencer or decision maker. You then have the amount of time that it takes to go from the ground floor to when they exit the elevator or lift to plant a seed. Hopefully they will invite you to present to them based on the strength of that one short pitch.

I have successfully pitched in elevators/lifts, hallways/corridors, stairways, sidewalks, while crossing the street, while at a salad bar, standing in a line/queue, while on the phone, and sitting next to someone on a plane. The point is that you never know when the opportunity will present itself. Practice your pitch over and over until you can say it without thinking about it. And practice it on different people to make sure that it makes sense and is coherent.

Practice your pitching without slides or props or other visual support. You never know when, where, or how you will be pitching. If your pitch is reliant on a slide or a prop, you might find yourself fumbling with your phone or computer, trying to pull up whatever you need, and end up burning the seconds or minutes that you have to persuade the listener. Also keep in mind that you only have a handful of seconds to create a powerful first impression; if you know what you are talking about and can say it off the top of your head without notes or visual assistance, then all the better.

If you have technology that can be quickly and effortlessly shown, then do it; just be aware that if it doesn't work then that is what the listener will remember.

Full presentations can start with a quick two-minute pitch at the top, to snapshot the long story short and give the audience an idea of what you are doing. Then you can start the longer format presentation. The longer presentation can include slides and product demonstrations if you have them; just remember to tell the story in an order that makes sense. Practice, practice, practice. There is no substitute for practicing before you present. Then after you've presented, practice some more.

As to time management, let's say, for example, that you are given a 30-minute meeting to present. Do not prepare 30 minutes of presentations and slides and demonstrations. A good rule of thumb is to prepare presentations for half of the allotted time. So, in this example you would prepare 15 (or 20 maximum) minutes of a presentation, for a 30-minute meeting. Leave room for questions during the presentation as well as questions and answers at the end.

Here is a thumbnail EXAMPLE of how much time should be spent on each part of the presentation:

▶ **Intro** (~5% of the available time)
Don't apologize—it is a common opener, but it is a poor start. Be confident but never arrogant.

▶ **The Opportunity/Problem** (~25%)
Do not pander or exaggerate; be factual.

▶ **What options are possible** (~15%)
Give a few examples of options. Do not make the mistake of speaking poorly of any alternative to what you are recommending. Be factual.

▶ **What I am doing** (~45%)
Do not hold back any secret ingredient (aka silver bullet or game changer) during your presentation. It is a common problem that the presenter will save the big "wow" of their solution for a follow-up presentation. If the audience doesn't hear the wow in your first pitch, there may not be a second presentation.

▶ **How you can be involved** (~10%)
Do not tell them what they will do. Welcome them to the party and invite them to be involved.

Start on time and finish on time (or a little early). Going over time should only happen if the audience asks you to stay and explain more. Even then, be sensitive to being over time. It is typically better to leave when you are ahead while they want more and schedule a follow-up.

Do not feel nervous or upset about any questions that might be asked of you. Questions expose holes in your presentation and tell you what was not clear or understandable to the listener (no matter how clear you thought that you made the point). Questions also give you an indication of what matters to the person asking the question. Write down all the questions that you were asked, and the answers that you gave, and then use those notes as preparation for future meetings (and work on clearer presentations and better answers for the future).

Build the materials that you will need (e.g., 2–3-page executive summary, slides, etc.). Practice that 60-second pitch until you can say it without thinking. THEN start working on expanded detail versions of that pitch so that when people ask you to give them more you can do 60 seconds on this detail and 60 seconds on that detail. THEN work on a 30-minute expanded version of that pitch, which gives more meaningful insight and detail. Explore and refine your questions.

STEP 12

SAVE YOUR WORK, UPDATE IT REGULARLY, AND REFER TO IT OFTEN

Revisit all of the above work regularly. Remember to save your work regularly and keep backups on separate secure devices. Once a day, or at a minimum once a week on a routine day at a routine time, review and update details for all of the above work. The last time that out of date documents created a problem for me was when I was asked to send my current business plan to a meeting deciding the placement of millions of dollars (in the dot.com era) and I was not ready in the moment. Since that day I have always had current documents ready to send whenever a shareholder, investor, or board member asks. It always makes a good impression when you are ready to send freshly updated documents when asked.

Every time you update the document, save a unique version in a common reference folder on your computer. Use a consistent naming convention and update the name every time to include the date that you modified it (or some other intuitive system that others, not just you, will understand if they need to find information).

You never know when you will need to give someone a copy of your plan. You might be given advance warning, but sometimes the call is unexpected. Do not be caught off guard with an out of date version! Be prepared, and you will have nothing to fear.

ASSIGNMENT Comb through your document. Save everything. If you write something and you aren't quite sure how it fits, either put the thought on the last empty page of the document or create a second document in the same folder just for thoughts that you aren't yet sure how to use. You do not want to find yourself in the situation where later on, you wish that you hadn't deleted that thought.

On future days when you open and edit the document, do a Save As and change the version date on the document so that it creates a new document that is saved in the same folder. It may happen that in the future you will want to refer to an earlier draft, and if anything happens to the file that you are working on that day, you can always go back to the most recent version rather than starting over.

Keep a backup somewhere other than on your computer. (You should regularly back up your entire hard drive.) If you are working on paper, you need to keep your binder safe and secure at all times. When you are able, you might have someone scan every page in the binder onto a file that you keep on a small portable computer stick for safekeeping. If you edit your document on a public computer, just make certain that you do not leave a copy of your document on the public hard drive.

Regularly update your writing, save copies, keep the dream alive, and work to make it real.

GRACE UNDER PRESSURE

There is no magic formula for how to be graceful under pressure. Some people are naturally good at it, others work hard to develop the ability, and the rest struggle with it (some to the point of running away when the going gets tough).

When I was a child, while our neighborhood was celebrating the 4th of July, a little girl caught on fire when she accidentally touched a sparkler[1] to her dress. Her dress immediately caught fire. In a fully understandable panic, she started running and screaming. Adults and children around her froze. My mother had been lying on a blanket in front of our house, up the road, on the other side of the street. As soon as the girl caught fire, my mother immediately jumped to her feet grabbing the blanket she had been sitting on, sprinted down the road, and wrapped the girl in the blanket, putting out the flames. Doctors at the hospital commented that my mother's swift action saved the little girl's life.

In a crisis, too many people freeze. I remember freezing as a child that 4th of July. Other people panic, react in fear, or get angry. Be the person who takes decisive, deliberate action. My mother saw and quickly evaluated what was happening (critical thinking), surveyed her options and available tools (problem solving), and took swift action (execution). Transaction time: less than a minute.

---

1 "A sparkler is a type of hand-held firework that burns slowly while emitting colored flames, sparks, and other effects." Wikipedia

ABOVE
Carol Wilson Hite

When I was around five years old my older brother picked me up from an activity, which was odd because my mother had told me that she would pick me up. My brother and I went home, and I started watching television. The phone rang and my older siblings started earnest conversations behind a closed door with whoever was on the phone. I was the youngest of the six kids, so I was not included in the hushed conversation. They were protecting me. Whoever it was who called (I don't know if it was a firefighter or police officer) explained that there had been an accident and they found our number from the license plate of the car. Our mom's car had exploded into a ball of flames on the road. She had just filled up the tank, so there was plenty of fuel to burn. When the fire was out they could not find a body and whoever was on the phone asked my siblings if they knew where our mother was at that moment. It turned out that she was standing with other onlookers in the crowd. They found her, and she explained that while she was driving she felt a bump in the rear left of the car. She saw a tire bouncing past her on the left. She looked in her rear-view mirror and saw flames barreling forward toward her inside the car. She opened the driver's door and rolled out onto the road, then the car flipped and exploded. She sat up, stood up, and joined the other drivers who had stopped their cars and stepped onto the road to watch the car burn until firefighters arrived. We later learned that the lug nuts on the new rear left tire had not been tightened. My mom had asked my brother to pick me up that afternoon because it was payday, which meant that she could finally go buy new tires to replace the bald tires that she had been worrying about on the car.

Again, she saw what was happening, quickly surveyed her environment (which is critical thinking), determined what to do (which is problem solving), and took deliberate action (which is execution). Transaction time: seconds, as time stopped with a crisis in motion.

Carol Wilson Hite (my mother) was never a leader of a corporation, or a manager of teams in a business, but she was an excellent example of staying calm, clear headed, and action oriented in a crisis. (I could tell many other stories about her!)

My mother never boasted about her calm composure under pressure. While growing up, whenever I was not as calm and collected as I should have been, she would say "Pauly, just remember that the true measure of a person is not how they behave when things are good."

How to respond well under pressure can be learned and practiced. Take the time to learn and practice. I'm still working on it, and I'm hopefully getting better over time. Being like my mom is my goal.

CRISIS
LEADERSHIP

"There's always an opportunity with crisis.
Just as it forces an individual to look inside himself, it
forces a company to reexamine its policies and practices."
—Judy Smith

If there is a health and safety emergency in your company, call the emergency numbers in your area immediately before doing anything else.

This framework is designed to help you think through a difficult moment that you are experiencing in your company. If you or someone you are trying to help is experiencing a personal crisis and you need someone to talk to, please call a crisis hotline[1] in the country where you are right now to ask for help. Your life matters. Please reach out and talk to someone now.

> "Ah Pauly. Don't be too worried about storms. In the vastness of the universe, our little planet and especially this storm in our little corner of this earth are smaller than the tip of a pin. Even more importantly, the sun is still shining completely unbothered by this storm. Every storm passes, you'll see."
> —Stella Geneva Thomas Wilson
> (my maternal grandmother)

Regarding your business:

Too often people just "do stuff" and wonder why things aren't getting any better. It is interesting to me that when people feel that they are experiencing a crisis in their company there are three basic approaches to the situation:

1. Doing nothing.

2. "Fighting fires" (meaning that you rush from one problem to the next).

3. Addressing, dealing with, and eliminating problems at the source.

The following is a 9-step framework for Crisis Leadership training that I have created over my career. The framework can be used to train teams around the world, across industries, and in structures of all sizes.

---

1 If you don't know who to call, here are a few crisis numbers that might help: In the USA, Canada, and Mexico for a mental health crisis call 2-1-1 for all other emergencies call 9-1-1; In the UK for mental health ring 116123 or for all other emergencies ring 9-9-9; In Australia for mental health dial 13 11 14 or for all other emergencies dial 0-0-0; In New Zealand for mental health call 0800 543 354 or for all other emergencies call 1-1-1.

For a list of suicide crisis numbers please go to:
https://en.wikipedia.org/wiki/List_of_suicide_crisis_lines

For a list of emergency numbers around the world visit:
https://en.wikipedia.org/wiki/List_of_emergency_telephone_numbers

Before you start this framework: If you have not already done so, please go back to the page called START HERE at the beginning of the book and complete parts 1, 2, 3, and 4 of the Preparatory Frameworks. If you are pressed for time, at a minimum read parts 1 and 2. Once that is completed, come back to this page and move forward to the following:

STEP 1 **Emergency Help, The Chairman, Board, Shareholders, and Lawyers**

STEP 2 **Critical Thinking and Problem Solving**

STEP 3 **Neutralizing and Stabilizing**

STEP 4 **Measures and Controls for Team and Execution**

STEP 5 **Champions and Canaries in the Coal Mine**

STEP 6 **Barriers and Roadblocks**

STEP 7 **Updates and Presentations**

STEP 8 **Take Care of Yourself and Your Team**

STEP 9 **Save Your Work, Update It Regularly, and Refer to It Often**

This framework will help leaders who are dealing with crises in their company to structure an execution-focused plan so that they can persuade shareholders, the board, and other leadership to support what they plan to do. The 9-step framework is as follows:

EMERGENCY HELP, THE CHAIRMAN, THE BOARD, SHAREHOLDERS, AND LAWYERS

If there is a health and safety emergency in your company call the emergency numbers in your area immediately before doing anything else.

As soon as immediate physical dangers have been addressed, contact the chairman and inform him or her about what is happening in detail. You do not want the chairman to find out about your crisis from the evening news or someone else through the grapevine. Call the chairman right now; the chairman should decide whether to call an emergency meeting of the board and whether to involve shareholders.

Next, get the company lawyer on the phone as soon as possible. Explain everything that you know in detail; this is to ensure that you are fully compliant with the law and taking every action required by law. Document everything with copies to the lawyer with details so that you are fully compliant with all laws. Do not hide or fail to disclose any details.

CRITICAL THINKING AND PROBLEM SOLVING

You need both right now.

As a reminder: Critical Thinking is the gathering of FACTS to inform your opinions and actions. Problem Solving is when you use critical thinking to puzzle through what you will do.

> "Those parties who are impacted by a crisis are often very good partners to help you think critically through the crisis."
> —Douglas Rosefsky

Work with your team, your leadership team, key employees who are your champions, the chairman, lawyers, accountants, finance professionals, bankers, etc.

If your crisis is not criminal or medical or in any way physical, then you are already in a better situation than you might think.

As to difficulties with a situation in your company, chances are you don't have enough information, so start with the verifiable facts that you do know. If you or your team has guesses, then pursue those guesses to validate or refute them with data and evidence.

> "Crises in a company are much more complex, with more dimensions, than most physical fires."
> —Douglas Rosefsky

Keep in mind that two things happening at the same time (which is correlation) does not mean that the one is what made the other thing happen (which is causation).

Philip Merilees' 1972 talk on chaos theory titled, "Does the flap of a butterfly's wing in Brazil set off a tornado in Texas?" articulated a much-referenced notion that seemingly little things could cause big things. The bottom-line is that when a crisis happens you need to understand what happened (big or small) so that you can repair it if you are able.

Very importantly, in a difficult moment you often do not have the luxury of waiting to understand the cause of a situation. You very often need to take action to address the symptoms before you understand the cause, not unlike an emergency room quickly deciding which life-threatening wounds to address first, and which painful but non-life-threatening wounds should be next.

I have had a number of surgeons in my classrooms over the years. Even though we might be running a business crisis simulation, it is interesting how often the surgeons will give similar instructions for the business. (I am not a doctor, but this is from my note taking when I listen to them speak.) Stop the bleeding so that you can repair the wounded organ. Reintroduce the blood flow and see if anything is leaking. If there is a leak, stop the blood flow again while you look for other damage, and assess if the sutures are holding. Search around the area to make certain that no other damage is visible. Look everywhere, lifting and feeling around not only at the source of the original obvious bleeding.

I have also had firefighters, other emergency response professionals, and military personnel in my classes. When you are dealing with a fire, for example, there are several things that you will do no matter what caused the fire. All fires need three things: 1. Heat, 2. Oxygen/ Air, and 3. Fuel. Removing potential sources of fuel and depriving any fire of oxygen (air) will typically extinguish the fire. But if removing fuel sources and smothering out oxygen is not an option and you don't know what type of fire you are dealing with, you might make it worse by attempting to put it out with a method that is appropriate for a different type of fire (for example, using water on an oil or grease fire will likely make it worse).

When you are in a crisis you need to 1. Take measures to neutralize the spread of the threat, regardless of what caused it, and 2. Work to understand what happened to cause it so that you can neutralize it. In that order. Repairing a punctured heart or lung is the first objective, the secondary priority would be figuring out what damaged the organ, and a tertiary, post-operation goal would be to understand what caused the wound in the first place.

The path to this discovery is rapid critical thinking, but it can become mired in emotionalism and finger pointing in the moment if you aren't careful. You and your team need to be dispassionate while being compassionate as you work to gather facts to inform your opinions that become plans that become action.

You should structure interviews that are simple to administer and track in advance as part of your SOP (Standard Operating Procedures). If you don't have such a thing, you will need to think about what you know of the crisis and ask your team to administer a simple three-question survey to all of their direct reports or affected parties. The questions should validate and explore what you think you know while opening the door to what you do not yet know. Have your team write down the answers. Then aggregate the answers and look for trends. Then construct a new set of questions and go again. By the third round you should be on the path to discovering what happened and what is at the heart of the cause of the crisis.

> **ASSIGNMENT** Write down everything that you know for a fact is true about the situation. Organize the details into a coherent story of what happened. Where there are gaps, make an Assignment for someone to figure it out. Then compose a clear action plan with unambiguous Assignments to those on your team who are best able to execute with positive results.

NEUTRALIZING AND STABILIZING

For 10 years at INSEAD, I taught a real-time role-play simulation course on turning around a failing company. The course simulates a series of crises, putting participants under constant pressure so as to train them how to respond calmly and professionally. By the second day of the course, all participants have been conditioned to anticipate the worst while they try to hope for the best. I work to get them to take action ahead of the problems that plague them, working to prevent fires or the spread of fires as they burn (or rage seemingly out of control), but most participants never get out of firefighting mode.

We bring in real people as role-players and put participants into a series of crisis situations to see how they will perform; the role-players then score the engagement and give feedback on what worked and worked less well. It is interesting to me how often people are paralyzed in the moment and are unable to take reparative action on the fly. Participants often feel paralyzed by a lack of quality information about what actually happened and why. They try to pause the moment while they gather facts (critical thinking), but when you have an angry person yelling at you it is tough to perform critical thinking. Participants often try the "no comment" approach, but this typically comes across poorly, as it implies that they don't know what happened or they are hiding something. The angry role-player typically wants participants to take action NOW and not hesitate or wait. The best-performing participants work to create psychological safety[2] in the moment, even before they fully understand the details of why they are even in the situation in the first place.

Interestingly, a meaningful percentage of angry role-players respond that what they really wanted in the crisis situation was 1. to be heard, and 2. to know that the team was trying to work through a solution with them even if it was clear that a good solution was not really possible.

Once you figured out (to the best of your ability) why something happened to cause a crisis, you perform corrective surgery to repair it correctly. But in the middle of a situation, the cause of the problem is your second priority ... your first situation is to create safety.

You have two things to deal with in this order:

1. The responses from humans, systems, and potentially the press, etc. to what happened.
2. What happened.

Neutralize the threat or problem, and begin the work to stabilize everything that is impacted. Focus on effectiveness, not efficiency.

---

2   Psychological safety is when individuals feel they can bring their authentic best selves to a situation. They show their real opinions and ideas because they feel safe doing so. Google executives maintain that psychological safety is the #1 factor in successful teams.

READ *Fearless Organizations: Creating Psychological Safety in the Workplace for Learning, Innovation, and Growth,* Amy Edmondson (2019)

Efficient refers to how you do what you do. Effect refers to what happened as a result of how you did what you did.

If an elite athlete was in an accident and is now fighting for his or her life, your first priority should be ensuring that they live, not trying to get them back into their sport ASAP. In business, people will commonly push a failing situation to perform rather than first working to understand what is broken and failing, performing necessary repairs to stabilize it, and ensuring a return to good health. Thus, the first order of business is to work out what is hurt inside the body of the failing moment. Think and take action like a trauma surgeon working to find everything that is threatening the life of their patient. Perform repairs to every vital broken thing, and ensure that it stabilizes and starts functioning again.

Once the situation is stable, take action to return it to normal functioning. For our athlete, this would be normal everyday living without pain or complications from the accident. In business, this is when you operate normally and make as much money as you spend (aka "break even").

Then our athlete can start planning and taking action to return to elite performance levels in their sport. The same goes for your business unit and company.

When you try to force a sick body or a broken situation to do more than it is able based on the realities of its condition you might make the situation worse. Heal, then return with strength.

ASSIGNMENT Create psychological safety. Create a space that encourages critical thinking (fact finding and discovery) and problem solving without attitude or being judgmental. Write down what you know and what you are doing to solve the situation.

STEP 4

MEASURES AND CONTROLS
FOR TEAM AND EXECUTION

> "The right team and execution can
> make gold out of rubbish. The wrong team and
> execution will make rubbish out of gold."
> —**Paul Kewene-Hite**

It is vital that you work to understand what you can control, what you cannot control but you can influence, and what you can neither control nor influence.

Inventory what needs to be done and score the inventory two ways:

1. **Priorities**

   Those who can prioritize accurately and then take action according to their priorities tend to succeed ahead of those who do not. Most people just do stuff and then wonder why so little progress was made on the things that matter most.

2. **Control, Influence, or Neither**

   Write a "C" for what is actually in the responsible person's control, an "I" for what the responsible person can influence but not control, and then an "N" for what is outside of the responsible person's control and influence. Then do the same for the person who has authorization (if they are a different person). (Important note: The only thing that anyone can actually control is his or her own thoughts and actions.)

   ▶ Then make assignments as to who is responsible and who has what authority.

During the uncertainty in and around a crisis, people need to know what they can and cannot do, and what is expected from them. Depending on the type and magnitude of the crisis, you might be highly prescriptive with the dos and don'ts, but you might give general guidelines and let them govern themselves. Some level of what needs to be done by whom, when, where, how, and why will be needed, so that people aren't left drifting in the mix as things happen around them.

> **ASSIGNMENT** Inventory your top 20 (or more) mission-critical activities. Put names of committed team members next to each activity. The critical activities that have no name next to it tell you whom you need to recruit to help you. Write at least one paragraph on this section. Explore and refine your questions.

CHAMPIONS AND CANARIES IN THE COAL MINE

Quickly identify two types of people who can help with the situation: champions and canaries in the coal mine.

▶ Champions

Look for individuals who can be effective and powerful allies as you work to take over the business. This is a person (or people) with credibility, power, and influence inside the organization. They can clear the paths, open doors, and protect your initiatives to give them time and resources necessary to succeed. A savvy champion can help you clear barriers and roadblocks.

▶ Canaries in the coal mine

Before electronic equipment that could warn you if there was an odorless and colorless gas in the mine that would kill you, miners would take happy but delicate singing birds into the mines. If the bird continued to sing happily, they knew that all was well but if the bird died, they knew to clear out and get to the surface. In groups of humans, including at work, there is typically a person whom everyone watches to see if they are happy about the company. If they are worried and leave, then others are more likely to do the same. So, it is helpful to identify the person or people whom others in the company watch and listen. Keep those people informed and on board, and the wider group is more likely to stay on board as well. One way to identify a canary is to listen for names that repeat positively in conversations, especially when people need help or insight into the company.

> **ASSIGNMENT** If you know the names of the people you need to bring onto your side, explain whom they are and what you plan to do to keep them informed and happy. If you do not know who they are then you need to explore how to find them and get to work. Write at least one paragraph on this section. Explore and refine your questions.

BARRIERS AND ROADBLOCKS

Anticipating and identifying the threats to success is very important. More than simply pointing at the potential barriers, identify what will be done about them. Be as honest and as clear-minded as possible about what might be in your way and what might be working to undermine your initiative. Work with your champion to identify and plan for overcoming barriers to your initiative.

Inside the company, the barriers and roadblocks might be as fundamental as a lack of resources and funding. Another might be a lack of authorization to pursue the work. Others inside the company might be threatened by the work that you propose to do or are doing. It could be that they are actively working to stop your progress and success for political reasons. Whatever the motivations or reasons, you need to identify what is happening and have a plan for how to deal with it.

Outside the company, there will also be challenges and competitive pressures, but this is normal business. You will need to have answers prepared in advance of presentations and discussions about what you see and plan to do about the challenges and competitive pressures.

Keep in mind that when people say that there are no challenges to what they are doing, that implies that either 1. They are naïve and fooling themselves, 2. What they are doing is of little value if it doesn't threaten anyone or the status quo, 3. They aren't trying hard enough if they are not meeting any resistance. Change and disruption sometimes makes others unhappy; anticipate who will be unhappy about what you are doing so that you can prepare and get ahead of what they might do in response. So resistance is not necessarily a negative or bad thing; it might mean that they are on the right path.

> **ASSIGNMENT** It is vital that you understand what might harm you and otherwise get in your way. Create a list. Very importantly you must identify not only that the barrier exists, but what you will do about each. This will be very sensitive information, especially if it is regarding a person, so do not distribute this information. As soon as you click send on an email or click print you need to expect that the information is public domain info and the person in question will see a copy of it. Write at least one paragraph on this section. Explore and refine your questions.

UPDATES AND PRESENTATIONS

STEP 7

> "I skate to where the puck is going to be, not where it has been."
> —National Hockey League all-time great **Wayne Gretzky**

Think very carefully about what messages you will share with whom.

If you have unions or other employee organizations in the company, you need to work with your lawyer and chairman to put together a message for them, as well as the employees.

Consider what messages you will give to your workers. Will you do a town hall? Where would you hold it? Who will be invited? What will you say? Will you be prepared for angry and potentially hostile questions from them? What will you say and do in response? Town halls are a potentially risky move when you have a crisis underway. Consult with the chairman and lawyer as well as your leadership team.

If you send a broadcast message out, be very careful about every word in that message. You need to know that anything that you send will be 100% outside of your control once you click send. Even if you put the word "confidential" in the email, it will be forwarded to others outside of your influence. As you are typing, you need to ask yourself about every word both in and out of context: "How will this read on the evening news?"

Speaking of the press, you need to think what messages you will share if a news crew arrives at your door. Will you turn them away? How will that look and sound on the radio and TV tonight when they say that you refused to speak with them? If you speak with them will you give details? If so, which details? If you speak with the press, here are a few considerations:

1. Keep your messages short and to the point. (Resist the urge to explain in long detailed sentences.) Every word that you speak can be used in follow-up questions. The more you say, the more you are giving people to misinterpret.

2. Stick to the facts as you know them to be. Do not speculate, and do not guess. If you are asked questions that you do not know how to answer, it is okay (in most cultures) to suggest that you have a follow-up conversation once you know more.

3. Do not cast blame and do not use words that imply guilt. Once you know with certainty what happened, you can think through the best way to explain it.

4. To the best of your ability use only positive words. Negative words (even simple clarifying words such as "no," "don't," and "can't") may intensify how people are feeling. Rather than saying what isn't or can't, say what is and can.

5. Do not repeat any negative words that the employees, interviewer, or anyone else might say. Pick a positive word in their question and build a positive response around it. Question, "How many dangerous machines are in your factory?" Do not say: "We don't have dangerous machines." Say something like: "All of our machines are safe when operated correctly."

6. If you decide to not give details about the crisis, keep in mind that saying "No comment" sound like A. you are hiding something, and/or B. you don't know. Sticking to a "no comment" line of response is difficult, so pay careful attention as you go.

7. In most cases, it is okay to suggest that the press return later when things are calmer so that you can answer questions more fully.

8. In most cultures, coming across as boring is better than coming across as emotional. Boring is stable. Emotional can come across as not thinking clearly and might add fuel to the emotions that others are already processing through around the crisis.

9. Use a tone that is appropriate for your culture and environment. Most cultures respond best to a calm, neutral tone. In most countries, a response that sounds boring is better than an emotional or excited response.
   ▶ People will not always remember the specific words and details of what you say but they will remember how they felt when you said it.

Before a crisis happens, practice answering difficult questions when you are being recorded on a camera with a microphone in your face. Hire a professional to train you. In a crisis people will be listening to every word that you say. If you have the luxury of a few minutes to prepare, practice, practice, practice, what you will say.

ASSIGNMENT Even if you only have a few minutes to prepare, practice what you will say and practice face-to-face with another person. Practicing in a room by yourself might help you feel calmer; do this if you feel that it is essential to your calming down, but a trusted person can give you feedback on how you sound. The person with whom you are practicing should ask you very difficult questions when you practice. (Note: If you are not in an active crisis, take the time to practice before you are in a real situation.)

STEP 8

TAKE CARE OF YOURSELF AND YOUR TEAM

In my experience, individual heroics are a poor indicator of winningness over time. Individuals who practice and collaborate as a unified team tend to win over time.

One form of heroics that might win in a moment but not over time is when a worker or leader stresses themselves to a breaking point. Take care of yourself. Your physical, mental, spiritual, and emotional health matters. Get enough sleep. Take time to exercise. Eat well. If you need someone to talk to, don't "tough it out" or "suck it up" or "be a man" (I know women who have suffered from this flawed mindset as well). Think of it in the context of the instructions that are given at the beginning of flights everywhere in the world, put the oxygen mask on yourself before assisting others. I am not the only person to have asked a flight attendant about the reasoning for the instruction. She told me "You won't be of any help to anyone when you are passed out because you don't have oxygen."

The same is true for your team: healthy, well rested, well fed team members will be more help to you than sleep deprived, undernourished people. If your situation is dire enough, bring in healthy foods and fresh fruit and designate a safe and secure resting area.

Importantly, create a psychologically safe work environment.

ASSIGNMENT Create a plan for yourself and your team: when you will arrive, take breaks, eat meals, exercise/go for walks, and go home, sleep. Think about how you can create psychological safety in your workplace.

SAVE YOUR WORK, UPDATE IT REGULARLY, AND REFER TO IT OFTEN

Revisit all of the above work regularly. Remember to save your work regularly and keep backups on separate secure devices. Once a day, or at a minimum once a week at a routine time on a routine day, review and update details for all of the above.

Every time you update the document, save a unique version in a common reference folder on your computer. Use a consistent naming convention and update the name every time to include the date that you modified it (or some other intuitive system that others, not just you, will understand if they need to find information.)

It may happen that someone will need to know something, or all things, in this framework. Do not be caught off guard with an out of date version! Be prepared, and you will have nothing to fear.

ASSIGNMENT Comb through your document. Save everything. If you write something that you aren't quite sure how it fits, either put the thought on the last empty page of the document or create a second document in the same folder just for thoughts that you aren't yet sure how to use. You do not want to find yourself in the situation where later on you wish that you hadn't deleted that thought.

On future days when you open the document, do a Save As and change the version date on the document so that it creates a new document that is saved in the same folder. It may happen that in the future you will want to refer to an earlier draft, and if anything happens to the file that you are working on that day you can always go back to the most recent version rather than starting over.

Keep a backup somewhere other than on your computer. (You should regularly back up your entire hard drive.) If you are working on paper, you need to keep your binder safe and secure at all times. When you are able you might have someone scan every page in the binder onto a file that you keep on a small portable computer stick for safekeeping. When you are able you might have your handwriting transcribed onto a computer document; you might check with a local library to see if you can use a computer there. If you edit your document on a public computer just make certain that you do not leave a copy of your document on the public hard drive.

Regularly update your writing, save copies, keep the dream alive and work to make it real.

PSYCHOLOGICAL SAFETY

In 1965, MIT professors Edgar Schein and Warren Bennis argued that psychological safety was essential for making people feel secure and capable of changing their behavior in response to shifting organizational challenges."[1]

Psychological Safety is a focus of Harvard Business School professor Amy Edmondson's very important life's work. Psychological safety is when individuals are able to bring their authentic best selves to a situation. They show their real opinions and ideas, because they feel safe doing so. They are confident that they will be heard with no negative impact on them or their status in the conversation or organization (or relationship) going forward.

After a multi-year study, analysts at Google determined that Psychological Safety is the #1 factor in successful teams. "The five keys to a successful Google team" are: 1. Psychological Safety, 2. Dependability, 3. Structure & Clarity, 4. Meaning of Work, and 5. Impact of Work.[2]

To create psychological safety in your work and life, Professor Edmondson offers **SAFE** as an acronym: Setting Limits, Approachability, Fallibility, and Engagement.

Setting Limits

Some people and organizations frame their rules of conduct and engagements as their "ethos." Ethos is the Greek word for character. Ethos is the rule or law of good conduct, and it is the driving guide by which decisions are made.

When I was the CEO of a small technology company, I was approached by a weapons manufacturer who wanted to integrate our tech to make safer training weapons. Our founders and shareholders (who held

	ACCOUNTABILITY	
COMFORT QUADRANT	**LEARNING** QUADRANT
PSYCHOLOGICAL SAFETY: **HIGH**	PSYCHOLOGICAL SAFETY: **HIGH**
ACCOUNTABILITY: **LOW**	ACCOUNTABILITY: **HIGH**
APATHY QUADRANT	**ANXIETY** QUADRANT
PSYCHOLOGICAL SAFETY: **LOW**	PSYCHOLOGICAL SAFETY: **LOW**
ACCOUNTABILITY: **LOW**	ACCOUNTABILITY: **HIGH**

PSYCHOLOGICAL SAFETY (HIGH / LOW)

ACCOUNTABILITY (LOW / HIGH)

---

1   Psychological Safety: The History, Renaissance, and Future of an Interpersonal Construct, Annual Review of Organizational Psychology and Organizational Behavior / Volume 1, 2014, / Edmondson, pp 23–43

2   Julia Rozovsky, Analyst, Google People Operations (Google's HR) (17 November 2015)

controlling interest in the company) voted against the opportunity, saying that involvement with weapons of war, even safer weapons, violated the ethos of the company. We did not do the deal, even though we needed the money.

Approachability

On my first day at a major technology company, a senior executive presented to a large group saying, among other things, that his door was always open and to stop by any time. Later that day, I was late for my first meeting (remember, this was my first day), and I ran down a hallway, looking for the meeting room. I saw his door open. I knocked, stuck my head inside, and asked if he could direct me to the meeting room. He stormed at the door, yelling at me, then yelling at his secretary that she needed to keep idiots like me from bothering him. I stammered rather naïvely, "But you said your door was always open, and it was actually open … " He slammed the door with such force that I was surprised the glass didn't explode. His secretary trembled as she told me where the meeting room was located and suggested that I avoid him and his door like the plague. I took her advice. Over the years I've learned from others who have said that their door was open, but then they were unkind when approached, that you need to show (not just say) that you are approachable. Be open and be kind.

Fallibility

People tend to mask their insecurities and weaknesses with bravado, arrogance, anger, and condescension. I've always loved the lyric in Sting's song "Shape of My Heart,"

where it says, "I'm not a man of too many faces, the mask I wear is one." Be the same person at home, work, and out with friends. Wear no masks; wear your own true face everywhere you go. This doesn't mean that you tell all of your secrets and troubles during a presentation to the board, it simply means that you should be normal and be yourself when you walk into a room. People respond to honesty. Truth resonates.

Engagement

There was a senior executive who regularly claimed full credit for my ideas and work in presentations to the top leadership. When I asked him about it, he said, "That is what you do when you are the boss. You should take the ideas from your team as your own as well. It is part of the privilege of being the boss. It is what leaders do." In a meeting with senior leaders a short time later, I presented my team and gave them credit for their ideas and praised their work. After the meeting, the above mentioned senior executive called me into his office and told me that I would never succeed in business if I kept giving credit to "underlings." I don't believe in "underlings" and I reject the condescension that goes along with referring to anyone in such a demeaning way. Share, and play well with others. Don't take other people's ideas or things. Be good, be kind, be generous and open. Praise and embrace the good work of others, and give credit where credit is due.

Psychological safety takes courage, focused deliberate work, and time. The investment will be well worth the effort. It isn't easy, but it does in fact start with you. Be SAFE.

READ THE BOOK *Fearless Organizations: Creating Psychological Safety in the Workplace for Learning, Innovation, and Growth*, Amy Edmondson (2019)

BUILDING AND REBUILDING
YOUR CAREER

"The greater danger for most of us lies not in setting our aim too high and falling short; but in setting our aim too low, and achieving our mark."

—Michelangelo

My first boss after university gave me a US$20 bill one morning and told me to go to a bookstore at lunch and buy a copy of the book *What Color is Your Parachute?* by Richard Nelson Bolles. On my lunch break I walked across the street to the mall, went into the bookstore, found the book, bought it, and took it back to my boss with the change. He looked at me and said, "You've misunderstood me. The book is for you. This isn't the right place for you. You should be doing more with your life. It is time for you to move on to bigger things." I remember standing in front of him unsure if I understood what he was saying. He had a goofy smile on his face. He said, "You're fired. You have two weeks on the payroll then I want you to fly onto bigger and better places than this." He awkwardly swooped his hand into the air as he said it. I did my work, and on breaks, in a daze, I started reading *What Color is Your Parachute?* trying to figure out my next step. It was a very strange experience. After a few days he stuck his head into my office and said, "How is it going? Find your next thing yet? By the way, just to be clear, my firing you is a compliment. You have greater potential than this place. I just don't want you to wake up one morning years from now asking yourself 'Why am I still here?'"

Years later, I had another employer slowly cancel my work piece-by-piece, little by little, over time, until I had very little work to do. After making a bid for my contract to be renewed, I was told that my contract would not be renewed and I had until the end of my contract to find my next opportunity. I should have seen it coming. In hindsight, I did see it coming, but I absolutely loved the work that I was doing, and I didn't want it to end. As part of my processing through the stages of grief over it, I read several books including *Who Moved My Cheese?*, Spencer Johnson (1998); I actually laughed out loud when I saw myself very clearly in one of the characters in the book. I decided to get over myself and look for new cheese (my next path forward).

You might be in a job where everything is shifting under and around you. You might feel like the end is coming. You might feel like you could continue coming in and sitting at the same desk moving the same papers from one side of the desk to the other for as long as you live, but maybe you want more. Or maybe things used to be better, and now they are getting progressively worse. Maybe you are out of a job entirely and need to find work ASAP. Whatever you might be experiencing at work (or no work) right now ... you are reading this workbook. So ... what should you do now?

This is not a framework designed to get you a job quickly; this is more of a "planning your path" framework, and one of the results may be better positioning for a new gig sooner than later. This framework is not exhaustive, but it is a place to start thinking things through.

Before you start this framework: If you have not already done so, please go back to the page called START HERE at the beginning of the book and complete parts 1, 2, 3, and 4 of the Preparatory Frameworks. Once that is completed, come back to this page and move forward to the following:

STEP 1 **Your Basic Idea and Big Play**

STEP 2 **Your 10-Year Plan**

STEP 3 **Your Offering and Value Proposition**

STEP 4 **Marketing, Business Development, and Sales of You**

STEP 5 **Your Barriers and Roadblocks**

STEP 6 **Your Execution**

STEP 7 **Your Call to Action or The Ask**

STEP 8 **Your Pitching and Presentations**

STEP 9 **Save Your Work, Update It Regularly, and Refer to It Often**

One more thought before you get going. My definition of courage is doing what must be done even though you are afraid. Reinventing and rebuilding takes courage. Use whatever anxieties, fears, and doubts you might be wrestling with as a fuel for your work. Everyone has fears. Imposter syndrome[1] is more common than you might think. We all experience FUD (fear, uncertainty, and doubt) but what we do with our FUD makes all of the difference. Use your FUD as fuel to get things done.

YOUR BASIC IDEA AND BIG PLAY STEP 1

The basic idea is to be able to: 1. Feed yourself and your family, 2. Pay your bills, 3. Get out of debt, 4. Stay out of debt, and 5. Live within your means.

The big play is to experience genuine happiness on the path to achieving your dreams and to accomplish something that is meaningful and brings you joy.

If you have seen the classic Jimmy Stewart movie *It's a Wonderful Life*, you will know (if not ... spoiler alert) that it took a painful and shocking process for the main character to realize that he was already living a meaningful and wonderful life despite his not having done the big adventurous things that he had always dreamt of doing.

---

1   Imposter syndrome is a term for when people doubt their accomplishments and fear being exposed as a fraud.

As I travel the world teaching and speaking about entrepreneurship, people often ask me about their dreams for their lives and whether or not they can achieve those dreams.

> **Read** *How Will You Measure Your Life?*, Clayton Christensen, James Allworth, and Karen Dillon (2012)

> **Read** *Questions Are the Answer: A Breakthrough Approach to Your Most Vexing Problems at Work and in Life*, Hal B. Gregersen (2019)

"How did you know what you wanted to do as a career?" I asked my father's younger brother, Tom Hite. He chuckled and said that he was still wondering what he should do when he grows up. At the time, he was retired from the US Navy with the rank of full Commander. After his retirement from the Navy, he launched a second career as a sales professional for a technology company that wanted to sell their products to the Navy. When I asked him about his post-Navy job he said, "I am fluent in Navy-English and regular English and I have learned technology-English, so I help both sides of the conversation understand each other. You could say that I'm an interpreter who is paid commission on the transactions that my translations make possible." During our conversation, he dreamed out loud about the dozen careers that interested him and what he wished he had time to explore and do in one lifetime. He loved his career in the Navy and would not change it, and he loved his new career in technology, selling to the Navy, and would not change it. He knew that he was lucky to have two careers that he loved, when most people struggle to find one.

I know people who have worked as lawyers, then shifted gears to become technology startup entrepreneurs, people who have left careers as accountants to become teachers of young school children, doctors and scientists who have become executives in large corporations, a private equity investor who became a high school administrator, and a high school administrator who became a private equity investor, and more. Don't be limited or defined by what you've been doing in years past, be emboldened by what you dream to accomplish.

Everyone has a dream. You might be a dentist who wants to teach Classics, or a truck driver who wants to be a real estate developer. Whatever your situation, take the opportunity to explore how you might pivot (shift and reorient your direction and trajectory) to find a new place that 1. Helps you feel fulfilled, and 2. Covers your needs financially (so that you can feed your family and pay your bills). You might also be exactly where you want to be, and you want more from it, or it has left you and you need to decide what to do now.

> **ASSIGNMENT** If you already use the cloud to back up all of your work securely, that is excellent. If you regularly use software that keeps track of versions of your work, so that you never invest hours editing the wrong version of a document, that is superb. If, however, for any reason, you are not yet able to back-up in the cloud or you do not have access to software that keeps track of versions of your documents, you will need to do these things manually. If you are working on a computer, create a folder with a logical name that you will not forget. Put that folder in an obvious location on the computer (not a clever place, but a clear and easy to remember place), that will still be obvious to you tomorrow and the next day. Create a new document and save it in the folder that you just created. Name the file something easy to remember and give it today's date; then every day you edit it, save a version with that day's date so that you can tell the difference between files. Always work on the most recent date

and version of the file. If you do not have a computer, buy a spiral binder with lined paper (or an equivalent that is available to you). Put your name and contact information on it and keep it in a safe place. Do all of your work in the document or binder.

ASSIGNMENT Write at least one paragraph on what you have done and what you are doing THEN what you would like to do next. Explore and refine your ambitions as questions.

ASSIGNMENT Once you identify a potential new career, create an inventory of the skills and characteristics of that would be required of someone in that job/career.

YOUR 10-YEAR PLAN

STEP 2

In 1998, when my oldest son was a year old, I remember opening a blank PowerPoint slide on my computer (while Joshua was asleep, draped over my shoulder) and typing on the left side, "1998: Silicon Valley Entrepreneur," and on the right side I typed "2008: Top 10 business school Professor." Then in the middle between the two I typed, "How do I get from here to there?"

Wayne Dyer published his book *The Power of Intention* in 2004. I would say that without knowing it, what I was doing in 1998 was putting the power of intention in play.

I started doing research into the backgrounds of professors at top US business schools, then in 1999 I added the *Financial Times* (FT)[2] top 30 business schools to see how many had Silicon Valley experience or had ever worked in technology companies, and what they did (ranging from degrees to jobs) in between those jobs and becoming professors. It was not easy research in 1998. These years later, the research would be much simpler thanks to the evolution of the Internet and how people document their lives on it. With what information I could find, I started mapping the possible paths from where I was to where I wanted to go. I mapped overlapping trends in types of roles in companies, graduate degrees earned, etc.

I started marking anticipated months and years by when I would need to do what (ranging from roles in companies to applying to PhD programs). I mapped specific programs based on those attended by professors with backgrounds and interests that seemed most similar to mine. I made telephone calls, trying to interview as many professors as I could to ask them about their paths to where they were now. It was not an easy project. It took me a few months of stolen moments in and around my work and time with my young family, but I came up with a 10-year road map from where I was to where I wanted to go.

My roadmap was not a do-or-die single line, must-do path; it had many potential paths with forks in the roads and projected dates for what I needed to do by when. I was focusing

---

2   I chose the *Financial Times* (FT) over USA-focused rankings such as the *U.S. News & World Report* (which despite the "*World Report*" part of the name only reports on and ranks US schools). The FT ranks all schools worldwide.

on what I could control, not the things outside of my control. For example, I yearned to be accepted at a top PhD program; I could take the examinations and apply, but I could not control being accepted. I could apply for jobs that I thought that I needed to advance my career, but I could not control whether or not I was hired.

I could, however, control whether or not I started a company. Factors in the economy and world that were outside of my control made things interesting. We had great highs and lows, and I focused on staying flexible on my path. I remember being thunderstruck when I read a quote by Jack Welch: "Strategy is not a lengthy action plan. It is the evolution of a central idea through continually changing circumstances." It hit my thinking powerfully, and the more I worked on what I was doing to achieve my dreams and things worked, or didn't work, the more I refined his quote to work with how my life was going. In time, I found myself developing a version of it into a mantra of my own as I tried thousands of locked doors, and walked through those few doors that were open to me: "Strategy is not a lengthy action plan etched in stone, it is the practical capacity to stay flexible around a central idea."

I was determined to make myself as appealing as possible in 10 years' time (by 2008), to be hired as a professor of entrepreneurship at a Financial Times top 10 business school. There were several possible paths, common trails that had forks in the road, and I realized that even if I never became a professor at a business school, I would become better as a result of the process.

I remember telling friends and family members about my 10-year plan, and the responses were occasionally supportive but not always encouraging. A few congratulated me on having the dream and wished me well with it. One of my favorite people on the planet laughed at my 10-year plan. In 1999, a person I love and respect told me, "Do you have any idea how many PhD graduates are not hired as professors? Even if you graduate from a top school with a PhD with top marks and an award-winning dissertation, the odds are against you. Adjust your plan. Pick a new dream." In 2001, a friend told me, "I don't mean to be rude," [which is a clue that the person is about to say something rude] "but why would any business school hire you? Don't they only hire successful people?" In 2005, a person I greatly admired told me "There is no way you can get there from here. Some dreams just aren't meant to happen. Don't misunderstand me—I admire your work toward your goal. I wish it was possible for you. I really do."

Those 10 years were not perfect, and I didn't make it onto several of the paths that I had intended, but I stayed flexible and worked very diligently, embracing every opportunity that was anywhere near one of those paths that I mapped in 1998 and continually updated over the years.

My wife Natasha and my kids were the anchor for me along the way. Natasha was 100% fault- tolerant and patient with all of my work to puzzle through and figure out where I/ we needed to go. She was patient and supportive with the things that didn't work, and she was the first to high-five me on the things that did work. I know for a fact that the most mission-critical team is at home. One of my favorite quotes from Natasha is something she said to a friend who asked her (in front of me) why she "put up with" the twists and turns of my career. Natasha didn't hesitate and said, "I've never confused our relationship with our bank account." She is a great example of an entrepreneur's ideal life partner.

In 2008, I was the CEO of a technology startup in Ireland. We worked hard in that company at 2 St Stephens Green in Dublin; I loved the team and what we were working to accomplish. I was also volunteering with Social Entrepreneurs Ireland (SEI) to help entrepreneurs and social ventures around Ireland puzzle through how to build and run successful social ventures. One day, out of the blue, Lynda Stopford and Seán Coughlan at SEI recommended me to Hans Wahl at INSEAD to join a panel as a speaker during an INSEAD Social Entrepreneurship Programme (ISEP) event in Paris, France. Out of the ISEP event in Paris, two things happened that proved to be powerful inflection points for me: 1. I volunteered to be an Entrepreneur-in-Residence (EiR) at INSEAD in Fontainebleau, France, and 2. The leader of ISEP, INSEAD Professor Filipe Santos and I started a series of conversations that led to Filipe offering me a job in 2009, working in the INSEAD Centre for Entrepreneurship (ICE) in Fontainebleau.

At Filipe's invitation, I started teaching weekend bootcamps for INSEAD MBAs on how to create a Startup company from nothing and I taught a Business Planning Workshop. Filipe asked me to chair the INSEAD Venture Competition (IVC); I volunteered in various professors' classes; I ran speaking events on campus; I did evening seminars on professional sales with my friend Scott Osborne, and more. INSEAD's Dean of Faculty Peter Zemsky asked me to learn how to teach a crazy course called Your First Hundred Days (YFCD, the C is the Roman numeral 100). I worked to learn YFCD as I team-taught with Affiliate Professor Patrick Turner. YFCD was a 24-hour-a-day, 12-day, real-time role-play course on how to acquire and then turn around a failing company. We brought in live role-players, held Socratic method team meetings with students, sent out and responded to thousands of emails, and we slept very little. We taught the course four times back-to-back. Patrick was a force of nature.

I thought that might be as close as I would ever get to my original dream of being a professor. Then in 2010, INSEAD offered me a full-time job as an Affiliate Professor of Entrepreneurship and Family Enterprise. At the time, INSEAD was #5 in the Financial Times business school rankings.

It could be argued that my willingness to volunteer opened the first doors at INSEAD. Then professors Filipe Santos and Peter Zemsky opened more doors for me once inside INSEAD. I would like to thank Filipe Santos and Peter Zemsky for seeing value in what I created at INSEAD, and in turn capturing that value for INSEAD—Filipe by hiring me into the Entrepreneurship Centre and starting me into the bootcamps et al, then Peter for getting me into YFCD and ultimately offering me the contract as an Affiliate Professor.

There was a lot of hard work involved in those years. There were also a lot of missed turns and wrong directions, and pivots, and extra work to get back on a productive path. There were many doors closed, and several doors opened. I experienced my share of bad luck, and my share of blessings and good fortune. Everything factored in the mix, and it all worked out. I'm thankful to those who opened doors when they could have kept them closed.

P.S. This was not the first time I achieved the seemingly impossible. I have my volunteer missionary work for The Church of Jesus Christ of Latter-day Saints in Thailand from 1983–1985, as well as the rock-solid support of my brother Steven J. Hite to thank for helping me evolve from an insecure kid who barely graduated high school in 1983, to registering for night classes at the Harvard Extension School in Cambridge, Massachusetts, USA in 1986, to graduating with a bachelor's degree from Harvard in 1991. What seems impossible in a given moment is very possible if you are willing to believe, work hard, and make sacrifices.

> **HINT** Sacrifice is giving up something good for something better.

> **ASSIGNMENT** Create a 10-year roadmap for you. It doesn't need to be a fancy ultra-complicated thing. Start the way that I started: I am here, and I want to get there. What do I need to do to get from here to there? Do some research about other people who are doing what you want to do. How did they get there? Sketch the details and mark the years (or months) between here and there and what you need to do in broad brushstrokes. Then begin filling in the finer details.

If you don't have 10 years, then make it 5 years, or 2 years, or 1 year, or 2 months; whatever amount of time you feel like you have and need to make the new you happen. Less time just means less time to develop the new and improved version of you that will be compelling and even irresistible to whoever is making decisions wherever you plan to go.

YOUR OFFERING AND VALUE PROPOSITION

STEP 3

Investors evaluate potential investees, schools evaluate prospective students, and companies evaluate potential employees, current employees, and everyone else who might be of use to the company in a way that is similar to how products and services are evaluated. What can they do and how will they make things better? How useful are they? Can they do what they say they can do? (These are your features and benefits.) Will they help or hurt what we need to accomplish? (These are how you are an asset or liability). Will they be a full-time employee (FTE), part-time employee (PTE), contractor? From their track record how long will they stay with us if we hire them? (This is your life cycle and forecast EOL or End of Life.) And so on.

As a worker in any organization, venture, or industry, or a student at any school, your involvement will create and capture value, or erode, decay, or destroy value. Whether it is a social venture, a movie production, or a Fortune 500 company, decision makers are regularly evaluating and deciding which people to bring on board based on the value that they can offer to the environment, and what needs to be accomplished. You will not be hired or admitted or given investment capital to start your company because you are passionate about your dream and really, really, really want to do whatever it is. You need to offer whoever is making the decision to open the door for you (or to keep it closed) something that will compel them to open the door for you. You need to SHOW, not only tell them, how you will create and capture value for what they are doing. What are you offering that will make what they are doing better?

If the idea of value creation and capture is new to you, think of it this way:

People sit at their desks doing work. They walk to the bathroom. Then back to their desk. They go to lunch. Then back to their desk. They get a drink of water. Then back to their desk. Then they go home. This repeats day-after-day. The company benefits a little; they need someone to move those papers from one box to another. The people benefit a little, they get a check in exchange for their time at that desk moving papers around. A meaningful percentage of people do some version of that job for most of their lives.

If, however, you want to make a powerful impact on your life, then you need to think about how you can make a powerful impact on a business. You need to think of how what you do in a given day makes the company more valuable. You might work on a project that is genuinely value creative, which is designed to grab the attention of customers and make more money for the company. Your boss loves your work on the initiative, and it is implemented. Your initiative attracts new customers who give more money to the company, and the company is seen by more people as being innovative and more impressive. Your work and initiative created value, secured more customers, made money, and increased brand awareness, which is all captured value. If you don't make more money or move up in the organization as a result of creating and capturing more value for the company, you are investing your time at the wrong company.

Early in my career I had a customer on the phone ask to speak with my boss to tell him how impressed he was with my work to help him. After speaking with my boss, the customer came back on the phone with me and said, "Get out now. I mean right now before you waste another minute of your talent and potential on that place. That guy, your so-called boss, is never going to give you the credit you deserve. Trust me on this one. From his response to me when I was expressing my appreciation for you it was clear that you are just another cog in the machine for him. You are creating huge value for that business and he is blowing it, rather than using it productively. You are a value creation engine. You are destined for more." That was the first time I had heard the words "value creation" as being a thing. The "using it productively" part of his sentence was the "value capture" part of the message that I puzzled over and connected with much later.

A question to consider is how do you become a value creator? A companion question is where is the optimal environment that will recognize your value creation and capture that value for both your benefit and the benefit of the organization?

You need to R&D both yourself and the prospective environment(s) so that value creation and capture becomes the way your days play out as your new daily routine. (Research and Development (R&D) is when someone investigates (researches) and then creates (develops) an offering (what you are able to do).) So, you need to do some R&D on you yourself and your dreams and goals. Invest some time and honest consideration into what you genuinely should be doing as a career.

Example: Let's say, for example, that you are tone-deaf, but your dream is to be a Grammy award-winning vocal artist. If years of singing your heart out in vocal training has not helped you carry a tune, but you remain passionate about the music industry, you might target another instrument than voice (keyboards, guitar, etc.) or something around the vocal artist (maybe a song writer or producer) that could keep you close to the music and still put a Grammy in your hand. (This is called a "pivot." Not all pivots are in the opposite direction, most are a little this way or that way.) My dream was to be a tenured academic faculty at a top business school. I never was an academic and I never received tenure ("tenure" for a professor means guaranteed employment through retirement), but I was a practitioner faculty at a top business school for 10 amazing years. I still lived my dream to be a professor, just differently than my original dream. I am blessed to have had the opportunity.

Do background research and talk to the most successful people you can get access to about how they got to where they are today. Map what they did and see how their path might somehow fit into your plan to get from where you are to where they are. Do that as many times as possible until you see a pattern on your personal map. Your path will most likely not look like anyone else's, and that is 100% okay. Once a path starts to materialize, you can begin seeking out the education and training you will need to be qualified to develop that idea and dream into a viable offering in the market.

ASSIGNMENT When you think about what you have to offer, make three inventories, detailed lists of:

1. Positive things you A. Know that you can deliver, and B. Believe that you have to offer, and that have never been fully understood or appreciated.
2. Positive things others recognize in you. (Be honest. Everyone has them.)
3. Weaknesses that you know that you need to neutralize and develop into strengths. (We all have them.)

Look closely at the details between the work you did on the Assignments in Steps 1 & 2 and then the above 3 lists. Make sure that you have not forgotten to list anything (either accidentally or on purpose (people often "conveniently" leave uncomfortable and inconvenient realities off self-evaluation inventories).

Looking at all of the information together, does it tell a story that you recognize? Does it paint the picture that you can work to define in greater detail? Work what you have written into a coherent statement of both where you are and what positive and powerful person you see yourself becoming in the future.

ASSIGNMENT Once you identify a potential new career, create an inventory of the skills and characteristics that would be required of someone in that job/career. Correlate what education and training you will need to develop your ability to perform into marketable features (on your CV or resume you would list these as "Skills") and benefits (on your CV or resume you would list these as "Strengths") that you can offer.

MARKETING, BUSINESS DEVELOPMENT, AND SALES OF YOU

You need to think about your path forward the way that businesses think about <u>marketing</u>, <u>sales</u>, and <u>business development</u>.

▶ **Marketing**
The research and planning to find out where the optimal opportunity is located, who the potential customers are, what is special about them, and how they do what they do (which is the "market"—a marketplace where things are bought and sold, traded and exchanged). Marketing then determines how to capture the attention of those people through advertising, trade shows, press, etc.

This is the work to identify where in the world, and in what company, institution, or venture of whatever type of engagement genuinely works for you. This might be your current employer, just somewhere else in the organization, or it might be a completely different life in an industry that is new to you.)

Next, identify what the decision makers inside that new-to-you, opportunity are looking for from anyone whom they will hire for that opportunity. Then puzzle through how to position yourself as that person. How will you package and message what you are offering them?

Look at your curriculum vitae or CV (your "résumé," in North America). If you don't have one, you need to build one; work with a professional if you are not happy with what you can do on your own with your CV/résumé. In a way, your CV/resume is a brochure about you. It describes your features and benefits. If someone invests in you and the features and benefits do not work as described, then they may not be happy. So be honest, without exaggeration. Very importantly, do not lie. You can be creative in how you word and message, but you cannot change the reality of what you did in your career before today. However, how you embrace your current reality is a control that can influence what happens from today forward.

▶ **Business development**
Building strategic relationships that open doors and remove barriers to the market. Biz Dev (business development) applies to everything that happens in a company, including marketing and sales, as well as operations, and engineering, and more.

What strategic relationships do you need to open doors to the future version of you? Is it more training and education? Or do you have the training and education already and just need help getting access to someone at the new company to give you an interview?

Networking (building meaningful relationships with others, thereby expanding who you know and who knows you) is not to be underestimated. If you don't know the right people who can open a door for you, you need to find them. Those people might be members of alumni associations (if you are also an alumnus or alumna), or professional associations (such as Rotary Club International), or online "business and employment oriented service" such as LinkedIn that you could join and curate connections that can introduce you to the person or people who can open a door to the conversation.

▶ **Sales**
The activity that results in the exchange of what you are offering for what you need and/or want others to do. The most common thing that we sell is our time. We show up and work a job, and in exchange we are paid for that time and effort. Sometimes, we volunteer our time and the exchange is valuable to us (and hopefully those whom we serve).

All of the other work that you are doing in this framework and in your life is what you will use in that moment of the sale (interviews, conversations, negotiations, etc.).

A company would do the marketing and business development to position in a market and open strategic doors so that sales could then walk through those doors to close deals. You need to do the same.

Build a timeline with the end in mind.[3] Then work backward to today. Do you have time to get the training and certifications that you need? Do you have time to develop the new skills that will be required? Will you need to travel to market yourself to the new company? Will you need to be willing to relocate if they require it? What are the considerations and factors?

ASSIGNMENT Marketing: Do the marketing development research on where in the world you should be positioned, and with which opportunity. Then do the marketing work of how you will need to position yourself to the decision makers around that opportunity.

Biz Dev: Do the business development research on what strategic activities you will need to do, and relationships you will need to engage to open the doors of the opportunity that you are targeting.

Sales: Do the sales research on what the exchange or transaction will look like once you are face-to-face with the opportunity. Will you do the work for free? Will you be paid? Will you pay? What will you be offering and then expecting in return?

---

3   This is also habit #2 in The 7 Habits of Highly Effective People, Steven R. Covey (1989)

YOUR BARRIERS AND ROADBLOCKS

For our purposes we'll say that the potential problems that you will encounter in making your new and improved future possible, come in two basic types: inside and outside.

▶ Inside

> "We have met the enemy and he is us."
> —from the comic strip **Pogo** by Walt Kelly

There is reality in the humorous yet sad observation that despite our best intentions we are very often our own worst enemy. Anticipate this reality and plan for what to do about it when (not if) your own behavior threatens to undo what good you are working to accomplish.

You might be your own worst enemy when it comes to pivoting and shifting into a bright new future version of you. The way you talk, the words you use, your attitude, negativity about yourself and others, speaking poorly of past employers (no future employer wants to hear about your bad last employer, and they do not want to become the next employer that you bad-mouth). Develop a positive, can-do mindset. Speak of the good about your past, even if there was very little good. Positive messaging inside of yourself (when you talk to yourself about yourself and everything else) is just as important as messaging outside of yourself with others about you and everything else.

You are what you eat. That goes for everything you think, listen to, watch, say, and with whom you spend your time. It is all food for your soul, and the relative quality of it all will make you weaker or stronger.

▶ Outside

Continuing with the reality that you are what you eat: your environment matters. Do you spend your time around people who are uplifting and encouraging? Are your friends cheering you on with hope for your future? Do you live your life in the company of positive can-do achievers or negative people who rarely do well? Choose your friends and environment carefully. Even if you feel limited by your environment, work to surround yourself, within that challenging environment, with others who are seeking to do good. Find the eagles.

Humans are judgmental. We play to our biases. In most places in the world, you cannot legally deny someone a job because of their skin color, or accent, or gender, or orientation, or religion, or tattoos, or clothes, etc. But it still happens. It shouldn't, but it does. They will say that you "weren't the right fit" or that they are looking for someone who is more this or that.

The key is to be so compelling that they cannot say no to you. You cannot control other people, but you can control yourself. Stay positive and proactive.

You might, for example, be older than the hiring manager expected for a candidate who would typically apply for an opportunity. Do your homework on what you have to offer them so that your age becomes less relevant. Show (don't just tell) them what you can do.

Ageism is a real thing, and it can unfairly harm a person who needs to work. An employer might miss out on a great employee because they could not see past the applicant's age. Being older and more experienced typically indicates that you are more expensive, so anticipate the objection and give them a solution before they can use it to block you. The future employer needs to understand why they should become your advocate and champion to anyone else who might resist or object to hiring you. Work to influence that judgment by making yourself a valued asset that they cannot resist bringing into their opportunity. I used age as an example here, but you can apply the principle to any of the other unfair biases that humans use against each other. Anticipate the arguments, but do not have a chip on your shoulder going in. Do not offer the argument or tell the hiring manager that they have a bias. Simply be prepared with evidence of your very real value and show it.

Be calm, happy, and positive, with a can-do attitude rather than just "an attitude." Develop a comfortable smile; no forced smiles. Do your homework and offer them what they need and cannot refuse.

ASSIGNMENT Write a paragraph on the things standing in your way. Focus on messaging what you can do about those barriers and roadblocks. Do not make the classic mistake of listing problems without exploring the counterbalance of what can be done about those problems. Think practically. For example, Barrier: I have no money and I am undereducated. Rather than saying: "I need money and education," say: "the following program offers the education that I need. I will apply for the following financial aid, grants, and scholarships."

YOUR EXECUTION

You need to articulate *WHY* you are doing WHAT you are doing, WHEN you are doing it, WHERE you are doing it, and HOW you are doing it. Most people just "do" but they cannot explain why, what, when, where, and how.

People "do stuff" and then wonder why they aren't going anywhere. For example, you might be taking classes as a community college or university, but don't seem to be any closer to graduating. This might be because you are taking classes that look interesting rather than taking the classes that the school will count toward a certificate or degree. Sometimes, the classes that you need to take are not interesting to you, but if you don't take and do well in those classes, you cannot graduate.

So you need to think: what MUST be done so that I can get from here to there?

Here is one way to think about it: If someone asks how a traditional clock works. Most people would make the mistake of saying "a clock tells time," when the question might be looking for mechanical detail. (This is the classic birds and bees question for parents with their children. The child might be asking if a baby comes from the mom's tummy or a stork, or they might be at the level of development where they are seeking information about the mechanics of where a baby comes from.) Do you, as the questioner, need to simply learn to tell time, or do you need to understand the mechanical detail of how a clock tells time as a way of learning how to tell time?

When asked how it tells time, people might say that the big hand points to the minutes and the little hand points to the hours. What you need to be able to do is open the clock face and point at a few representative cogs and springs and demonstrate that you understand how that cog and that spring operate in the system of moving pieces that in turn move the hands that signal time. Again, you may not need to invest in glorious detail, just representative examples. Another analogy would be to think of it like skipping stones across a pond. You can point to the area around the pond and the body of water, and then touch on a few details that would be struck across the surface where a skipped stone might hit from one side to the other side. The level of detail that is needed, in this case, is whatever you need so that you can work in the right direction to accomplish your goals and dreams.

ASSIGNMENT Write a list detailing why you will do what you will do when, where, and how. Explore and refine your questions. Do not worry if the list is intimidating. You climb a mountain one step at a time. Humans have been climbing mountains for as long as there have been humans. You can do it.

YOUR CALL TO ACTION OR THE ASK

In business **The Ask** or the **Call to Action** is put to others to tell them what you need them to do. In my experience, the weakest calls to action tell that something should happen, while the most powerful calls to action SHOW what should happen with supportive telling.

"I need the job." vs. "Here are three examples of what I will accomplish in this position ... "

"I am the right person for this job." vs. "Here are four examples showing why I am the ideal candidate for this opportunity ... "

The first Ask (or Call to Action) that you need to consider is to ask yourself to commit to a path of making changes in your life that will put you into a more powerful and happy place in your future.

Then invest in the work to reinvent yourself. Then when you engage any and all people along your way, ask them to work with you as you progress along your path until you achieve your goal. Do not wait for others to ask you, you need to develop the courage to ask for help.

The ability to ask for help from others is a superpower, and not everyone can do it.

HINT In a business, you can't always tell who or what is in trouble by looking at an employee, or a department, or a business unit. But a rule of thumb is that the employees that never ask for help may be in trouble. Even the most competent and powerful employees and people need help sometimes, and they ask for help when they need it so that they can get their work done.

ASSIGNMENT Write at least one paragraph on this section. Explore and refine your questions. Write as many Asks as you think will be necessary and write to whom that Ask will be relevant and directed.

YOUR PITCHING AND PRESENTATIONS

> "Everyone has a plan 'til they get punched in the mouth."
> —**Mike Tyson**, former heavyweight boxing champion of the world

▶ Pitching

A pitch is a short format presentation. It should be quick, clear, and to-the-point. An elevator or lift pitch is typically no more than one or two minutes (the time it would take to get from one floor in a building to a few floors up).

▶ Presentations

A presentation is a longer format pitch, but has a similar structure.

Classic blunder (one that took me years to stop doing): Do not go into detail about negative things. No one will want to bring your negativity into their space.

I experienced a powerful moment in 1986, when I was taking a night school class at Harvard. I had been called to the office of Dr. Donald Bacon. The note said that he wanted to discuss a paper that I had submitted in his class. (The assignment had been to rewrite, in my own words, the Chapter 24: Conclusion of Nathaniel Hawthorne's *The Scarlet Letter*). I was convinced that I was in deep trouble and that he was going to call me out as the fraud that I felt I was, even daring to take a night class at Harvard. Sitting in his office, he asked me a simple question, "Tell me if the following is a complete sentence: 'Horse stands'." I did not know the answer. I panicked and started a long wandering sob story that never answered his question and made excuses conjuring a murky mess that made everything worse. I will never forget the compassion on his face when he looked at me. In my notes, I wrote down that he said, "Well Paul, I am very sorry to hear that story. You have a decision to make. Will you limit your future by empowering what you consider to be the weaknesses of your past? Or will you embrace the opportunity that you have to change your future?" This was an important moment in my life. At another point he said, "If we work together, I believe that you could learn to write a great paper, even an award-winning paper. I see gold inside the often-confusing writing that you have submitted in this paper. The fixes are achievable; you just need to learn how. I can work with you, if you will let me. I can also make suggestions for classes with friends of mine who can help you."

In business, and life, we are not always so blessed and lucky. In most interviews and conversations if you go into negative detail about your past or present, or pretty much anything, people will simply close the door that you needed opened.

> "I am not a product of my circumstances.
> I am a product of my decisions."
> —Stephen Covey

> **HINT** Presentations tend to too heavily message the problem/
> opportunity and have too little practical detail on what can be done
> and what you are actually doing (aka execution). It is true that the
> listener needs to believe that you are addressing an authentic prob-
> lem (do not solve a non-problem, and do not be a solution looking
> for a problem to solve) but remember that the listener needs to
> believe that you know what you are doing (execution level detail).

Explain the opportunity and give representative detail into what you are doing about that opportunity.

Next, it is too common in the world of business that people don't practice their presentations in advance. People often work on their materials up to the moment before presenting and then walk into the room and start. Practice your pitch and presentations before giving them. There is no substitute for practice. Make sure that the first time that you pitch, or present is during practice rather than in front of the person whom you need to persuade. You only get one chance at a first impression. In case you feel that practice will make you less spontaneous in the moment, keep in mind that practice will make you better in a moment. For example, professional athletes practice SO THAT they will be better able to be more powerfully and effectively spontaneous in a moment.

The opportunity to persuade a key influencer or decision maker might happen at any moment. The quick two-minute pitch is called an elevator pitch or lift pitch because you might be in an elevator or lift when you realize that you are standing next to a key influencer or decision maker. You then have the amount of time that it takes to go from the ground floor to when they exit the elevator or lift to plant a seed. Hopefully they will invite you to present to them based on the strength of that one short pitch.

I have successfully pitched in elevators/lifts, hallways/corridors, stairways, sidewalks, while crossing the street, while at a salad bar, standing in a line/queue, while on the phone, and sitting next to someone on a plane. The point is that you never know when the opportunity will present itself. Practice your pitch over and over until you can say it without thinking about it. And practice it on different people to make sure that it makes sense and is coherent.

Practice your pitching without slides or props or other visual support. You never know when, where, or how you will be pitching. If your pitch is reliant on a slide or a prop, you might find yourself fumbling with your phone or computer, trying to pull up whatever you need, and end up burning the seconds or minutes that you have to persuade the listener. Also keep in mind that you only have a handful of seconds to create a powerful first impression; if you know what you are talking about and can say it off the top of your head without notes or visual assistance, then all the better.

That being said, if you have technology that can be quickly and effortlessly shown, then do it; just be aware that if it doesn't work then that is what the listener will remember.

Full presentations can start with a quick two-minute pitch at the top, to snap shot the long story short and give the audience an idea of what you are doing. Then you can start the longer format presentation. The longer presentation can include slides and product demonstrations if you have them, just remember to tell the story in an order that makes sense. Practice, practice, practice. There is no substitute for practicing before you present. Then after you've presented, practice some more.

As to time management, let's say, for example, that you are given a 30-minute meeting to present. Do not prepare 30 minutes of presentations and slides and demonstrations. A good rule of thumb is to prepare presentations for half of the allotted time. So in this example you would prepare 15 (or 20 maximum) minutes of a presentation, for a 30-minute meeting. Leave room for questions during the presentation as well as questions and answers at the end.

Here is a thumbnail EXAMPLE of how much time should be spent on each part of the presentation:

▶ **Intro** (~5% of the available time)
Don't apologize—it is a common opener, but it is a poor start. Be confident but never arrogant.

▶ **The Opportunity/Problem** (~25%)
Do not pander or exaggerate; be factual.

▶ **What options are possible** (~15%)
Give a few examples of options. Do not make the mistake of speaking poorly of any alternative to what you are recommending. Be factual.

▶ **What I am doing** (~45%)
Do not hold back any secret ingredient (aka silver bullet or game changer) during your presentation. It is a common problem that the presenter will save the big "wow" of their solution for a follow-up presentation. If the audience doesn't hear the wow in your first pitch, there may not be a second presentation.

▶ **How you can be involved** (~10%)
Do not tell them what they will do. Welcome them to the party and invite them to be involved.

Start on time and finish on time (or a little early). Going over time should only happen if the audience asks you to stay and explain more. Even then, be sensitive to being over time. It is typically better to leave when you are ahead while they want more and schedule a follow-up.

Do not feel nervous or upset about any questions that might be asked of you. Questions expose holes in your presentation and tell you what was not clear or understandable to the listener (no matter how clear you thought that you made the point). Questions also give you an indication of what matters to the person asking the question. Write down all the questions that you were asked, and the answers that you gave, and then use those notes as preparation for future meetings (and work on clearer presentations and better answers for the future).

ASSIGNMENT Write at least one paragraph that will become a maximum 2-minute pitch that you will memorize and practice until you can deliver it effortlessly and naturally.

Then rewrite your CV starting with a statement of what you will do for your next venture. Create an inventory of your skills and strengths. Then write a sentence or two for each job that you have worked, highlighting percentages and other measurements for how you met or exceeded expectations and goals. Use only positive words. Make absolutely certain that there are no typos or grammar mistakes on the document.

SAVE YOUR WORK, UPDATE IT REGULARLY, AND REFER TO IT OFTEN

Revisit all of the above work regularly. Remember to save your work regularly and keep backups on separate secure devices. Review and update details for all of the above once a day, or at a minimum once a week.

Every time you update the document, save a unique version in a common reference folder on your computer. Use a consistent naming convention and update the name every time to include the date that you modified it (or some other intuitive system that others, not just you, will understand if they need to find information.)

It may happen that someone will need to know something, or all things, in this framework. Do not be caught off guard with an out of date version! Be prepared, and you will have nothing to fear.

ASSIGNMENT Comb through your document. Save everything. If you write something that you aren't quite sure how it fits, either put the thought on the last empty page of the document or create a second document in the same folder just for thoughts that you aren't yet sure how to use. You do not want to find yourself in the situation where later on you wish that you hadn't deleted that thought.

On future days when you open the document, do a Save As and change the version date on the document so that it creates a new document that is saved in the same folder. It may happen that in the future you will want to refer to an earlier draft, and if anything happens to the file that you are working on that day you can always go back to the most recent version rather than starting over.

Keep a backup somewhere other than on your computer. (You should regularly back up your entire hard drive.) If you are working on paper, you need to keep your binder safe and secure at all times. When you are able you might have someone scan every page in the binder onto a file that you keep on a small portable computer stick for safekeeping. When you are able you might have your handwriting transcribed onto a computer document; you might check with a local library to see if you can use a computer there. If you edit your document on a public computer just make certain that you do not leave a copy of your document on the public hard drive.

Regularly update your writing, save copies, keep the dream alive and work to make it real.

YOUR TEMPUS MIRABILE (TIME OF WONDERS)

Isaac Newton returned home to Woolsthorpe-by-Colsterworth, England, between 1665–1666 to wait out the Great Plague. I'm not sure what his school chums were doing with their days, but the 22-year-old Isaac Newton invested his time at home working on his questions: he formalized what would become Calculus, he performed groundbreaking work on Optics, and he made breakthroughs on his Theory of Universal Gravitation. He later referred to that time as his Annus Mirabilis (Year of Wonders or Year of Miracles). I imagine that for others it was a scary time; a far cry from what most would have called a year of wonders. Isaac Newton did not cure the plague; he worked on what was in his control: his own thinking and work. The greatest mind of his time, one of the greatest minds of any time, worked on what he could control, puzzling through those things that were in line with his interests, abilities, and questions. (He was a mathematician, physicist, astronomer, theologian, and author.)

The rest of us should learn from his example. We may not develop something as massive as the Theory of Universal Gravitation, but we can do work that will make a difference even if only in our own lives.

During the 2020 COVID19 lockdown in New Zealand, I was at home with my family focusing on those things that were in my

control. Our family took the rare opportunity of dedicated time at home to focus on several things: 1. When my regularly scheduled work vaporized, my wife and I created new work and opportunities, and in the process, we found exciting new life for two new businesses that we incorporated in New Zealand. 2. I woke up at 4am most mornings to dedicate uninterrupted time to completing this workbook, 3. My wife closed her door for several hours every day to finish her thesis for her Master's degree at INSEAD. 4. Our adult daughter Sasha had been living in Indonesia as a missionary, but lockdowns around COVID19 brought her home to New Zealand very suddenly in the 9th month of her scheduled 18 month volunteer work; that sadness became a blessing to the work of this book, as she helped me think through the details of every page. She also wrote music and invested time in meaningful conversations over the Internet with friends around the world. 5. Our youngest son Elijah learned to play the piano, worked on writing stories, memorized the countries of the world, focused on his math skills, made short movies and took photos, and more. 6. We worked together on our land, we played games as a family, we sat around the table talking and investing time in each other.

In our own way, we tried to live in line with the example of the young Mr. Newton by focusing on those things in our control that were in line with the questions that we could meaningfully address.

As we anticipate what life will be like when we move forward into our new normal beyond COVID19, my sincerest hope is that we will take the lessons with us of focusing on what we can control, investing time in the people and projects that matter, and working to achieve a more enlightened and deliberate use of our time and energies.

Whatever the circumstances of this moment for you, at whatever point in the future when you are reading this message, I hope the same for you—that you will embrace your priorities, focus on those things in your control, and work to achieve your own time of wonders and miracles.

Years later, when Sir Isaac Newton reflected on his Year of Wonders, he said "For in those days I was in the prime of my age for invention & minded Mathematicks & Philosophy more then than at any time since."[1]

Imagine how our world would take shape if all 7.53 billion of us (or even 1%, 75.3 million of us) focused for a time on our best thinking and work. Just imagine what the world would be like if each of us created our own personal time of wonders. We would each create the better world that stories are written about, that movies are made about, that people talk about and hope for. The world would be better for each of us, and therefore, for all of us.

---

1   The full passage by Sir Isaac Newton is: "In the beginning of the year 1665 I found the Method of approximating series & the Rule for reducing any dignity of any Binomial into such a series. The same year in May I found the method of Tangents of Gregory & Slusius, & in November had the direct method of fluxions & the next year in January had the Theory of Colours & in May following I had entrance into ye inverse method of fluxions. And the same year I began to think of gravity extending to ye orb of the Moon & (having found out how to estimate the force with wch [a] globe revolving within a sphere presses the surface of the sphere) from Kepler's rule of the periodic times of the Planets being in sesquialterate proportion of their distances from the center of their Orbs, I deduced that the forces wch keep the Planets in their Orbs must [be] reciprocally as the squares of their distances from the centers about wch they revolve: & thereby compared the force requisite to keep the Moon in her Orb with the force of gravity at the surface of the earth, & found them answer pretty nearly. All this was in the two plague years of 1665–1666. For in those days I was in the prime of my age for invention & minded Mathematicks & Philosophy more then than at any time since."

LIFESTYLE
ENTREPRENEURSHIP

"What we achieve inwardly will change outer reality."

—Plutarch

Lifestyle entrepreneurship is when you work enough to live, rather than living to work.

In my experience, few lifestyle entrepreneurs are wealthy (unless they made their money before focusing on their lifestyle, or they inherited wealth, or their spouse/life partner has money or a career that pays well, etc.). Most lifestyle entrepreneurs do not focus on monetary wealth; they do enough to make what they need, and then do what they want with their time. The liberation of time is the focus of a lifestyle entrepreneur.

When I lived and worked in France, I remember taking my bicycle's tire to be repaired. The bike shop near my home was small, crowded to overflowing with bikes to be repaired, and the lone worker in the shop was easygoing and happy to take my tire. He said it would be repaired in two days' time, when I could pick it up. Two days later I arrived at the door to find it locked in the middle of the day. A handwritten sign on the door read: "allé à l'ouest" (which translates as "gone to the west.") I checked the shop whenever I was able over the month that followed, and eventually the door was once more unlocked. I took my daughter Sasha to translate for me. I was expecting a story about something like a death in the family that took him to the west for a month, but he said that he decided to visit the west of France because he had saved enough money to go. He said that he came back when he ran out of money.

So he would now work until he had enough money, and then he would take another trip. It turns out that he worked enough to finance the life that he wanted to live. As the shop owner and only worker, he had the luxury of opening when he wanted and closing when he wanted. His was the only bike repair shop in a village where many people ride bikes, which meant that he was never short of options for making money. He prioritized his personal time over working to make more money. Importantly, the mindset of his customer base was understanding and flexible around things like putting a sign on a shop door and not returning for a month. Everyone got it, was used to it, and therefore did not have a problem with it. I learned to work around this reality as part of life in France.

There is a misconception in the world that all entrepreneurs are anti-corporation, anti-"the man," anti-working for someone else, and anti-job, etc. The truth is that most entrepreneurs love working; they crave the security of a paycheck and benefits such as health insurance and retirement accounts. When most entrepreneurs work to build a startup, or to buy a company, or to turn around a failing company etc., they are toiling to make their small company big with a goal of a regular salary with good benefits for everyone. A lifestyle entrepreneur, by contrast, does not want the work that they do to become a big company with infrastructure and a regular 9am to 5pm, Monday to Friday work week,

UNLESS they can still have the lifestyle that they want while all of that happens around them. The lifestyle entrepreneur wants freedom of movement and the flexibility of time.

When I hear people say "I could never be an entrepreneur, I'm risk averse" I chuckle. The typical difference between someone working a job and an entrepreneur is not the absence of risk or the aversion to risk, but the willingness to do what needs to be done to push through the risk and the aversion to risk.

Some people don't feel anxious when their bank balance is low, they don't lose sleep when bills are overdue. They just work some more until they can make a few payments on their bills, then they put some fuel in the tank of their car and drive to the west for a month.

I have known many people over the years who do not want to spend more time working than they spend living their lives. The time to get to work, time at work, time to get home from work, and then time sleeping, is a majority of the day for most people. The small amount of time in a typical day not working or sleeping is too small for some people. Lifestyle Entrepreneurship is a path for people who want the focus of their lives to be the non-work living of their lives.

Structure can help you create flexibility in your life (sounds odd, but it is true).

Consider this framework:

Before you start this framework: If you have not already done so, please go back to the page called START HERE at the beginning of the book and complete parts 1, 2, 3, and 4 of the Preparatory Frameworks. Once that is completed, come back to this page and move forward to the following:

STEP 1 **A Firm Foundation**

STEP 2 **The Basic Idea**

STEP 3 **The Offering**

STEP 4 **Value Proposition**

STEP 5 **Business Modeling**

STEP 6 **Financial Modeling**

STEP 7 **Execution**

STEP 8 **Capital Modeling**

STEP 9 **Marketing, Business Development, and Sales**

STEP 10 **Barriers and Roadblocks**

STEP 11 **Make It Happen**

STEP 12 **Save Your Work, Update It Regularly, and Refer to It Often**

This framework does not include everything that needs to be considered, but it is a good place to start.

A FIRM FOUNDATION

A lifestyle career sounds like it doesn't need structure, but it does. The right structure and execution will be important to achieving your goal of a career that offers you the flexibility of time.

It could be that you are good with money. Maybe you are very frugal. Maybe you do your own taxes successfully. All of that is good news. Most people, however, are not good with money, are not frugal, and cannot do their own taxes. In which case, an accountant is likely to be an important partner in your lifestyle business.

A lawyer to help you set things up correctly could also be important. They would help you puzzle through where you should create your lifestyle venture; especially if you need to incorporate, which may or may not be the case, but a lawyer can tell you. Where you incorporate may or may not be where you operate; again, a lawyer can help you with these details.

You need to think very carefully about your cost of living where you live and run your life-style business. Is it in an expensive area? Think about the cost of your home and whether it is too big or too small to suit the requirements of your lifestyle (not wants but actual needs and requirements). Then there is the question of location; is it close to where you need to be? Can you do what you need to do from home so that you can be nearer to where you want to be? Consider how you get around (a car, motorcycle, bike, bus, walking, etc.) and whether that mode of transportation is what best fits the lifestyle that you want for yourself.

You should also evaluate your propensities to consume and save; this is how much you spend or save of every dollar (or euro, pound, peso, yen, baht, etc.) that hits your hands. This is vital to understand but it is difficult to be honest and objective about. (Most people think that they are better with money than they are in actual fact.) If you are always short of money then you will probably need to seek out advice and training on money manage-ment, budgeting, and how to live on less money.

Once you have done the above, you are ready to explore your basic idea.

ASSIGNMENT If you already use the cloud to back up all of your work securely, that is excellent. If you regularly use software that keeps track of versions of your work, so that you never invest hours editing the wrong version of a document, that is superb. If, however, for any reason, you are not yet able to back-up in the cloud or you do not have access to software that keeps track of versions of your documents, you will need to do these things manually. If you are working on a computer, create a folder with a logical name that you will not forget. Put that folder in an obvious location on the computer (not a clever place, but a clear and easy to remember place), that will still be obvious to you tomorrow and the next day. Create a new document and save it in the folder that you just created. Name the file something easy to remember and give it today's date; then every day you edit it, save a version with that day's date so that you can tell the difference between files. Always work on the most recent date and version of the file. If you do not have a computer, buy a spiral binder with lined paper (or an equivalent that is available to you). Put your name and contact information on it and keep it in a safe place. Do all of your work in the document or binder.

THE BASIC IDEA

STEP 2

This is not the idea that you want a lifestyle gearing around the freedom of time; that is a given since you are working on this framework. The basic idea that you need to consider is what work will be able to purchase your freedom of time for you.

This is your equivalent of the bike shop in France.

What can you do that will pay your bills and leave you some money left over every day? As with the French bicycle repair shop, it doesn't need to be a complicated business. It helps if it is something that you love, something that you are skilled at, or are highly motivated to learn. It needs to be something that others will pay you to do, and something that can be done on a flexible schedule.

This might be opening a repair shop that you own as a sole proprietor, or tutoring academics or teaching musical instruments, a substitute teacher, consulting to businesses on your specialty, being a handyman or casual laborer, etc. You need to think: What can I do that others will pay me to do that can be done in flexible time?

THE OFFERING

STEP 3

Once you decide on the basic idea, you need to articulate some meaningful detail around it so that people will be inspired and motivated to engage you to do it for them. It might be electrical work, plumbing, fence building, math tutoring, legal advice (from your phone while you sit on a beach), tax preparation (from a mountain lodge with a stable internet connection). You need to define what it is that you are qualified and able to do, and what you can charge for it.

Key: What you charge and how often you do it MUST cover your cost of living.

With this section, be as specific as possible regarding the details, features, and benefits.

A key detail here is that you need to think about the standard requirements that your customers expect (whether you agree with those requirements or not). Be sure to offer enough of the standard expectations. Then consider what differentiators might set you apart from others.

> **ASSIGNMENT** This is where you will inventory the features and benefits of what you will be offering to others. Be certain that you list the things that you will do that are normal and ordinary parts of this type of service or product. Then include the things that you will do that are special, or in some way unique (so that clients will choose you rather than the alternatives.) If there are times of year or seasons when you will do the work and other times you will not, include those considerations in this section. Write at least one paragraph on this section. Explore and refine your questions.

VALUE PROPOSITION

STEP 4

You need to understand what value you are offering to those for whom you will do your work. Why would they turn to you for what you are offering? Why would they pay you to do it?

This is a message that needs to be clearly articulated on a business card, on a website, and in any other form of communication that is appropriate for what you are doing.

Keep in mind that your primary competitor is nothing, meaning your intended customer deciding to do nothing rather than something.

> **ASSIGNMENT** Write what is special about what you are offering. Why would someone pay you to do this activity or for your product over the alternatives? Write at least one paragraph on this section. Explore and refine your questions.

BUSINESS MODELING

Your business model is how you will make money (meaning revenue and more specifically, profit, which is the money left over after you pay for everything), as well as how you will otherwise finance and operate your lifestyle business. When you are asked about your business model, the underlying question is how you will become and then stay a viable business.

This might be as simple as selling your time (e.g., a lawyer, a plumber, etc.), it might be by project (e.g., plumber again, artists, engineers, etc.), or it might be a thing that you are making and selling, or it might be fruit and vegetables from your property, etc.

Be careful with how you think about this. What is your time worth and what does it cost you to do what you do? If you spend $100 so that you can make $50 then your time as a lifestyle entrepreneur will be very brief (you will run out of money and maybe go bankrupt). This might sound obvious, but this is a very common problem among hopeful lifestyle entrepreneurs (spending more money than is made is actually a woefully common problem in many businesses).

I have a friend who invested hours in making beautiful clay figures at home. The cost of materials for the clay alone was more than what she could sell them for, plus each figure took hours to create. They were beautiful, people loved them, and she sold so many that it looked like she was successful. She struggled, however, with the reality that she was losing money on every figure. It is a tough thing to fathom when you are making sales but losing money to do it.

Your business model is the beating heart of your venture. Do not assume that how you will make revenue and profit[1] and otherwise finance your lifestyle business is obvious. When you are asked about your business model you need to have a better response than "we will sell what we make." You need to be prepared with a robust response to questions about your business model, even if that question is from your family, or your accountant, or the people to whom you owe money.

Google's business model is an interesting example. I remember visiting Google's office when it was a startup. They had a monitor over the reception desk that showed every search that was happening real-time. I remember the tempo of it … search (pause) search (pause) search. I thought to myself "Wow, people are actually using it." I sat in the lobby doing searches to watch them pop up on the monitor over the desk. As of now, there are more than 3.5 billion searches every day. People who use Google's search engine do not pay to perform their search. At Google, search is a vehicle that is leveraged to do much more than display results for the definition of a word or a website or a restaurant near you, and Google is much more than an Internet search company.

Google makes its money through Google AdWords, AdSense, Google Play store, Google Cloud, and more. Businesses pay Google to display their information in search results

---

1   Revenue is the money that you make from the sale of goods and services. Profit is the money that is left over after you make all of your payments, settle your debts, and in all ways account for your costs and expenses.

(AdWords). AdSense is interesting, because both Google and website publishers make a little money when an ad is placed by Google on a website and someone, somewhere on the planet, clicks on it. When an app is purchased on the Google Play store, Google makes a little money. Google does not make money on Android itself (the smart device operating system), interestingly, but it does make money on the ecosystem around it. An interesting feature of Google's business model is that, in addition to free searches, they have several offerings that do not generate revenue directly. As with search, these offerings create value in the Google brand by generating good will and loyalty. Take, as only one of dozens of possible examples, Google for Startups Accelerator (formerly Google's Launchpad Accelerator). Google for Startups Accelerator spends money to help startup companies around the world for free. It is an initiative that creates good will, healthy brand awareness and loyalty for Google; it also keeps Google current on what is happening with the best startups globally. I am an unpaid volunteer Anchor Mentor in the Google for Startups Accelerator, and there are hundreds of volunteers like me who work with Google to level the playing field for founders and startups around the world.

Here is a non-Internet example: How does BMW make money? Selling cars is the obvious response. They also make money on dealership franchises, parts, service and maintenance, leasing, rentals, and merchandise, among others.

Here is another: Star Wars has made more money on licensing and merchandise than on ticket sales for the movies themselves.

Here is another: "Razor and Blades" is a common expression in business. Companies will give away the handle of a razor used for shaving (even though it cost them money to design, engineer, and manufacture it) because there is more money to be made on selling the blades that attach to the end of the handle because the blades wear out and need to be replaced more frequently than the handle. An application of this expression would be a printer. Let's say, for example, that your offering is a 3D printer. You sell the printer for money (maybe at a discount so that people buy your printer over the competition); you then make additional revenue by selling the printer cartridges for your 3D printer. You could also sell a service contract to maintain the printer, and software to design what you print. Then software advertising might help you sell other 3D printer-related offerings.

The above being said, when you think about the business you are starting, how will you make money? Simple sales of what you are offering? Is there any other way? Maybe there could be other products or a service around the offering that you are selling? Is there a way to sell other products and services through your offering? Will you sell B2C (Business to Consumer, meaning you will sell and ship your offering directly from your business to your consumer), B2B (Business to Business), or B2G (Business to Government)? Some detail would be helpful.

ASSIGNMENT Articulate all the ways that you will make money (revenue and profit). Don't just say "sell product"—you need to be specific about how you will sell, and various ways that money will be made. Write at least one paragraph on this section. Explore and refine your questions.

FINANCIAL MODELING

> "Never, EVER, run out of cash!"
> **—Patrick Turner,**
> INSEAD Professor of Entrepreneurship

You need to think about the money, even if it seems like it will be comparatively small amounts. The better you are at measuring and protecting what money you have, the greater flexibility of time you will have over time.

If you can build a Cashflow from scratch, then you can explain the details when you are asked to defend the numbers during any meeting. When you present, have an updated copy of your Cashflow, and be prepared to explain the details to those who ask.

Work to frame a financial model going forward that progresses you from where you are to where you plan to go. Building a Cashflow (as well as an SG&A, P&L, Balance Sheet, along with Budgets for MDF/SDF, T&E/T&S, etc.) is fundamental for understanding your initiative. At this point you may not know what those words and acronyms mean, which is okay. You will, however, need to invest some effort in learning their meaning so that you can use them comfortably in sentences as well as comfortably answer questions about them when asked. The definitions are below.

In the business world it is very common for people to assume that other people will know how to build and read the numbers, so they invest very little study into it. Basic financial skills are very important for all people in business. Not everyone needs to be a Certified Public Accountant or Chartered Accountant but being able to build and read a Cashflow should be a required skill for all business professionals.

If an investor, board of directors, or shareholder calls you to a meeting to discuss your venture, grab an updated Cashflow on the way to the meeting. The other financial instruments such as a Profit and Loss (P&L), Balance Sheet, Sales General and Administrative (SG&A) etc., are also important but the Cashflow is the most critical. If you don't understand your cash position over time, you do not understand your business.

Good financial planning is key to persuading shareholders, the board, and leadership that you know what you are doing. If you don't (yet) know how to do it yourself, work side-by-side with a finance-professional to build complete financials. I say side-by-side so that you see how it is done, you fully understand the numbers, and can understand and explain the details. (If you can build a Cashflow from scratch then you can explain the details when you are asked to defend the numbers during any meeting.)

Here are a few overly simplified definitions of business words that you need to know:

▶ **Finance vs. Accounting**
   <u>Finance</u> looks forward to what will happen.
   <u>Accounting</u> looks back at what happened.

- ▶ **Payment vs. Expense**
  A Payment is when money leaves the company and is given to someone else.
  An Expense is the agreed responsibility to make a payment at some future date.

- ▶ **Revenue vs. Profit**
  Revenue is all money that comes into the company from sales.
  Profit is the money that is left over after you have paid all of your
  expenses and taxes.

- ▶ **Sources & Uses**
  Source is where you will get money.
  A Use is how the money will be spent.

- ▶ **Budget**
  A Budget is the amount of money (and time) that must be invested in order to do
  what must be done. Importantly budgeted amounts need to factor for how much
  money (and time) is actually available.[2]

- ▶ **Cashflow**
  A Cashflow is the financial detail of how a company is being operated; money
  coming in, all money measured impacts on debts and assets, and all money
  going out.[3]

- ▶ **Free Cashflow**
  Free Cashflow (not to be confused with the document that is called "a Cashflow")
  is the money that you have left over after all capital expenditures (aka CapEx,
  which is the money spent on fixed assets).

- ▶ **Working Capital**
  Working Capital = **Current Assets** minus **Current Liabilities**. Assets are tangible
  things that have value such as property, inventory, cash, etc. Liabilities are things
  that you need to pay such as debt, taxes, wages, rent, utilities, etc.

- ▶ **Professional Fees**
  Professional Fees are cash paid to professionals who are not your employees, such
  as lawyers, accountants, designers, engineers, etc.

- ▶ **CapEx vs OpEx**
  CapEx is Capital Expenditure, which is money spent on fixed assets.
  OpEx is Operating Expenditure, which is the money spent to operate the company.

---

2 Budgeting is incredibly valuable and essential for running your entrepreneurial venture and making
   sure that you never run out of cash. Your budgets should be planned, reviewed, and updated
   routinely as a team. Be sure to remind everyone that a budget is more than a plan for how much
   money will be spent, it is a reconciliation of how much must be spent in order to accomplish your
   plan compared to how much money there is to spend in the bank account. Monthly budgeting
   meetings, accounting back a month, and financially planning forward a quarter are good practices.

3 This is a window into all money that comes in and leaves the company. (You should typically have
   an 18 to 24-month Cashflow, with the next 13 weeks by week, and the rest of the months by month.)
   Be sure to use mathematics rather than simply typing in numbers.

- ## Fixed Assets
  Fixed Assets are physical things such as land, buildings, equipment, vehicles, etc.

- ## Burn Rate and Runway
  Burn Rate is the amount of money that you spend in a month.
  Runway is the number of months that you have until you are out of money.

- ## Break Even, and Profitability
  Break Even is when the same amount of money comes in as goes out.
  Profitability is when you have money left over after paying everything.

- ## Pro forma
  Pro forma is Latin for "as a matter of form" or "for the sake of form" and is a word put on financials to show that the numbers are educated guesses or projections.

- ## T&E or T&S
  T&S/T&E[4] is Travel & Subsistence or Travel & Expenses (occasionally referred to as Travel & Entertainment). This budget is for rental cars, trains, planes, hotels, lunches and dinners, etc. T&E is used in North American English and in North American influenced regions. T&S is used in British English and in British influenced regions.

- ## MDF and SPIF
  MDF is an acronym for Market Development Fund and is the money that you spend to take your offering to market.
  SPIF stands for Sales Promotion Incentive Fund and is a powerful tool for motivating the point of sale to inspire them to advocate for your offering over the competition (the seller and/or buyer). This could be, and is not limited to, a payment made to the salesperson or a discount/rebate offered to the customer.

ASSIGNMENT Build a Cashflow. Do not assume that you will simply hire someone else to do it for you. Learn to build a Cashflow from a blank spreadsheet if you can; at a minimum, find someone on your team or work together as a team right now to build a basic Cashflow. Then write at least one paragraph on the details inside of the Cashflow, possibly including the details listed above. Explore and refine your questions. If you need to partner with a finance professional to help you, do it; but learn how to read financial documents, how to tell the stories of the numbers, and how to read along as others go through the numbers.

---

4   Watch this budget very carefully and put rules on all expenses and what can be claimed to make people responsible and hold people accountable. It happens at times that people (especially inside of large companies) game their expense reports so that they claim more money than they legitimately spend on real business. This line item can be value destructive when you are a fledgling venture that is carefully watching every dollar in the bank account.

EXECUTION

A typical, critical mistake made by first-time entrepreneurs is ignoring the "boring" execution details of what needs to be done to make the dream a reality. Thinking through and documenting these details is the equivalent of creating a recipe with a list of ingredients for the meal you want to prepare and eat. Execution modeling is a step-by-step inventory of what needs to be done so that your lifestyle venture will become real. When you present to potential investors or potential team members, the right people will NEED to know that you know what needs to be done. If you went into a kitchen to cook a meal from raw ingredients, what is the order of operations that you would follow? What is the first activity that you need to do? What is the second activity? What is the third? Do the same thing for your startup. Inventory the activities that must be done in order. Be as specific and as detailed as possible.

Begin by inventorying what activities MUST be done and then put your name next to which of those activities you can credibly perform (not what you are simply willing to try but don't really know how to do). Once that is done, you will see the gaps around must-do activities that have no name assigned to them. That tells you whom you need to find to help you. Even as a Lifestyle business, you will need others from time to time, maybe not as full-time employees (FTE) or part-time employees (PTE), but maybe as contract workers or pay-for-hire (such as a lawyer or accountant) to do a specific thing that you need, as and when you need it, etc.

A way to think about execution, is not unlike explaining *how* a clock tells time not just *that* it tells time. Imagine opening the face of a traditional clock to expose the clockworks showing the gears, springs, and other moving parts. It would be ideal if you could document and explain every detail, but at a minimum, be prepared to give representative detail on what mechanisms move and how to make the hands move, and in turn, tell time. Do that for the details of the company that you are working to build.

> **ASSIGNMENT** Inventory your top 20 (or more) mission-critical activities. Put your name next to each activity that you can perform as a professional level. The critical activities that have no name next to it tell you whom you need to recruit to help you. Write at least one paragraph on this section. Explore and refine your questions.

CAPITAL MODELING

You may have savings that you plan to use, you might need loans from a bank, and you may be eligible for grants from an agency, government, or other organization. Right now, you need to determine what capital (primarily cash) you will be required to pay overtime for what you need (equipment, etc.) to do your work, and from where that support will come. Keep in mind that although capital is typically money, it might also be money equivalents (e.g., access to and use of buildings, equipment, etc.) Make sure to fully understand what capital is required to get your venture to the point where it can self-sustain (which is at break-even—when you are bringing in as much money as is going out) and reach profitability (which is when more money is coming in than is going out).

If you think that you will need to raise investment capital, then you might read the capital section in the Startup Framework.

If your capital needs are simple, and you won't be going to professional investors to raise money, then keep going here.

ASSIGNMENT Write at least one paragraph on this section. Explore and refine your questions. Do you have savings that will fund what you need to buy? Will you take out a loan? (Be careful getting into debt! Debt is an enemy to Lifestyle entrepreneurship!) Do you know how much you will need to spend on what you need? Or will you be raising money? If so, go to the Startup Framework and look at the step for Capital Modeling.

MARKETING, BUSINESS DEVELOPMENT, AND SALES

Now that you have a meaningful amount of detail around what you will be doing, you can better plan how you will perform your marketing, business development, and sales. If you do this planning too early you will just end up redoing it as you evolve the other details in the earlier steps.

▶ **Marketing**
The research and planning to determine where the optimal customers are located, who those people are, what is special about them and the market. Marketing then determines how to capture the attention of those customers through advertising, trade shows, press, etc.

- ▶ **Business development**

  Building strategic relationships that open doors and remove barriers to the market for everything that happens in the company, including marketing, and sales, as well as operations, and engineering, and more.

- ▶ **Sales**

  The activity that results in the exchange of what you are offering for what you need (this is most commonly money but could be other things). This could be in person (traditional sales) through to taking credit cards on a website or inside a mobile application (digital transactions).

ASSIGNMENT Write at least one paragraph for marketing, one paragraph for business development and one paragraph for sales. Explore and refine your questions.

BARRIERS AND ROADBLOCKS

Anticipating and identifying the threats to your lifestyle venture's success is very important. More than simply pointing at the potential barriers, identify what you will do about them. Be as honest and as clear-minded as possible about what might be in your way and what might undermine your initiative. Work with those who believe in you and are invested in your success to identify and plan for overcoming barriers to your initiative. Anticipating and identifying the threats to your initiative's success is very important. More than simply pointing at the potential barriers and roadblocks, it is important that you identify what will be done about them.

Inside the venture, the barriers and roadblocks might be as fundamental as lack of resources and funding. If you have legal responsibilities for others, those responsibilities are not enemies to your quest for a lifestyle occupation. Those responsibilities are necessities, and you need to do what is right and honor those responsibilities and obligations.

The barrier might be someone else who is reliant on your work for their life and lifestyle (such as a spouse, life partner, parents, children, etc.). If so, think carefully about whether pursuing a lifestyle career in any way compromises others. Do not cause harm in pursuit of your lifestyle career.

But the most significant barrier and roadblock might simply be you and your fears, uncertainty, and doubt (FUD). If you are the only barrier, and you pursuing your lifestyle entrepreneurship dream in no way threatens to harm those for whom you are responsible, then push through your fears.

"We have met the enemy and he is us."
(From the comic strip Pogo by Walt Kelly, who borrowed it from a 1970 Earth Day poster.)

There is reality in the humorous yet sad observation that, despite our best intentions, we are very often our own worst enemy. Anticipate this reality, and plan what to do about it when (not if) your own behavior threatens to undo the good you are working to accomplish.

Outside the venture, there will also be challenges and competitive pressures, but this is normal. Others outside your lifestyle business might be threatened by the work that you propose to do or are doing. They might actively work to stop your progress and success (as they would for any threat to them and their business). Anticipate the external or outside barriers. You will need to have answers prepared before making presentations and having discussions about what you see and what you plan to do about it.

If you think there are no challenges to what you are doing, that implies that either 1. You are naïve and fooling yourself, 2. What you are doing is of little value because it doesn't threaten anyone or the status quo, 3. You aren't trying hard enough, so you are not meeting any resistance. Change and disruption always ruffles someone's feathers. So, resistance is not necessarily a negative or bad thing; it might mean that you are on the right path.

> **ASSIGNMENT** It is vital that you understand what might harm you and otherwise get in your way. Create a list. Very importantly you must identify not only that the barrier exists, but what you will do about each one. This will be very sensitive information, especially if it is regarding a person, so do not distribute this information. As soon as you click send on an email or click print you need to expect that the information is public domain info and the person in question will see a copy of it. Write at least one paragraph on this section. Explore and refine your questions.

MAKE IT HAPPEN

STEP 11

"Go confidently in the direction of your dreams! Live the life you've imagined." —**Thoreau**

It might sound obvious but there is a point when you need to invest the hard work to make your dreams a reality. Dreaming is easier than doing. I fully appreciate and understand that life can be complicated, and that telling someone to "do it" does not make "doing it" any easier.

Over the years I have heard an abundance of explanations as to why it is not possible for someone to pursue their dreams. Many people have confided and explained to me in detail why they need to work a "normal" job rather than pursuing their dream career. Having responsibilities is the most common explanation (e.g., aging parents, young children, children at university, debt, etc.). I have seen the anguish on people's faces as they have asked me for my understanding, and a few have asked for permission. One fellow asked me with tears in his eyes to absolve him of the guilt that he felt for not pursuing his dream. I offer no judgement, and I cannot offer absolution. I am simply another entrepreneur on the path encouraging others to join a path.

You need to protect those who rely on you for shelter, food, medicines, etc. Do not ignore your responsibilities. Having responsibilities does not, however, mean that you cannot follow an entrepreneur's path. There is more than one way to be an entrepreneur. As a professor I worked as an entrepreneur inside of a business school. I have worked as an entrepreneur inside big companies, earning a stable paycheck, so that I could pay down my debt. My wife and I engaged startups when we had little kids. We moved to the other side of the world with young children (a 10 year old, eight year old, and one who was 5 months old) to join a startup; we didn't have a lot of money in the bank, but we were willing to figure it out together. I have worked as an entrepreneur from home, puzzling through how to build a path forward that works for the lifestyle I want to live.

Make big life decisions with the people who are on your team; the most critical members of your team are at home. You will be stronger and more able when you work together.

It might take careful planning, and time. Pay down, and pay off, your debt. Get out of debt, stay out of debt, and live within your means. Learn to live within your means by recalibrating and realigning what demands there are on your income (e.g., the car you drive, the house you live in, the discretionary spending that you make, etc.).

You can shape your own path, if you plan and work to achieve it.

Read the interlude **A THOUGHT ABOUT THE GRASS THAT IS GREENER**.

SAVE YOUR WORK, UPDATE IT REGULARLY, AND REFER TO IT OFTEN

Revisit all of the above work regularly. Remember to save your work regularly and keep backups on separate secure devices. Once a day, or at a minimum once a week at a routine time on a routine day, review and update details for all of the above.

Every time you update the document, save a unique version in a common reference folder on your computer. Use a consistent naming convention and update the name every time to include the date that you modified it (or some other intuitive system that others, not just you, will understand if they need to find information.)

It may happen that someone will need to know something, or all things, in this framework. Do not be caught off guard with an out of date version! Be prepared, and you will have nothing to fear.

ASSIGNMENT Comb through your document. Save everything. If you write something that you aren't quite sure how it fits, either put the thought on the last empty page of the document or create a second document in the same folder just for thoughts that you aren't yet sure how to use. You do not want to find yourself in the situation where later on you wish that you hadn't deleted that thought.

On future days when you open the document, do a Save As and change the version date on the document so that it creates a new document that is saved in the same folder. It may happen that in the future you will want to refer to an earlier draft, and if anything happens to the file that you are working on that day you can always go back to the most recent version rather than starting over.

Keep a backup somewhere other than on your computer. (You should regularly back up your entire hard drive.) If you are working on paper, you need to keep your binder safe and secure at all times. When you are able you might have someone scan every page in the binder onto a file that you keep on a small portable computer stick for safekeeping. When you are able you might have your handwriting transcribed onto a computer document; you might check with a local library to see if you can use a computer there. If you edit your document on a public computer just make certain that you do not leave a copy of your document on the public hard drive.

Regularly update your writing, save copies, keep the dream alive and work to make it real.

A THOUGHT ABOUT THE GRASS THAT IS GREENER

"After a time, you may find that having is not so pleasing a thing after all as wanting. It is not logical but is often true."
—**Spock** in *Star Trek* (Season 2, Episode 1: "Amok Time," 1968)

I've lived in six countries, five of those with my wife and kids. It has been fantastic raising my children across countries around the world. My children have learned languages, explored cultures, and luxuriated in all of the abundant benefits that you could imagine from life around the world. They did not, however, have the opportunity to luxuriate in the abundant benefits of growing up in a single house in the same neighborhood and going to the same school with the same kids that they had known their whole lives. My kids assure me that they are happy with the life that they lived growing up across the USA, Ireland, France, Singapore, and New Zealand. I am happy about the life that we have lived while, from time to time, yearning for the life that we did not live.

I have had many people tell me that they "would love" and "would give anything" to live around the world raising their kids the way that we have done. More often than not, I simply say something along the lines of "Yeah it has been great" but I always think to myself "the reality is that you like the idea of it. If you would actually 'give anything', then you would be doing it." (I have actually said that out loud a time or two and now in print.)

There is strength in embracing the benefits of the life that you are living and the experiences that you are having, rather than pining for what you don't have. No matter the inadequacies of it, there are always lessons to learn and good to draw from your life as it is now.

That being said ... if you want more education, a shift in career, a new neighborhood or country, don't just pine for it. Do something about it.

You can make your own path to wherever you want to go. That is not the question. The more salient question from my perspective is whether or not you will be happier once you arrive wherever it is that you yearn to go.

If you are running away, escaping, hating your present because you believe that an alternative future will be better, I believe that your negative motivation is going to contaminate your destination.

People have mistakenly assumed that my motivation for moving to Ireland, France, Singapore, and New Zealand was to "get out" and "stay out" of the USA. That is far from the truth. Every move that I have made over my career was following the opportunities that I was working hard to create ... opening every door and embracing opportunities. For me, and therefore my family, my work to create and embrace paths just happened to lead around the world.

The life over the fence in other people's gardens is lush and green because of the regular and consistent hard work that the people who live there have invested to cultivate and curate a lush green garden. A beautiful garden takes focused and deliberate work every single day. If someone who wants to have, but doesn't want to actually work for that beautiful garden were to move into a house with a lush green garden, and then they did not invest the work to maintain that garden, it would be only a matter of time before that garden will be just as dead as the garden where they lived before.

Work to achieve the dream. Be positive and proactive. You can taste the emotions of the chef in the food they cook. Gardens reflect the moods of the gardener. The paths that you stay on or the paths that you work to create and take throughout your lifetime will be filled with your motivations, emotions, and very importantly, your willingness to embrace and engage opportunities.

If you in fact would "give anything" to live a certain way of life, then by all means give everything to it and make it happen.

SOCIAL
ENTREPRENEURSHIP

"There is no greater thing you can do with
your life and your work than follow your passions—in a
way that serves the world and you."

—Sir Richard Branson

Congratulations on your interest in creating a social impact venture. It is a great adventure and can be very exciting! It can also cause anxiety and worry if you have never done it before, or if you have done it before and it didn't go well, or if you did it before and it went well but you aren't sure why or whether you can be so lucky again.

Before we get started with your framework let me say that I have worked with social ventures around the world, and I know that the best non-profit social ventures are very similar to for-profit companies. I have been called in to help puzzle through why social ventures are failing (or have failed) and very often it is because they did not have even basic business rigor built into the daily operations. Most social ventures are fueled by passion and belief, which is fantastic, but if you are not disciplined you will run out of cash and shut down ... then you won't be able to perform the good that drives you. If you run your social venture like a for-profit the probability of your surviving and thriving and doing good over time dramatically increases.

A few differences between a non-profit and a for-profit venture are that in non-profits:

1. All money that is not paying salaries and bills is put directly into social impact initiatives.

2. Philanthropic investors do not expect equity ownership or classic returns on investment.

3. The founders and others who invest their time and passion into the venture are focused on meaningful social impact rather than personal wealth creation.

▶ A Social Venture—or— Social Impact Venture

This is a non-government organization (NGO) or legally organized non-profit or not-for-profit (either a non-profit or charity) that operates with the singular and sole purpose of having meaningful social impact. (Examples of this range from The Salvation Army, to Social Entrepreneurs Ireland (SEI) that helps social entrepreneurs and their ventures around Ireland.)

▶ A For-Profit with Social Spillovers

This is a legally incorporated for-profit company, not a non-profit or not-for-profit, that operates to make profit for its shareholders AND has CSR (Corporate Social Responsibility) initiatives that have a spillover effect that benefits society and/or the earth. (Examples of this range from the clothing company Patagonia to the restaurant chain Hard Rock Café.)

> **A COMMON BLUNDER** Sometimes entrepreneurs work to create a social venture that would have greater potential as a for-profit with social spillovers. Conversely, entrepreneurs sometimes work to create a for-profit that would be better positioned as a pure social venture. You will need to research and decide the approach that works best for your venture and the good you hope to accomplish.

▶ **This framework works**

Most of the people whom I have taught had never been involved in a startup or social venture before. I am confident that even if you have never done a startup or social venture before, this framework will help you during your early steps to be a social impact entrepreneur. There is more to do than what is in this framework, but this is a kick-off point for you to think through your first planning of how to frame a social impact venture that can succeed.

The following is a 19-step framework for Social Entrepreneurship training. The foundation of the framework is my personal experience and knowledge of what is expected from strategic others[1] and what works in practice. This framework is not exhaustive but is designed to kick-start planning and execution to give you a path forward.

Before you start this framework: If you have not already done so, please go back to the page called START HERE at the beginning of the book and complete parts 1, 2, 3, and 4 of the Preparatory Frameworks. Once that is completed, come back to this page and move forward to the following:

PREAMBLE **Write Everything Down**

STEP 1 **A Firm Foundation**

STEP 2 **The Basic Idea**

STEP 3 **The Big Play**

STEP 4 **The Offering**

STEP 5 **Value Proposition**

STEP 6 **Go to Market**

STEP 7 **Team and Execution**

STEP 8 **Business Modeling**

STEP 9 **Financial Modeling**

STEP 10 **Execution and Fundable Event Timelines**

STEP 11 **Capital Modeling**

STEP 12 **Barriers and Roadblocks**

STEP 13 **Founderitis**

STEP 14 **Boards: Advisory and Governance**

STEP 15 **Marketing, Business Development, and Sales**

STEP 16 **Call to Action or The Ask**

STEP 17 **Executive Summaries and Business Plans**

STEP 18 **Pitching and Presentations**

STEP 19 **Save Your Work, Update It Regularly, and Refer to It Often**

---

1   By "strategic others" I mean anyone who matters to what you are working to accomplish. These people might be investors, bankers, lawyers, boards of directors, shareholders, executives, workers, unions, the press, suppliers, customers, the government, etc.

The purpose of the framework is to help individuals and teams structure to their ideas into an execution-ready condition so that they can: A. Persuade those with resources (e.g., capital when as philanthropic funds or grants, etc.), and B. allow the individual and teams to actually launch their social venture. This framework can be taught in-person or via technology or worked on privately by an individual or team. The 19-step framework is as follows:

WRITE EVERYTHING DOWN
PREAMBLE

It is common that people have a bright idea, then they think and dream about it (most likely talking themselves out of it), but never write down the details. Then they forget. At the time the idea seemed so obvious, so clearly brilliant but an hour later, or the next morning ... it is gone. Get into the habit of writing down all of your bright ideas.

Once you have an idea for a social venture, the first thing that you need to do is write down all of your thoughts about it. Don't worry about the structure of the writing yet, write down everything that you can think of that you want the social venture to do. If writing does not work for you then record yourself talking, if you can't do that then draw pictures, if you can't do that then ask someone to help you with one of the options. Once you've documented your thoughts then get started with the 19-step framework and refer to your documented thoughts as you go. Do not delete any of your thoughts, drawings, or recordings. Use all of it as a reference as you work. Special note: Stay flexible around the central idea. Things will be evolving and moving around. Keep track of the details. Let's get started.

ASSIGNMENT If you already use the cloud to back up all of your work securely, that is excellent. If you regularly use software that keeps track of versions of your work, so that you never invest hours editing the wrong version of a document, that is superb. If, however, for any reason, you are not yet able to back-up in the cloud or you do not have access to software that keeps track of versions of your documents, you will need to do these things manually. If you are working on a computer, create a folder with a logical name that you will not forget. Put that folder in an obvious location on the computer (not a clever place, but a clear and easy to remember place), that will still be obvious to you tomorrow and the next day. Create a new document and save it in the folder that you just created. Name the file something easy to remember and give it today's date; then every day you edit it, save a version with that day's date so that you can tell the difference between files. Always work on the most recent date and version of the file. If you do not have a computer, buy a spiral binder with lined paper (or an equivalent that is available to you). Put your name and contact information on it and keep it in a safe place. Do all of your work in the document or binder.

A FIRM FOUNDATION

Once you have decided to create a social impact venture, seek out qualified legal and accounting guidance on questions such as where to incorporate, where to operate, agreements between the founders on ownership, and other legal and financial issues. These are critical questions that people take for granted as they enthusiastically rush to create their product. Where you incorporate will impact the taxes that you pay, access to support from the government including grant money, and more. Where you operate will impact the cost of operating your company, your access to skilled employees, and more. Building a solid foundation when you start will save the trouble of realizing later that you should have incorporated in a different country or state, that you should have incorporated as a different type of legal entity, or that you should have opened an office somewhere else. Then you will have to move everything around and you may lose money and key employees. Start with interviewing lawyers and accountants who understand the type of business you plan to create. Seek their counsel before you do anything.

If you don't have money to pay a lawyer, do not worry. Approach a law firm that understands what you are planning to do and ask them for help. (Or approach a law firm and ask them if they understand what you are working to do or if they can recommend another firm that does.) Contrary to lawyer jokes and their poor reputation, lawyers are human beings, and most are caring, professional people who will listen to you and who might be able to help you as part of the CSR (Corporate Social Responsibility) program at their firm. They may even help you pro-bono. The American Bar Association Model Rule 6.1 says "a lawyer should aspire to render at least (50) hours of pro bono public legal services per year." What you need might fit within the lawyer's or law firm's pool of hours to help without charge.

ASSIGNMENT Identify a lawyer and accountant whom you can approach and with whom you can work. Identify where you will incorporate and where you plan to operate as a company (where you will have an office and employees). Write at least one paragraph on this section. Explore and refine your questions.

THE BASIC IDEA

"Do well by doing good."—**often attributed to Benjamin Franklin**

If you have an idea to work on, that is good news. If you aren't sure if your idea is good enough, take a chance on it and start working; you can always pivot—try it from a different angle or approach, taking it in a different direction—or you can view the exploration as practice and start over with a completely different idea if this first idea doesn't fly for some reason. Do not overthink it. Chances are you have had several excellent ideas over the years, but if you are like most people you talked yourself out of those ideas saying something along the lines of "If it is such a good idea, then someone would have done it by now." The truth is that you might be the someone who thought of it.

In the Silicon Valley the conventional wisdom is that if you are and I are talking about it then there are other teams of people within driving distance who are already working on it. Don't worry about other people working on an idea that is similar to your idea; competition is validation. You could still be the one to win with the execution of that idea so embrace it and see what you can do with it.

If you cannot think of "a once in a lifetime idea," you might look around you. What doesn't exist (as far as you can tell) that would make your life better? Look at your home life, your hobbies, your work, and think, "what does not exist that would be really helpful?" or "I have an idea of how to make that already helpful thing even better."

I know from experience that people have more ideas than they give themselves credit for. I have led hundreds of trainings around the world with groups of colleagues, friends, and strangers, and at the beginning of the brainstorming ideas section of the training people say they have no good ideas. But then we talk about it, and within an hour we have dozens of ideas for products and startup companies.

It is very important to realize a couple of things about an idea to start things off:

1. The idea will change. It will morph and evolve, and in the end, it might be very similar to the original idea, or it might be radically different, or you might abandon it completely in preference for a new idea that evolves out of your work on that original idea. All of those outcomes are perfectly okay.

2. If you, or anyone who works with you, are too attached to the details of your original idea, it could become a problem when the idea evolves and changes. It is very important that you become attached to doing something entrepreneurial, rather than being attached to a specific idea or particular detail. This is why the original idea is important but not more important than picking your best idea (whatever it is) and getting started ... then see what happens over time.

There are the fundamental 5 vital areas of need: 1. Everyone is born, 2. Everyone needs to breathe clean air, 3. Everyone needs to eat healthy food and drink clean water, 4. Everyone eliminates what their body does not use of what they eat and drink, 5. Everyone dies. You need to consider how far away your idea falls from those fundamental 5 vital areas of need. The father away from the 5 you go the less your idea is a need and becomes a want or even worse a curio, a useless thing looking for someone who cares.

If you are genuinely stuck and cannot think of an idea, not to worry, there are resources that you can explore.

> **READ** Here is a *Harvard Business Review* article that you might read to get things started: "Reclaim Your Creative Confidence," Tom Kelley and David Kelley, *Harvard Business Review* (HBR) (December 2012)

Once you have an idea to work on, keep in mind that the idea will evolve, move around, and potentially change completely. Do not anchor too tightly onto the specifics of the idea, but stay flexible around the central idea.

The idea is important but not the most important ingredient in the creation of a startup. A powerful idea is very helpful, but there are an abundance of examples in the world of weak ideas that succeed and great ideas that do not. Do not let the lack of a great idea (in your opinion) get in the way of you starting a company.

This framework is geared around execution, and we will get to the formation of the right team later in the steps.

ASSIGNMENT Explore your basic idea. This is not yet the documenting of your features and benefits, this is simply stating what it is that you plan to do (e.g., cleaning water in villages in Myanmar, providing viable seedlings to farmers in Africa, protecting rescued children in Vietnam, etc.) Write at least one paragraph on this section. Explore and refine your questions.

THE BIG PLAY

STEP 3

The people who will work to support you and your social venture will need to understand:

1. Is your venture a one-trick pony? Meaning, will your venture ever do more than whatever you have decided to do as a first activity?

2. How the first activity (and the hopeful follow-on activities that you are lining up) fits into a bigger opportunity.

For example, let's say you decide to focus on clean drinking water for a specific village in Africa. (This is an example only, and it is the type of focused detail that you will explore in Step 4. Step 3 is where you will broaden your focus and look around and above what you will be offering to see how big your scope will be.) Once successful, will you work to clean the water in other villages in the region and country? Or will you stay in that one village then work on other activities for the village such as growing food crops that will feed the people in the village? This will significantly drive the purpose of your venture as a solution for the lives of people in the village, and not a water cleaning solution for people across the region, country, or continent. "No, but wait," you say, "once we clean water, plant crops and feed the village, we will then do the same in other villages in the region and country."

Or you say, "that is correct, because we will stay in that first village and work to build better housing for the people and then build a school, and so on." So the next questions are:

3. Are you working on a geographic focus? If so, how narrow is the focus?

4. Are you working on a specific solution? If so, how specific is the solution? And how can, and how will it be applied to where?

If you plan on proving your new solution in a specific geography and then take it to the world, that vision for a bigger play will shape the planning forward. If you plan to bring in other existing solutions to focus on meaningful social impact in one geography, that focus will inform your planning forward.

There are no right or wrong responses to these questions; refine the questions until they reveal the direction and focus.

> **ASSIGNMENT** Write at least one paragraph on this section. Think, what is the bigger play for what you are working to accomplish? How does this tree (your initiative) more fully complete the forest, or potentially elevate what is now a stand of

THE OFFERING

STEP 4

Once you decide on the basic idea and your intention for the bigger play you need to articulate some meaningful detail into what you will offer to your intended audience; this is your product, service, and/or platform. Remember to include the standard features and benefits that are required for your type of offering, do not focus exclusively on special or differentiated features and benefits.

If your social venture is gearing around any type of science or technology, it will be helpful to use my framework for an **Offering Requirements Document (ORD)**. My ORD is a specially customized science and technology development framework based on a traditional Market Requirements Document (MRD).

You should consider whether or not or which of the following factors in your offering:

Invention ▶ Uncommon. This is when you work to achieve what has never been before. This can be done but it is comparatively rare, and it is often the most expensive in both cost and time.

Innovation ▶ Common. This is when you take an existing thing and materially change, modify, adapt, and reposition it into a new and improved thing. The key here is that innovation is done to something that already exists. This is significantly more common than invention and typically less expensive in both cost and time. Importantly, innovation does not necessarily stay positioned where it is at the moment; part of the innovation is that it might be repositioned and/or relocated.

Renovation ▶ Common. Renovation makes material modifications and adaptations to something that already exists, but it differs from innovation in two respects: 1. The renovated thing is typically intended to stay positioned where it already is, and 2. The primary goal is to uplift and refresh the thing so that it can be revived and stay relevant.

Revolution ▶ Uncommon. This is when you engage (maybe even fight against) the way that things are to effect significant change from the status quo, so that things can become what they should be. Revolution commonly requires invention as well as innovation, and the renovation of many things rather than effecting change to only one specific thing.

Nothing ▶ *This fifth option is the most common.* Most companies do more of the same, even when they know that they need to change. Doing something just to be doing something, or because you can, is also not good enough, and might be value destructive rather than value creative. Do not break something that is working and should not be changed. Think about this carefully; this question circles back to question #1: WHY are you doing whatever it is that you plan to do?

With the above being said, at the beginning of your explanation of what you hope to do and accomplish, I suggest that you first identify whether (and why) you intend to invent, innovate, renovate, or revolutionize, as part of creating a startup.

Next, in the context of that declared intention, you need to give some detail about the thing itself that you intend to work on and accomplish. Create as much definition to what it currently is and what it can and should become (it is helpful if you can connect it back to the "why").

Keep in mind that the "what" will likely evolve over time, and that is normal. You will be experimenting and exploring, trying different approaches, possibly pivoting once or more, until you find the right combination to open the lock on this opportunity.

> **ASSIGNMENT** Write at least one paragraph in your own words about what you plan to do. Then identify whether or not this work will require invention of something new, an innovation or renovation of an existing thing, or an revolution to overthrow something. Explore and refine your questions.

VALUE PROPOSITION

Now that you have inventoried the features and benefits, you need a simple-to-understand statement of why anyone will care about it and who they are to you (e.g., employees, volunteers, customers, suppliers, etc.) You might need multiple statements of value; do not assume that one statement fits all purposes, each stakeholder may have a unique perspective on what about what you are doing is valuable to them.

So, establishing the value of the offering to intended beneficiaries (i.e., most critically, the social venture itself, but also anyone who engages your venture) is key. Why would someone do whatever you need them to do rather than doing nothing differently? You need to think about value from several perspectives: the venture's leadership who will sign off on your initiative and allocate resources to make it happen, as well as your target beneficiaries.

This is another opportunity to think in the context of standards and differentiators. People have standard motivations, such as needing a product or service or solution that actually works as advertised and as suits their needs. But they are also motivated by the values around the offering that are different and set your offering apart from any other offerings.

When putting together and puzzling through the value of the offering and why anyone would buy it, think about their specific requirements and pain points.

For example, as to the value proposition for your own venture itself: Answer the question of how this offering meaningfully improves a specific situation or circumstance? Will it make a process more efficient and/or effective? If so, how?

As another example, regarding the value proposition for your target audience, address the question of whether your offering satisfies their fundamental needs and requirements? Once that is established (hopefully easily and quickly), start thinking about their motivations. Are they motivated at all? (Keep in mind that the most common competition is "nothing," meaning the audience does nothing to change what they are currently doing.) If they are motivated to change, what is behind that motivation? Everyone has a drive that is separate and distinct. There might be something that is causing your intended audience to be frustrated or stressed or to lose sleep. You need to figure out what that is so that you can address it.

ASSIGNMENT Write at least one sentence but no more than three sentences for each target audience on this section. Your value proposition or why-to-buy statement needs to be easy to say in 30 seconds and easy for your audience to remember. You are creating the hook. Your goal is for your target audience to say, "Wow, you can do that? Tell me more!" Explore and refine your questions. (Special note: This will change and evolve as you do the work in the rest of this framework. Check back routinely to make sure that this proposition is still relevant, and make updates as needed.)

GO TO MARKET

You need to think about and plan around delivering your offering to the target beneficiary (aka your customer) and market. Where, to whom, how, and when the offering will be delivered, should be detailed to a meaningful degree.

It is often helpful to think backward from the hands of the beneficiary. How did the offering make it into their hands so that they can start using it? Then take one step at a time back to where you are now. Are you building something for your target audience? Will you be manufacturing a physical product that you will be delivering to them? Will it be software that is downloaded from the cloud or used at-will via a web browser and delivered from a cloud-based server (including the delivery of installers and plug-ins)? Does whatever it is need to be delivered in person? You need to think through all of the moving parts as if you were building the clockworks inside of a mechanical watch.

TAM VS. TASM

In addition to the above, I would like to recommend an exercise to you. You may have heard of a TAM, *T-A-M* stands for <u>Total Addressable Market</u>. The *S* in TASM (sometimes called SAM) is the addition of the word: <u>Serviceable</u>.

► The **Total Market** is the big number of all people and money spent on products, services, and solutions similar to the one that you will be creating.

► The **Addressable Market** is the percentage of the Total to whom you can deliver a targeted meaningful message designed to inspire the customer to buy and use what you are offering.

    People will often draw a big circle and call it the Total and then draw a circle inside the big circle and call it the Addressable, and then declare a percentage of that number to represent the number of users or the amount of money that they hope to secure.

► You should add one more circle in the center, and that is the **Serviceable Market** number. Serviceable means that you can serve or deliver your offering to that number of customers (which could be discrete products or number of simultaneous users and clicks, etc.). This is a critical number to understand.

    When you are presenting to a government for a grant, or a philanthropist for financial support, or to your team, the most relevant number is not the Total, it is the relationship and connection between the numbers that represent the Addressable and the Serviceable Markets. The amount of money that you will be investing in the Addressable correlates to the amount of money invested in the Serviceable.

Let's say that you spend so much in the Addressable that you have a higher conversion to cash (meaning paying customers) than you have capacity to serve; then you have either overinvested in the Addressable or underinvested in the Serviceable. What matters is that you "right size" the investment for both in a coordinated effort so that you convert to cash (achieve paying customers) at a comparable rate to the amount of product or capacity of the service that you have to offer.

Understanding this relationship is critical to for-profit ventures, and it is even more vital for social ventures. This exercise will indicate whether or not you are wisely investing what money and resources you have. The better you are at prudent expenditure and getting good results, the easier it will be to secure grants and philanthropic investment.

If you were to build a TASM now, meaning a plan for your Total, Addressable, Serviceable Market, how big is the Total? (Don't anchor too much on this big number, as it matters but not as much as the next numbers.) How big is the Addressable Market? Who are the customers? Where are they? How will you put a meaningful message to them? At what cost? And how big is your Serviceable Market? Meaning how much serviceable capacity do you anticipate needing to create so that you can profitably deliver to paying customers? Once you start measuring this way, you will have a better chance of impressing key influencers and decision makers because you know what you are doing.

> **ASSIGNMENT** Write at least one paragraph identifying WHO the target audience is for your offering and WHERE they are located. Then give some meaningful detail in at least one paragraph on HOW you will deliver your offering to them; be certain to factor for special timing considerations that will impact adoption (e.g., this could be anything ranging from budgeting cycles to known deadlines on their end to the impact of holidays in a market.) Then construct a TASM with numbers and details so that when you present you can explain the relationship between the investment made and how many of any given thing can be accomplished. Explore and refine your questions.

TEAM AND EXECUTION

> "The right team and execution can
> make gold out of rubbish. The wrong team and
> execution will make rubbish out of gold."
> —Paul Kewene-Hite

Be inclusive and embrace diversity. Be an equal opportunity and equal pay for equal work employer. A typical, critical mistake made by first time entrepreneurs is ignoring the "boring" execution details of what needs to be done to make the startup a reality. Thinking through and documenting these details is the equivalent of creating a recipe with a list of ingredients for the meal you want to prepare and eat. Execution modeling is a step-by-step inventory of what needs to be done so that your startup will become real. When you present to potential investors or potential team members, the right people will NEED to know that you know what needs to be done. If you went into a kitchen to cook a meal from raw ingredients, what is the order of operations that you would follow? What is the first activity that you need to do? What is the second activity? What is the third? Do the same thing for your startup. Inventory the activities that must be done in order. Be as specific and as detailed as possible.

Performing the above activities-based inventory of what must be done is a good way to figure out whether or not you already have the team that you need, and who is missing and needs to be found and brought on board your startup. Begin by inventorying what activities MUST be done and then put your name next to which of those activities you can credibly perform (not what you are willing to try but don't really know how to do). If there are others already committed to your startup then list their names next to those activities that they can credibly perform. Once done you will see the gaps around must-do activities that have no name assigned to it. That tells you whom you need to find to complete your startup team. Those whom you need to find could be new hires as full-time employees (FTE) or part-time employees (PTE), contract workers, volunteers, etc.

A way to think about team and execution: When you are explaining what you plan to do to create a new company it is not unlike explaining how a clock tells time not that it tells time. Imagine opening the face of a traditional clock to expose the clockworks showing the gears, springs, and other moving parts. It would be ideal if you could document and explain every detail but at a minimum be prepared to give representative detail on what mechanism moves and how to make the hands move and in turn tell time. Do that for the details of the company that you are working to build.

ASSIGNMENT Inventory your top 20 (or more) mission critical activities. Put names of committed team members next to each activity. The critical activities that have no name next to it tell you whom you need to recruit to help you. Write at least one paragraph on this section. Explore and refine your questions.

BUSINESS MODELING

This is a classic and vital for-profit detail that most social impact entrepreneurs rarely talk about. Most non-profit and not-for-profit ventures rely heavily on donations and grants, but there are some that do sell products to produce income that is then put back into the social venture's good work. If you have any service or product that you will sell, you need to think about the business model for those things. Do not fall into the common trap of doing a little of this and that and hoping you have enough money to pay your bills. You need to think like a for-profit and make sure that you always have enough money in the bank and focus on bringing more money into your social venture than you spend. Then you can put the money that you have left over back into the venture (or return it to the government if that is required) and pay your bills and workers and build more value for society.

Society will not benefit from your social impact venture running out of money and closing its doors.

As with a for-profit, the money that comes into a non-profit is called "revenue." The difference between the revenue and any expenses (and losses) is called "income." Revenue can come from many sources. Thrift stores that are associated with non-profits such as The Salvation Army, Goodwill, St Vincent de Paul, and Deseret Industries, are examples of social ventures that:

1. Receive donations.

2. Sell the donations.

3. Use revenue from sales to pay the expenses to operate the stores, pay the workers, and do other social impact work with what is left.

Thus the "business model" for non-profit thrift stores is based on social impact, rather than returns to shareholders, as are for-profit businesses. If the Salvation Army, Goodwill, St Vincent de Paul, and Deseret Industries did not run their operations like businesses, they would not survive.

When I was the CEO of a for-profit startup in Dublin, Ireland, I volunteered with Social Entrepreneurs Ireland (SEI) specifically to help Irish social impact ventures to think like for-profits so that they could survive and thrive, helping the people and country of Ireland. I have continued to help social ventures around the world, and I know for a fact that running a not-for-profit like a for-profit business is vital to success.

ASSIGNMENT Articulate how you will make money. Don't just say "sell product"—you need to be specific about how you will sell, and various ways that money will be made. Write at least one paragraph on this section. Explore and refine your questions.

FINANCIAL MODELING

"Never, EVER, run out of cash!"
—**Patrick Turner**,
INSEAD Professor of Entrepreneurship

This is another excellent example of what non-profits and not-for-profits need to do to survive and thrive. Far too many social ventures fail because they do not engage finance and accounting as practically and seriously as a for-profit. If you run out of cash and go bankrupt, you will not be able to do the good that your social venture is designed to accomplish.

If you can build a Cashflow from scratch, then you can explain the details when you are asked to defend the numbers during any meeting. When you present, have an updated copy of your Cashflow, and be prepared to explain the details to those who ask.

Work to frame a financial model going forward that progresses you from where you are to where you plan to go. Building a Cashflow (as well as an SG&A, P&L, Balance Sheet, along with Budgets for MDF/SDF, T&E/T&S, etc.) is fundamental for understanding your initiative. At this point you may not know what those words and acronyms mean, which is okay. You will, however, need to invest some effort in learning their meaning so that you can use them comfortably in sentences as well as comfortably answer questions about them when asked. The definitions are below.

In the business world it is very common for people to assume that other people will know how to build and read the numbers, so they invest very little study into it. Basic financial skills are very important for all people in business. Not everyone needs to be a Certified Public Accountant or Chartered Accountant but being able to build and read a Cashflow should be a required skill for all business professionals.

If an investor, board of directors, or shareholder calls you to a meeting to discuss your venture, grab an updated Cashflow on the way to the meeting. The other financial instruments such as a Profit and Loss (P&L), Balance Sheet, Sales General and Administrative (SG&A) etc., are also important but the Cashflow is the most critical. If you don't understand your cash position over time, you do not understand your business.

Good financial planning is key to persuading shareholders, the board, and leadership that you know what you are doing. If you don't (yet) know how to do it yourself, work side-by-side with a finance-professional to build complete financials. I say side-by-side so that you see how it is done, you fully understand the numbers, and can understand and explain the details. (If you can build a Cashflow from scratch then you can explain the details when you are asked to defend the numbers during any meeting.)

Here are a few overly simplified definitions of business words that you need to know:

▶ **Finance vs. Accounting**
  Finance looks forward to what will happen.
  Accounting looks back at what happened.

▶ **Payment vs. Expense**
A <u>Payment</u> is when money leaves the company and is given to someone else.
An <u>Expense</u> is the agreed responsibility to make a payment at some future date.

▶ **Revenue vs. Profit**
<u>Revenue</u> is all money that comes into the company from sales.
<u>Profit</u> is the money that is left over after you have paid all of your expenses and taxes.

▶ **Sources & Uses**
<u>Source</u> is where you will get money.
A <u>Use</u> is how the money will be spent.

▶ **Budget**
A <u>Budget</u> is the amount of money (and time) that must be invested in order to do what must be done. Importantly budgeted amounts need to factor for how much money (and time) is actually available.[2]

▶ **Cashflow**
A <u>Cashflow</u> is the financial detail of how a company is being operated; money coming in, all money measured impacts on debts and assets, and all money going out.[3]

▶ **Free Cashflow**
<u>Free Cashflow</u> (not to be confused with the document that is called "a Cashflow") is the money that you have left over after all capital expenditures (aka CapEx, which is the money spent on fixed assets).

▶ **Working Capital**
<u>Working Capital</u> = **Current Assets** minus **Current Liabilities**. <u>Assets</u> are tangible things that have value such as property, inventory, cash, etc. <u>Liabilities</u> are things that you need to pay such as debt, taxes, wages, rent, utilities, etc.

▶ **Professional Fees**
<u>Professional Fees</u> are cash paid to professionals who are not your employees, such as lawyers, accountants, designers, engineers, etc.

▶ **CapEx vs OpEx**
<u>CapEx</u> is Capital Expenditure, which is money spent on fixed assets.
<u>OpEx</u> is Operating Expenditure, which is the money spent to operate the company.

---

2   Budgeting is incredibly valuable and essential for running your entrepreneurial venture and making sure that you never run out of cash. Your budgets should be planned, reviewed, and updated routinely as a team. Be sure to remind everyone that a budget is more than a plan for how much money will be spent, it is a reconciliation of how much must be spent in order to accomplish your plan compared to how much money there is to spend in the bank account. Monthly budgeting meetings, accounting back a month, and financially planning forward a quarter are good practices.

3   This is a window into all money that comes in and leaves the company. (You should typically have an 18 to 24-month Cashflow, with the next 13 weeks by week, and the rest of the months by month.) Be sure to use mathematics rather than simply typing in numbers.

▶ Fixed Assets

<u>Fixed Assets</u> are physical things such as land, buildings, equipment, vehicles, etc.

▶ Burn Rate and Runway

<u>Burn Rate</u> is the amount of money that you spend in a month.
<u>Runway</u> is the number of months that you have until you are out of money.

▶ Break Even, and Profitability

<u>Break Even</u> is when the same amount of money comes in as goes out.
<u>Profitability</u> is when you have money left over after paying everything.

▶ Pro forma

<u>Pro forma</u> is Latin for "as a matter of form" or "for the sake of form" and is a word put on financials to show that the numbers are educated guesses or projections.

▶ T&E or T&S

T&S/T&E[4] is <u>Travel & Subsistence</u> or <u>Travel & Expenses</u> (occasionally referred to as Travel & Entertainment). This budget is for rental cars, trains, planes, hotels, lunches and dinners, etc. T&E is used in North American English and in North American influenced regions. T&S is used in British English and in British influenced regions.

▶ MDF and SPIF

<u>MDF</u> is an acronym for Market Development Fund and is the money that you spend to take your offering to market.
<u>SPIF</u> stands for Sales Promotion Incentive Fund and is a powerful tool for motivating the point of sale to inspire them to advocate for your offering over the competition (the seller and/or buyer). This could be, and is not limited to, a payment made to the salesperson or a discount/rebate offered to the customer.

ASSIGNMENT Build a Cashflow. Do not assume that you will simply hire someone else to do it for you. Learn to build a Cashflow from a blank spreadsheet if you can; at a minimum, find someone on your team or work together as a team right now to build a basic Cashflow. Then write at least one paragraph on the details inside of the Cashflow, possibly including the details listed above. Explore and refine your questions. If you need to partner with a finance professional to help you, do it; but learn how to read financial documents, how to tell the stories of the numbers, and how to read along as others go through the numbers.

---

4   Watch this budget very carefully and put rules on all expenses and what can be claimed to make people responsible and hold people accountable. It happens at times that people (especially inside of large companies) game their expense reports so that they claim more money than they legitimately spend on real business. This line item can be value destructive when you are a fledgling venture that is carefully watching every dollar in the bank account.

FUNDABLE EVENT TIMELINES

Now that you have done your team and financial modeling, with your list of 20 or more mission-critical activities, you should put that list of activities on a timeline (for example 18 to 24 months). Creating a Gantt chart of mission-critical activities (highlighting milestones and fundable events) then harmonizing it with a Cashflow is good planning and good for presentations.

You can build your Gantt chart in a spreadsheet if you don't have project management software. What matters is that you can see the bars that represent the start and stop dates for each activity. On each bar you should name the activity as well as who is responsible along with the associated costs.

When you build a Cashflow you should then harmonize it with the Gantt chart to ensure that the activities and costs over the same months align month-by-month.

When you are building the timeline, with the completed Gantt on the top of the page and the Cashflow lined up below it, decision makers can quickly see that your financial and activities-based planning is complimentary in their construction.

The next thing that I suggest that you do is identify the **Milestones** (the moments in time when you complete an activity or task) on the Gantt chart. Then, differentiate between which milestones simply mark the completion of a task and which milestones are actually evidence that you are right in what you intended, planned, and executed. (This could be a working prototype or a village agreeing to be your first installation and reference site, etc. This is very different from finishing the writing for a business plan for example, which does not prove that you are right but just that you finished what you started.) The type of milestone that is evidence that you are right, is called a **Fundable Event** and it is very important for a few reasons.

▶ Evidence that you are right shows that the entrepreneurial venture is making progress!

▶ Evidence that you are right will be the proof that you need for continued funding and support from the company leadership and board.

▶ Evidence that you are right can be correlated to value creation (increasing value) and value capture (when the company is able to hold onto and make use of the value). Fundable events correlate to the increase in the value of what you are doing, and potentially increase the value of the company itself.

Governments, philanthropists, boards, and others who hold the keys to your future funding will be watching for the Fundable Events so that they can know that the work is progressing and that your corporate entrepreneurial venture is deserving of continued support.

When you have the Fundable Event Timeline planned out, and you regularly update it (you should update it at a minimum of once a week) then you and those who are supporting you can use it to keep track of progress and timings that might change over time.

Governments, philanthropists, boards, and other financial supporters might use the Fundable Event Timeline to plan when they will transfer resources and capital support to your initiative (just as an investor would do for a startup); when you hit your deliverables (the milestones and especially the fundable events) then you have a measurable defense for expecting ongoing support.

ASSIGNMENT Write at least one paragraph on this section. Explore and refine your questions. Create a Gantt chart identifying all of your activities (when each activity is intended to start and stop). Then put the Gantt chart and your Cashflow summary on the same page making sure that the months line up as shown in the following template (and on page 410). (You should have built a Cashflow in step 9.) Highlight the milestones that prove that you are right to call them Fundable Events; e.g., this is when the machine you are building actually works, it is when a stranger who has no connection to you purchases your product, etc. A fundable event is not when you simply finish what you started, such as writing a business plan or building a Cashflow with numbers that look good or designing a brochure that makes you happy, etc.

TEMPLATE

Cashflow Summary

	Month 1, Year 1	Month 2, Year 1	Month 3, Year 1	Month 4, Year 1	Month 5, Year 1	Month 6, Year 1	Month 7, Year 1	Month 8, Year 1	Month 9, Year 1	Month 10, Year 1	Month 11, Year 1	Month 12, Year 1
Opening Cash Balance												
Total CapEX												
Total OpEx												
Total Cash Out												
Total Cash In												
Closing Cash Balance												

Execution Timeline (Gantt Chart)

ACTIVITY	OWNER	ASSOCIATED COSTS US$	Month 1, Year 1	Month 2, Year 1	Month 3, Year 1	Month 4, Year 1	Month 5, Year 1	Month 6, Year 1	Month 7, Year 1	Month 8, Year 1	Month 9, Year 1	Month 10, Year 1	Month 11, Year 1	Month 12, Year 1

Note: Milestones mean that you finished what you started. Fundable Events are validation that you are right.

CAPITAL MODELING

Every venture needs people. And people need money. You might need an office, office furniture, computers, phones, etc. Then you need to pay for electricity, insurance, travel etc. (as you explored in Step 9). Modeling the money and money equivalents (e.g., office space, furniture, computers, etc.) that you need is essential. Do not fall into the common trap of "just doing stuff" and hoping everything works out. If you can measure what you need, you can approach those who can donate or otherwise make it available to your venture.

So, make sure to fully understand what capital is required to get your venture to the point where it can be self-sustaining, which is at break-even (meaning you are bringing in as much money as is going out). Those who are invested in your success will ask you what you need to take your dream for a social impact venture from where you are now to the point of self-sufficiency. Be prepared with an answer. It will be helpful to have a best case, base case, and worst case for your financials and capital requirements. If you can be successful with the worst case or base case numbers, then present those. It is typically best to NOT present the best-case numbers.

When you think about the timing and costs associated with investment from others you need to understand that money has the same three states as water: liquid, solid, and vapor.

▶ **Liquid**
This is when money is transportable, or otherwise in a state that it can be moved from one person or entity to another by either electronic transfer from one bank account to another, or from one person to another as some form of recognized currency. Example: When you have coins and bank notes in your pocket and use it to buy something at a store you are <u>liquid</u>, as your money is available for use. People will say "I'm not liquid at the moment." Which typically means "I have money, but I don't have access to it right now."

▶ **Solid**
This is when money is not available or for some reason, not liquid. The money might be in stocks or bonds, or otherwise invested into something that makes it not accessible, or portable, or moveable. But the idea is that it will expand as ice expands when water is frozen (because of interest or other successful growth by performance of the stock or investment or real estate, etc.). When an investor gives you money in exchange for equity (aka ownership) in your company, the idea is that their money will grow or expand (like ice) as you are successful as a company.

▶ **Vapor**
When ice is melted, a percentage of the ice becomes liquid (water) and a percentage is lost as vapor (e.g., steam). With money, the <u>Vapor</u> is any fee or charge or tax or disadvantageous exchange rate, etc., meaning there is some loss of value that could equal part, or potentially all of their money that was invested in a failed stock.

When a philanthropist (for example) pledges to invest into your social venture, they might be liquid in the moment and need to move quickly back into a solid before they incur taxes or other penalties on that money. Or they might need time to "liquidate" or otherwise liberate their money from other investments (stocks, bonds, real estate, etc.) so that they can give cash to your social venture, which means that to invest in you they are going from a solid, to a liquid (with hopefully as little vapor as possible). The expectation is that their money will grow and expand during its time as a solid with your social venture in a way that creates value for society and/or the earth.

> **ASSIGNMENT** Write at least one paragraph on this section. Explore and refine your questions. Will you be seeking grants and philanthropic support? Have you identified a grant and/or a philanthropist? When will you start the process?

BARRIERS AND ROADBLOCKS

Anticipating and identifying the threats to your venture's success is very important. More than simply pointing at the potential barriers, identify what will be done about them. Be as honest and as clear-minded as possible about what might be in your way and what might be working to undermine your initiative. Work with those who believe in you and are invested in your success to identify and plan for overcoming barriers to your initiative. Anticipating and identifying the threats to your initiative's success is very important. More than simply pointing at the potential barriers and roadblocks, it is important that you identify what will be done about them.

Inside the venture, the barriers and roadblocks might be as fundamental as lack of resources and funding. Those who are volunteers or on your payroll might be ill suited for the work, or they might actively work to create failure in your venture. Whatever the motivations or reasons, you need to identify what is happening, and have a plan for how to deal with all of it.

"We have met the enemy and he is us." From the comic strip Pogo by Walt Kelly, who borrowed it from a 1970 Earth Day poster. There is reality in the humorous yet sad observation that, no matter how well intentioned, we are very often our own worst enemy. Anticipate this reality, and plan what to do about it when (not if) our own behavior threatens to undo the good we are working to accomplish.

Outside the venture, there will also be challenges and competitive pressures, but this is normal. You might lack the authorization to pursue the work as you intend. Others outside the venture might be threatened by the work that you propose to do or are doing. It could be that they are actively working to stop your progress and success for political reasons. Anticipate the external or outside barriers. You will need to have answers prepared in advance of presentations and discussions about what you see and plan to do about it.

Keep in mind that you say that there are no challenges to what they are doing, that implies that either 1. You are naïve and fooling yourself, 2. What you are doing is of little value if it doesn't threaten anyone or the status quo, 3. You aren't trying hard enough if you are not meeting any resistance, 4. Change and disruption always ruffles someone's feathers. So resistance is not necessarily a negative or bad thing; it might mean that you are on the right path.

ASSIGNMENT It is vital that you understand what might harm you and otherwise get in your way. Create a list. Very importantly you must identify not only that the barrier exists, but what you will do about each. This will be very sensitive information, especially if it is regarding a person, so do not distribute this information. As soon as you click send on an email or click print you need to expect that the information is public domain info and the person in question will see a copy of it. Write at least one paragraph on this section. Explore and refine your questions.

STEP 13

FOUNDERITIS

> "Founders' attachment, overconfidence, and naïveté may
> be necessary to get new ventures up and running, but
> these emotions later create problems."
> —Noam Wasserman

READ "The Founder's Dilemma," Noam Wasserman, *Harvard Business Review* (HBR) (February 2008)

Founderitis is when a founder behaves in value destructive ways. Companies can be meaningfully harmed or even destroyed by the bad behavior of a founder. You need to take measures in the beginning when things are still good and healthy to protect everyone and everything from unforeseen value-destructive behavior in the future. Work with a good lawyer NOW on a rules-of-engagement agreement between the founders and shareholders to protect the company (and families of founders and shareholders) from what might go wrong in the future.

Founders who cause harm to the companies that they found and work to build are rarely as candid as American Apparel's founder Dov Charney who told Marketplace in 2014, "My biggest weakness is me. I mean, lock me up already! It's obvious! Put me in a cage, I'll be fine. I'm my own worst enemy."[5]

You might find out too late that someone is value destructive. Again, take measures at the start when things are still early and being formed. Sit down with a qualified lawyer and

---

5 Marketplace.org with Kai Ryssdal 20 January 2014, updated 27 March 2015 "American Apparel CEO Dov Charney on pushing boundaries and his biggest weakness"

document the rules for good conduct and what happens if one or more of the founders become value destructive. Hopefully you will never need to take action. Hopefully everyone will be rational and behave well.

Finding examples of well-known founders who harmed their successful companies is not that difficult. For every name brand person who fails their company, there are countless regular people who harmed their ventures (and those involved and around it) before they qualified for big press coverage.

> "We have met the enemy and he is us."
>
> From **Pogo** by Walt Kelly, who borrowed it from a 1970 Earth Day poster

There is reality in the humorous yet sad observation that no matter how well intentioned, we are very often our own worst enemy. Anticipate this reality and plan for what to do about it when (not if) our own behavior threatens to undo what good we are working to accomplish.

> **ASSIGNMENT** You and your co-founders (if you have them) need to put in writing what will happen if you or the partners become value destructive. Consider designating an arbiter or another independent, such as an independent senior industry expert or lawyer. This will need to be someone who agrees to function as an arbiter. Write at least one paragraph on this section. Explore and refine your questions.

BOARDS: ADVISORY AND GOVERNANCE

At the very beginning, you can organize a few people who are not legally affiliated with the social venture but are qualified to help guide you. This is called an Advisory Board. Advisors typically volunteer their time, but sometimes they ask for compensation.

> **HINT** If a person asks for money to give you advice when you need to protect what little money you have to run the social venture, that person likely does not have your social venture's best interests as a priority.

Once the venture is showing signs of viability (that it will actually survive and hopefully thrive), then you should organize (constitute) a Board of Directors (in some jurisdictions this is called a Board of Governors). This is not the Executive Leadership (sometimes called an Executive Board) but it is responsible for the company as a whole. The CEO (Chief Executive Officer) reports to the Chairman of the Board of Directors. The Chairman is ideally an independent outsider (not the CEO, or an investor) so that they can be as objective as possible. It is ideal if the Chairman has deep industry expertise. The Board of Directors, including the Chairman, should be an uneven number so that there are no split-votes. The

Founders and Investors/Shareholder would typically have an even number of seats. If you are a Founder, be brave enough to put trusted non-employees non-Founders in your seats.

> **ASSIGNMENT** Identify up to four people by name who could serve as volunteers on your board of advisers; make sure that these are people who understand what you are doing, they understand the industry, and you have access to them. Then identify an odd number of seats for your board of directors (3, 5, 7, etc.). Identify a potential chairman of the board (e.g., ideally an independent senior industry expert to whom you have access). Write at least one paragraph on this section. Explore and refine your questions.

MARKETING, SALES, AND BUSINESS DEVELOPMENT

Yes, social entrepreneurship ventures do <u>marketing</u>, <u>sales</u>, and <u>business development</u>. You still need to know where the right people are, how to persuade them, and establish strategic relationships to open doors.

Definitions for marketing and sales and business development are not always the same from organization to organization. Sometimes marketing and sales is one integrated organization, and other times they are separated, and sometimes they struggle to work together. Business development is sometimes part of marketing, sometimes part of sales, and other times it stands on its own.

I believe that one of the reasons why people sometimes struggle to differentiate between the three is because in the beginning the three were one integrated function. People wanted to exchange what they had for what other people had so they created marketplaces in town squares or villages and figured out how to transact with each other for goods and materials or money. Over time, people have artificially separated the three.

We will need to stay flexible within the definitions; you will need to work with the definitions of the three as your company defines them.

For the purpose of this startup entrepreneurship training, we will define the three neutrally, as follows:

▶ **Marketing**
The research and planning of where in the world the optimal customers are located and who those people are in that market. Then determining the means by which to capture the attention of paying customers (via the sundry activities that we typically associate with marketing, such as advertising, trade shows, press, etc.)

▶ **Sales**

The activities that result in the exchange of your offering for what you need from the other person. This might be money; it might be authorization; it might be any number of things that you need.

▶ **Business development**

The securing of strategic relationships that open doors and remove barriers. For example, let's say that you are developing a device designed to help medical patients better manage their pain during therapies. Business development (sometimes called "Biz Dev") would secure an agreement with a recognized medical research facility to perform a study to determine if your device actually does help people manage their pain during therapies.

You should identify the key activities that must be done for marketing, sales, and business development. If you already identified these activities in your team modeling and they are already reflected in your Gantt chart and fundable event timeline, then very well done! There is always more to do so you should continue to build the list of activities.

ASSIGNMENT Write at least one paragraph for marketing, another for sales, and another for business development. Give one or two specific examples of what you will do for marketing, one or two for sales, and one or two for business development. More than simply saying you will do it, SHOW what will be done and what will happen as a result. Do not write, "Do marketing." Give a detailed example of why what specific type of marketing will be done where, when, how, and by whom. Be prepared to be challenged on every detail that you write. Explore and refine your questions.

CALL TO ACTION OR THE ASK

In preparation for your presentations to potential lawyers, bankers, investors, strategic hires, and others, you need to identify the message(s) that will inspire key influencers and decision makers that you know what you are doing so that they will want to join you.

In business, the moment when you ask the listener for what you need from them is sometimes called a **Call to Action** or **The Ask** or **The Question**, but the intent of all three terms is the same.

Keep in mind that what is clear and motivates one listener may or may not be clear and motivate anyone else. Every person has their own requirements, mandates, needs, wants, hopes, stresses, pressures, and so on. Do your best to figure out what motivates the person to whom you are extending (what is often called "putting") The Ask or Call to Action.

For example, Steve Jobs (co-founder of Apple) asked John Sculley (the person who became CEO of Apple after Steve Jobs): "Do you want to sell sugared water for the rest of your life?

Or do you want to come with me and change the world?" That Call to Action from Steve Jobs worked for John Sculley, but it might or might not have worked for anyone else. Steve Jobs did his homework on what motivated John Sculley and that specific Call to Action or Ask worked on him in that situation.

As another example, if you are presenting to an investor and you bias your presentation heavily toward revenue and profit but never mention shareholder value, they may not fund your startup if their priorities are shareholder value. Or it could be the other way around if their top priority is revenue and profit. You need to puzzle through and figure out the critical motivations of your audience BEFORE you present the details and call them to action. Do not assume that your priorities or the primary benefits of your initiative are aligned with their priorities, or that you understand their priorities because to you this or that argument "makes sense."

Another thing to keep in mind is that if you are presenting to a group, everyone in that room is going to have their own biases and opinions. Figure out as much as you can about every influencer and decision maker who might be in the room during your presentation and Call to Action. It is okay to strategically lace messages throughout the presentation that speak to what each person in the room needs to hear; just be certain that all of those messages are truthful and consistent with what you are actually doing.

When you extend or put The Ask, depending on the culture and context, you can then briefly issue a call to action for each person in the room in the appropriate order of who matters most.

Sometimes, in some cultures, the messages in the body of the presentation are all that most need, and the formal Ask would only be issued to the most relevant and important person in the room. So be sure that you know what is most appropriate before you enter the room to present.

> **ASSIGNMENT** Write at least one clean sentence for EACH person that you need to persuade to support your initiative. Never give the same pitch twice; what works for one person may or may not work for any other person. Explore and refine your questions.

EXECUTIVE SUMMARIES AND BUSINESS PLANS

"Everyone has a plan 'til they get punched in the mouth."
—**Mike Tyson,** former heavyweight boxing champion of the world

Hopefully you have been writing down all of your thoughts while going through each of the steps to this point. I have found great value in keeping track of all ideas or thoughts whether they seem relevant to me at the time or not.

You will need to complete a written <u>executive summary</u> (a document that takes the same amount of time to read as to drink a glass of water) that will help influencers and decision makers understand enough that they will 1. want to know more, and 2. be interested (or even excited) to support you and the initiative. A <u>business plan</u> is a long, more detailed executive summary.

▶ Executive Summary

An Executive Summary, not to be confused with a full Business Plan, is ideally two pages and no longer than three pages in length. It should have the most representative and most relevant details, which are explained in greater detail in the full business plan. Make sure that every word in the Executive Summary is relevant to persuade the reader that you know what you are doing to build and run the company. The Executive Summary should inspire the reader to ask you for more information.

▶ Business Plan

A Business Plan is a longer, more detailed document than an Executive Summary. A typical length for a business plan is 20–30 pages. When writing business plans you should bias the writing very heavily to execution detail; show what you will do, when, where, how, and why. State the problem, build out the execution detail around the solution to the problem, put some financials in so that the costs are understood, and call the reader to action. Use multiple proofreaders and listen to their feedback. Questions and comments give you insight into what is understandable and working (or not), so be grateful and never impatient with questions and comments.

(I once submitted a 30-page business plan to a government body, not realizing that they required a minimum of 100 pages because more pages demonstrated thorough and complete investigation and consideration. In the business world, a 100+ page business plan to an investor or leadership team might imply that you are overthinking or cannot succinctly say what you need to say.)

There is no single magic format or outline for business plans and executive summaries. You should write the details in a way that will flow most naturally and persuade the reader, while also providing a document that will help guide your running of the company.

The goal for an executive summary and business plan, along with all supportive financials, should be to use it as practice. Stay flexible, move with what happens, and update your documentation regularly so that you are ready at a moment's notice to share and present. Do not get caught with a summary or plan that is out of date; that moment might be the game changer. Keep updating, practicing, learning, and adapting to change as you go forward.

> **ASSIGNMENT** All of the topics explored in this framework can be used in your executive summary and business plan. Create your 2–3-page executive summary first in a separate document (name it uniquely and always save the date in the file name every time you update it). Once your executive summary is completed, save a copy of it as a different file (using "Save As … ") with the date in the file name in the same folder. Then, begin the work of meaningfully expanding the detail in each section until you have a 20–30-page full business plan.

PITCHING AND PRESENTATIONS

▶ Pitching

A pitch is a short format presentation. It should be quick, clear, and to the point. An elevator or lift pitch is typically no more than one or two minutes (the time it would take to get from one floor in a building to a few floors up). Quickly state your name, what you do for your company (this should take a few seconds only) and then get straight into the pitch. Your pitch should clearly state that there is an opportunity (aka a problem), something that can be done about the opportunity, what you are doing about it, and how the listener can be involved. Keep the pitch to the point and positive.

▶ Presentations

A presentation is a longer format pitch but has a similar structure.

> **HINT** Presentations tend to too heavily message the problem/ opportunity and have too little practical detail on what can be done and what you are actually doing (aka execution). It is true that the listener needs to believe that you are addressing an authentic problem (do not solve a non-problem, and do not be a solution looking for a problem to solve) but remember that the listener needs to believe that you know what you are doing (execution level detail). Explain the opportunity and give representative detail into what you are doing about that opportunity.

It is common in the world of business that people don't practice their presentations in advance. People often work on their materials up to the moment before presenting and then walk into the room and start. Practice your pitch and presentations before giving them. There is no substitute for practice. Make sure that the first time that you pitch, or present is during practice rather than in front of the person whom you need to persuade. You only get one chance at a first impression. In case you feel that practice will make you less spontaneous in the moment, keep in mind that practice will make you better in a moment. For example, professional athletes practice SO THAT they will be better able to be more powerfully and effectively spontaneous in a moment.

The opportunity to persuade a key influencer or decision maker might happen at any moment. The quick two-minute pitch is called an elevator pitch or lift pitch because you might be in an elevator or lift when you realize that you are standing next to a key influencer or decision maker. You then have the amount of time that it takes to go from the ground floor to when they exit the elevator or lift to plant a seed. Hopefully they will invite you to present to them based on the strength of that one short pitch.

I have successfully pitched in elevators/lifts, hallways/corridors, stairways, sidewalks, while crossing the street, while at a salad bar, standing in a line/queue, while on the phone, and sitting next to someone on a plane. The point is that you never know when the opportunity will present itself. Practice your pitch over and over until you can say it without thinking about it. And practice it on different people to make sure that it makes sense and is coherent.

Practice your pitch without slides or props or other visual support. You never know when, where, or how you will be pitching. If your pitch is reliant on a slide or a prop, you might find yourself fumbling with your phone or computer, trying to pull up whatever you need, and end up burning the seconds or minutes that you have to persuade the listener. Also keep in mind that you only have a handful of seconds to create a powerful first impression; if you know what you are talking about and can say it off the top of your head without notes or visual assistance, then all the better.

That being said, if you have technology that can be quickly and effortlessly shown, then do it; just be aware that if it doesn't work then that is what the listener will remember.

Full presentations can start with a quick two-minute pitch at the top, to snapshot the long-story-short and give the audience an idea of what you are doing. Then you can start the longer format presentation. The longer presentation can include slides and product demonstrations if you have them, just remember to tell the story in an order that makes sense. Practice, practice, practice. There is no substitute for practicing before you present. Then after you've presented, practice some more.

As to time management, let's say, for example, that you are given a 30-minute meeting to present. Do not prepare 30 minutes of presentations and slides and demonstrations. A good rule of thumb is to prepare presentations for half of the allotted time. So, in this example you would prepare 15 (or 20 maximum) minutes of a presentation, for a 30-minute meeting. Leave room for questions during the presentation as well as questions and answers at the end.

Here is a thumbnail EXAMPLE of how much time should be spent on each part of the presentation:

▶ **Intro** (~5% of the available time)
Don't apologize—it is a common opener, but it is a poor start. Be confident but never arrogant.

▶ **The Opportunity/Problem** (~25%)
Do not pander or exaggerate; be factual.

▶ **What options are possible** (~15%)
Give a few examples of options. Do not make the mistake of speaking poorly of any alternative to what you are recommending. Be factual.

▶ **What I am doing** (~45%)
Do not hold back any secret ingredient (aka silver bullet or game changer) during your presentation. It is a common problem that the presenter will save the big "wow" of their solution for a follow-up presentation. If the audience doesn't hear the wow in your first pitch, there may not be a second presentation.

▶ **How you can be involved** (~10%)
Do not tell them what they will do. Welcome them to the party and invite them to be involved.

Start on time and finish on time (or a little early). Going over time should only happen if the audience asks you to stay and explain more. Even then, be sensitive to being over time. It is typically better to leave when you are ahead while they want more and schedule a follow-up.

Do not feel nervous or upset about any questions that might be asked of you. Questions expose holes in your presentation and tell you what was not clear or understandable to the listener (no matter how clear you thought that you made the point). Questions also give you an indication of what matters to the person asking the question. Write down all the questions that you were asked, and the answers that you gave, and then use those notes as preparation for future meetings (and work on clearer presentations and better answers for the future).

> **ASSIGNMENT** Build the materials that you will need (e.g., 2–3-page executive summary, slides, etc.). Practice that 60-second pitch until you can say it without thinking. THEN start working on expanded detail versions of that pitch so that when people ask you to give them more you can do 60 seconds on this detail and 60 seconds on that detail. THEN work on a 30-minute expanded version of that pitch, which gives more meaningful insight and detail. Explore and refine your questions.

STEP 19

SAVE YOUR WORK, UPDATE IT REGULARLY, AND REFER TO IT OFTEN

Revisit all of the above work regularly. Remember to save your work regularly and keep backups on separate secure devices. Once a day, or at a minimum of once a week on a routine day at a routine time, review and update details for all of the above work. The last time that out-of-date documents created a problem for me was when I was asked to send my current business plan to a meeting deciding the placement of millions of dollars (in the dot.com era) and I was not ready in the moment. Since that day I have always had current documents ready to send whenever a shareholder, investor, or board member asks. It always makes a good impression when you are ready to send freshly updated documents at a moment's notice.

Every time you update the document, save a unique version in a common reference folder on your computer. Use a consistent naming convention and update the name every time to include the date that you modified it (or some other intuitive system that others, not just you, will understand if they need to find information).

You never know when you will need to give someone a copy of your plan. You might be given advance warning, but sometimes the call is unexpected. Do not be caught off guard with an out of date version! Be prepared, and you will have nothing to fear.

ASSIGNMENT Comb through your document. Save everything. If you write something and you aren't quite sure how it fits, either put the thought on the last empty page of the document or create a second document in the same folder just for thoughts that you aren't yet sure how to use. You do not want to find yourself in the situation where later on, you wish that you hadn't deleted that thought.

On future days when you open and edit the document, do a Save As and change the version date on the document so that it creates a new document that is saved in the same folder. It may happen that in the future you will want to refer to an earlier draft, and if anything happens to the file that you are working on that day, you can always go back to the most recent version rather than starting over.

Keep a backup somewhere other than on your computer. (You should regularly back up your entire hard drive.) If you are working on paper, you need to keep your binder safe and secure at all times. When you are able, you might have someone scan every page in the binder onto a file that you keep on a small portable computer stick for safekeeping. If you edit your document on a public computer, just make certain that you do not leave a copy of your document on the public hard drive.

Regularly update your writing, save copies, keep the dream alive, and work to make it real.

DOING SOMETHING THAT MATTERS

My wife Natasha and I moved to the Silicon Valley before "dot.coms," and we left after "dot.bombs," so we lived the full cycle of that wild and crazy time.

I remember coming home from work one day, anguishing about the banality of the job that I was doing day after day. I remember saying to Natasha that the company and products that I was losing sleep over, into which I was at that point investing my life, just didn't matter. The products were not feeding the hungry or healing the sick. The products did not make anything better on planet earth. The primary purpose of our products was to increase our company's profit margins and generate more value for shareholders, but our products were not special. They were just more technology looking for someone who cared. What was worse, people around us in the Silicon Valley were making huge money out of thin air, doing little more than being in the right place at the right time.

I remember pressing the heels of my palms into my eyes, saying under my breath to my wife that I didn't want my life to be spent this way. I wanted to invest it into doing something relevant, something authentic, something that actually mattered.

I knew the word "social" in the context of society and being social. I knew the word "impact" as in doing something that could be felt, and an object or force coming in contact with another. But Social Impact was not incorporated into my vocabulary until much later.

I knew people who were working to help people in different ways, but at that early point in my career, I had not yet connected with the reality that it is possible for a for-profit company to have meaningful social impact, or at least, meaningful social spillovers.

The first time I heard a successful business professional speak about a for-profit company having meaningful impact (not just a spillover) on society and the earth, was Ray C. Anderson. In the early 2000s, he was a speaker at the Sustainable Business Symposium (SBS), which was a joint initiative between the University of Oregon's Lundquist College of Business, the Planning Public Policy and Management Department, and the law school.

In addition to her full-time job, every year for years, my mother-in-law Vera Moore volunteered her time tirelessly to pull together a meaningful SBS. Ray was the keynote speaker that Vera arranged that year, and on the day of the SBS, she asked if I would pick him up at the airport and deliver him to the event on time. Ray was the Founder and Chairman of Interface, Inc., which is one of the world's largest makers of modular carpets for commercial and residential applications. I will never forget the story he told the group about his "spear in the chest" moment when he realized that he and Interface Inc. needed to work toward having a zero-footprint impact on the planet. (He wrote a book about it called *Mid-Course Correction*, Ray Anderson (1998). You might also read the book that inspired Ray's "spear in the chest" moment: *The Ecology of Commerce*, Paul Hawking (1993)). I was fortunate to have some meaningful one-on-one time with Ray twice that day, when I picked him up and then in the car when we took him back off at the airport.

He opened my eyes to the fact that a capitalist could be socially responsible and have a meaningful, positive impact.

In no small part due to Ray's inspiring speech and our personal conversations, I started to think about business differently. Business could be used to deliberately make profit and build value for shareholders, and at the same time, do something that matters for society; it wasn't an "either or" scenario.

A little while later, I learned the principle of a Double Bottom Line—the first bottom line being value to the company and shareholders, and the second being value to society. The potential of a Double Bottom Line was a thunderous awakening for me. Then I learned about a Triple Bottom Line[1] which is, 1) profit, 2) people (aka social responsibility), and 3) planet (aka the environment). These ideas profoundly impacted the way that I thought about business, corporate social responsibility (CSR), and not only what is possible but what I needed to actively work to accomplish.

I have since worked to help people create for-profits that have Double and Triple Bottom Lines. We have worked to accomplish meaningful social spillovers where CSR initiatives do genuine good in the world. I've helped create pure social ventures with a primary focus on doing social good, from cleaning water to delivering medications to people with limited options and resources in the developing world.

Even if your for-profit took a small percentage of its profit and donated it to a qualified organization that is doing good in the world, that would help. I recommend that you create an ethos in your company that you, as a company, will do no harm, and that you will seek out opportunities to do good. Give your employees time every week where they can work on passion projects or volunteer in the community, helping children and adults, doing math tutoring at a community center, teaching the illiterate how to read, visiting the elderly, volunteering at a local hospital ... something.

There are Social Entrepreneurs all over the world doing excellent work as they sacrifice to make the world better.

There are For-Profit Entrepreneurs and Capitalists all over the world doing excellent work to make a better world.

In 2006, my brother and sister-in-law (Steven and Julie Hite) incorporated a US Federal 501(c)3 and continued doing their meaningful and vital work to help HIV and AIDS orphans and vulnerable children in Uganda with their NGO (non-governmental organization), TRUE Africa. TRUE is an acronym for Technology and Research for Universal Education. Their daughters, Melissa Seager and Rachel Eng (with the support of their husbands and engagement by their children), have become passionately involved. TRUE Africa continues to grow from strength to strength. Steven and Julie were both professors at Brigham Young University when they decided to engage their passions and aspirations to do good in the world. Since the founding of TRUE Africa in 2006, they have dedicated every moment they can find to helping children in Uganda. They inspire me.

My brother and sister-in-law, along with Ray Anderson, helped me realize that rather than waiting for an opportunity to come my way while working whatever job I might be doing at a moment, I can create opportunities to do good. In 2007, while I was the CEO of a for-profit startup in Dublin, Ireland, I started volunteering with Social Entrepreneurs Ireland (SEI) to help Social Entrepreneurs around Ireland learn how to run their social ventures with the business

---

1   In 1994 British management consultant and sustainability expert John Elkington coined the phrase Triple Bottom Line.

rigor of for-profits so that they could not only survive, but they could learn to thrive. Those hours volunteering were enormously gratifying.

I know from experience that when a venture (whether for-profit or non-profit) is run like a for-profit, they have a better chance of succeeding. It is a win for everyone when workers are regularly paid, they can pay their rent or their mortgage, they can pay their bills, they can cool and heat their homes as needed, they can put shoes on the feet of their children, they can see the doctor and buy medications as needed, they can eat regularly, and they can sleep at night. Stability at home makes happy, productive workers who create and capture value for their companies, and happy workers are more likely to get involved in their communities (especially if you make community engagement part of your business).

When a for-profit makes responsible decisions that are in the best interest of the communities where it operates and its workers live, that creates social benefit. That company also pays taxes that are used to develop and maintain infrastructure and pay for vital services in the community and country. The best capitalists understand their role and responsibilities in the system of systems in which they operate.

One of my friends from Harvard comes from very humble beginnings and he has built for himself a very successful career as an impact investor. Brian Heywood is the CEO and Founding partner of Taiyo Pacific Partners in Seattle, Washington USA. Taiyo's mission is "Protecting, Unlocking, and Creating Value in Misunderstood Markets." Brian has been a guest speaker during my teaching at INSEAD. He once told a classroom of participants at INSEAD, "As a capitalist and investor, when I get involved in an opportunity, I work to create and capture value for all parties in the mix; that includes the company, the shareholders, the workers, through to everyone in the ecosystem who relies on that business working to its fullest potential. Free market capitalism is about money as well as preserving and promoting value across the board." Brian is a pure capitalist, and he understands that his considerable success in business includes responsibility to the company and shareholders, as well as those making the system of systems work in every business he engages for profit.

I remember being interviewed on camera years ago. During the interview, I could see a venture capitalist named Steve Eskenazi waiting for me off to the side. I knew that he was a venture capitalist in San Francisco. I recognized him from his photo. I had been trying to get a meeting with him for months. He was in very high demand. He had seen me present on stage at the DEMO conference moments before. He waited patiently as I stood being interviewed. When the interview ended, he walked up and said, "Hello, my name is Steve Eskenazi. I enjoyed your presentation. I'm a big believer in Benjamin Franklin's credo, 'Do well by doing good'. Could we sit down somewhere and talk about how we might work together to do just that?" Free market capitalists and investors very often work toward creating meaningful positive impact on the world.

No matter which type of entrepreneurship journey you embrace, we can all do well by doing good.

VOLUNTEERS

"When I was a boy and I would see scary things in the news, my mother would say to me, 'Look for the helpers. You will always find people who are helping.' "

—Mr. Rogers

When my youngest son was very little, he was very interested in understanding how to tell the difference between good guys and bad guys. "Is he a good guy?" he would ask, pointing at some man in a crowd. He wanted to know if you could tell from a hairstyle, or clothing, or anything else that you could see from a safe distance. It was difficult for my little boy to understand that what a person looks like has very little to do with what kind of human being they are on the inside. "But if I get lost," he asked earnestly, "how do I know who to ask for help?" He asked a very good question. How do you find the right person to help you?

I believe that all people are born good, and that despite the fact that we all make mistakes, the vast preponderance of people on planet earth are, in fact, good. I believe that most people would inconvenience themselves to help someone in their moment of need. That being said, there are people who will not help, and there are, unfortunately, people who will harm you. I personally believe that the "bad guys" are few in number. Fortunately, time and experience have also proven to my son that there are, in fact, more good people than bad in the world.

Mr. Rogers' mother was onto something important. When you wonder if there is good in the world, look for the helpers. I have learned that keeping someone happily engaged as a helper (aka volunteer) is more difficult than getting them to help in the first place. In all of my volunteering over the years, a meaningful percentage of people disconnect after they start, because they don't feel that the investment of their time and effort is producing a benefit that matches their sacrifice. Worse yet, they might see value in the helping but they don't feel supported in their work, or the work and benefit is being mismanaged, so they disconnect intellectually, emotionally, spiritually, and then leave physically.

I have had fantastic experiences volunteering, and I have had disappointing and frustrating experiences volunteering. It is frustrating when you sacrifice your time to help others, and the effort is unorganized or chaotic. I once offered a Saturday to help our little town but when I arrived no one knew what was happening. When I walked up to a person with the word "Supervisor" written on the back of her shirt, thinking she would be in charge and know who was supposed to do what, I asked what to do. She said "Oh, uhm, whatever. Yeah, okay, so here take this shovel and dig over there." I asked about the purpose of the digging, how deep, what size, etc. "Just dig okay?" She waved her hand and walked away from me. I walked over to the general area that she had indicated, and a few other people were half-heartedly digging around in the ground, so I asked them what we were digging. "No idea. She just said dig." It was frustrating. I asked "But are we digging a garden? Are we putting in a set of pipes for a sprinkling system? What are we digging?" One of the other volunteers stopped and said, "I dunno man. But now that you ask, it seems ridiculous that we are digging for no clear reason." We tried talking to the "supervisor" who was increasingly frustrated and unhappy. She offered no better instructions, and she was unwilling to accept my offer to help organize and figure out what we were all supposed to do, so I went home. I still have no clear understanding of what was supposed to be happening other than volunteering to help our town.

I have helped people organize volunteers. A few simple things will help your efforts to organize volunteers. Simple, clear instructions will help you and the volunteers have a better experience.

Before you start this framework: If you have not already done so, please go back to the page called START HERE at the beginning of the book and complete parts 1, 2, 3, and 4 of the Preparatory Frameworks. Once that is completed, come back to this page and move forward to the following:

PREAMBLE **Write Everything Down**

STEP 1 **There Is an Opportunity (aka a Problem)**

STEP 2 **Something Can Be Done About It**

STEP 3 **This Is What You Can Do and Why**

PREAMBLE

WRITE EVERYTHING DOWN

It is common that people have a bright idea, then they think and dream about it (most likely talking themselves out of it), but never write down the details. Then they forget. At the time, the idea seemed so obvious and so clearly brilliant, but an hour later, or the next morning ... it is gone. Get into the habit of writing down all of your bright ideas.

Once you have an idea for your volunteering initiative, the first thing that you need to do is write down all of your thoughts about it. Don't worry about the structure of the writing yet; write down everything that you can think of that you want the social venture to do. If writing does not work for you, then record yourself talking. If you can't do that then draw pictures. If you can't do that then ask someone to help you with one of the options. Once you've documented your thoughts, get started with the 3-step framework and refer to your documented thoughts as you go. Do not delete any of your thoughts, drawings, or recordings. Use all of it as a reference as you work. Special note: Stay flexible around the central idea. Things will be evolving and moving around. Keep track of the details. Let's get started.

> **ASSIGNMENT** If you already use the cloud to back up all of your work securely, that is excellent. If you regularly use software that keeps track of versions of your work, so that you never invest hours editing the wrong version of a document, that is superb. If, however, for any reason, you are not yet able to back-up in the cloud or you do not have access to software that keeps track of versions of your documents, you will need to do these things manually. If you are working on a computer, create a folder with a logical name that you will not forget. Put that folder in an obvious location on the computer (not a clever place, but a clear and easy to remember place), that will still be obvious to you tomorrow and the next day. Create a new document and save it in the folder that you just created. Name the file something easy to remember and give it today's date; then every day you edit it, save a version with that day's date so that you can tell the difference between files. Always work on the most recent date and version of the file. If you do not have a computer, buy a spiral binder with lined paper (or an equivalent that is available to you). Put your name and contact information on it and keep it in a safe place. Do all of your work in the document or binder.

THERE IS AN OPPORTUNITY (AKA A PROBLEM)

The world is overflowing with opportunities to help those in need. That is not the question. What are you willing to do about it? Which opportunity? Of everything that needs to be done, why are you pursuing that specific opportunity?

Once you have identified an opportunity, you need to refine the message about it into a simple-to-explain set of sentences.

A classic blunder with opportunities is to paint an intense, sad, bleak, picture about it so that the listener understands in full, glorious detail just how bad the situation really is. Don't overdo the details of the opportunity. In all of the nitty-gritty details, you need to find a few things:

1. **Something meaningful that is representative of the rest of the details.**
   What you present to volunteers needs to be manageable in its scope. Be honest, don't downplay the reality, but resist the urge to go into full graphic detail. If you paint a picture that is too overwhelming, it could be off-putting for potential helpers who may decide that it is such a big problem that no matter how much they help they couldn't possibly make any real difference. People need to believe that their effort can make a difference that their time and sacrifice will matter.

2. **Something that can be repaired, fixed, or something (anything) that can be done about it.**
   If nothing can be done to fix it, pick something else that can be addressed in some meaningful way.

For example, let's say that there is a little old lady who lives up the street. She lives alone, no family lives near her, she receives no visitors, she is in her 90s, and her health is managed with medications (when she can get them) and she is not getting any younger. Her house is looking run down, and her yard is going to seed (she was once a keen gardener, but she can't work the earth anymore). She is a sweet person who would never dream of asking anybody for anything. If you were going to rally volunteers in the neighborhood to help her, how would you position the opportunity? If you knock on a neighbor's door and tell them everything, saying that they need to help here several hours every day to do everything that she needs done, how would you expect them to respond? (All of the details of her situation would be too much for most people.)

As another example, let's say that your neighborhood has seen better times. Bars on doors and windows are the norm. Walking outside is not as safe as any of the families on the street would hope. Unemployment is high. Every family is struggling to pay their bills. What can be done for the people on that street? How do you message the reality on that street in a way that motivates without creating anxiety for the potential volunteer? Telling a potential volunteer that they need to convert that mean street into Sesame Street would likely be overwhelming.

Paint a realistic picture without pandering or creating anxiety for the potential volunteers.

ASSIGNMENT Think of your opportunity. Write a few clear sentences about the honest situation so that when volunteers show up, they don't feel deceived or overwhelmed by the reality of it. 1. Inventory the details inside of what needs to be done, 2. Prioritize what matters most, 3. Score each thing that needs to be done as "C" (for Control, meaning something within our control can be done about it), "I" (for Influence, meaning we can't control it but we can work to influence what happens with it), and "NIC" (for Neither in our Influence or Control). When speaking with potential helpers (government, businesses, private individuals), focus your message on those items that are highest in priority with the letter "C." Then the second focus would be on high priority items with an "I." Those details with an "NIC" are not to be ignored, especially if they are a high priority, but you will work on puzzling through the "NICs" as able.

Create a message around the situation for the highest priority Cs. Frame them realistically but hopefully.

SOMETHING CAN BE DONE ABOUT IT

Now that you have an inventory of what needs to be done, complete with priorities and scoring what can be controlled, influenced, and neither controlled nor influenced, you are ready to formulate what can be done.

Make the messages around what can be done clear and unambiguous. If any of the activities are time-sensitive, illustrate the details of the impact of time. If there are associated costs, give details. If there are quality requirements, make those details clear.

ASSIGNMENT For each high priority "C," articulate what can or needs to be done in some meaningful detail. Once done move on to the "Is." Be aware that if any "NICs" are high priority, people may want to understand why those things are not being addressed. Have a reasoned explanation ready. You never know what someone might be able to offer as a solution for a NIC; "NICs" might be upgradeable to "Is" or "Cs" if the right person is involved (which is why you should never ignore or count out a "NIC.")

Identify implications for cost, quality, and time. Keep in mind that you can rarely have all three. At least one and often two will "pay" for the third. If cost is the priority, then time and quality will pay for the savings on cost. If time is the priority, then cost and quality will likely pay for getting things done on time. If quality is the priority, then time and cost will pay for the quality. Then if you bundle the priorities, the impact on the one goes up; if cost and time are the priority then quality pays, etc. For example, if you only have a dollar but you need to plant a whole garden, it will take more time and have a lower quality (unless you can find more money or donated plantings which will cost someone else money and will take time to recruit their donations to your project).

THIS IS WHAT YOU CAN DO AND WHY

Don't just throw volunteers at any old task. When someone asks you how they can help, don't just hand them a shovel and tell them to start digging. When people understand what they are digging and why digging matters, especially if the cause grips their heart powerfully, they will dig through the center of the earth with their hands if they need to.

When the volunteer sees what is possible, and why it is necessary, the sacrifice and time invested in their work will be filled with purpose. Show them why they are doing the specific things that you need them to do; understanding the impact of their sacrifice will become their fuel for sustained effort.

ASSIGNMENT If the volunteer has a passion for gardening, ask them to be involved in the little old lady's garden. Get them involved in building a garden along the sidewalks in the struggling neighborhood; have them make the garden something that produces vegetables for the community.[1]

Take the time to understand the motivations of the volunteer and, to the best of your ability, match their drive and talents to what needs to be done.

If a person has no specific skills or motivations other than to help, gauge their attitude and aptitude, and assign them to work on the highest priority activities that need the most help. SHOW them why that activity matters, explain what needs to be done by when, give them the tools they will need, and let them at it.

ASSIGNMENT Set up a feedback system so that volunteers can easily update you on what is happening and can ask for help when they need it. Be responsive. Be grateful. Show appreciation. Show everyone involved the successes that are being achieved. Be their support and cheerleading section. Keep things real, keep everything practical, and make every communication full of reasoned hope.

> "Volunteers do not necessarily have the time;
> they just have the heart."
> —Elizabeth Andrew

---

1   Look into the excellent work of Ron Finley. He is a community activist and a self-proclaimed "Gangster Gardener" who teaches people how to grow their own food. He transformed his community with curb-side gardens. He has a Ted talk as well as a course on masterclass.com that you should check out.

DON'T FEAR MESSES

Don't quit on things just because they appear messy.

EXAMPLE 1 **The Rubik's Cube**

My sister-in-law Julie's little brother, Mark, showed me how to solve a Rubik's cube when I was a young adult. He was watching Saturday morning cartoons, and I was using a butter knife to pop out the pieces so that I could put them back in order. "You'll ruin it" he said to me, not turning away from his cartoon. "Huh?" I responded. "You'll ruin the Rubik's cube if you pop the pieces out like that," he said calmly, while watching the TV. "Watch your cartoons," I chided. "What do you know about Rubik's cubes? This thing is really hard." He held out his hand without turning from his entertainment. I sat looking at his hand. He flexed his fingers in encouragement and I put the cube in his open palm. "Don't ruin it," I said with no small irony, considering that the moment before I had a knife jammed in it trying to break it apart. He glanced at the cube briefly and solved it perfectly in a handful of seconds. He handed it back to me while still looking at the TV. I sat in stunned silence. "It isn't difficult once you know what you are doing," he said. "Every color has only one place where it belongs. You just turn the colors on their paths to put each color back into its place."

EXAMPLE 2 **The Artist**

Rochelle Heywood is an uncommonly gifted watercolor artist. I have a painting of a samurai in my office that startles people when they realize that it is watercolor and not an oil painting. I once told Rochelle how much I admired her work, adding that every time I have tried to watercolor it has looked like a big black and blue blob. Rochelle responded, "If you saw any of my work in the middle of the process, you'd think it was somewhere between a Rorschach Test and a baby's finger painting. Up until the final moments, the watercolors are matter unorganized. Then there is a gathering that happens when the colors come together and I begin to see on the paper the image I had in my mind, or the object that inspired it."

EXAMPLE 3 The Shortsighted Quitter

During one of my startup trainings, I had a participant quit. His team had been working on the financials for their startup, and the numbers were not painting a hopeful picture. In frustration, the participant declared the training a waste of his time and started walking out. I asked him to stay, saying that I would sit down with him and his team to go through the financials. He said that with those numbers he would never be a millionaire from that startup, so it wasn't worth his time, and he left. I sat down with the team without him, we discussed their assumptions, and we made changes (to many things) until the numbers and business model worked. That team won the bootcamp and went on to create the startup. Over the years, a few others have also quit the startup bootcamp in frustration, saying similar things when the details looked messy around the idea or the numbers or various assumptions.

There are times when a mess is simply a mess and it would be best to start over. But the practiced and expert eye can look at assumptions and details to see what can be modified and updated. At times the problem is less the mess than the need to summon the will and ability to push through the mess to produce success. If more than one person is in the mix, then it takes everyone working together to make a mess into something good; thrashing around and making more messes will ruin what might have had a chance to work out.

Entrepreneurs look to see what everyone else is running away from, and they look for the opportunity so that they can take action to do something about whatever it is. An entrepreneur is the person who sees order inside the mess. An entrepreneur is a person in the developing world gathering coconut husks to sell to a company that makes doormats out of the fiber. An entrepreneur sells fruit from a cart on the street so that they can feed their family. Entrepreneurs are mothers with children, juggling a thousand activities in a day. Entrepreneurs are barbers, scientists, lawyers, builders, artists, plumbers, electricians, farmers, politicians, teachers, engineers, ad infinitum. All entrepreneurs deal with messes (some inherited, some that happen outside of their control and influence, and some of their own creation), bringing order where there was none or when it is just difficult to see.

While writing and compiling the frameworks into what has become this workbook, there were times when the mess of it felt overwhelming. More times than I can count I felt like giving up on it. The fact that you are reading it is proof that I resisted the urge(s) to delete the files and give up. I worked and pushed through the messes of it all and got it over the line.

It takes grit. Messes can be cleaned up. Sometimes, whatever it is you are working on is already in its order, and you just need to learn to see the patterns; sometimes, it requires an artist's perspective and touch on the mess to make it look real; sometimes, it is a base assumption that needs to be tweaked for the mathematics of it to work.

You can survive and thrive regardless of the messes that happen. Happily work the finger painting of your mess, whatever it is, until the samurai appears.

SALES:
THE ART OF
PERSUASION

"Your attitude, not your aptitude,
will determine your altitude."

—**Zig Ziglar**

W e all sell, all of the time.

I want to see this movie—did you see the trailer? Here let me show it to you then let's go tonight ...

Let's eat at this restaurant. I ate there two weeks ago. They have an amazing dish called ...

Oh! You should go to my university. I loved everything about it, and I'd go again in a heartbeat. This is what I loved about it and you will too ...

Clean your room. This is the 100th time that I have asked you. Do it now or there will be no TV or video games for a week ...

I couldn't keep my eyes off you from across the room ...

We may not think of it as sales, but every time we recommend or ask or encourage or explain or threaten ... we are selling. We pitch (which is the sales technique of persuading quickly), and we present (which is persuading by explaining in lengthy detail). Both pitching and presenting are designed to persuade and negotiate with someone to do something that they might otherwise not do or might not understand that they should do until you present the opportunity to understand.

Sales is a reality that is hardwired into how humans have survived since the beginning.

"Do not eat the berry from that plant. My brother ate those berries and died. Here, eat these berries from this bush instead. Give me animal skins for the winter and I will show you more plants that are safe to eat."

A persuasive person will be able to sell a product to someone who does not want or need whatever it is that they are selling (e.g., selling ice to polar bears during the winter). A win-win is when the person who is persuading (the seller) and the person who is listening (the buyer) both win in the transaction.

There are those who will lie or cheat to advance their win and your loss, but in my experience, exploiter personalities are the exception, not the rule, no matter what the mythology implies. The same goes for other similarly reviled professions (e.g., lawyers, politicians, tax auditors, etc.). People are good; it's just a tiny percentage of rotten eggs that create a majority of the stink that perpetuates bad reputations.

sale (noun) 1. The act of selling

sales (plural noun) 1: operations and activities involved in promoting and selling goods or services

sell (verb) 1. To deliver or give up in violation of duty, trust, or loyalty and especially for personal gain, 2a. to give up to another for something of value, 2b. To offer for sale

persuade (verb) 1: to move by argument, entreaty, or expostulation to a belief, position, or course of action, 2: to plead with: URGE

Regardless of the dictionary definitions, when people use the words **sale** and **sell**, what they typically mean is the act of persuasion to motivate some form of exchange (I give you what I have in exchange for what you have).

When you are planning how to sell, consider the following:

Before you start this framework: If you have not already done so, please go back to the page called START HERE at the beginning of the book and complete parts 1, 2, 3, and 4 of the Preparatory Frameworks. Once that is completed, come back to this page and move forward to the following:

STEP 1 **Sales, Marketing, and Business Development**

STEP 2 **Tail-Waggers vs. Influencers vs. Decision Makers**

STEP 3 **The Offering and Value Proposition**

STEP 4 **Go to Market**

STEP 5 **Barriers and Roadblocks**

STEP 6 **Call to Action or The Ask**

STEP 7 **Pitching and Presentations**

STEP 8 **Tracking Progress and Taking Action**

STEP 9 **Save Your Work, Update It Regularly, and Refer to It Often**

SALES, MARKETING, AND BUSINESS DEVELOPMENT

During an interview to hire a salesperson, ask them what drives and motivates them to do sales. If they say something along the lines of how they love helping people and making sure that they have everything that they need, that person has an account manager personality. If they say that they love the freedom to work deals and to make as much money as possible, that is a hunter outbound sales personality. If they say something along the lines of how they understand that without sales there is no revenue and without revenue the company cannot pay its bills and pay its employees, which means that employee home mortgage payments are missed and the children of employees aren't being fed, that is a sales team leader personality. The professional at the top of your sales organization needs to be an integrator personality who can see and reach across the departments inside the company as much as they work with their team to close deals to make profitable revenue.

The best sales professionals invest as much time inside their company (building relationships, networking, sitting down with everyone from engineering to marketing so that they fully understand and learn what is what) so that when they are out in the world working with potential customers developing sales opportunities they authentically know what they are talking about. The better they understand what they are selling, the better they can sell it. Be wary of the sales guy who is resented or hated by everyone inside the company because they are selling incorrectly (engineering will hate them for making promises that they cannot make happen, marketing will resent them for working different markets than where they have identified and invested in cultivating the opportunity for sales to sell, etc.). This applies for all types of companies, non-profits, and sole-proprietor one-person initiatives. Invest the time that you need inside (even if that inside is inside you) so that you understand what can actually be delivered to the customer before you sit with a customer to persuade them to commit.

Marketing, sales, and business development people, however, do not communicate and collaborate as much as they should. In some companies they ignore each other, in some organizations they fight. When they collaborate and coordinate, magic can happen. When the three work seamlessly with the entire organization, genuinely powerful things are possible.

I have found that a good litmus test for a sales professional is whether they are hated by the engineers. If the sales guy is running around doing things that give engineers headaches then you might have a bigger problem than engineers being unhappy; that could have legal implications along the lines of Sarbanes-Oxley[1], as well as other contractual messes that might occur. Get everyone on the same page and working together.

Another good litmus test for a sales professional is to see how the marketing team feels about them. If the sales professional's work lines up with the work of marketing, then you are doing things correctly. If, however, the salesperson is ignoring the work of marketing, then the company is likely wasting time, resources, and money. The issue here is that sales

---

1   Sarbanes-Oxley (SOX) is a law that was passed in 2002 by the US Congress. SOX is designed to protect against fraudulent financial reporting and it created strict rules for accountants, auditors, and corporate officers. Be careful because the implications stretch across organizations. Be SOX compliant.

and marketing often have different ideas of where the market is, who will care, how to motivate them, etc. Work to bring the two into alignment.

You may have noticed that the definitions and roles of <u>marketing</u> and <u>sales</u> and <u>business development</u> are not always the same from company to company. Sometimes marketing and sales is one integrated organization and other times they are separated, and sometimes they struggle to work together. Business development is sometimes part of marketing, sometimes part of sales, and other times it stands on its own.

I believe that one of the reasons why people sometimes struggle to differentiate between the three is because in the beginning the three were one integrated function. People wanted to exchange what they had for what other people had, so they created marketplaces in town squares or villages and figured out how to transact with each other for goods and materials or money. Over time, people have artificially separated the three.

We will need to stay flexible within the definitions; you will need to work with the definitions of the three as your company defines them.

For the purpose of this startup entrepreneurship training we will define the three neutrally, as follows:

> **Marketing**
> The research and planning of where in the world the optimal customers are located and who those people are in that market. Then determining the means by which to capture the attention of paying customers (via the sundry activities that we typically associate with marketing, such as advertising, trade shows, press, etc.)

> **Sales**
> The activities that result in the exchange of the offering for money. This could be in person (traditional sales), or through to taking credit cards on a website or inside a mobile application (digital transactions).

> **Business development**
> The securing of strategic relationships that open doors and remove barriers. For example, let's say that you are developing a device designed to help medical patients better manage their pain during therapies. Business development (sometimes called "Biz Dev") would secure an agreement with a recognized medical research facility to perform a study to determine if your device actually does help people manage their pain during therapies.

You should identify the key activities that must be done for marketing, sales, and business development. If you already identified these activities in your team modeling and they are already reflected in your Gantt chart and fundable event timeline, then very well done! There is always more to do so you should continue to build the list of activities.

STEP 2

TAIL-WAGGERS VS. INFLUENCERS VS. DECISION MAKERS

It is a very common problem that people do not know who makes the buying decision, who is influencing that decision, and who is just excited to be in the conversation but can neither influence nor decide what will happen. It is ideal if you can figure it out before the conversation, but once the conversation starts you need to puzzle through who will just wag their tail happy to be there, who can influence, and who can decide. Sometimes the influencer is so important that you won't ever meet the decision maker. Sometimes the decision maker won't meet without their influencer.

Sometimes the decision maker is not who you think it should be. The admin to the boss may be an influencer, at times they might actually be the decision maker rather than the boss. You need to figure it out.

▶ Don't assume you know who has influence

A friend of mine once struggled mightily to figure out who was the influencer and decision maker in a company that he had identified as a potential customer. He was invited back to present repeatedly, and the crowd was always excited by the technology that he was showing, but the sale was not progressing, and he could not figure out why. One day he asked, point blank, if they would make a purchase and he figured out very quickly that none of them had any influence or decision-making authority. It was a room of tail-waggers who were very happy to see the newest advancements in technology. What is more, no one in that group had any idea who did make purchasing decisions in their own company. Weeks of presentations had not resulted in a sale, and he realized that he had wasted a lot of time and opportunity. He stopped presenting to that group and started knocking on doors and making calls trying to find the right people. It took him a few days of persistence, but he eventually found a person whom several people had indicated was the decision maker. That decision maker pointed him to his administrative assistant, suggesting that my friend present to her. My friend made the presentation to her. She was very neutral and appeared unimpressed. She thanked him for his time, and he left. He was deflated by the experience. Several days later that admin called saying that the decision maker kindly requested a formal presentation to a group. My friend made the presentation to all new faces in the company, the decision maker sat in the back of the room. The company made a large order from my friend.

▶ Don't underestimate the Admin

Here is another powerful administrative assistant story. I was helping a company make a multi-million-dollar decision selecting a technology that was going to materially impact the next several years of their business. We had been meeting with salespeople from various companies to work through which technology would be best. After one particularly impressive presentation, the decision maker gave some very encouraging feedback to the salesperson and he left smiling, undoubtedly optimistic about his chances to make a multi-million-dollar deal with us. As the decision maker and I left the conference room, we were talking about how impressed we were with the salesperson and his presentation. The decision maker's admin chimed in saying that she didn't trust the salesman. The decision maker stepped over to her desk and asked why. She explained that before the meeting started, she had heard him speaking rather loudly and rudely to someone on the phone. She said, "The things he said were authentically scary. I worry for whomever he was talking to on that call. Then when you walked up he was all sweetness and light. I've been sitting here wondering if I should call someone to try to stop something bad from happening." We didn't go with that technology and salesperson. We kept hunting for alternatives. We also sat down with our lawyer to see what our options were regarding the call that the administrative assistant had overheard.

▶ Don't be the Donut Guy

There was a guy who brought donuts to our company every Friday for months. The donuts were excellent and eagerly anticipated every Friday morning. One Friday morning there were no donuts. The following Friday, again, there were no donuts. I asked a colleague if I just missed the donuts, or if donut guy had not shown up yet that day, or maybe he had changed the timing of the donut delivery. My colleague looked at me with surprise and asked, "What donut guy?" I said "You know, the guy who used to bring donuts every Friday morning. I don't know his name; he was just the donut guy who delivered donuts and hung out with people chatting while we ate the donuts." My colleague laughed out loud. "That guy was a salesman hoping to get your attention. He wanted to sell his tech to you!" I was stunned. "What? What company? What technology?" My colleague said that their company logo was on the cover of the donut boxes. I realized that I had never seen the lid of the boxes when they were closed. I always arrived after the donuts arrived and left before they were finished. I feel badly for donut guy. All of those donuts, and he knew my name. Every Friday for weeks, standing in the room eating donuts with us all, he never said a word to me about his company or technology. All of those donut receipts submitted as expenses, and no sale to report. Do not be the donut guy!

> **ASSIGNMENT** Once you have worked with marketing to identify the market and customers, and you have worked with business development to have doors opened and barriers removed, work to identify the decision makers and their influencers. Then work on an approach that you believe will persuade the influencers and decision makers to go with you. Expect the unexpected. Take direction and never underestimate who and what factors will matter in the decision making process. Treat everyone with respect.

THE OFFERING AND VALUE PROPOSITION

You need to think and plan in the context of standards and differentiators. People have standard motivations to buy, such as needing a product or service or solution that actually works as advertised and suits their needs. There might be specific features that must exist in the offering, and without those features there is simply no way that they can buy it. After the buyer establishes that your offering meets the standards that they require, they can be persuaded by the features that differentiate your offering from the competition. Do not make the mistake of leaving out a standard because you don't like it or believe that it matters; whatever it is might be essential to the potential customer. For example: long after floppy disk drives became irrelevant on personal computers, some companies and governments still required floppy disk drives to ensure backward compatibility with content on floppy disks and/or because their internal processes were slow to update. Companies that continued to offer floppy drives continued to sell successfully even though that standard feature was outmoded and replaced by other technology. Find out what the buyer has on their list of must have standards so that you don't waste the opportunity of offering something that they cannot even consider buying.

When putting together and puzzling through the value of the offering and why anyone would buy it, think about their specific requirements and pain points.

As an example, when I worked at a technology company, we were presenting for a significant contract worth millions of dollars. We figured out that a primary motivation was around the fact that they had a unified global P&L anchored on a single currency and they needed to purchase in that single currency everywhere in the world. We figured out how to make it possible for the client to buy in their single currency anywhere in the world, and that very heavily biased them toward buying our technology. So what motivated them was less about the specific features and benefits of the technology itself. As long as the technology met the basic technical specifications, it was how they bought the technology that differentiated our offering and motivated them to buy from our company versus the other companies that presented to them at the same time.

You need to offer something that has specific value that correlates to the bona fide problems and pains being experienced by the potential buyer. If they don't see relief in what you are offering, they will be less motivated to pay attention to you.

Figure out what causes the potential buyer to lose sleep at night. If what you are selling does not scratch the buyer's itch or solve their problems then you are a solution looking for a problem that doesn't exist for that buyer.

▶ Do your homework

That could mean doing research before you sit down with the buyer, and it could mean asking good questions and listening to the buyer's responses. Do not make the common mistake of not listening because you are busy thinking of some terribly clever thing that you want to say. Ask good questions, then listen to what is said. Then shape your response accordingly.

▶ Never give the same pitch twice

What message works for one person may or may not work for the next person. Puzzle through and figure out what motivates the person whom you are working to persuade. If, for example, you try to dazzle a potential buyer with your amazing technology and they are motivated purely by price, then your razzle-dazzle technology pitch is less likely to result in a sale. If price is their motivation, see how you can fit a solution into their budget; if you can fit some cool technology into the budget then maybe you have a chance.

Think of what you are offering in the following ways:

> ▶ What about the offering is standard, meaning it is required in order to be eligible and/or it ensures normal functioning and no barriers to authorization for the transaction?

> ▶ What differentiators in the offering are relevant to the person who is buying?

> ▶ What is the value of the offering to everyone involved in the potential transaction?

The following definitions are relevant due to the fact that during pitches and presentations sales people too commonly throw around buzzy words such as "innovative" and "revolutionary" when what they are selling is, in fact, neither. The best sales professionals develop credibility by understanding what a customer actually needs and then using accurate words without hyperbole that fit the reality of what they are selling.

Invention ▶ Uncommon. This is when you work to achieve what has never been before. This can be done but it is comparatively rare, and it is often the most expensive in both cost and time.

Innovation ▶ Common. This is when you take an existing thing and materially change, modify, adapt, and reposition it into a new and improved thing. The key here is that innovation is done to something that already exists. This is significantly more common than invention and typically less expensive in both cost and time. Importantly, innovation does not necessarily stay positioned where it is at the moment; part of the innovation is that it might be repositioned and/or relocated.

Renovation ▶ Common. Renovation makes material modifications and adaptations to something that already exists, but it differs from innovation in two respects: 1. The renovated thing is typically intended to stay positioned where it already is, and 2. The primary goal is to uplift and refresh the thing so that it can be revived and stay relevant.

Revolution ▶ Uncommon. This is when you engage (maybe even fight against) the way that things are to effect significant change from the status quo, so that things can become what they should be. Revolution commonly requires invention as well as innovation, and the renovation of many things rather than effecting change to only one specific thing.

Nothing ▶ *This fifth option is the most common.* Most companies do more of the same, even when they know that they need to change. Doing something just to be doing something, or because you can, is also not good enough, and might be value destructive rather than value creative. Do not break something that is working and should not be changed. Think about this carefully; this question circles back to question #1: WHY are you doing whatever it is that you plan to do?

> **ASSIGNMENT** Why would someone buy whatever you are selling? Especially, why should they do what you want them to do rather than doing nothing differently? Write at least one paragraph in your own words about what you plan to offer. Identify whether or not this work will include an actual invention of something new, an innovation or renovation of an existing thing, or a revolution to overthrow something. Explore and refine your questions.

> **ASSIGNMENT** Write at least one sentence but no more than three sentences for each potential customer you plan to approach. Your value proposition or why-to-buy statement needs to be easy to say in 30 seconds and easy for your audience to remember. You are creating the hook. Your goal is for your target audience to say, "Wow, you can do that? Tell me more!" Explore and refine your questions. (Special note: This will change and evolve as you do the work in the rest of this framework. Check back routinely to make sure that this proposition is still relevant, and make updates as needed.)

STEP 4

GO TO MARKET

You need to plan how to deliver your offering to the target customer and market (whether it is internal to your company or external). Where, when, how, and to whom the offering will be delivered should be detailed to a meaningful degree.

It is often helpful to think backward from the hands of the customer. How did the offering make it into their hands so that they can start using it? Then take one step at a time back to where you are now. Will you be manufacturing a physical product? Will it be software that is downloaded from the cloud or used at-will via a web browser and delivered from a cloud-based server (including the delivery of installers and plug-ins)? Is it a service that will be delivered over the cloud or in person? Think through all of the moving parts as if you were building the clockworks inside of a mechanical watch.

Let me give you a high-level example that begins with the goal and works backwards. In the business world, this is commonly called "Reverse Engineering"—taking a process or product apart to see how it was built so that you can build the same thing without starting from scratch. Of course, this timeline is for example only and will differ for every product and market as every delivery involves unique considerations that must be factored into planning.

Let's say that your startup will be designing, engineering, manufacturing, and then delivering a physical electronic device to the market. (I'll use a physical product that needs to be manufactured as an example, because it tends to be more complicated than engineering and delivering software.) Let's further assume that there are seasonality considerations for your target market.

1. **Product in stores (online as well as brick-and-mortar)**
   Let's say that you need to have the product in stores (online and in physical locations) by November (for example), so that you can hit the big selling season for your product in late November through late-December.

2. **Pallets[2] of finished goods shipping to distribution, fulfillment, and stores**
   Which means that you need to have pallets of boxes of your physical product in distribution by October so that it can be delivered to stores in October and November.

3. **Active manufacturing**
   Which means that you should be actively manufacturing by August or no later than September so that you can begin shipping in September to hit distribution in October.

4. **Raw materials to manufacturing**
   Which means that you need to have all raw materials, casts, tools, and manufacturing BOMs (Bill of Materials) and specifications, etc. to the manufacturer by August, but ideally in July for manufacture in August.

5. **Testing complete**
   Which means that you need to have the product finalized and tested and ready for manufacturing no later than July.

6. **Active Beta and Alpha testing along with bug regression and fixes**
   Which means that you should have been in beta testing no later than May, and alpha testing (for example) as early as February or March, giving your team time for bug regression and fixes. This is also the time that you should be ordering all of the raw materials to make sure that they arrive at the manufacturer's facility on time.

7. **Technical Specifications and other engineering completed**
   The freeze on modifications to all technical specifications for the product should happen by February, with engineering and design completed by that time.

8. **Research and Development (R&D)**
   You need to work with engineering to ensure that you have time to complete that work between now and January-February, which also means working with Marketing and all other internal parties to ensure that the device that you are making is correctly planned and aligned with all relevant expectations.

---

2   A pallet is a type of low profile platform typically made of wood, but at times, other materials. Boxes and other materials are stacked on the pallet, which is then movable by a forklift from one part of a factory to another, and then loaded onto trucks, etc.

9. **Marketing and Sales Activities well in advance**

Then you have considerations for all marketing and sales activities. You need to advertise to stores and distribution so that they can order the product and have it in stores in time, and that needs to be done far in advance. You also need to plan when you will advertise to the customer, so that they are motivated to buy once the product is in stores and online.

TAM VS. TASM

In addition to the above, I would like to recommend an exercise to you. You may have heard of a TAM, *T-A-M* stands for <u>Total Addressable Market</u>. The *S* in TASM (sometimes called SAM) is the addition of the word: <u>Serviceable</u>.

▶ The **Total Market** is the big number of all people and money spent on products, services, and solutions similar to the one that you will be creating.

▶ The **Addressable Market** is the percentage of the Total to whom you can deliver a targeted meaningful message designed to inspire the customer to buy and use what you are offering.

People will often draw a big circle and call it the Total and then draw a circle inside the big circle and call it the Addressable, and then declare a percentage of that number to represent the number of users or the amount of money that they hope to secure.

▶ You should add one more circle in the center, and that is the **Serviceable Market** number. Serviceable means that you can serve or deliver your offering to that number of customers (which could be discrete products or number of simultaneous users and clicks, etc.). This is a critical number to understand.

When you are presenting to a Board of Directors, or a CEO or CFO, or an investor, or to your team, the most relevant number is not the Total, it is the relationship and connection between the numbers that represent the Addressable and the Serviceable Markets. The amount of money that you will be investing in the Addressable correlates to the amount of money invested in the Serviceable.

Let's say that you spend so much in the Addressable that you have a higher conversion to cash (meaning paying customers) than you have capacity to serve; then you have either overinvested in the Addressable or underinvested in the Serviceable. What matters is that you "right size" the investment for both in a coordinated effort so that you convert to cash (achieve paying customers) at a comparable rate to the amount of product or capacity of the service that you have to offer.

If you were to build a TASM now, meaning a plan for your Total, Addressable, Serviceable Market, how big is the Total? (Don't anchor too much on this big number, as it matters but not as much as the next numbers.) How big is the Addressable Market? Who are the customers? Where are they? How will you deliver a meaningful message to them? At what cost? And how big is your Serviceable Market? That is, how much serviceable capacity do you anticipate needing to create so that you can profitably deliver to paying customers? Once you start measuring this way, you will have a better chance of impressing key influencers and decision makers because you know what you are doing.

> **ASSIGNMENT** Write at least one paragraph identifying WHO the target audience is for your offering and WHERE they are located. Then give some meaningful detail in at least one paragraph on HOW you will deliver your offering to them; be certain to account for special timing considerations that will impact adoption (this could be anything from budgeting cycles to known deadlines on their end to the impact of holidays in a market.) Then construct a TASM with numbers and details so that when you present you can explain the relationship between the investment made and how many people you addressed and how many you can serve. Explore and refine your questions.

BARRIERS AND ROADBLOCKS
STEP 5

Anticipating and identifying the threats to success is very important. More than simply pointing at the potential barriers, identify what will be done about them. Be as honest and as clear minded as possible about what might be in your way and what might be working to undermine your sale.

Inside the company, the barriers and roadblocks might be as fundamental as a lack of support, resources, and funding. Another might be a lack of authorization to pursue the sale. Others inside the company might be threatened by the sales initiative that you propose to do or are doing. It could be that they are actively working to stop your progress and success for political reasons. Whatever the motivations or reasons, you need to identify what is happening and have a plan for how to deal with it.

Outside the company, there will also be challenges and competitive pressures, but this is normal business. You will need to have answers prepared in advance of presentations and discussions about what you see and plan to do about the challenges and competitive pressures.

Keep in mind that when people say that there are no challenges to what they are doing, that implies that either 1. They are naïve and fooling themselves, 2. What they are doing is of little value if it doesn't threaten anyone or the status quo, 3. They aren't trying hard enough if they are not meeting any resistance. Change and disruption sometimes makes others unhappy; anticipate who will be unhappy about what you are doing so that you can prepare and get ahead of what they might do in response. So resistance is not necessarily a negative or bad thing; it might mean that they are on the right path.

> **ASSIGNMENT** It is vital that you understand what might harm you and otherwise get in your way. Create a list. Very importantly you must identify not only that the barrier exists, but what you will do about each. This will be very sensitive information, especially if it is regarding a person, so do not distribute this information. As soon as you click send on an email or click print you need to expect that the information is public domain info and the person in question will see a copy of it. Write at least one paragraph on this section. Explore and refine your questions.

CALL TO ACTION OR THE ASK

In preparation for your presentations to potential customers you need to identify the message(s) that will inspire key influencers and decision makers that you know what you are doing so that they will want to join you.

The moment when you ask the listener for what you need from them is sometimes called a **Call to Action** or **The Ask** or **The Question** but the intent is the same.

Keep in mind that what is clear and motivates one listener may or may not be clear and motivate anyone else. Every person has their own requirements, mandates, needs, wants, hopes, stresses, pressures, and so on. Do your best to figure out what motivates the person to whom you are extending (what is often called "putting") The Ask or Call to Action.

For example, Steve Jobs (co-founder of Apple) asked John Sculley (the person who became CEO of Apple after Steve Jobs): "Do you want to sell sugared water for the rest of your life? Or do you want to come with me and change the world?" That Call to Action from Steve Jobs worked for John Sculley, but it might or might not have worked for anyone else. Steve Jobs did his homework on what motivated John Sculley and that specific Call to Action or Ask worked on him in that situation.

Another thing to keep in mind is that if you are presenting to a group, everyone in that room is going to have their own biases and opinions. Figure out as much as you can about every influencer and decision maker who might be in the room during your presentation and Call to Action. It is okay to strategically lace messages throughout the presentation that speak to what each person in the room needs to hear; just be certain that all of those messages are truthful and consistent with what you are actually doing.

When you extend or put The Ask, depending on the culture and context, you can then briefly issue a call to action for each person in the room in the appropriate order of who matters most.

Sometimes, in some cultures, the messages in the body of the presentation are all that most need, and the formal Ask would only be issued to the most relevant and important person in the room. So be sure that you know what is most appropriate before you enter the room to present.

> **ASSIGNMENT** Write at least one clean sentence for EACH person that you need to persuade to support your initiative. Never give the same pitch twice; what works for one person may or may not work for any other person. Explore and refine your questions.

PITCHING AND PRESENTATIONS

▶ Pitching

A pitch is a short format presentation. It should be quick, clear, and to the point. An elevator or lift pitch is typically no more than one or two minutes (the time it would take to get from one floor in a building to a few floors up). Quickly state your name, what you do for your company (this should take a few seconds only) and then get straight into the pitch. Your pitch should clearly state that there is an opportunity (aka a problem), something that can be done about the opportunity, what you are doing about it, and how the listener can be involved. Keep the pitch to the point and positive.

▶ Presentations

A presentation is a longer format pitch but has a similar structure.

> **HINT** Presentations tend to too heavily message the problem/opportunity and have too little practical detail on what can be done and what you are actually doing (aka execution). It is true that the listener needs to believe that you are addressing an authentic problem (do not solve a non-problem, and do not be a solution looking for a problem to solve) but remember that the listener needs to believe that you know what you are doing (execution level detail). Explain the opportunity and give representative detail into what you are doing about that opportunity.

It is common in the world of business that people don't practice their presentations in advance. People often work on their materials up to the moment before presenting and then walk into the room and start. Practice your pitch and presentations before giving them. There is no substitute for practice. Make sure that the first time that you pitch, or present is during practice rather than in front of the person whom you need to persuade. You only get one chance at a first impression. In case you feel that practice will make you less spontaneous in the moment, keep in mind that practice will make you better in a moment. For example, professional athletes practice SO THAT they will be better able to be more powerfully and effectively spontaneous in a moment.

The opportunity to persuade a key influencer or decision maker might happen at any moment. The quick two-minute pitch is called an elevator pitch or lift pitch because you might be in an elevator or lift when you realize that you are standing next to a key influencer or decision maker. You then have the amount of time that it takes to go from the ground floor to when they exit the elevator or lift to plant a seed. Hopefully they will invite you to present to them based on the strength of that one short pitch.

I have successfully pitched in elevators/lifts, hallways/corridors, stairways, sidewalks, while crossing the street, while at a salad bar, standing in a line/queue, while on the phone, and sitting next to someone on a plane. The point is that you never know when the opportunity will present itself. Practice your pitch over and over until you can say it without thinking about it. And practice it on different people to make sure that it makes sense and is coherent.

Practice your pitching without slides or props or other visual support. You never know when, where, or how you will be pitching. If your pitch is reliant on a slide or a prop, you might find yourself fumbling with your phone or computer, trying to pull up whatever you need, and end up burning the seconds or minutes that you have to persuade the listener. Also keep in mind that you only have a handful of seconds to create a powerful first impression; if you know what you are talking about and can say it off the top of your head without notes or visual assistance, then all the better.

That being said, if you have technology that can be quickly and effortlessly shown, then do it; just be aware that if it doesn't work then that is what the listener will remember.

Full presentations can start with a quick two-minute pitch at the top, to snapshot the long story short and give the audience an idea of what you are doing. Then you can start the longer format presentation. The longer presentation can include slides and product demonstrations if you have them, just remember to tell the story in an order that makes sense. Practice, practice, practice. There is no substitute for practicing before you present. Then after you've presented, practice some more.

As to time management, let's say, for example, that you are given a 30-minute meeting to present. Do not prepare 30 minutes of presentations and slides and demonstrations. A good rule of thumb is to prepare presentations for half of the allotted time. So, in this example you would prepare 15 (or 20 maximum) minutes of a presentation, for a 30-minute meeting. Leave room for questions during the presentation as well as questions and answers at the end.

Here is a thumbnail EXAMPLE of how much time should be spent on each part of the presentation:

▶ **Intro** (~5% of the available time)
Don't apologize—it is a common opener, but it is a poor start. Be confident but never arrogant.

▶ **The Opportunity/Problem** (~25%)
Do not pander or exaggerate; be factual.

▶ What options are possible (~15%)

Give a few examples of options. Do not make the mistake of speaking poorly of any alternative to what you are recommending. Be factual.

▶ What I am doing (~45%)

Do not hold back any secret ingredient (aka silver bullet or game changer) during your presentation. It is a common problem that the presenter will save the big "wow" of their solution for a follow-up presentation. If the audience doesn't hear the wow in your first pitch, there may not be a second presentation.

▶ How you can be involved (~10%)

Do not tell them what they will do. Welcome them to the party and invite them to be involved.

Start on time and finish on time (or a little early). Going over time should only happen if the audience asks you to stay and explain more. Even then, be sensitive to being over time. It is typically better to leave when you are ahead while they want more and schedule a follow-up.

Do not feel nervous or upset about any questions that might be asked of you. Questions expose holes in your presentation and tell you what was not clear or understandable to the listener (no matter how clear you thought that you made the point). Questions also give you an indication of what matters to the person asking the question. Write down all the questions that you were asked, and the answers that you gave, and then use those notes as preparation for future meetings (and work on clearer presentations and better answers for the future).

> **ASSIGNMENT** Build the materials that you will need (e.g., 2–3-page executive summary, slides, etc.). Practice that 60-second pitch until you can say it without thinking. THEN start working on expanded detail versions of that pitch so that when people ask you to give them more you can do 60 seconds on this detail and 60 seconds on that detail. THEN work on a 30-minute expanded version of that pitch, which gives more meaningful insight and detail.

TRACKING PROGRESS AND TAKING ACTION

"Do what you say you're going to do.
And try to do it a little better than you said you would."
—Jimmy Dean

Keep track of every phone call, every email, every message, promise, and exchange of any kind. If you keep track, you are better able to know what happened and what comes next. Plus, you do not want to end up on the wrong side of a he said, she said debate.

If you and your company can afford it, consider investing in a CRM (Customer Relationship Management) system. A cautionary note is that CRMs are only effective if you use them. Many people do not have the patience to sit and type information into the system. You need everyone on board and entering their information. Garbage in, garbage out. Do not waste the company's money on a system that will not be used.

If you do not have a CRM, or if you have flexibility in the CRM, develop a scoring system for the status of sales from concept to close, and money in the bank. Devise a logic that works for you; something that will help you know what you should pay attention to and when you should move on. The scoring system might be as simple as (keep in mind that this is for example ONLY):

100% = Product has been delivered, and money has been confirmed as having been deposited in the bank

90% = A signed agreement

80% = A written agreement is being negotiated with a gentlemen's agreement (verbal agreement)

70% = The decision maker has put in writing that they intend to do the deal

60% = We have presented to the decision maker and we have been invited back

50% = We have presented to the decision maker and we are waiting to hear

40% = We have presented to a confirmed influencer and have an appointment with a decision maker.

30% = We are still working to identify the decision maker and influencer.

20% = We have presented to "tail wagers" in the organization who are excited and giving positive feedback

10% = We have identified a potential customer, or we are circling back to a potential (or past) customer

0% = Well and truly dead, with no possible hope for a future opportunity

Meet at least weekly with everyone inside the company who in any way helps progress the probability to close opportunities. Some companies call these meetings "War Rooms," and others simply call them Sales Meetings. Make the date and time predictable and consistent. For example, you might have the meetings every Tuesday. The people who stay in the room the whole time might be the internal forecasting and operations teams who need visibility on the probabilities of potential sales over time so that they can plan. Then, each sales person or head of sales area has a time to deliver their updates. Structure and timing is critical so that people feel that the meeting is meaningful and helpful. Make certain that what you need from the sales team is understood in advance; hopefully they submitted their updates in the system or via email the day before (on Monday for example) so that the meeting is less about new information and more about how to problem solve how everyone can help progress the sales opportunities to close and put money in the bank.

During the meetings, make action item assignments[3]. Within an hour of each meeting, send a summary email to everyone with items discussed and action items. Make sure that everyone knows that if you don't hear any corrections to those notes and action items (say within two hours from when it is sent), you will assume their agreement to the details. At the next meeting, ask for status updates on the action items, and hold people accountable. Adjust the percentages based on the results of those meetings.

Important note: Everyone needs help. In my experience, it is often a warning sign when a person or team says that they don't need help.

Accountability and empowerment is key to success.

> **ASSIGNMENT** If you do not have a CRM, identify a CRM that best suits the needs of your business and sales process. If you cannot afford a CRM, develop a simple and stable method of receiving updates and tracking progress, using tools such as spreadsheets and email. Plan regular sales meetings with all people in the company who need to understand the status of opportunities so that they can plan accordingly. Communicate openly and regularly so that no one is the dark on any opportunities. Make Assignments. Keep everyone accountable and empowered.

---

3   An **Action Item** sometimes called an AI means that an assignment is made to an individual or individuals. AIs are sometimes called other things such as **Action Required** (AR) and **Follow-up Items**, etc. Whatever you call it the Action Item typically has a specified deadline along with detail as to what is expected.

SAVE YOUR WORK, UPDATE IT REGULARLY, AND REFER TO IT OFTEN

Revisit all of the above work regularly. Remember to save your work regularly and keep backups on separate secure devices. Once a day, or at a minimum once a week at a routine time on a routine day, review and update details for all of the above.

Every time you update the document, save a unique version in a common reference folder on your computer. Use a consistent naming convention and update the name every time to include the date that you modified it (or some other intuitive system that others, not just you, will understand if they need to find information.)

It may happen that someone will need to know something, or all things, in this framework. Do not be caught off guard with an out of date version! Be prepared, and you will have nothing to fear.

ASSIGNMENT Comb through your document. Save everything. If you write something that you aren't quite sure how it fits, either put the thought on the last empty page of the document or create a second document in the same folder just for thoughts that you aren't yet sure how to use. You do not want to find yourself in the situation where later on you wish that you hadn't deleted that thought.

On future days when you open the document, do a Save As and change the version date on the document so that it creates a new document that is saved in the same folder. It may happen that in the future you will want to refer to an earlier draft, and if anything happens to the file that you are working on that day you can always go back to the most recent version rather than starting over.

Keep a backup somewhere other than on your computer. (You should regularly back up your entire hard drive.) If you are working on paper, you need to keep your binder safe and secure at all times. When you are able you might have someone scan every page in the binder onto a file that you keep on a small portable computer stick for safekeeping. When you are able you might have your handwriting transcribed onto a computer document; you might check with a local library to see if you can use a computer there. If you edit your document on a public computer just make certain that you do not leave a copy of your document on the public hard drive.

Regularly update your writing, save copies, keep the dream alive and work to make it real.

A LESSON ON DISRUPTION FROM ANTS

In 1984–1985, I was living in Thailand as a missionary. One Sunday, I was outside the church contemplating a line of red ants. I kept dragging my finger across the long line of ants and watching them scramble in disarray, until one ant re-established the line and the other ants then marched along the line again. A friend of mine came over to ask me what I was doing. I said that I was thinking about how people need to be more like ants. He said that he didn't understand. I said, "We all march along in our lives, then if anything disrupts our path we scatter just like the ants. BUT, what ants do better than people is they don't sit around crying or complaining about the disruption, they just

get back on the line when another ant shows the way." I dragged my finger across the line, and we watched the predictable pattern of behavior play out. I pointed to my lunch off to the side of that line of ants. I said, "My lunch has been sitting there for 15 minutes. I broke the line down here, and they scattered but they didn't swarm my lunch. I broke the line up here, and they didn't swarm my lunch. They are obsessed with that original line." We just sat watching the ants for a few minutes.

"You see that one ant on my food? He found the food after the first great disruption. I'm waiting for him to tear off a piece of food, return to the line and see if others will follow his new line." My friend listened, gesturing for me to continue. "Don't misunderstand me," I said, "that long line of ants is headed to a growing wealth of food in their home. All of those little pieces that they are carrying will become part of a massive store of food that is larger still than my heaping plate of food. Every ant is contributing to the survival and well-being of all of the ants in their colony. Both approaches are working. My point is that no ants are sitting around crying about the disruptions that they experienced. They are all getting on with it, one over there is doing its thing and hundreds more are on this line. People need to be like these ants; fully embracing their path, weathering the storms of disruptions, and being the leaders, and following the leaders to get back on the path or find a new purpose and a new source of what they are seeking, and then blazing a new path back to the main path to benefit every ant." As we sat there, that lone red ant worked and toiled, and eventually tore off a huge piece of food that it then faithfully carried back to the line. Moments later, a new line was created with regular traffic back and forth to my plate of food.

After that conversation, my friend forever called me มดแดง (Red Ant).

Disruptions happen. People scatter. People cry and complain. A few work to re-establish the path, and a few seek new paths to new sources.

Which are you? Which would you like to be?

Be the clear voice for others, listen for the healthy voices of others. Find your way back to the path. As needed, find a productive new path and then connect your new healthy path to the main path to share the wealth of what you've found.

Over my career, there have been disorienting disruptions, and I've realigned on or near the primary path. At times, I've gone off-roading and orienteering, looking for a new plate of food.

The fact that I have been able to build all of the frameworks in this workbook is because, in my professional career, I have proactively sought out new paths in and around the well-worn paths and disruptions that have happened from time to time.

I have been (and continue to be) that lone red ant on that plate of food, off to the side of the solid steady line.

READ *Who Moved My Cheese?* Spencer Johnson (1998)

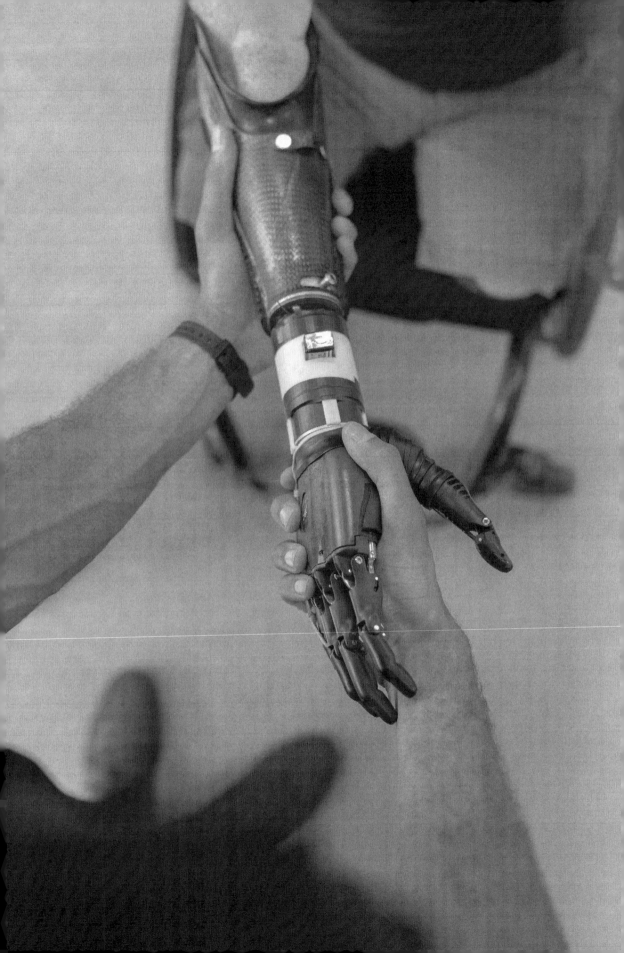

OFFERING REQUIREMENTS DOCUMENT (ORD)

"Great things are done by a
series of small things
done together."

—Vincent van Gogh

This framework is an adapted and enhanced version of a traditional **Market Requirements Document (MRD)** and is called an **Offering Requirements Document (ORD)**[1]. The ORD is part of my system of frameworks for entrepreneurship and good business practice. Too many people and businesses simply "do stuff" when working to develop their dreams and ideas into viable business-ready offerings. This framework, in concert with the appropriate business and entrepreneurship framework, will help you evolve your ideas into an offering that has a chance at viable business success.

▶ This ORD is specially designed for planning an offering around existing science and technology as well as software development. Use the correct language through this framework as needed.

---

1   In Old and Middle English "ord" was the point of the spear, the beginning of the weapon, as well as the vanguard.

AN APP, SOFTWARE APPLICATION, TECHNOLOGY, PLATFORM, OR SERVICE, OR SOLUTION?

Rather than being one of the offerings in the world that is unclear as to whether they are a Technology (aka "tech"), an "App," or Solution, or Platform, or Service, evaluate and decide that now.

What Technology, an Application, and an "App" have in common is that they are self-contained things that perform a specific function or set of functions. The difference between an "App" and an Application is that an App is typically small and self-contained on a smart-device (e.g., a "smart phone," tablet, etc.) while an Application is a larger and more robust feature-complete set of software that might reside on a personal computer, a server, in the Cloud, etc. "Technology" might be software, but not necessarily an App or Application. Technology is more commonly a physical thing, whether or not it uses software. Your technology could be a new molecule that could become a pharmaceutical. If however, it is a combination of traditional non-high technology ("no tech" or "low tech") and high technology, it might be better categorized as a solution.

A service can be either human or machine (software, hardware, or other) or a combination of things. A service is performed at one time, or several times, or for a defined period, or perpetually ongoing (e.g., a subscription or other ongoing agreement) until some future date when it could be terminated. It is an activity done by someone or something outside of the customer for the customer.

A platform, as with a stage in the performing arts, is a place that hosts or in some way makes other things possible, by facilitating the other thing's success (and might be one time, or a defined number of times, or ongoing as a subscription, until terminated). Decide in the beginning (you might change it later in the process) whether or not you are building a product, a service, or a platform.

A solution is an ensemble or group of some combination of applications, technologies, platforms, and services that are specially configured to address a specific need.

ASSIGNMENT Write three to five sentences on whether you are creating technology, a solution, a platform, or a service.

> **SPECIAL NOTE** For simplicity going forward, the word "widget" (which is the traditional, generic, economic term for anything produced, not to be confused with the contemporary use of the word for software tools in an operating system) will be used as a proxy (place holder) for whatever you are creating whether it is technology, an App, an application, service, platform, or solution.

WILL YOUR WIDGET INCLUDE ANYTHING THAT COULD BE PROTECTED AS PROPRIETARY INTELLECTUAL PROPERTY (IP)?

Not all widgets have a special, new, and protectable something in them. You need to think carefully about whether what you are creating with this widget has any technology or method in it that could be protected (e.g., a technology or method patent). You will need to work with lawyers to validate that you do have something that qualifies as IP, and then to do the work to legally protect it.

ASSIGNMENT Write at least one sentence stating that you have no IP, or a paragraph or more (with very specific examples) on what you believe to be legally protectable IP.

DESCRIBE THE WIDGET IN ONE PARAGRAPH. (WHAT DOES IT DO?)

You need to be able to explain the widget in simple, clear sentences. Think of this two ways: 1. What would you say to a non-technical person so that they would understand the offering? Then 2. What would an expert in the field need to hear so that they understand the offering? Use both in your description.

ASSIGNMENT Write at least one paragraph introducing what your widget does. This will be important to show executive leadership and potential investors and shareholders. This could be a description of the objective for it. This paragraph will capture the reader's interest or inspire them. Do NOT get into specific features. That is coming up next. This section is a few paragraphs defending your widget's reason for being. If there is a "requirement" for it (institutional, industrial, governmental, communal, personal, etc.), include the details here.

DETAIL ITS FEATURES AND BENEFITS, ESPECIALLY IDENTIFYING NEEDS VS. WANTS, AS WELL AS WHAT IS REQUIRED VS. DESIRED BY THE END-USER

Develop an inventory of features and benefits that are required for your type of widget, then inventory the special or differentiated features and benefits. This is where you articulate what your widget will actually do. Very importantly, you should understand the difference between what the intended end-user actually NEEDS, as opposed to what they or you WANT from the product, service, or platform to do. Also keep in mind that there may be fundamental requirements that your product, service, or platform MUST meet in order for it to be used. This is vital for the potential sales of your offering; for example, a government or business may not be able to buy from you if you do not have certain standard features, even if you personally think those features are unnecessary. You need to include those features even if you do not personally believe in them.

ASSIGNMENT Make a list of >20 features (make the list as exhaustive as possible); stack rank them by priority, group/mark each as Standard vs. Differentiated, then write at least one or more sentences to explain how the feature behaves when a user uses it, and to what effect. This is an inventory of features with editorial commentary about each feature's benefits.

CREATE A STORYBOARD OF HOW THE WIDGET IS USED, BY WHOM, WHEN, AND WHY

If you have ever read a comic in a newspaper, or a graphic novel in a book, or even picture-based instructions for assembling a toy or piece of furniture where it has squares on a page that are filled with drawings that take you step-by-step through the story, that is a storyboard.

This is when you SHOW a compelling use-case for your widget (to the best of your ability) pictographically, so that others can better visualize what it will look and act like. Don't worry if you aren't an artist; just do your best. Draw the significant moments in the use of your product, service, or platform. Don't worry about showing action or movement; this is a snapshot of the meaningful transitional steps to show other people the basic idea of how the IP works. If you have a working version of your widget, you could use actual photographs in each frame.

Sample storyboard

Draw inside this square ...

Sample smart device outline for manual wireframing

ASSIGNMENT Sketch (keep in mind that functional understanding is more important than making it pretty) or use photographs in a series on pieces of paper. This is when you SHOW the widget (to the best of your ability) pictographically so that others can better visualize what the widget looks like and how it performs. Think from the perspective of the things that must be done (i.e., activities), not job titles (i.e., functions).

IDENTIFY THE TARGET MARKET, INCLUDING TOTAL, ADDRESSABLE, AND SERVICEABLE MARKET

The "total market" is the big number of all the conceivable people, or the amount of revenue, or the number of products used, or consumed in a period of time. The "addressable market" number (not to be confused with the total) is a subset of the total market that is equal to the number of people inside the total to whom you know how/where to put a message (e.g., you have their contact information, you know what magazines they read, where they shop, what airlines they fly, etc.). Then the serviceable market is how many people (from the addressable number) to whom you can provide the product or service or platform at a given time (e.g., how many simultaneous users hitting a server at once? Think, for example, if you need to build one product at a time for each customer, how many of those custom builds can you do at a time? Think like a hotel with finite capacity: if you have 100 rooms with a maximum or double occupancy, your serviceable limitation is 200 people, at two people per room per night and not more ... if >100 people as single occupancy all want their own room, you can only serve 100 people.).

Then think conversion to cash ratios ... when you advertise to the addressable, anticipate that you will convert at approximately 0.8% (round up to 1% to simplify the mathematics). The better you are at addressing the market, the higher the conversion percentage to your serviceable. This will tell you if you have created sufficient serviceable capacity or if you need to invest more. It will also tell you if your addressable is too big or too small.

> **SPECIAL NOTE** If the total/addressable/serviceable market is too small then you may struggle to capture the interest of investors and/or potential acquirers.

Then you need to think what it will cost to convert any of those people whom you have addressed to make a sale. This is called the cost of acquisition or cost of sales. It sounds obvious, but companies of all sizes make this mistake: if you spend more to acquire a customer or make a sale than the amount of money that you will profit on a sale, it's not good business.

> **ASSIGNMENT** Write at least one paragraph on the following: Where is the market? What is the group inside that market that will buy your offering? How many potential customers are there? Do you know how/where to put a message in front of them to persuade them to buy your offering? What is the cost of putting that message, and what is the total cost of acquisition (cost of sale)?

SCOPE YOUR USP, WHY TO BUY, CALL TO ACTION (WHEN AND WHERE DO YOU CONVERT TO CASH?)

It is key that you articulate the value of the offering to intended users (i.e., most critically the company itself, but also any customers). Why would someone buy it and/or use your widget? Especially, why should they do what you want them to do rather than doing nothing? You need to think about value, USP, and why-to-buy from several perspectives: the shareholders, board of directors, the company leadership who will sign off on your initiative and allocate resources to make it happen, investment committee, as well as your target customers.

ASSIGNMENT Describe who the customer is, why they need it, and what is unique about their requirement. You would also comment on market size here. Use numbers from credible sources to establish market size. USP/Call to Action: Put forward a simple message that explains that there is a genuine problem and that this solution is the fix for it.

GO TO MARKET ... HOW DO YOU GET YOUR WIDGET FROM HERE TO THERE?

Who is the customer? Where are they located on planet earth? What are the considerations for who they are, where they are, how and when they will buy what you are selling? It is essential that you factor for as many considerations as possible (e.g., seasonality, forecasting, procurement, supply chain, manufacturing, inventory controls, logistics, delivery, support, etc. as appropriate) to demonstrate that you know how to deliver what you will be selling. It is helpful to reverse engineer delivery to the customer back to where you are now. What are the things that need to happen to get from here to there? Remember to factor for competition, which might be other widget, or might be apathy, budgetary cycles, holiday seasons, market behaviors and pressures, and more.

ASSIGNMENT Write three to five sentences articulating where, when, why, and how you will take your offering to market. (Think, how much will it cost? Can it be done cheaper? Who are powerful others that would be invested in your success? Can you partner with them?)

LICENSING (INCLUDING ROYALTIES) PER SEAT, AND PRICING (SINGLES, MULTI-PACKS, SITE LICENSES)

A "seat" is a single installation of your application (think of a person seated while using your offering one at a time). How does licensing work per seat?

Do you have some part of your offering that can be downloaded from the internet and installed for free? Is there a cost to download/install per seat? If so, what is the MSRP (Manufacturer's Suggested Retail Price) for each unit (or however you are measuring one widget or thing that will be sold)? Will there be small charges/payments made transactionally as they use your widget? Or is the only revenue that you will make from it once they buy it from you? (Think in-app purchases in software; will there be opportunities to sell more to the user while or after they use what you sold to them?)

Can a user purchase a multi-user license to use your application on multiple devices or for multiple people to use it on their phones? Can a company or institution purchase a site license so that they can install it 100 or 1,000 times? What is the pricing structure? (This information will help the engineer know how to design the application's awareness of serialization (requiring a unique code to operate. One code allows one app, a multi-user code works for multiples, etc.)

ASSIGNMENT Write a paragraph explaining whether or not there is anything about your application (e.g., technology that you need to use to make it work, branding or co-branding, etc.) that will require that you make payments to them or share your revenue?

CONFIGURATIONS AND BUILDS

A "configuration" is a version of the offering that includes and excludes selected features depending on the intended purpose of that specific offering. There may be a "one-size fits all" configuration where you include every feature and benefit, regardless of where and how it is used. There may be several different configurations. Each configuration would typically be assigned a unique Stock Keeping Unit (SKU) so that you can keep track of which is which. If you will have more than one SKU then you should develop an easy-to-understand method to the numbers and letters in the SKU itself. This is what you would list in a catalogue or brochure for reference and ordering so that those who purchase what you are offering are sure to receive the correct version.

A "build" is a version number or batch number for when you compiled or put together a specific configuration or SKU. A batch number will help you track everything from quality control and support to expiration dates (if they apply). The build number would likely be printed or coded onto the offering in some way, so that it can be referenced in the future. It would also be put on any packaging, as appropriate, for quick reference.

All of that being said, will there only be one version or type of your offering? Will there be a feature-rich premium version and a feature-lite basic version? Will there be a difference between your offering for professionals or amateurs, corporate or home users, researchers or practitioners, and so on? Will the offering be to different markets around the world, and for different groups within a market? If so, how?

One more thing to consider: "OEM" and "white label" or "private Label." OEM (pronounced O-E-M) means "Original Equipment Manufacturer." OEM is misleading as it sounds backward from its actually meaning. An OEM is when company B sells and distributes the product of company A (the original equipment manufacturer), with the catch that company B puts their name and branding on company A's product. White label (aka private label) is the same relationship but is typically used for software while OEM is typically used for physical things (and the terms are often used interchangeably).

> **ASSIGNMENT** Write at least one solid paragraph on the different types of configurations and builds that you anticipate for this widget. Will there be a consumer version and a prosumer version (professional/consumer hybrid) and a professional version? Will it be sold stand-alone or integrated into other widgets? Will it be branded by you, white labeled or OEMed?
>
> Write at least one paragraph on the configurations and requirements for the application. (Using an app, for example, what type of phone or version of the operating system is required? Does it require a 5G network?) In most basic terms, think of it this way: do you want your app to run on any generation phone? This will be important for the engineer/developer to know because it will impact how they develop the application. Or do you want to use the current operating system version as the base line, and go forward from now? This backward-compatibility decision is a bigger question than you might realize, as there are tons of older phones running the older operating system still in use.)

LIFE CYCLE ... HOW LONG IS ITS PRODUCTIVE LIFE? WHEN IS ITS EOL?

▶ **EOL = End of Life**

Very few things in this world last forever, especially if they are part of the natural world or the technology world (some technology may continue in use as a curiosity, such as in museums, rather than for practical performance). Nature decays and technology becomes outdated and outmoded. How long does your offering have from the start of its useful life to the end of its useful life? This is more than an expiration date, this is the moment in time when using your offering will no longer be possible. Think of a piece of software that is designed for a computer from 30 years ago that no longer has the ability to run on a computer built with today's technology. Think of a race car or motorcycle or bicycle from 50 years ago trying to compete with this year's new technology in a race. Think of a professional athlete wearing shoes from a hundred years ago when competing today. In their time, those offerings may have been very compelling or even the best available. But today, they are not competitive and have been replaced with the latest offerings that are more compelling.

An important consideration is whether or not you or a competitor will be the one to release the next offering to replace your planned or current offering.

ASSIGNMENT Write a paragraph about how long you anticipate this offering to be relevant in this first iteration. When will it need to be refreshed or enhanced? (Note: To maximize the odds of investors or execs buying in, plan a few generations forward, over a few years.)

Make a statement regarding the natural end of the productive life of your offering, and whether a new iteration of the offering is planned, and when it will be released. This is usually when support for the product ends (no more updates, etc.). At a minimum, EOL positioning is usually accompanied with a statement, and sometimes references to a plan for what will replace it (if anything).

FORECASTING, PROCUREMENT, SUPPLY CHAIN, INVENTORY CONTROL, AND PORTION CONTROL

This section applies if your widget has any connection to a physical item that needs to be supplied to the manufacturer or user of the widget. This might be a physical product sold, a device that you need to supply, etc.

Forecasting, procurement, supply chain, inventory control, and portion control[2] are among the secrets to success for companies that make things (from hardware to food). These are the inner workings of the clock that move the hands that in turn, tell time. People often gloss over these details because 1. They aren't glamorous and exciting, and 2. They don't know how to do it, 3. They just don't want to do it, or 4. They don't understand why it matters.

You can have customers lined up and down the street, but if you have too few of your widgets to sell, you have a problem. If you have too many of the wrong ingredients/parts, or not enough essential ingredients to make your widget, then you have a problem. It may sound obvious, but you need to have the right number of everything when you need it. It is both art and science; call it scientifically applied art or artfully applied science. Either way, it requires careful attention and execution. This is relevant during the research and development (R&D) process as well as when you are manufacturing and shipping your offering. Do not fall into the common trap of doing a little of this or that, buying what you think you need, a little here and a few there.

Figure out how many of what you will need to make and when. Then identify the optimal source from whom to buy the ingredients/parts. Then figure out the best, most cost-effective way to get those ingredients/parts to you. Then put some intelligence into how to store and track what you have. Finally, you need to invest careful execution into tracking how much of what is used when, throughout the production process.

---

2   Portion control in food is how much of which ingredient is used. When a cook uses a little of this and a little of that rather than exact measurements it creates a problem for 1. The person who is tracking inventory to better forecast what we have and what needs to be ordered, 2. It complicates the process for others who need to cook the same dishes and replicate the flavors and food experience, 3. It can create an inconsistent dining experience for customers. Interestingly a similar problem happens when building other things from houses to toys to automobiles to technology of any type. How many of which raw materials are used matters; if the builder or manufacturer simply uses a little or this and that then it creates inconsistencies and problems for the forecasters trying to keep track and order more through to the user experience.

ASSIGNMENT Create an inventory of what components are needed to both perform R&D, as well as to manufacture the necessary numbers of your offering. This is called a BOM (Bill of Materials). Then inventory the associated costs to manufacture and deliver your offerings (when added to the BOM, this is called the COGS or Cost of Goods Sold).

Then work with a forecasting professional (or do it yourself if you know how) to create a spreadsheet that plans forward what components and parts you will need, and when. Forecast as far forward as possible, then regularly update your forecasts (at a minimum, monthly).

Then plan and create a detailed list of the optimal supplier(s) for what you need, and when you need it.

Then plan and write out the optimal logistics of delivery from the supplier(s) to your point of manufacture (or other locations as needed).

Then plan and write a paragraph on how you will control your inventory wherever it will be stored until used.

Then plan and write a paragraph on how much of what will be used when, by whom, where, and why.

Factor for the EOL impact of all components that are used in the offering as well as the offering itself.

MANUFACTURING

This section applies if you need to make any of the physical items explored in Section 12 above.

The word manufacture means to make by hand. Almost all things that are made by hand are made with the assistance of some type of tool or machine. In the modern world, many things are made entirely by machines; either with or without the engagement of people.

Think carefully about where to manufacture. Pick a partner that demonstrates genuine care and attention to you and your offering. The details of your offering and how it is manufactured impact functionality, performance, durability, service and maintainability, as well as cost.

Do not make the mistake of underestimating the importance and costs of manufacturing; this goes for small numbers of validation units through to mass production volumes of the offering.

ASSIGNMENT Write a paragraph detailing who will manufacture your offering in all phases, from single validation units through to mass production. Keep in mind that building one at a time is more expensive. "Economies of scale" means that your costs go down when you produce more. Plan where your economies of scale in manufacturing come into play in the context of the details in section 12 above.

PACKAGING

This section primarily applies to a physical offering, but it could also apply to the way that you make your software visually appealing wherever it might be displayed.

▶ For physical things

Many things that are manufactured are then put in some type of packaging. The primary purpose of packaging is to protect the offering from damage when it is being moved from one place to another, between the moment that it is finished manufacturing and when it is opened by the end user. Some companies choose to invest in decorative packaging to increase the shelf appeal of their offering to catch the eye of buyers and incentivize purchase.

Keep in mind that every cut and fold on paper or other materials has a cost. Resist overengineering your packaging. Also please consider the environmental impact of the packaging that you choose, and the experiences of whoever is unpacking your offering.

▶ For software only

Think carefully about iconography (what the icon for your app looks like) and how it fits into the branding and positioning for your software. This could be featured in all advertisements ranging from banner advertisements and video ads, and traditional advertising.

> **ASSIGNMENT** Write a paragraph detailing the packaging, primarily including its functional details, as well as the materials and aesthetics.

DISTRIBUTION, FULFILLMENT, AND RETURNED MERCHANDISE

You need to think about how your widget will make it from you to the end user. Will they download it from your website and server? Is it purchased in a physical store? Is it shipped directly to the customer (customers can range from restaurants to corporations to hospitals to scientific lab)? Will you need to physically ship them a drive of some type?

ASSIGNMENT Write at least one paragraph on how your offering will make its way into the hands of the person who will use it.

This part of this section primarily applies to software that is associated with a physical thing.

The words "distribution" and "fulfillment" are often used interchangeably (and often confusingly), but they are different. Both have warehouses and deliver boxes based on orders. Distributors, however, focus on delivering products to other businesses, while fulfillment focuses on delivering to individual people. Distributors may, at times, also offer the service of fulfilling orders.

ASSIGNMENT Write at least one paragraph on how you will distribute or fulfill orders. Will you do it yourself? Will you contract with a company to do it for you? Will the manufacturer distribute and/or fulfill orders for you?

Then you need to figure out how you will handle RMAs (Returned Merchandise Authorizations or returned merchandise). Plan for the possibility that customers will want or need to return what you sold to them (whether or not what you sold them works or is defective). If your offering cannot be repaired or dealt with wherever it is in the world, you might opt to 1. have it returned to some location that will handle your RMAs for you, then potentially repair and prepare it for re-sale, or 2. do what many companies do—abandon the product and simply offer a refund or ship a replacement. Remember to factor for RMAs in your financials.

ASSIGNMENT Write at least 3–5 sentences on how you will handle RMAs. Keep in mind that not all distributors and fulfillment houses handle RMAs.

MAINTENANCE

How will you or the end-user of your offering fix, repair, or update the widget as needed?

Will your widget be "unbreakable" (meaning it self-diagnoses and self-repairs)?

If your widget is not part of the IoT (Internet of Things), so you cannot see and interact with it remotely, and it's lack of connectedness means that a person needs to drive out to wherever it is located and personally find it and then put their hands on it personally, how will you know its status and effect maintenance and repairs?

Will you need to offer your users a maintenance plan or Service Level Agreement (SLA)? If so, consider the following:

▶ Updates and fixes to the thing; how often they will happen, who will do them, how will you get updates and fixes to the customer (push or pull, meaning will you force updates at them with reminders (aka push) or do they need to go find it and do it themselves (aka pull)).

▶ How do you plan to support the widget and its user? Will there be a website with FAQ (frequently asked questions)? Do you have a natural language processing chat-bot? Can they email someone? Will there be a number through which they can call a real person?

▶ As appropriate for your software, think through the three basic levels of SLAs: corporate/company, customer/user, and service. How will you ensure that each of those three are taken care of?

> **ASSIGNMENT** Build a timeline (e.g., decision tree, Gantt chart, project management software, etc.) of what will happen, and when (starting from today until EOL). Then write at least one paragraph detailing what type of service and support might be required, and how you would deliver it (e.g., in person, via chat-bot or live text chat, email, phone call, etc.)? Then how will you deliver updates, fixes, etc.? Then factor for how far into the future beyond EOL you will continue to deliver maintenance updates, support, etc.

COMPETITIVE LANDSCAPE (WHAT ARE THE ALTERNATIVES?) SWOT.

Make a list of features and benefits for each competitor for your widget. Score what every potential competitor currently has on offer. Be brutally honest about what others are offering; it is common for people to downplay and sometimes ignore compelling competitor's features and benefits because they threaten your offering.

Perform a **SWOT** (Strengths Weaknesses Opportunities Threats) analysis. It is useful to do a SWOT analysis for the offering, as well as the company that you are building. Think inside and outside of the offering, as well as inside and outside of the company. Keep in mind that the single greatest competitor is nothing (people doing nothing or changing nothing), and the second greatest competitor is often a weakness in the offering itself (for example, inferior quality of a component, or the absence of a key feature that is a strength in a competitor's offering that you are not yet able to offer), or in your company (the human beings in your company, being human).

ASSIGNMENT You might start with a simple table that lists all competitors across the top, and then **all** features down the left-hand side (do not conveniently leave off features that you don't like or those that threaten you and your offering). Then do a simple binary (yes or no, on or off) scoring of what your offering has compared to what you know about the competition. Keep in mind that you do not know what the competitors are currently working to develop; do not assume that they are doing nothing to evolve or improve. Then start your SWOT by listing all strengths, then what is currently weak, what is currently threatening, and then the opportunities (how to neutralize the threats by downgrading them to weaknesses, how to make weaknesses strengths, and then how to capitalize on strengths).

RESEARCH AND DEVELOPMENT (R&D) COSTS

Having now done all of the above, you are ready to puzzle through what it is going to cost to do it all to make your widget a reality.

ASSIGNMENT Work with a finance professional to puzzle it through. (Remember that **finance** is planning forward what you believe will happen, and **accounting** is looking back at what has happened.) Show your work! Show it to bankers, investors/shareholders, boards, the CFO and others who need to understand the financial implications, and all impacted teams need to understand what will happen and what it will cost. Prepare a minimum of high-level financial impacts for the next 18 months.

Comb through your document. Save everything. If you write something and you aren't quite sure how it fits, either put the thought on the last empty page of the document or create a second document in the same folder just for thoughts that you aren't yet sure how to use. You do not want to find yourself in the situation where later on, you wish that you hadn't deleted that thought.

On future days when you open the document, do a Save As and change the version date on the document so that it creates a new document that is saved in the same folder. It may happen that in the future you will want to refer to an earlier draft, and if anything happens to the file that you are working on that day, you can always go back to the most recent version, rather than starting over.

Keep a backup somewhere other than on your computer. (You should regularly back up your entire hard drive.)

Regularly update your writing, save copies, keep the dream alive, and work to make it real.

BE THE BLESSING IN OTHER PEOPLE'S LIVES

In the 200,000+ years of humans on our beautiful spinning blue ball in our far corner of the galaxy, we are the luckiest people to ever live.

Our world itself is amazing, inspirational, powerful, and beautiful. As humans, we have our challenges (some of our issues are authentic doosies), and we have our moments of amazing, inspirational, powerful beauty.

For most of the time that humans have inhabited our planet, not much changed. For most of our 200,000 years—thousands of generations—clothing, shelter, tools, weapons, hunting methods, farming practices, etc. evolved so slowly and changed so little that one generation to the next most likely didn't notice much of a difference. Children dressed and lived lives that were more or less the same as their parents, and then their children did the same. The big moments like fire, the wheel, irrigation, spears, etc. and moving from the Stone Age to Bronze to Iron etc. might have been sudden bursts of discovery like those we experience and have come to expect today, but they were more likely very gradual.

It has been during the last few thousand years of our 200,000 years that big leaps in progress have changed how humans do what we do. If you look at the last few hundred years, the evolutionary changes have been startling. Changes in the two hundred years or so since the industrial revolution have been staggering. The advances of humans in the last hundred plus years have been almost unfathomable. The changes in the last couple of decades alone have been so rapid that it has been tough to keep pace with them. As months pass, things happen so fast that staying current is almost a job itself.

If I had been born a few hundred years ago, I would have lived my life in the coal mines of Scotland, or Wales, or in the fields of Ireland. That would have been my existence as it had been for generations before—sons going into the mines with their fathers, then those sons becoming fathers who took their sons into the mine. My specifying mines and fields is just my ancestral example, and the point is not the mines or fields themselves per sé. I live on a property with animals in the countryside of New Zealand, and I do it by choice; when you don't have a choice that is when there is a problem. I know that people today still work in mines and fields. My point is that a few hundred years ago, my options as a human on planet earth would have been dramatically more limited and narrow than they are now. A few hundred years ago, I would not have had the rights of self-determination that I have today; I would not have had the rights to education and upward mobility in society that we have today; neither would women, or people of color, or countless others.

In our time, people have greater liberty and choice. And yet we still hold each other back; there is still slavery in our time, as well as brutal poverty in parts of the world which includes the burdens of food insecurity and safety problems, and we still create an abundance of our own problems socially and politically. Still, for the

majority of us, we have greater access to education, employment, and a spectrum of opportunities, as well as mobility globally, than the vast majority of people who have ever lived. We still have work to do, and more advancement to make, but the rights of a vast preponderance of people, regardless of any demographic detail, are so far advanced today that our lives and choices are almost not recognizable in the context of our ancestor's lives.

We were not born at any other time over the last 200,000 years; we were born now. I cannot believe the good fortune that I had to be born in an era when a kid from a working poor family in Middle America could figure out how to graduate from Harvard University. The fact that I could work in an office and get paid a king's ransom compared to my ancestors is incredible.

I married someone from the other side of the world, and we have traveled the world together, raising our kids across countries and cultures. I've helped build companies around the world, becoming a professor at a top business school. I've worked with CEOs, leaders, and a broad range of people from over 90 countries around the world. It boggles my mind.

What impresses me the most about it all is that I'm not better than any of my ancestors. I cannot imagine how hard it would have been to live, survive, and figure out how to thrive a thousand or a hundred thousand years ago. But my ancestors did survive, and their children survived, and the evidence of their successful struggle is that I was born. Our lives are a different kind of hard compared to theirs. Our work to survive and thrive is not harder than the ancients or even those hundreds of years ago. I can't imagine what it took to raise a child to adulthood when around every tree and in all of the tall grass something threatened one's survival every day all day ... for a couple hundred thousand years.

I am, we all are, simply blessed to have been born in our time.

What compounds it all for me, is that there are thousands of blessings that have made my life as it is today possible. Yes, I've worked hard, I've puzzled and explored, but I highly doubt that I've worked with greater diligence or commitment than my ancestors did. Having thought about it a great deal over the years, I believe that my life is the product of a succession of blessings. I've tried to count them, but there are simply too many, the numbers are too high. Not everything has gone smoothly; there have been a few nosedives, and a lot of turbulence, some of it severe. But at the end of the day, I have been blessed that when thousands of people could have said no to me, they said yes. Doors that could have stayed closed had someone with their hand on the latch, and they decided to open the door

for me. Plenty of doors have stayed closed rather than been opened, but doors have in fact been opened.

When I look around me in the world, I look for ways that I can open doors for others.

Years ago, my young family and I were driving down a road somewhere in the world. We were driving behind a truck packed with men who were day laborers off to do some manual labor somewhere for someone. My oldest son Joshua, who was then a boy, said, "Dad! Look at the truck with all those men in the back! I wonder how many of those men would be doctors or scientists or artists if only their luck was better. Let's stop the truck and be the luck in their lives." I had talked about this for years, and to hear my young son reflect what he heard from me was like listening to the sweetest music.

Countless people have been the blessings and luck in my life. Here are a few as an example: In early 1964 a doctor sent my mom home from the hospital because she had a cold, saying they would need to reschedule her planned hysterectomy. Two weeks later she returned to the hospital because she was over her cold, but they canceled her surgery because she was pregnant with me. (I always smile when I have a cold.) My oldest childhood friend Mark Probert was a great blessing in my young life; he listened to years of my thinking out loud. When I was little my older sisters and brother protected me during our father's storms. My mother made innumerable sacrifices to provide and care for me. My mother's mother (Grandma Wilson) was a beacon of hope and inspiration from my earliest memories and she continues to be. When I could not pay for my volunteer missionary work in Thailand, my sister Melissa and brother-in-law Jeff covered my expenses for two years even though they couldn't afford it. My brother Steven and sister-in-law Julie took me in and gave me a path when I was clueless about where to go to university; they were busy with their own young family, school, and work but they took the time to help me. Without Steven's coaching and mentoring there is no way I would have gone to Harvard. When I was having an existential crisis during college Melissa and Jeff gave me a place to stay while I sifted and sorted through what I needed to do.

Dr. Donald Bacon, one of my teachers at Harvard, helped me understand that my past can inform but does not need to define my future. Brian Heywood offered authentic friendship when I felt alone at Harvard. Brian has been a guest speaker in my classes at INSEAD, we are in regular contact and friends to this day. Clayton Christensen was a very important friend to me at Harvard; he was my Bishop (what The Church of Jesus Christ of Latter-day Saints calls our unpaid volunteer clergy). Knowing Clay impacted me profoundly for the better. Years later I went to hear Clay speak when he was visiting the Silicon Valley and Stanford; out of an ocean of people he waved to me, and when I walked up he called me by name and gave me a warm hug. The same thing happened again years later in Singapore. His door was always open. My brother-in-law Manahi Taber-Kewene has been an engaged, loving, and compassionate friend for me since the moment we first met. Brent Knudsen was the first successful business professional who took the time to explain to me in simple understandable terms how business actually works; we are friends to this day. Curt Walton and Mark Ryvola were stable friends when the caprice of the dot.com era was not going my way; we are still good friends today. Kendall Simmons was an engaged and helpful friend for me during an unstable time, he opened the door to a job when I needed it. Kendall and I are in regular contact to this day and excellent friends. Stefan Schaefer was my friend when I was searching for my career path during dot.coms and after dot.bombs; we traveled the world together working to connect with entrepreneurial opportunities and we are still good friends. My wife Natasha has been daily proof since our wedding in 1993 that whom you marry and invest your life with changes everything; she has lifted me higher than I dared dream possible. When a friend was challenging her for tolerating the ups and downs of my entrepreneurial career Natasha told her: "I have never confused our relationship with our bank account." She is the ideal wife and life partner for an entrepreneur.

> "If I have seen further
> it is by standing on the
> shoulders of Giants."
> —Sir Isaac Newton

We can be the luck in other people's lives. We can be the blessings and answers to prayers. We can make a difference. If only we will open doors when we have the decision in our hands that rest on the latch. If only we will say yes when we might say no. Very importantly, we need to open doors for ourselves; we keep so many doors closed because of our fears, uncertainties, and doubts (FUD). Do not block your own path—get out of your own way. Then help others. Seek out opportunities to serve and break down the walls and barriers that constrict and bind others. Build bridges.

It might be presumptuous and a step too far for me to hope that this workbook has been a blessing in your life ... But my hope is that the frameworks in this book have in some meaningful way helped open a door for you that was previously closed.

I wish for you every success and happiness.

RESOURCES[1]

BOOKS

Anderson, Ray. *Mid-Course Correction.* Peregrinzilla Press, 1999.

Christensen, Clayton. *The Innovator's Dilemma.* Harvard Business Review Press, 2016 (originally published 1997).

Christensen, Clayton, James Allworth, and Karen Dillon. *How Will You Measure Your Life?* Harper Business, 2012.

Covey, Steven R. *The 7 Habits of Highly Effective People.* Simon & Schuster, Anniversary edition, 2020 (originally published 1989).

Dyer, Wayne. *The Power of Intention.* Hay House Inc., 2005.

Edmondson, Amy. *Fearless Organizations: Creating Psychological Safety in the Workplace for Learning, Innovation, and Growth.* Wiley, 2018.

Falcão, Horacio. *Value Negotiation: How to Finally Get the Win-Win Right.* FT Press, 2012.

Gregersen, Hal B. *Questions are the Answer: A Breakthrough Approach to Your Most Vexing Problems at Work and in Life.* Harper Business, 2018.

Hawking, Paul. *The Ecology of Commerce.* Harper Business, 2010 (originally published, 1993).

Johnson, Spencer. *Who Moved My Cheese?* G. P. Putnam's Sons, 1998.

Karlgaard, Rich. *Late Bloomers.* Currency, 2019.

Kelley, Tom, and David Kelley. *Creative Confidence: Unleashing the Creative Potential Within Us All.* Currency, 2013.

Kim, W. Chan, and Renée Mauborgne. *Blue Ocean Strategy.* Harvard Business Review Press, Expanded edition, 2015 (originally published 2004).

Nelson, Richard N. *What Color Is Your Parachute?* Ten Speed, 2018 (originally published 1970).

Ray, Michael. *The Highest Goal: The Secret That Sustains You in Every Moment.* Berrett-Koehler Publishers, 2004.

Terwiesch, Christian, and Karl Ulrich. *Innovation Tournaments: Creating and Selecting Exceptional Opportunities.* Harvard Business Review Press, 2009.

Zeisberger, Claudia, Michael Prahl, and Bowen White. *Mastering Private Equity: Transformation via Venture Capital, Minority Investments and Buyouts.* Wiley, 2017.

ARTICLES

Christensen, Clayton. "What Is Disruptive Innovation?" *Harvard Business Review* (HBR), December 2015.

Govindarajan, Vijay, and Jay Terwilliger. "Yes, You Can Brainstorm Without Groupthink" *Harvard Business Review* (HBR), July 2012.

Gregersen, Hal "Better Brainstorming" *Harvard Business Review* (HBR), March–April 2018.

Gregersen, Hal "Use Catalytic Questioning to Solve Significant Problems" *Harvard Business Review* (HBR), July 2013.

Edmondson, Amy. "Psychological Safety: The History, Renaissance, and Future of an Interpersonal Construct" *Annual Review of Organizational Psychology and Organizational Behavior,* pp 23–43, Volume 1, 2014.

Kelley, Tom, and David Kelley. "Reclaim Your Creative Confidence" *Harvard Business Review* (HBR), December 2012.

Kim, W. Chan, and Renée Mauborgne. "Blue Ocean Strategy" *Harvard Business Review* (HBR), October 2004.

Mintzberg, Henry. "The Fall and Rise of Strategic Planning" *Harvard Business Review* (HBR), January-February 1994.

Wasserman, Noam. "The Founder's Dilemma" *Harvard Business Review* (HBR), February 2008.

Wedell-Wedellsborg, Thomas. "Are You Solving the Right Problems?" *Harvard Business Review* (HBR), January–February 2017.

TALKS

Does the flap of a butterfly's wing in Brazil set off a tornado in Texas?, Philip Merilees' (1972).

RADIO PROGRAMS

"American Apparel CEO Dov Charney on pushing boundaries and his biggest weakness," Marketplace.org with Kai Ryssdal (2014, updated 2015).

---

1   Word definitions used throughout are from Merriam-Webster Dictionary Online, merriam-webster.com

FUNDABLE EVENT TIMELINE

Cashflow Summary

	Month 1, Year 1	Month 2, Year 1	Month 3, Year 1	Month 4, Year 1	Month 5, Year 1	Month 6, Year 1	Month 7, Year 1	Month 8, Year 1	Month 9, Year 1	Month 10, Year 1	Month 11, Year 1	Month 12, Year 1
Opening Cash Balance												
Total CapEX												
Total OpEx												
Total Cash Out												
Total Cash In												
Closing Cash Balance												

Execution Timeline (Gantt Chart)

ACTIVITY	OWNER	ASSOCIATED COSTS US$	Month 1, Year 1	Month 2, Year 1	Month 3, Year 1	Month 4, Year 1	Month 5, Year 1	Month 6, Year 1	Month 7, Year 1	Month 8, Year 1	Month 9, Year 1	Month 10, Year 1	Month 11, Year 1	Month 12, Year 1

Note: Milestones mean that you finished what you started. Fundable Events are validation that you are right.

FUNDABLE EVENT TIMELINE

Cashflow Summary

	Month 1, Year 1	Month 2, Year 1	Month 3, Year 1	Month 4, Year 1	Month 5, Year 1	Month 6, Year 1	Month 7, Year 1	Month 8, Year 1	Month 9, Year 1	Month 10, Year 1	Month 11, Year 1	Month 12, Year 1
Opening Cash Balance												
Total CapEX												
Total OpEx												
Total Cash Out												
Total Cash In												
Closing Cash Balance												

Execution Timeline (Gantt Chart)

ACTIVITY	OWNER	ASSOCIATED COSTS US$	Month 1, Year 1	Month 2, Year 1	Month 3, Year 1	Month 4, Year 1	Month 5, Year 1	Month 6, Year 1	Month 7, Year 1	Month 8, Year 1	Month 9, Year 1	Month 10, Year 1	Month 11, Year 1	Month 12, Year 1

Note: Milestones mean that you finished what you started. Fundable Events are validation that you are right.

ACKNOWLEDGMENTS

REGARDING THE STARTUP FRAMEWORK

I would like to make a special mention thanking a colleague and friend of mine: former INSEAD Professor of Entrepreneurship Filipe Santos. As of this writing, Filipe is Dean and Fundação Amélia de Mello Professor at Católica-Lisbon School of Business and Economics. Filipe is a research academic, a leader, and a successful entrepreneur inside of schools.

The first time I taught my startup framework to a group of MBA students it was thanks to Filipe. Up to that point my Startup framework was something that I used personally. When I met Filipe I was the CEO of a startup in Ireland. Filipe invited me to get more involved at INSEAD, specifically in the INSEAD Centre for Entrepreneurship (ICE) in Fontainebleau, France and in Singapore. Filipe asked me what I could do with a 48-hour weekend with INSEAD MBA students to help them better understand what it means to be an entrepreneur. One October weekend in 2009 I climbed onto a bus that was full of INSEAD students. A career professional entrepreneur named Peter Sage joined the students and me. Together we made the trip to a chateau in the Loire Valley. For 48 hours we worked to build startups. It was exciting and a great deal of fun. I have since taught my startup bootcamp hundreds of times in more than 24 countries around the world to thousands of people of all ages and education levels. Filipe giving me the opportunity that first weekend, and the weekends that followed, was a game changer for me.

REGARDING THE SCIENCE AND TECHNOLOGY FRAMEWORK

I would like to make a special mention regarding two colleagues and friends of mine: Former INSEAD Professor of Entrepreneurship Filipe Santos and INSEAD Adjunct Professor of Entrepreneurship Bill Magill. Filipe, Bill, and I put my science and technology framework into a program at INSEAD called the Sci-Tech Commercializer. Bill and I delivered the Commercializer together in Paris and Fontainebleau, France to INSEAD MBA students and scientists from France, Germany, and the BeNeLux (Belgium, the Netherlands, and Luxembourg). I delivered the Commercializer alone in Singapore with scientists in Singapore. It was a powerful time of exploring and building startup muscle around existing science and technology. The Sci-Tech Commercializer won the 2012 Association for MBA Innovation award.

REGARDING THE ACQUISITIONS, TURNAROUNDS, AND CRISIS LEADERSHIP FRAMEWORKS

Three adjuncts professors at INSEAD greatly influenced my opinions about acquisitions, turnarounds, and crisis leadership. Patrick Turner, Timothy Bovard, and Douglas Rosefsky.

Patrick and Timothy created the course Your First Hundred Days (YFCD, the C is the Roman numeral 100) which is a course on how to acquire and turn around a failing 120-year-old family business. Learning the course from Patrick had a profound impact on me for the better. Timothy's sharing of all of the very real details inside the course was a game changer for the course, every student who took the course, and me.

Timothy's masterful teaching of INSEAD's acquisitions course (named Realizing Entrepreneurial Potential or REP) was another power tool in INSEAD's belt. I was a volunteer judge in REP for several years, and the experience was transformational for me. I love listening to Timothy teach; I always leave inspired.

YFCD brings in outside professionals onto campus as volunteer role-players to engage students; simulating and testing their ability to problem solve and be professional under pressure. Doug Rosefsky volunteered as a Banker role player during my teaching in France. I then I taught him how to teach YFCD to MBA and EMBA students at INSEAD in France and Singapore. Working with Doug as a role-player and then teaching side-by-side with him expanded and enhanced the way that I thought about banks and bankers, CFOs, acquisitions, turnarounds, and crisis leadership. I learned things from him that meaningfully influenced my teaching, coaching, and consulting for the better.

REGARDING THE SOFTWARE DEVELOPMENT FRAMEWORK

I would like to make a special mention of INSEAD's Deputy Dean and Professor of Strategy Peter Zemsky. The first time I taught the Software Development framework to a group of MBA students was thanks to Peter who inspired and supported the program. Before Peter engaged me to teach software development as a bootcamp at INSEAD this framework was an informal set of steps I used privately in my own work and with companies. Peter is a very innovative entrepreneur who is a research academic and a leader in a top business school. He is proof positive that entrepreneurship can be powerfully engaged inside of a school.

REGARDING THE DEDICATION

While writing a dedication and acknowledgements I realized that I began writing an entire book dedicated to the people who have positively impacted my life. Thank you to all of my students, event and conference attendees, colleagues, friends, and family members who have encouraged me (many repeatedly, several nagging) to write a book on my experience and how to be an entrepreneur. Thank you all for the doors opened, bridges built, and pathways cleared.

INDEX

ABOUT THE AUTHOR

PAUL KEWENE-HITE* is a graduate of Harvard University, a career professional entrepreneur, an Affiliate Professor of Entrepreneurship and Family Enterprise at INSEAD, and co-founder, with his wife Natasha, of the business consulting practice *Mātanga Hāpai* in New Zealand.

At INSEAD, he won the Dean's Award for Excellence in Teaching multiple times. He has taught in the MBA, EMBA, and Executive Education programs. Since 2009 he has taught INSEAD's popular course Your First Hundred Days, which is a real-time role-play crisis leadership simulation on how to acquire and turnaround a failing company. Among other successful original courses based on frameworks in this book, Paul created INSEAD's very popular Startup Bootcamp (based on his Startup framework) and has taught it in 24 countries around the world.

Before joining INSEAD, Paul held roles in companies ranging from technical support to CEO. In addition to various roles in small companies, his big company experience was as a Technology Evangelist at Apple, and Director of New Business Development and Strategic Planning at NEC.

Paul has helped people at all education and experience levels successfully create companies, and build successful new initiatives inside organizations, across various industries around the world. One of Paul's key drivers is helping people work toward their potential in business and in life.

He is an educator, trainer, coach, consultant, and a frequent public speaker. He is an Anchor Mentor for Google's Accelerators worldwide.

He is married with three children. After living in the USA, Ireland, France, Thailand, and Singapore, Paul now resides in the countryside of New Zealand with his wife and youngest son.

Paul is a Muay Thai enthusiast. He loves languages and is fluent in Thai.

---

*   People often ask how to pronounce the family name: Kewene-Hite. All letters *e* in "Kewene" are pronounced quickly and sound the same, like the short letter *e* sound in the words: jet *set*. The emphasis is on the first syllable and sounds like: KEH-weh-neh. "Hite" sounds like the word *height* as in how tall or an elevation. Hite is Paul's original family name and Kewene is his wife Natasha's original family name; they combined their family names when they married in 1993.

Printed in Great Britain
by Amazon